BOOK OF COMMON WORSHIP
DAILY PRAYER

Book of
Common Worship
Daily Prayer

Prepared by

The Theology and
Worship Ministry Unit

for the

Presbyterian Church (U.S.A.)

and the

Cumberland Presbyterian Church

Commended by the 205th General
Assembly (1993) of the Presbyterian
Church (U.S.A.) and the 163rd General
Assembly (1993) of the Cumberland
Presbyterian Church for use in worship.

Published by

Westminster/John Knox Press
Louisville, Kentucky

For Acknowledgments, see pages 511–517.

Published by Westminster/John Knox Press
Louisville, Kentucky

This book is printed on acid-free paper that meets the American National Standards Institute Z39.48 standard. ∞

Book design by Susan E. Jackson

Interior illustrations by Aavidar Design Inc.

PRINTED IN THE UNITED STATES OF AMERICA

2 4 6 8 9 7 5 3 1

Library of Congress Cataloging-in-Publication Data

Presbyterian Church (U.S.A.)
   [Book of common worship. Selections]
  Book of common worship, daily prayer / prepared by the Theology and Worship Ministry Unit for the Presbyterian Church (U.S.A.) and the Cumberland Presbyterian Church.
     p.   cm.
  ISBN 0-664-22032-0

  1. Presbyterian Church (U.S.A.)—Liturgy—Texts. 2. Cumberland Presbyterian Church—Liturgy—Texts. 3. Presbyterian Church (U.S.A.)—Prayer-books and devotions—English. 4. Cumberland Presbyterian Church—Prayer-books and devotions—English. 5. Presbyterian Church—United States—Liturgy—Texts. 6. Reformed Church—United States—Liturgy—Texts. I. Presbyterian Church (U.S.A.). Theology and Worship Ministry Unit. II. Cumberland Presbyterian Church. III. Title.
BX8969.5.P74 1993b
264'.05137013—dc20

                              93-4547

CONTENTS

PRAYERS FOR VARIOUS OCCASIONS

PREFACE

Across the centuries, prayer in the morning and evening has played an important role in shaping Christian piety. The practice has its roots in ancient Judaism and was continued by the early Christians. The sixteenth-century Reformation gave renewed attention to daily prayer as a valuable discipline of the Christian life. So also in our time, Christians are once again discovering the value of spiritual disciplines and the practice of daily prayer. It is an important recovery in the contemporary liturgical renewal movement and is evidenced in every major Christian tradition.

The intent of the *Book of Common Worship, Daily Prayer* is to provide a readily accessible resource that will assist in the practice of daily prayer. The book consists of those portions of the full text edition of the *Book of Common Worship* (Louisville: Westminster/John Knox Press, 1993) that are useful in maintaining this discipline. Most of the material is a revision of the previously published *Daily Prayer* (Supplemental Liturgical Resource 5; Philadelphia: Westminster Press, 1987).

As the words "common worship" in the title suggest, the liturgical forms that follow reflect a tradition shared in common with the whole church, past and present. This book, therefore, is appropriately ecumenical in scope, transcending sectarian divisions and reflecting the contributions of the contemporary liturgical movement that is shaping the major Christian traditions.

As common worship, daily prayer is basically communal in nature. Even when one is engaged in private prayer one is not alone. Whether a group of Christians is gathered in prayer or one Christian is praying alone, in praying the church's prayer one is joined in prayer with all the faithful of every place and time. An important value of using a daily lectionary, of participating in elements of a liturgy that are shared by other Christians, of praying with the whole church for specific parts of the church, is that it conveys a sense of solidarity with all of the baptized.

The significance of daily prayer is that it follows the natural cycle of the day. The earliest tradition is prayer in the morning and evening.

In the morning, we bless God for the new day, focusing our prayers upon the day that has just begun with all of its promised activity and relationships. We petition God for guidance in the tasks immediately before us and for strength to fulfill our vocation as Christ's disciples. Our prayers encompass concerns of both church and world, as well as the immediate concerns of those assembled for prayer or of the person praying.

Evening prayer traditionally takes place as daylight fades and the shadows lengthen. Since the beginning of civilization, people have lit lamps as darkness approached. Lighting the lamps has always been more than a utilitarian act, for associated with it are the ancient symbols of darkness, light, and fire. In the quietness of the gathering darkness, after the pressures and busy activities of the day are set aside, we reflect on the day that is spent. It is a time to give thanks for the blessings of the day just ended, to commit ourselves anew into the protective care of God, to bring before God tasks completed or left undone or done amiss, and to pray once again for a broken world in need of God's redeeming grace. The lighting of the candles reminds us that Jesus is the light of the world and the rising smoke of incense suggests that our prayers rise before God as a fragrant offering. By employing sight, sound, and smell, evening prayer engages our whole body in prayer.

While morning and evening are the principal times of

prayer, this book also provides prayer at midday and at the close of day, for occasions when these are called for.

In midday prayer we are conscious of being in God's world and praise God for the wonders of creation and the opportunities for service. We celebrate the life Christ gives that we may live life fully in his service, drawing upon the power of the Holy Spirit to fulfill the moral and ethical responsibilities of Christian discipleship.

In prayer at the close of day we prepare for sleep. Death and resurrection are clear accents in this time of prayer. We surrender our lives into God's keeping, anticipating our own death, confident that God will "raise us to new life" in the morning as we look toward our resurrection in Jesus Christ.

Prayer punctuating the cycle of each day helps us fulfill the injunction of Paul, "pray without ceasing" (1 Thessalonians 5:17). It helps deliver us from the inclination to divide life into separate compartments and opens our lives to allow the faith to permeate all we are and do. Daily prayer helps us engage our whole life—all our thoughts, words, and actions—as a vocation offered to God in humble service.

Daily prayer is to be seen in relationship with worship on the Lord's Day. The services in this book are not proposed as services for a congregation gathered on the Lord's Day to hear the scripture proclaimed and to celebrate the Eucharist. The intent of these services is different: services of daily prayer do not focus upon proclaiming the Word but upon prayer. It is in the uniqueness of each—Word and prayer—that they are able to support and feed each other. The Word proclaimed and sacraments celebrated will undergird daily prayer. So also the practice of daily prayer will quicken our appetite for the Lord's Day feast when the week culminates and we come with anticipation to hear the Word proclaimed and to be renewed at the Lord's table.

Morning and evening prayer engages us in a variety of ways.

First, daily prayer engages us in praying the psalms. The psalms have been a fundamental part of daily prayer for centuries. The psalter is a book of prayers, and through the ages has shaped the prayers of Jews and Christians alike. In stressing the importance of praying the psalms, Dietrich Bonhoeffer wrote that what is truly important is

> not what we want to pray . . . , but what God wants us to pray. If we were dependent entirely on ourselves, we would probably pray only the fourth petition of the Lord's Prayer. But God wants it otherwise. The richness of the Word of God ought to determine our prayer, not the poverty of our heart.[1]

Because of the central place of the psalms in daily prayer all of the psalms appointed in the lectionary are included in this volume in a form that invites use in varied ways. This version is an inclusive language revision of the psalter in the *Book of Common Prayer* and is arranged for singing to simple psalm tones contained in this book or to other common tones available to the user. Singing the psalms can engage us in praying the psalms more readily than simply reading them.

Second, daily prayer engages us in a prayerful, quiet reflection on a reading from scripture. Daily lectionaries provide us with a systematic discipline of Bible reading that leads us into more scripture than is possible on the Lord's Day. Use of a daily lectionary commends itself because it enables us to become familiar with the whole of the scriptures, and to hear the voice of God in portions of the Bible with which we are less familiar.

(The daily lectionary included in this volume is shared, with slight alterations, with Episcopalians and Lutherans, and derives from the *Book of Common Prayer*. It has been used among Presbyterians for about twenty years.)

Third, daily prayer engages us in thanksgiving, supplication, intercession, and penitence. Prayers focusing on the concerns of the moment are set in the context of prayers that derive from the heritage of liturgical prayer. As noted above, the focus of prayer varies with the time of day.

---

[1] Dietrich Bonhoeffer, *Psalms: The Prayer Book of the Bible*. Minneapolis: Augsburg Publishing House, 1970, pp. 14, 15.

This book contains a rich variety of prayer texts, both ancient and modern. The prayer forms of thanksgiving and intercession in morning and evening prayer combine fixed prayer, silence, and free prayer. These prayers, together with the prayers in the section of alternative texts for seasons and festivals, the section of prayers for various occasions, and the prayers for preparing for worship, provide a treasury of prayers that can broaden the range of our concerns and quicken prayers within us to express concerns that otherwise might not arise within our minds and hearts.

Fourth, daily prayer engages us in silent contemplation. Silence provides a time of calm in the rush of life. At the beginning of a service of prayer, silence helps us center our whole person on God in prayer. Silence at appropriate places during the service helps us contemplate the words of the psalm and of the scripture reading and enables us to give particular focus to our prayers. These moments of silence provide a time in this frenetic world for us to be still and open our lives before God.

This book provides resources for daily prayer in a variety of situations. Congregations are discovering the value of gathering for prayer on a regular basis or during a particular liturgical season. Opening meetings of church boards and committees with evening prayer sets the deliberations to follow within the framework of prayer. Small groups within a congregation find that morning or evening prayer is an appropriate way to begin gatherings. The whole congregation is enriched when it has a staff that assembles for morning prayer at the start of each day, and is perhaps joined by others who wish to participate in the discipline of daily prayer in a group.

Governing bodies such as presbyteries that punctuate their meetings with morning and evening prayer discover that their work becomes an offering to God.

Church retreats are given depth when each day is marked with the rhythm of prayer: morning, midday, evening, and the close of day. The vigil of the resurrection is a fitting way for those gathered in retreat to welcome the Lord's Day and to renew the baptismal covenant.

In the discipline of daily prayer families are bonded together in Christ. Prayers for use at mealtime help us to bless God for providing food to sustain our lives.

In maintaining a personal discipline of daily prayer, the spiritual life of individuals is deepened, and they are enriched by knowing that they are joined with others in their prayers. Many find prayer at the close of day, or a prayer selected from that service, a fitting way to end the day upon retiring for the night.

As a discipline that has enriched the life of faith across the centuries, the services in this book commend themselves to groups and individuals who vow to make daily prayer an important part of life before God.

THEOLOGY AND WORSHIP MINISTRY UNIT

ABBREVIATIONS

PH   *The Presbyterian Hymnal: Hymns, Psalms, and Spiritual Songs.* Louisville, Ky.: Westminster/John Knox Press, 1990.

PS   *The Psalter—Psalms and Canticles for Singing.* Louisville, Ky.: Westminster/John Knox Press, 1993.

...   (in prayers) indicates a pause for silent prayer.

[ ]   Square brackets, or horizontal brackets extending the width of the page, are used to designate optional elements or sections.

▼   A triangle is used to indicate continuation of text.

PREPARATION FOR WORSHIP

PREPARATION FOR WORSHIP

PRAYERS FOR USE BEFORE WORSHIP

The following prayers may be used by worshipers as they prepare for the service.

1

Eternal God,
you have called us to be members of one body.
Join us with those
who in all times and places have praised your name,
that, with one heart and mind,
we may show the unity of your church,
and bring honor to our Lord and Savior,
Jesus Christ.   **Amen.**   [1]

2

Everlasting God,
in whom we live and move and have our being:
You have made us for yourself,
so that our hearts are restless
until they rest in you.
Give us purity of heart and strength of purpose,
that no selfish passion may hinder us
    from knowing your will,
no weakness keep us from doing it;
that in your light we may see light clearly,   ▼

and in your service find perfect freedom;
through Jesus Christ our Lord,
who lives and reigns with you and the Holy Spirit,
one God, now and forever. **Amen.** [2]

3

Almighty God,
you pour out the spirit of grace and supplication
on all who desire it.
Deliver us from cold hearts and wandering thoughts,
that with steady minds and burning zeal
we may worship you
in spirit and in truth;
through Jesus Christ our Lord. **Amen.** [3]

4

God of grace,
you have given us minds to know you,
hearts to love you,
and voices to sing your praise.
Fill us with your Spirit,
that we may celebrate your glory
and worship you in spirit and in truth;
through Jesus Christ our Lord. **Amen.** [4]

5

O Lord our God,
you are always more ready to bestow your good gifts upon us
than we are to seek them.
You are more willing to give
than we desire or deserve.
Help us so to seek that we may truly find,
so to ask that we may joyfully receive,
so to knock that the door of your mercy may be opened for us;
through Jesus Christ our Lord. **Amen.** [5]

6

Almighty God, you built your church
upon the foundation of the apostles and prophets,
with Jesus Christ himself as the cornerstone.
Join us together by their teaching,
so that we may be a holy temple
in whom your Spirit dwells;
through Jesus Christ our Lord.   **Amen.**   [6]

7

Almighty God, we pray for your blessing
on the church in this place.
Here may the faithful find salvation,
and the careless be awakened.
Here may the doubting find faith,
and the anxious be encouraged.
Here may the tempted find help,
and the sorrowful comfort.
Here may the weary find rest,
and the strong be renewed.
Here may the aged find consolation
and the young be inspired;
through Jesus Christ our Lord.   **Amen.**   [7]

8

O God,
light of the minds that know you,
life of the souls that love you,
strength of the thoughts that seek you:
Help us so to know you
that we may truly love you,
so to love you
that we may fully serve you,
whose service is perfect freedom;
through Jesus Christ our Lord.   **Amen.**   [8]

9

Bless us, O God,
with a reverent sense of your presence,
that we may be at peace
and may worship you with all our mind and spirit;
through Jesus Christ our Lord.   **Amen.**   [9]

10

God of mercy,
grant that the Word you speak this day
may take root in our hearts,
and bear fruit to your honor and glory,
for the sake of Jesus Christ our Lord.   **Amen.**   [10]

11

O Jesus, our great high priest,
be present with us
as you were present with your disciples,
and make yourself known to us in the breaking of bread.
Amen.   [11]

13

Loving God,
you have so made us that we cannot live by bread alone,
but by every word that proceeds from your mouth.
Give us a hunger for your Word,
and in that food satisfy our daily need;
through Jesus Christ our Lord.   **Amen.**   [13]

14

To your name, Lord Jesus,
help me to bow the knee
and all its worshiping,
bow the head
and all its thinking,
bow the will
and all its choosing,

bow the heart
and all its loving.   **Amen.**   [14]

15

We praise you, we worship you, we adore you.
You hold the heavens in your hand,
all stars rejoice in your glory.
You come in the sunrise and the song of morn
and bless the splendor of the noonday.
The stars in their courses magnify you,
day and night tell of your glory.
Your peace blows over the earth
and the breath of your mouth fills all space.
Your voice comes in the thunder of the storm
and the song of the wind whispers of your majesty.
You satisfy all things living with your abundance
and our hearts bow at your presence.
Accept us, your children, Eternal Father,
and hearken to our prayer.
Bend over us, Eternal Love, and bless us.   **Amen.**   [15]

16

Eternal God,
you are the power behind all things:
behind the energy of the storm,
behind the heat of a million suns.

Eternal God,
you are the power behind all minds:
behind the ability to think and reason,
behind all understanding of the truth.

Eternal God,
you are the power behind the cross of Christ:
behind the weakness, the torture and the death,
behind unconquerable love.

Eternal God,
we worship and adore you.   **Amen.**   [16]

17

Grant unto us, O God, the fullness of your promises.
Where we have been weak, grant us your strength;
where we have been confused,
    grant us your guidance;
where we have been distraught,
    grant us your comfort;
where we have been dead, grant us your life.
Apart from you, O Lord, we are nothing,
in and with you we can do all things. **Amen.** [17]

18   *Christina Rossetti (1830–1894)*
As the wind is your symbol, so forward our goings.
As the dove, so launch us heavenwards.
As water, so purify our spirits.
As a cloud, so abate our temptations.
As dew, so revive our languor.
As fire, so purge out our dross. **Amen.** [18]

19   *Desiderius Erasmus (1466–1536)*
O Lord Jesus Christ,
the Way, the Truth, and the Life:
Do not let us stray from you, the Way,
nor to distrust you, the Truth,
nor to rest in anything other than you, the Life. **Amen.** [19]

20

Come, O Holy Spirit.
Come as Holy Fire and burn in us,
come as Holy Wind and cleanse us within,
come as Holy Light and lead us in the darkness,
come as Holy Truth and dispel our ignorance,
come as Holy Power and enable our weakness,
come as Holy Life and dwell in us.
Convict us, convert us, consecrate us,
until we are set free from the service of ourselves,
to be your servants to the world. **Amen.** [20]

21 *John Henry Newman (1801–1890)*

Give me, O my Lord,
that purity of conscience
which alone can receive your inspirations.
My ears are dull,
so that I cannot hear your voice.
My eyes are dim,
so that I cannot see the signs of your presence.
You alone can quicken my hearing
and purge my sight,
and cleanse and renew my heart.
Teach me to sit at your feet
and to hear your word.   **Amen.**   [21]

22 *Dag Hammarskjöld (1905–1961)*

Great and good God,
give us pure hearts that we may see you,
humble hearts that we may hear you,
hearts of love that we may serve you,
hearts of faith that we may live in you,
reverent hearts that we may worship you,
here and in the world out there,
through Jesus Christ our Lord.   **Amen.**   [22]

23 *Richard of Chichester (1197–1253)*

Thanks be to you, Lord Jesus Christ,
for all the benefits which you have won for us,
for all the pains and insults which you have borne for us.
O most merciful Redeemer, Friend and Brother,
may we know you more clearly,
love you more dearly,
and follow you more nearly,
day by day.   **Amen.**   [23]

24   *Howard Thurman (1900–1981)*

Lord, open unto me

    Open unto me—light for my darkness.

    Open unto me—courage for my fear.

    Open unto me—hope for my despair.

    Open unto me—peace for my turmoil.

    Open unto me—joy for my sorrow.

    Open unto me—strength for my weakness.

    Open unto me—wisdom for my confusion.

    Open unto me—forgiveness for my sins.

    Open unto me—love for my hates.

    Open unto me—thy Self for my self.

Lord, Lord, open unto me! **Amen.** [24]

25   *Augustine of Hippo (354–430)*

O loving God,

to turn away from you is to fall,

to turn toward you is to rise,

and to stand before you is to abide forever.

Grant us, dear God,

in all our duties your help;

in all our uncertainties your guidance;

in all our dangers your protection;

and in all our sorrows your peace;

through Jesus Christ our Lord. **Amen.** [25]

26   *Augustine of Hippo (354–430)*

O God, full of compassion,

I commit and commend myself to you,

in whom I am, and live, and know.

Be the goal of my pilgrimage, and my rest by the way.

Let my soul take refuge

from the crowding turmoil of worldly thought

beneath the shadow of your wings.

Let my heart, this sea of restless waves,

find peace in you, O God. **Amen.** [26]

27   *William Temple (1881–1944)*

Almighty and eternal God,
so draw our hearts to you,
so guide our minds,
so fill our imaginations,
so control our wills,
that we may be wholly yours,
utterly dedicated unto you;
and then use us, we pray, as you will,
but always to your glory
and the welfare of your people,
through our Lord and Savior, Jesus Christ.   **Amen.**   [27]

28   *William Laud (1573–1645)*

Gracious God,
we pray for your holy catholic church.
Fill it with all truth in all peace.
Where it is corrupt, purify it;
where it is in error, direct it;
where in any thing it is amiss, reform it.
Where it is right, strengthen it;
where it is in want, provide for it;
where it is divided, reunite it;
for the sake of Jesus Christ your Son our Savior.
Amen.   [28]

29   *Attributed to Benedict of Nursia (c. 480–547)*

O gracious and holy God,
give us diligence to seek you,
wisdom to perceive you,
and patience to wait for you.

Grant us, O God,
a mind to meditate on you;
eyes to behold you;
ears to listen for your word;   ▼

a heart to love you;
and a life to proclaim you;
through the power of the Spirit
of Jesus Christ our Lord.   **Amen.**   [29]

30   *Alcuin of Tours (c. 735–804)*

Eternal Light, shine into our hearts;
Eternal Goodness, deliver us from evil;
Eternal Power, be our support;
Eternal Wisdom, scatter the darkness of our ignorance;
Eternal Pity, have mercy upon us,
that with all our heart and mind and strength
we may seek your face
and be brought by your infinite mercy to your
    holy presence;
through Jesus Christ our Lord.   **Amen.**   [30]

31   *Sarum Primer (c. 1514)*

God be in my head, and in my understanding;
God be in my eyes, and in my looking;
God be in my mouth, and in my speaking;
God be in my heart, and in my thinking;
God be at my end, and at my departing.   **Amen.**   [31]

32   *Maria Ware (1798)*

Lord, hear;
Lord, forgive;
Lord, do.
Hear what we speak not;
forgive what we speak amiss;
do what we leave undone;
that not according to our words, or our deeds,
but according to your mercy and truth,
all may work for your glory,
and the good of your kingdom,
through Jesus Christ.   **Amen.**   [32]

Attributed to Francis of Assisi (1181–1226)

Lord, make me an instrument of your peace.
Where there is hatred, let me sow love;
where there is injury, pardon;
where there is doubt, faith;
where there is despair, hope;
where there is darkness, light;
where there is sadness, joy.

O Divine Master, grant that I may not seek so much
to be consoled as to console,
to be understood as to understand,
to be loved as to love.
For it is in giving that we receive,
it is in pardoning that we are pardoned,
and it is in dying that we are born to eternal life.
Amen. [33]

Patrick of Ireland (389–461)

May the strength of God pilot us.
May the power of God preserve us.
May the wisdom of God instruct us.
May the hand of God protect us.
May the way of God direct us.
May the shield of God defend us.
May the host of God guard us against the snares of evil
and the temptations of the world.

May Christ be with us,
Christ before us,
Christ in us,
Christ over us.
May your salvation, O Lord,
be always ours this day and forevermore. **Amen.** [34]

35 *Clement of Rome (d.c. 99)*

O God Almighty,
Father of our Lord Jesus Christ:
Grant us, we pray,
to be grounded and settled in your truth
by the coming down of the Holy Spirit into our hearts.
That which we know not, reveal;
that which is wanting in us, fill up;
that which we know, confirm;
and keep us blameless in your service;
through the same Jesus Christ our Lord.   **Amen.**   [35]

37 *Patrick of Ireland (389–461)*

I bind unto myself today
the strong name of the Trinity,
by invocation of the same,
the Three in One, and One in Three.

I bind this day to me forever,
by power of faith, Christ's incarnation;
his baptism in the Jordan river;
his death on the cross for my salvation.
His bursting from the spiced tomb;
his riding up the heavenly way;
his coming at the day of doom
I bind unto myself today.

I bind unto myself today
the virtues of the star-lit heaven,
the glorious sun's life-giving ray,
the whiteness of the moon at even,
the flashing of the lightning free,
the whirling wind's tempestuous shocks,
the stable earth, the deep salt sea
around the old eternal rocks.

I bind unto myself today
the power of God to hold and lead,
God's eye to watch, God's might to stay,

God's ear to hearken to my need,
the wisdom of my God to teach,
God's hand to guide, God's shield to ward,
the word of God to give me speech,
God's heavenly host to be my guard.

Christ be with me, Christ within me,
Christ behind me, Christ before me,
Christ beside me, Christ to win me,
Christ to comfort and restore me,
Christ beneath me, Christ above me,
Christ in quiet, Christ in danger,
Christ in hearts of all that love me,
Christ in mouth of friend and stranger.
I bind unto myself the name,
the strong name of the Trinity,
by invocation of the same,
the Three in One, the One in Three,
of whom all nature has creation,
eternal Father, Spirit, Word.
Praise to the Lord of my salvation,
salvation is of Christ the Lord.   **Amen.**   [37]

The Law of God

38

In preparation for worship, the people may wish to meditate on the law of God.

The Law of God   *Ex. 20:1–17*

God spoke all these words, saying,
I am the Lord your God.

You shall have no other gods before me.

You shall not make for yourself an idol,
whether in the form of anything that is in heaven above
or that is on the earth beneath,
or that is in the water under the earth.   ▼

You shall not bow down to them or worship them.

You shall not make wrongful use of the name of the Lord your God.

Remember the sabbath day, and keep it holy.

Honor your father and your mother.

You shall not murder.

You shall not commit adultery.

You shall not steal.

You shall not bear false witness against your neighbor.

You shall not covet your neighbor's house;
you shall not covet your neighbor's wife,
or anything that belongs to your neighbor.

39

In preparation for worship, the people may wish to meditate on the summary of the law.

Summary of the Law   *Matt. 22:37–40*

Our Lord Jesus said:
You shall love the Lord your God
with all your heart,
and with all your soul,
and with all your mind.
This is the greatest and first commandment.
And a second is like it:
You shall love your neighbor as yourself.
On these two commandments
hang all the law and the prophets.

DAILY PRAYER

An Outline of Morning Prayer

Opening Sentences
Morning Psalm or Morning Hymn
Psalm(s)
    Psalm
    Silent Prayer
    [Psalm Prayer]
Scripture Reading
    Silent Reflection
    [A Brief Interpretation of the Reading, or a Nonbiblical
        Reading]
Canticle
    Canticle of Zechariah or Other Canticle
Prayers of Thanksgiving and Intercession
    Thanksgivings and Intercessions
    Concluding Prayer
    Lord's Prayer
[Hymn or Spiritual]
Dismissal
    [Sign of Peace]

> When a person is worshiping alone, or in a family
> group, or when circumstances call for an abbreviated
> order, the following is suggested:

Psalm
Scripture Reading
    Silent Reflection
Prayers of Thanksgiving and Intercession

MORNING PRAYER

OPENING SENTENCES

All may stand.

O Lord, open my lips.

And my mouth shall proclaim your praise.

And one of the following, or a seasonal alternative
(pp. 65–104), is said:

1   *Lam. 3:22–23*

The Lord's unfailing love and mercy never cease,
fresh as the morning and sure as the sunrise.

2   *Ps. 74:16, 17*

You created the day and the night, O God;
you set the sun and the moon in their places;
you set the limits of the earth;
you made summer and winter.

3   *Ps. 5:2b–3*

I pray to you, O Lord;
you hear my voice in the morning;
at sunrise I offer my prayer
and wait for your answer.

4   *Rom. 11:33, 36*

O depth of wealth, wisdom, and knowledge of God!
How unsearchable are God's judgments,   ▼

how untraceable are God's ways!
The source, guide, and goal of all that is,
to God be glory forever!   **Amen.**

5   *Rev. 19:6, 7*

Alleluia!
For the Lord our God the Almighty reigns.
Let us rejoice and exult and give God the glory.

6   *Heb. 13:15*

Through Jesus let us continually offer up a sacrifice
    of praise to God,
the fruit of lips that acknowledge God's name.

7   *Rev. 4:11*

You are worthy, our Lord and God,
to receive glory and honor and power
for you created all things,
and by your will they existed
and were created.

MORNING PSALM OR MORNING HYMN

> One of the morning psalms (95:1–7; 100; 63:1–8;
> 51:1–12) or a morning hymn is sung.

Psalm 95:1–7   Tone 2; PH 215; PS 89, 90

Refrain: **Let us shout for joy** *
            to the Rock of our salvation.

R

1 Come, let us sing to the LORD; *
      let us shout for joy to the Rock of our salvation.

2 **Let us come before God's presence with thanksgiving** *
      and raise a loud shout to the LORD with psalms.   R

3 For the Lord is a great God, *
      and a great Sovereign above all gods.

4 **The Lord holds the caverns of the earth,** *
   and sustains the heights of the hills.

5 The sea belongs to God, who made it, *
   whose hands have molded the dry land.   **R**

6 **Come, let us bow down, and bend the knee,** *
   and kneel before the Lord our Maker.

   [Unison]

7 **For the Lord is our God,**
   and we are the people of God's pasture and the sheep
       of God's hand. *
   Oh, that today you would hearken to God's voice!   R

Psalm 100   Tone 3; PH 220; PS 97–101

Refrain: **Shout for joy to God, all the earth,** *
             Alleluia! Praise the Lord!

R

1 Be joyful in the Lord, all you lands; *
   ²serve the Lord with gladness
   and come before God's presence with a song.

3 **Know this: The Lord alone is God;** *
   we belong to the Lord, who made us,
   we are God's people and the sheep of God's
       pasture.   R

4 Enter God's gates with thanksgiving;
   go into the holy courts with praise; *
   give thanks and call upon the name of the Lord.

5 **For good is the Lord,**
   whose mercy is everlasting; *
   and whose faithfulness endures from age to age.   R

Psalm 63:1–8   Tone 6 or 8; PH 198, 199; PS 53, 54

Refrain: **O God, you are my God; ***
earnestly will I seek you.

R

1   O God, you are my God; eagerly I seek you; *
my soul thirsts for you, my flesh faints for you,
as in a barren and dry land where there is no water.

2   **Therefore I have gazed upon you in your holy place, ***
that I might behold your power and your glory.

3   For your loving-kindness is better than life itself; *
my lips shall give you praise.

4   **So will I bless you as long as I live ***
and lift up my hands in your name.   R

5   My soul is content, as with marrow and fatness, *
and my mouth praises you with joyful lips,

6   **when I remember you upon my bed, ***
and meditate on you in the night watches.

7   For you have been my helper, *
and under the shadow of your wings I will rejoice.

8   **My soul clings to you; ***
your right hand holds me fast.   R

Psalm 51:1–12   Tone 7; PH 195, 196; PS 47

Refrain: **Create in me a clean heart, O God, ***
and renew a right spirit within me.

R

1   Have mercy on me, O God, according to your
loving-kindness; *
in your great compassion blot out my offenses.

2 **Wash me through and through from my wickedness** *
        and cleanse me from my sin.   R

3 For I know my transgressions, *
        and my sin is ever before me.

4 **Against you only have I sinned** *
        and done what is evil in your sight.

   And so you are justified when you speak *
        and upright in your judgment.

5 **Indeed, I have been wicked from my birth,** *
        a sinner from my mother's womb.   R

6 For behold, you look for truth deep within me, *
        and will make me understand wisdom secretly.

7 **Purge me from my sin, and I shall be pure;** *
        wash me, and I shall be clean indeed.

8 Make me hear of joy and gladness, *
        that the body you have broken may rejoice.

9 **Hide your face from my sins** *
        and blot out all my iniquities.   R

10 Create in me a clean heart, O God, *
        and renew a right spirit within me.

11 **Cast me not away from your presence** *
        and take not your holy Spirit from me.

   [Unison]

12 **Give me the joy of your saving help again** *
        and sustain me with your bountiful Spirit.   R

   All may be seated.

PSALM(S)

   One or more additional psalms (pp. 167–390, 459–506)
   are sung or said.

Silence for reflection follows each psalm.

A psalm prayer may follow the silence.

SCRIPTURE READING

At the conclusion of the reading of scripture (pp. 459–506), the reader may say:

The Word of the Lord.

Thanks be to God.

Silence follows for reflection on the meaning of the scripture.

The scripture may be briefly interpreted, or a nonbiblical reading may be read.

CANTICLE

The Canticle of Zechariah or another canticle (pp. 137–158; PS 158–191) may be sung or said.

All may stand.

Canticle of Zechariah   *Benedictus; Luke 1:68–79*
                                  PH 601, 602; PS 158–160

Refrain: **You have come to your people ***
            and set them free.

Or

            In the tender compassion of our God *
            the dawn from on high shall break
            upon us.

R

Blessed are you, Lord, the God of Israel; *
    you have come to your people and set them free.
You have raised up for us a mighty Savior, *
    born of the house of your servant David.   R

Through your holy prophets, you promised of old
to save us from our enemies, *
   from the hands of all who hate us,

to show mercy to our forebears, *
   and to remember your holy covenant.   **R**

This was the oath you swore to our father Abraham: *
   to set us free from the hands of our enemies,
free to worship you without fear, *
   holy and righteous before you,
   all the days of our life.   **R**

And you, child, shall be called the prophet
      of the Most High, *
   for you will go before the Lord to prepare the way,
to give God's people knowledge of salvation *
   by the forgiveness of their sins.   **R**

In the tender compassion of our God *
   the dawn from on high shall break upon us,
to shine on those who dwell in darkness
      and the shadow of death,*
   and to guide our feet into the way of peace.   **R**

PRAYERS OF THANKSGIVING AND INTERCESSION

Satisfy us with your love in the morning,

and we will live this day in joy and praise.

One of the following, a seasonal litany (pp. 65–104), or
other prayers of thanksgiving and intercession, may be said:

1

Sunday

Mighty God of mercy, we thank you for the resurrection
dawn bringing the glory of our risen Lord who makes every
day new. Especially we thank you for
   the beauty of your creation . . .   ▼

the new creation in Christ and all gifts of healing
and forgiveness . . .
the sustaining love of family and friends . . .
the fellowship of faith in your church. . . .
Merciful God of might, renew this weary world, heal the
hurts of all your children, and bring about your peace for
all in Christ Jesus, the living Lord. Especially we pray for
those who govern nations of the world . . .
the people in countries ravaged by strife or warfare . . .
all who work for peace and international harmony . . .
all who strive to save the earth from destruction . . .
the church of Jesus Christ in every land. . . .   [434]

2

Monday

We praise you, God our creator, for your handiwork in
shaping and sustaining your wondrous creation. Especially
we thank you for
the miracle of life and the wonder of living . . .
particular blessings coming to us in this day . . .
the resources of the earth . . .
gifts of creative vision and skillful craft . . .
the treasure stored in every human life. . . .
We dare to pray for others, God our Savior, claiming your
love in Jesus Christ for the whole world, committing ourselves to care for those around us in his name. Especially we
pray for
those who work for the benefit of others . . .
those who cannot work today . . .
those who teach and those who learn . . .
people who are poor . . .
the church in Europe. . . .   [435]

3

Tuesday

Eternal God, we rejoice this morning in the gift of life,
which we have received by your grace, and the new life you

give in Jesus Christ. Especially we thank you for
    the love of our families . . .
    the affection of our friends . . .
    strength and abilities to serve your purpose today . . .
    this community in which we live . . .
    opportunities to give as we have received. . . .
God of grace, we offer our prayers for the needs of others
and commit ourselves to serve them even as we have been
served in Jesus Christ. Especially we pray for
    those closest to us, families, friends, neighbors . . .
    refugees and homeless men, women and children . . .
    the outcast and persecuted . . .
    those from whom we are estranged . . .
    the church in Africa. . . .   [436]

4

Wednesday

God of all mercies, we praise you that you have brought us
to this new day, brightening our lives with the dawn of
promise and hope in Jesus Christ. Especially we thank you for
    the warmth of sunlight, the wetness of rain and snow,
        and all that nourishes the earth . . .
    the presence and power of your Spirit . . .
    the support and encouragement we receive from others . . .
    those who provide for public safety and well-being . . .
    the mission of the church around the world. . . .
Merciful God, strengthen us in prayer that we may lift up
the brokenness of this world for your healing, and share in
the saving love of Jesus Christ. Especially we pray for
    those in positions of authority over others . . .
    the lonely and forgotten . . .
    children without families or homes . . .
    agents of caring and relief . . .
    the church in Asia and the Middle East. . . .   [437]

5

Thursday

Loving God, as the rising sun chases away the night, so you
have scattered the power of death in the rising of Jesus
Christ, and you bring us all blessings in him. Especially we
thank you for

the community of faith in our church . . .

those with whom we work or share common concerns . . .

the diversity of your children . . .

indications of your love at work in the world . . .

those who work for reconciliation. . . .

Mighty God, with the dawn of your love you reveal your
victory over all that would destroy or harm, and you bright-
en the lives of all who need you. Especially we pray for

families suffering separation . . .

people different from ourselves . . .

those isolated by sickness or sorrow . . .

the victims of violence or warfare . . .

the church in the Pacific region. . . .   [438]

6

Friday

Eternal God, we praise you for your mighty love given in
Christ's sacrifice on the cross, and the new life we have
received by his resurrection. Especially we thank you for

the presence of Christ in our weakness and suffering . . .

the ministry of Word and Sacrament . . .

all who work to help and heal . . .

sacrifices made for our benefit . . .

opportunities for our generous giving. . . .

God of grace, let our concern for others reflect Christ's
self-giving love, not only in our prayers, but also in our
practice. Especially we pray for

those subjected to tyranny and oppression . . .

wounded and injured people . . .

those who face death . . .
those who may be our enemies . . .
the church in Latin America. . . .   [439]

7

Saturday

Great and wonderful God, we praise and thank you for the gift of renewal in Jesus Christ. Especially we thank you for
    opportunities for rest and recreation . . .
    the regenerating gifts of the Holy Spirit . . .
    activities shared by young and old . . .
    fun and laughter . . .
    every service that proclaims your love. . . .
You make all things new, O God, and we offer our prayers for the renewal of the world and the healing of its wounds. Especially we pray for
    those who have no leisure . . .
    people enslaved by addictions . . .
    those who entertain and enlighten . . .
    those confronted with temptation . . .
    the church in North America. . . .   [440]

Individual prayers of thanksgiving and intercession may be offered.

There may be silent prayer.

The leader then says one of the following prayers, or a similar prayer. For seasonal alternatives see pages 65–104.

1

Eternal God,
our beginning and our end,
be our starting point and our haven,
and accompany us in this day's journey.
Use our hands
to do the work of your creation,
and use our lives   ▼

to bring others the new life you give this world
in Jesus Christ, Redeemer of all.   [441]

Amen.

2

As you cause the sun to rise, O God,
bring the light of Christ to dawn in our souls
and dispel all darkness.
Give us grace to reflect Christ's glory;
and let his love show in our deeds,
his peace shine in our words,
and his healing in our touch,
that all may give him praise, now and forever.   [442]

Amen.

3

Eternal God,
your touch makes this world holy.
Open our eyes to see your hand at work
in the splendor of creation,
and in the beauty of human life.
Help us to cherish the gifts that surround us,
to share your blessings with our sisters and brothers,
and to experience the joy of life in your presence.
We ask this through Christ our Lord.   [443]

Amen.

4

Eternal God,
you never fail to give us each day all that we ever need,
and even more.
Give us such joy in living
and such peace in serving Christ,
that we may gratefully make use of all your blessings,
and joyfully seek our risen Lord
in everyone we meet.
In Jesus Christ we pray.   [444]

Amen.

5

O God,
you are the well-spring of life.
Pour into our hearts the living water of your grace,
that we may be refreshed to live this day in joy,
confident of your presence
and empowered by your peace,
in Jesus Christ our Lord.   [445]

Amen.

6

Eternal God,
you call us to ventures
of which we cannot see the ending,
by paths as yet untrodden,
through perils unknown.
Give us faith to go out with courage,
not knowing where we go,
but only that your hand is leading us
and your love supporting us;
through Jesus Christ our Lord.   [446]

Amen.

7

God our creator,
yours is the morning and yours is the evening.
Let Christ the sun of righteousness
shine forever in our hearts
and draw us to that light
where you live in radiant glory.
We ask this for the sake
of Jesus Christ our Redeemer.   [447]

Amen.

All sing (musical settings: PH 571, 589, 590; PS 192–195) or say:

Or

Our Father in heaven,	Our Father,
hallowed be your name,	who art in heaven,
your kingdom come,	hallowed be thy name,
your will be done,	thy kingdom come,
on earth as in heaven.	thy will be done,
Give us today	on earth as it is in heaven.
our daily bread.	Give us this day
Forgive us our sins	our daily bread;
as we forgive those	and forgive us our debts,
who sin against us.	as we forgive our debtors;
Save us from	and lead us not
the time of trial	into temptation,
and deliver us from evil.	but deliver us from evil.
For the kingdom,	For thine is the kingdom,
the power,	and the power,
and the glory are yours	and the glory,
now and forever. Amen.	forever. Amen.

[HYMN OR SPIRITUAL]

DISMISSAL

The leader dismisses the people using one of the following:

1   *1 Tim.* 6:21
The grace of God be with us all, now and always.

Amen.

Bless the Lord.

The Lord's name be praised.

2   *Rom. 15:13*

May the God of hope fill us with all joy and peace
through the power of the Holy Spirit.

Amen.

Bless the Lord.

The Lord's name be praised.

3   *1 Tim. 1:17*

To God be honor and glory forever and ever.

Amen.

Bless the Lord.

The Lord's name be praised.

4   *2 Peter 3:18*

May we continue to grow in the grace and knowledge
of Jesus Christ, our Lord and Savior.

Amen.

Bless the Lord.

The Lord's name be praised.

A sign of peace may be exchanged by all.

An Outline of Evening Prayer

Service of Light   Or   Opening Sentences
    Opening Sentences   Evening Hymn
    Evening Hymn: Hymn to
        Christ the Light
    Thanksgiving for Light
    Evening Psalm
        Psalm 141
        Silent Prayer
        Psalm Prayer

Psalm(s)
    Psalm
    Silent Prayer
    [Psalm Prayer]
Scripture Reading
    Silent Reflection
[A Brief Interpretation of the Reading,
    or a Nonbiblical Reading]
Canticle
    Canticle of Mary or Other Canticle
Prayers of Thanksgiving and Intercession
    Concluding Prayer
    Lord's Prayer
[Hymn or Spiritual]
Dismissal
    [Sign of Peace]

When a person is worshiping alone, or in a family group, or when circumstances call for an abbreviated order, the following is suggested:

Psalm
Scripture Reading
    Silent Reflection
Prayers of Thanksgiving and Intercession

Evening Prayer

Evening prayer may begin with the service of light.

If evening prayer is not to include the service of light, the service begins on page 53.

Service of Light

The room should be dimly lit. A large lighted candle may be carried in procession to a prominent place as the opening sentences are sung or said. Or a lamp or candle already in place may be lighted as the people gather.

Opening Sentences

One of the following is sung or said.

All may stand.

1   *See John 1:5; 8:12; Luke 24:29*
Jesus Christ is the light of the world,

the light no darkness can overcome.

Stay with us, Lord, for it is evening

and the day is almost over.

Let your light scatter the darkness

and illumine your church.

2

Light and peace in Jesus Christ our Lord.

Thanks be to God.

3 *See Rev. 22:20*

Advent

The Spirit and the church cry out:

Come, Lord Jesus.

All those who await his appearance pray:

Come, Lord Jesus.

The whole creation pleads:

Come, Lord Jesus.

4 *See Isa. 9:2, 6; John 1:4–5, 14*

Christmas–Epiphany

The people who walked in darkness
have seen a great light.

**The light shines in the darkness,
and the darkness has not overcome it.**

Those who dwell in the land of deep darkness,
on them has the light shined.

**We have beheld Christ's glory,
glory as of the only Son of the Father.**

For to us a child is born, to us a Son is given.

**In him was life,
and the life was the light of all people.**

5 *See 2 Cor. 6:2; Ps. 85:4; 80:3*

Lent

Behold, now is the acceptable time;

now is the day of salvation.

Turn us again, O God of our salvation,

that the light of your face may shine on us.

May your justice shine like the sun;

and may the poor be lifted up.

6

Easter–Pentecost

Jesus Christ is risen from the dead.

Alleluia, Alleluia, Alleluia!

We are illumined by the brightness of his rising.

Alleluia, Alleluia, Alleluia!

Death has no more dominion over us.

Alleluia, Alleluia, Alleluia!

EVENING HYMN

Hymn to Christ the Light   *Phos Hilaron*
PH 548, 549; PS 167–169

As the hymn is sung, additional candles may be
lighted from the flame of the large candle and the
lights turned up.

O radiant Light, O Sun divine,
of God the Father's deathless face,
O image of the Light sublime,
that fills the heavenly dwelling place.

O Son of God, the source of life,
praise is your due by night and day.
Our happy lips must raise the strain
of your esteemed and splendid name.

Lord Jesus Christ, as daylight fades,
as shine the lights of eventide,
we praise the Father with the Son,
the Spirit blest and with them one.

THANKSGIVING FOR LIGHT

The thanksgiving for light may be sung or spoken.

The Lord be with you.

And also with you.

Let us give thanks to the Lord our God.

It is right to give our thanks and praise.

The leader continues, using one of the following prayers:

1

We give you thanks and praise, O God,
for you are without beginning and without end.
Through your Son, Jesus Christ,
you have created and preserved the world;
Father of Christ and the giver of the Spirit,
you rule over all creation.
The day you have made for the works of light
and the night for our refreshment and strength.

O Lord of love and source of all good,
receive our evening sacrifice of praise.

You have guided us through this day
to the beginning of night;
grant us, in Christ, an evening filled with peace
and a night free from sin;
and when at last we come to our own end,
bring us into the everlasting life of your kingdom,
where you live and reign with Jesus Christ,
    your Son,
in the unity of the Holy Spirit,
God, forever and ever.   [448]

Amen.

2

We praise you, O Lord our God, Ruler of
   the universe,
by whose word the shadows of evening fall.
Your wisdom opens the gates of morning;
your understanding orders the changes of time
   and seasons;
your will controls the stars as they travel through
   the skies.
You are the Creator of both night and day,
making light recede before darkness,
and darkness before light.
You cause day to pass,
and bring on the night,
setting day and night apart.
You are the Lord of hosts.

Living and eternal God, rule over us always,
to the end of time.
Blessed are you, O Lord,
whose word makes evening fall.   [449]

Amen.

3

Blessed are you, Lord God of all creation.
In the beginning you separated light from darkness
and placed all your works in our hands.
You have given us the light of day
that we might see your wonders
in all we say and do;
you give us the gentle darkness of the night
that we might rest from our burdens
and be refreshed in body and spirit.

Break through the darkness of our sins
with the splendor of your mercy and love.
Send your light to dispel our fears and anxieties
and fill us with hope and joy.   ▼

Glory, praise, and honor are yours, O God,
through Jesus Christ our Lord,
in the power of the Holy Spirit,
now and forever.   [450]

Amen.

4

We give you thanks and praise, O God of
  endless light,
through our Lord Jesus Christ.

In him your light shines in our hearts
and reveals the light that never fades.
As daylight comes to an end
and darkness begins to fall,
we thank you for the light of day,
created for our work and pleasure,
and bless you for the gift of this evening light.

All praise to you, O God,
through Jesus Christ, your Son:
through him all glory and honor is yours,
with the Holy Spirit,
in the holy church
now and forever.   [451]

Amen.

5

Advent

Blessed are you, O Lord our God, Ruler of the universe,
creator of light and darkness.
In this holy season,
when the sun's light is swallowed up
by the growing darkness of the night,
you renew your promise to reveal among us
the splendor of your glory,

made flesh and visible to us in Jesus Christ,
  your Son.
Through the prophets
you teach us to hope for his reign of peace.

Through the outpouring of your Spirit
you give sight to our souls,
that we may see your glory
in the presence of Christ.
Strengthen us where we are weak,
support us in our efforts to do your will,
and free our tongues to sing your praise,
for to you all honor and blessing are due,
now and forever.   [452]

Amen.

6

Christmas–Epiphany

Blessed are you, O Lord our God,
for you have made our gladness greater and increased
  our joy
by sending to dwell among us
the Wonderful Counselor, the Prince of Peace.
Born of Mary,
proclaimed to the shepherds
and acknowledged to the ends of the earth,
your unconquered Sun of righteousness
gives light in darkness and establishes us in freedom.

All glory in the highest be to you,
through Christ, the Son of your favor,
in the abiding presence of your Spirit,
this night and forever and ever.   [453]

Amen.

Texts 452 and 453 are by John Allyn Melloh, S.M., and are copyright © 1979 G.I.A. Publications, Inc., Chicago, Illinois. Altered with permission. All rights reserved.

7

Lent

Blessed are you, O Lord our God,
the Shepherd of Israel,
their pillar of cloud by day,
their pillar of fire by night.
In these forty days
you lead us into the desert of repentance
that in this pilgrimage of prayer
we might learn to be your people once more.
In fasting and service
you bring us back to your heart.
You open our eyes to your presence in the world
and you free our hands
to lead others to the wonders of your grace.

Be with us in these journey days,
for without you we are lost and will perish.
To you alone be dominion and glory,
forever and ever.   [454]

Amen.

8

Easter–Pentecost

Blessed are you,
O Lord, Redeemer God.
You destroyed the bonds of death
and from the darkness of the tomb
drew forth the light of the world.
You led us through the waters of death,
and made us children of light
singing Alleluias
and dancing to the music of new life.

Texts 454 and 455 are by John Allyn Melloh, S.M., and are copyright © 1979 G.I.A. Publications, Inc., Chicago, Illinois. All rights reserved.

Pour out your Spirit upon us
that dreams and visions
bring us ever closer to the kingdom of Jesus Christ,
our risen Savior.
Through him and in the Holy Spirit
all glory be to you, almighty God,
this night and forever and ever.   [455]

Amen.

EVENING PSALM   *Psalm 141:1–5, 8–10*
                                    PH 249; PS 144, 145

While Psalm 141 is being sung, incense may be
burned.

Refrain: **Let my prayer rise before you**
            as incense,*
            the lifting of my hands
            as the evening sacrifice.

R

1 O LORD, I call to you; come to me quickly; *
       hear my voice when I cry to you.

2 **Let my prayer be set forth in your sight as**
       incense, *
       the lifting up of my hands as the evening
       sacrifice.

3 Set a watch before my mouth, O LORD,
           and guard the door of my lips; *
           4 let not my heart incline to any evil thing.

   Let me not be occupied in wickedness with
           evildoers, *
   nor eat of their choice foods.   R

5 Let the righteous smite me in friendly rebuke;
       let not the oil of the unrighteous anoint my head; *
       for my prayer is continually against their
           wicked deeds.   ▼

8 But my eyes are turned to you, Lord GOD; *
    in you I take refuge;
    do not strip me of my life.   **R**

9 Protect me from the snare which they have laid
    for me *
    and from the traps of the evildoers.

10 Let the wicked fall into their own nets, *
    while I myself escape.   **R**

After the psalm, the leader says:

Let us pray.

Pause for silent prayer.

Holy God,
let the incense of our prayer ascend before you,
and let your loving-kindness descend upon us,
that with devoted hearts we may sing your praises
with the church on earth and the whole
    heavenly host,
and glorify you forever and ever.   [456]

Amen.

The service may continue with evening prayer,
beginning with the psalm(s) on page 54.

Or, when an evening meal or other evening activity follows, the service may be concluded with:
    a brief lesson from scripture
    the Lord's Prayer
    an additional hymn (optional)
    a grace or blessing

Evening Prayer

When evening prayer begins with the service of light (pp. 43–52), the opening sentences and the evening hymn are omitted. The service proceeds with the psalm(s) on page 55.

Opening Sentences

All may stand.

1   *Ps. 24:34*

Our help is in the name of the Lord,

who made heaven and earth.

Or

2   *See Ps. 70:1*

O God, come to our assistance.

O Lord, hasten to help us.

Or

3

Light and peace in Jesus Christ our Lord.

Thanks be to God.

And one of the following, or a seasonal alternative (pp. 65–104), is said:

1   *Dan. 2:22–23*

God reveals deep and mysterious things,
and knows what is hidden in darkness.
God is surrounded by light.
To you, O God, we give thanks and praise.

2   *Ps. 139:11–12*

I could ask the darkness to hide me
or the light around me to become night,
but even darkness is not dark for you,
and the night is as bright as the day;
for darkness is as light with you.

3   *Rev. 21:23–24*

The city of God has no need of sun or moon,
for the glory of God is its light,
and its lamp is the Lamb.
By its light shall the nations walk,
and the rulers of earth shall bring their treasures into it.

4   *Rev. 22:5*

In the city of God, night shall be no more;
they need no light of lamp or sun,
for the Lord God will be their light,
and they will reign forever and ever.

5   *Zech. 14:5c, 7, and 1 John 1:5*

God will come, and there shall be continuous day,
for at evening time there shall be light.
God is light;
in God there is no darkness at all.

6   *2 Cor. 4:6*

God who said, "Out of darkness the light shall shine!"
is the same God who made light shine in our hearts
to bring us the knowledge of God's glory
shining in the face of Christ.

7   *2 Sam. 22:29, 33*

You are my lamp, O Lord.
My God lightens my darkness.
This God is my strong refuge
and has made my way safe.

EVENING HYMN

An evening hymn is sung.

IF THE SERVICE OF LIGHT IS USED, THE
SERVICE CONTINUES HERE FROM PAGE 52.

All may be seated.

PSALM(S)

One or more psalms (pp. 167–390) are sung or said.

Silence for reflection follows each psalm.

A psalm prayer may follow the silence.

SCRIPTURE READING

At the conclusion of the reading of scripture (pp. 459–506), the reader may say:

The Word of the Lord.

Thanks be to God.

Silence follows for reflection on the meaning of the scripture.

The scripture may be briefly interpreted, or a nonbiblical reading may be read.

CANTICLE

The Canticle of Mary (Magnificat) or another canticle (pp. 137–158) may be sung or said.

All may stand.

The Canticle of Mary   *The Magnificat; Luke 1:46–55*
                              PH 600; PS 161–163

Refrain: **My soul proclaims the greatness**
                of the Lord,*
           my spirit rejoices in God my Savior.

R
My soul proclaims the greatness of the Lord,
my spirit rejoices in God my Savior, *
    for you, Lord, have looked with favor on your
        lowly servant.
From this day all generations will call me blessed: *
    you, the Almighty, have done great things for me
    and holy is your name.   ▼

You have mercy on those who fear you, *
   from generation to generation.   **R**

You have shown strength with your arm, *
   and scattered the proud in their conceit,
casting down the mighty from their thrones *
   and lifting up the lowly.
You have filled the hungry with good things, *
   and sent the rich away empty.   **R**

You have come to the aid of your servant Israel, *
   to remember the promise of mercy,
the promise made to our forebears, *
   to Abraham and his children for ever.   **R**

PRAYERS OF THANKSGIVING AND INTERCESSION

The prayers of thanksgiving and intercession may take
the form of a litany (A) or of the prayers appointed for
each day of the week (B) or of a seasonal litany (pp. 65–
104).

A

The litany on pages 399–402 may be sung.

B

The following prayers may be used:

Ps. 141:2

Let my prayer rise before you as incense,

the lifting of my hands as an evening sacrifice.

If Psalm 141 has been previously sung, the following
verses are used:

Ps. 25:1–2

To you, O Lord, I lift my soul.

O God, in you I trust.

One of the following, or other prayers of thanksgiving

and intercession, are said:

1

Sunday

We lift our voices in prayers of praise, holy God, for you have lifted us to new life in Jesus Christ, and your blessings come in generous measure. Especially we thank you for

the privilege of worship and service in this congregation . . .

the good news of the gospel of Jesus Christ for us . . .

food and drink to share in the Lord's name . . .

our calling to discipleship. . . .

We hold up before you human needs, God of compassion, for you have come to us in Jesus Christ and shared our life so we may share his resurrection. Especially we pray for

the healing of those who are sick . . .

the comfort of the dying . . .

the renewal of those who despair . . .

the Spirit's power in the church. . . .   [457]

2

Monday

We rejoice in your generous goodness, O God, and celebrate your lavish gifts to us this day, for you have shown your love in giving Jesus Christ for the salvation of the world. Especially we give thanks for

the labors of those who have served us today . . .

friends with whom we have shared . . .

those whom we love and who have loved us . . .

opportunities for our work to help others . . .

all beauty that delights us. . . .

Gracious God, we know you are close to all in need, and by our prayers for others we come closer to you. We are bold to claim for others your promises of new life in Jesus Christ, as we claim them for ourselves. Especially we pray for

those in dangerous occupations . . .

physicians and nurses . . .

those who are ill or confined to nursing homes . . .   ▼

those who mourn . . .
the Roman Catholic Church. . . .   [458]

3

Tuesday

Eternal God, we thank you for being with us today, and for
every sign of your truth and love in Jesus Christ. Especially
we thank you for

the gift of peace in Christ . . .
reconciliation in our relationships . . .
each new insight into your love . . .
energy and courage to share your love . . .
the ministries of the church. . . .

Gracious God, we remember in our own hearts the needs of
others, that we may reach up to claim your love for them,
and reach out to give your love in the name of Christ.
Especially we pray for

racial harmony and justice . . .
those imprisoned . . .
strangers we have met today . . .
friends who are bereaved . . .
Orthodox and Coptic churches. . . .   [459]

4

Wednesday

Give us your peace, O God, that we may rejoice in your goodness to us and to all your children, and be thankful for your
love revealed in Jesus Christ. Especially we thank you for

people who reveal your truth and righteousness . . .
courage to be bold disciples . . .
those who show hospitality . . .
surprises that have blessed us . . .
the unity of the church of Jesus Christ. . . .

Give us your peace, O God, that we may be confident of
your care for us and all your children, as we remember the
needs of others. Especially we pray for

friends and relatives who are far away . . .
neighbors in special need . . .

those who suffer hunger and thirst . . .
those who work at night while others sleep . . .
Episcopal and Methodist churches. . . .   [460]

5

Thursday

We give you our praise and thanks, O God, for all gifts of love we have received from you, and for your persistent mercy in Jesus Christ. Especially we thank you for
work we have accomplished pleasing to you . . .
the faithful witness of Christian people . . .
the example of righteousness we see in parents
    and teachers . . .
the innocence and openness we see in children . . .
all works of Christian compassion. . . .
We give you our cares and concerns, O God, because we know you are kind and care for your children in every circumstance. Especially we pray for
those who struggle with doubt and despair . . .
people afflicted with disease . . .
those called to special ministries . . .
people neglected or abused . . .
Baptist, Disciples of Christ, and other free
    churches. . . .   [461]

6

Friday

Merciful God, we praise you that you give strength for every weakness, forgiveness for our failures, and new beginnings in Jesus Christ. Especially we thank you for
the guidance of your spirit through this day . . .
signs of new life and hope . . .
people who have helped us . . .
those who struggle for justice . . .
expressions of love unexpected or undeserved. . . .
Almighty God, you know all needs before we speak our prayers, yet you welcome our concerns for others in Jesus Christ. Especially we pray for   ▼

those who keep watch over the sick and dying . . .
those who weep with the grieving . . .
those who are without faith and cannot accept
    your love . . .
the aged who are lonely, distressed or weak . . .
Reformed, Presbyterian, and Lutheran
    churches. . . .   [462]

7

Saturday

God of glory, we praise you for your presence in our lives,
and for all goodness that you shower upon your children in
Jesus Christ. Especially we thank you for
    promises kept and hope for tomorrow . . .
    the enjoyment of friends . . .
    the wonders of your creation . . .
    love from our parents, our sisters and brothers,
        our spouses and children . . .
    pleasures of living. . . .
God of grace, we are one with all your children, for we are
sisters and brothers of Jesus Christ, and we offer our prayers
for all whom we love. Especially we pray for
    those we too often forget . . .
    people who have lost hope . . .
    victims of tragedy and disaster . . .
    those who suffer mental anguish . . .
    ecumenical councils and church agencies. . . .   [463]

Individual prayers of thanksgiving and intercession may
be offered.

There may be silent prayer.

The leader then says one of the following prayers, or a
similar prayer. For seasonal alternatives see pages 65–
104.

1

As you have made this day, O God,
you also make the night.
Give light for our comfort.
Come upon us with quietness and still our souls,
that we may listen for the whisper of your Spirit
and be attentive to your nearness in our dreams.
Empower us to rise again in new life
to proclaim your praise,
and show Christ to the world,
for he reigns forever and ever.   [464]

Amen.

2

Great God, you are one God,
and you bring together what is scattered
and mend what is broken.
Unite us with the scattered peoples of the earth
that we may be one family of your children.
Bind up all our wounds,
and heal us in spirit,
that we may be renewed as disciples
of Jesus Christ, our Master and Savior.   [465]

Amen.

3

God of all who fear you,
make us one with all your saints
and with any who are in need.
Teach us to befriend the weak,
and welcome the outcast,
that we may serve the Lord Jesus Christ
and live to offer him glory.
In his holy name we pray.   [466]

Amen.

4

God our shepherd,
you have brought us through this day
to a time of reflection and rest.
Calm our souls,
and refresh us with your peace.
Keep us close to Christ
and draw us closer to one another
in the bonds of his wondrous love.
We pray through Christ our Lord.   [467]

Amen.

5

To you, O God
we give up the burdens of this day,
trusting your love and mercy.
To you, O God,
we surrender ourselves,
trusting our risen Lord to lead us always
in the way of peace,
today, tomorrow, and forever.   [468]

Amen.

6

Protect your people, O God,
and keep us safe
until the coming of your new dawn
and the establishment of your righteous rule.
By your Holy Spirit,
stir up within us a longing
for the light of your new day,
and guide us by the radiance of Jesus Christ
your Son, our risen Lord.   [469]

Amen.

7

Abide with us, O Lord,
for evening comes and the day is almost over.
Abide with us,
for the days are hastening on
and we hasten with them.
Abide with us and with all your faithful people,
until the daystar rises and the morning light appears,
and we shall abide with you forever. [470]

Amen.

All sing (musical settings: PH 571, 589, 590; PS 192–195) or say:

Or

Our Father in heaven,
hallowed be your name,
your kingdom come,
your will be done,
on earth as in heaven.
Give us today
our daily bread.
Forgive us our sins
as we forgive those
who sin against us.
Save us from
the time of trial
and deliver us from evil.
For the kingdom,
the power,
and the glory are yours
now and forever. Amen.

Our Father,
who art in heaven,
hallowed be thy name,
thy kingdom come,
thy will be done,
on earth as it is in heaven.
Give us this day
our daily bread;
and forgive us our debts,
as we forgive our debtors;
and lead us not
into temptation,
but deliver us from evil.
For thine is the kingdom,
and the power,
and the glory,
forever. Amen.

[HYMN OR SPIRITUAL]

DISMISSAL

The leader dismisses the people using one of the following:

1 *Phil. 4:23*

May the grace of the Lord Jesus Christ be with us all.

Amen.

Bless the Lord.

The Lord's name be praised.

2 *2 Thess. 3:16*

May the Lord, who is our peace,
give us peace at all times and in every way.

Amen.

Bless the Lord.

The Lord's name be praised.

3 *Phil. 4:7*

May the peace of God, which surpasses all understanding,
guard our hearts and minds in Christ Jesus.

Amen.

Bless the Lord.

The Lord's name be praised.

A sign of peace may be exchanged by all.

ALTERNATIVE TEXTS FOR SEASONS AND FESTIVALS: MORNING AND EVENING PRAYER

ADVENT

MORNING PRAYER

OPENING SENTENCES

1   *See Isa. 55:12*

The mountains and the hills shall break forth into singing,
and all the trees of the forest shall clap their hands.
For behold, our Lord and Ruler is coming to reign forever.
Alleluia!

2   *Ps. 85:10–11*

Love and faithfulness will meet;
justice and peace will embrace.
Faithfulness will spring from the earth
and justice will look down from heaven.

3

The Lord shall come when morning dawns,
and earth's dark night is past.
As the sentry waits for daybreak,
so my soul hopes for the Lord.

4

Like the sun in the morning sky,
the Savior of the world will come.
Like rain on the meadow,
he will descend.

MORNING HYMN

Seasonal hymn (alternative to the morning psalm):

"Sleepers, Wake!" A Voice Astounds Us   PH 17

CANTICLE

While traditionally sung in morning prayer throughout
the year,

Canticle of Zechariah (pp. 137–138)   PH 601, 602;
                                             PS 158–160

is particularly appropriate when sung during Advent.
Other canticles include:

Canticle of Thanksgiving (pp. 144–145)   PS 175
Seek the Lord (pp. 145–146)   PS 176
The New Jerusalem (p. 146)   PS 177
A Canticle of Creation (pp. 149–151)   PS 180, 181
A Canticle of Praise   PS 182
The Desert Shall Blossom (p. 144)   PH 18

PRAYERS OF THANKSGIVING AND INTERCESSION

Prayer concluding thanksgiving and intercession

1

God of all wisdom,
our hearts yearn for the warmth of your love,
and our minds search for the light of your Word.
Increase our longing for Christ our Savior,
and strengthen us to grow in love,
that at the dawn of his coming
we may rejoice in his presence
and welcome the light of his truth.
This we ask in the name of Jesus Christ.   [471]

Amen.

O Christ, splendor of the glory of God,
and perfect image of the Eternal One who begot you,
we praise you for the infinite love which sent you among us;
we confess you as the light and life of the world;
and we adore you as our Lord and our God,
now and forever.   [472]

Amen.

3

Holy God,
the mystery of your eternal Word
took flesh among us
when Mary, without reserve, entrusted her life to you.
Strengthen us by the example of her humility,
that we may always be ready to do your will
and welcome Christ into our lives,
who lives and reigns forever and ever.   [473]

Amen.

LITANY FOR ADVENT—O ANTIPHONS

May be used December 17 through 23.

O Wisdom,
coming forth from the mouth of the Most High,
pervading and permeating all creation,
you order all things with strength and gentleness:
Come now and teach us the way to salvation.

Come, Lord Jesus.

O Adonai,
Ruler of the house of Israel,
you appeared in the burning bush to Moses
and gave him the law on Sinai:
Come with outstretched arm to save us.

Come, Lord Jesus. ▼

O Root of Jesse,
rising as a sign for all the peoples,
before you earthly rulers will keep silent,
and nations give you honor:
Come quickly to deliver us.

Come, Lord Jesus.

O Key of David,
Scepter over the house of Israel,
you open and no one can close,
you close and no one can open:
Come to set free the prisoners
who live in darkness and the shadow of death.

Come, Lord Jesus.

O Radiant Dawn,
splendor of eternal light,
Sun of justice:
Come, shine on those who live in darkness
and in the shadow of death.

Come, Lord Jesus.

O Ruler of the nations,
Monarch for whom the people long,
you are the Cornerstone uniting all humanity:
Come, save us all,
whom you formed out of clay.

Come, Lord Jesus.

O Immanuel,
our Sovereign and Lawgiver,
desire of the nations and Savior of all:
Come and save us, O Lord our God.

Come, Lord Jesus.

After a brief silence, the leader concludes the litany:

God of grace,
ever faithful to your promises,
the earth rejoices in hope of our Savior's coming
and looks forward with longing
to his return at the end of time.
Prepare our hearts to receive him when he comes,
for he is Lord forever and ever.   **Amen.**   [131]

EVENING PRAYER

OPENING SENTENCES

1   *Isa. 40:5*

The glory of the Lord shall be revealed,
and all people shall see it together.

2   *See Isa. 45:8*

Drop down the dew from above, O heavens,
and let the clouds rain justice.
Let the earth's womb be opened,
and bring forth a Savior.

3   *Ps. 96:11, 13*

Let the heavens be glad and let the earth rejoice,
for the Lord comes to judge the earth,
to judge the world with justice
and the nations with truth.

4   *Matt. 3:2*

Repent, for the kingdom of heaven is at hand.

EVENING HYMN

Seasonal alternative to "Hymn to Christ the Light"
(Phos Hilaron):

O Come, O Come, Emmanuel   PH 9

CANTICLE

While traditionally sung in evening prayer throughout the year,

Canticle of Mary (pp. 139–140)   PH 600; PS 161–163

is particularly appropriate when sung during Advent. Other canticles include:

Christ, the Head of All Creation (p. 155)   **PS 186**
Jesus Christ Is Lord (p. 156)   **PS 187**

PRAYERS OF THANKSGIVING AND INTERCESSION

The Litany for Advent—O Antiphons (pp. 67–69) is appropriate to use from December 17 through 22.

Prayer concluding thanksgiving and intercession

1

God of the prophets,
you sent your messenger into the wilderness of Jordan
to prepare human hearts for the coming of your Son.
Help us to prepare for Christ's coming,
and to hear the good news and repent,
that we may be ready to welcome the Lord,
our Savior, Jesus Christ.   [474]

Amen.

2

God of hope and joy,
the day draws near when the glory of your Son
will brighten the night of the waiting world.
Let no sorrow hinder the joy
of those who seek him.
Let no sin obscure the vision of wisdom
seen by those who find him.
We ask this through Christ our Lord.   [475]

Amen.

3

God of grace,
ever faithful to your promises,
the earth rejoices in hope of the Savior's coming
and looks forward with longing
to his return at the end of time.
Prepare our hearts to receive him when he comes,
for he is Lord forever and ever.   [476]

Amen.

CHRISTMAS

MORNING PRAYER

OPENING SENTENCES

1   *Luke 2:14*

Glory to God in the highest,
and peace to God's people on earth.   Alleluia!

2   *Luke 2:10, 11*

Behold I bring you good news of a great joy;
for to you is born in the city of David
a Savior, who is Christ the Lord.

3   *John 1:14*

The Word became flesh and dwelt among us,
and we beheld his glory.   Alleluia!

MORNING HYMN

Seasonal hymn (alternative to the morning psalm):

O Morning Star, How Fair and Bright   PH 69
Break Forth, O Beauteous Heavenly Light   PH 26

CANTICLE

While traditionally sung in morning prayer throughout the year,

Canticle of Zechariah (pp. 137–138)   PH 601, 602;
                                         PS 158–160

is particularly appropriate when sung during Christmas. Other canticles include:

We Praise You, O God (pp. 141–142) PH 460; PS 170, 171
Glory to God (p. 142)   PH 566, 575, 576; PS 173
A Canticle of Creation (pp. 149–151)   PS 180, 181
A Canticle of Praise   PS 182
God's Chosen One (pp. 143–144)

PRAYERS OF THANKSGIVING AND INTERCESSION

Prayer concluding thanksgiving and intercession

All-powerful and unseen God,
the coming of your light into the world
has brightened weary hearts with peace.
Teach us to proclaim the birth of your Son Jesus Christ,
who lives and reigns with you in the unity
    of the Holy Spirit,
one God, forever and ever.   [151]

Amen.

LITANY FOR CHRISTMAS: A

The Word was made flesh,

Alleluia, Alleluia!

and dwelt among us,

Alleluia, Alleluia!

Jesus, Son of the living God, splendor of the Father,
    Light eternal:

Glory to you, O Lord!

Jesus, King of glory, Sun of righteousness,
    born of the Virgin Mary:

Glory to you, O Lord!

Jesus, Wonderful Counselor, mighty God,
    everlasting Lord:

Glory to you, O Lord!

Jesus, Prince of Peace, Shepherd of souls,
    perfect in holiness:

Glory to you, O Lord!

Jesus, Friend of all, Protector of the poor,
    Treasure of the faithful:

Glory to you, O Lord!

Jesus, Good Shepherd, inexhaustible Wisdom, our Way,
    our Truth, and our Life:

Glory to you, O Lord!

Jesus, joy of the angels, and crown of all the saints:

Glory to you, O Lord!   [148]

    After a brief silence, the leader concludes the litany:

Christ is born! Give him glory!
Christ has come down from heaven! Receive him!
Christ is now on earth! Exalt him!
O earth, sing to the Lord!
O you nations, praise him in joy,
for he has been glorified!   **Amen.**   [149]

EVENING PRAYER

OPENING SENTENCES

1

    Today Christ is born;
    today salvation has appeared;
    today angels are singing and archangels rejoicing;
    today the just exult and say:
    Glory to God in the highest.   Alleluia!

In this, O God, your love was revealed among us,
that you sent your only Son into the world
so that we might live through him.

EVENING HYMN

Seasonal alternatives to "Hymn to Christ the Light"
(Phos Hilaron):

Of the Father's Love Begotten	PH 309
Lo, How a Rose E'er Blooming	PH 48

CANTICLE

While traditionally sung in evening prayer or prayer at
the close of day throughout the year,

Canticle of Mary (pp. 139–140)	PH 600; PS 161–163
Canticle of Simeon (p. 140)	PH 603–605; PS 164–166

are particularly appropriate when sung in evening prayer
during Christmas. Other canticles include:

Christ, the Head of All Creation (p. 155)	PS 185
Jesus Christ Is Lord (p. 156)	PS 186

PRAYERS OF THANKSGIVING AND INTERCESSION

Prayer concluding thanksgiving and intercession

1

Eternal God,
in Jesus Christ your light shines in our darkness,
giving joy in sorrow
and comfort in loneliness.
Fill us with the mystery of your Word made flesh,
until our hearts overflow with praise and joy,
for he is the beginning and the end of all that exists,
living forevermore.   [478]

Amen.

2

O God,
you loved the world so much
that you gave your only Son for us.
Increase and strengthen our faith
and fix it firmly on the mystery of your Word made flesh,
that we may triumph over all evil
through Christ who reigns now and forever.   [479]

Amen.

LITANY FOR CHRISTMAS: B

All the ends of the earth
have seen the salvation of our God. Alleluia!

Shout to the Lord, all the earth. Alleluia!

O Christ, splendor of God's eternal glory,
the mighty Word, sustaining the universe:
Renew our lives by your presence.

Lord, have mercy.

O Christ, born into the world in the fullness of time
for the liberation of all creation:
Release all into your promised freedom.

Lord, have mercy.

O Christ, begotten of the Father before all time,
born in a stable at Bethlehem:
May your church be a sign of hope and joy.

Lord, have mercy.

O Christ, truly God and truly human,
born to a people in fulfillment of their expectations:
Fulfill our desires in you.

Lord, have mercy. ▼

O Christ, born of the Virgin Mary,
child of wonder and splendor,
mighty God of all ages, Prince of Peace:
May the whole world live in peace and justice.

Lord, have mercy.   [150]

After a brief silence, the leader concludes the litany:

All-powerful and unseen God,
the coming of your light into our world
has brightened weary hearts with peace.
Teach us to proclaim the birth of your Son Jesus Christ,
who lives and reigns with you in the unity
    of the Holy Spirit,
one God, forever and ever.   **Amen.**   [151]

EPIPHANY
MORNING PRAYER

OPENING SENTENCES

1   *Isa. 60:1, 3, 6*

Arise, shine, for your light is come!
The glory of the Lord is risen upon you!
Nations shall come to your light,
and rulers to the brightness of your dawn.
They shall come from Sheba, bearing gold and incense,
singing the praise of God.

2

For Baptism of the Lord

Sealed with the sign of the Spirit,
Jesus rises from the waters.
The Baptizer knows him and foretells:
This is the Lamb of God
who takes away the sin of the world.

MORNING HYMN

Seasonal hymn, alternative to the morning psalm:

Brightest and Best of the Stars of the Morning   PH 67

CANTICLE

Alternatives to Canticle of Zechariah:

We Praise You, O God (pp. 141–142) PH 460; PS 170, 171
Glory to God (p. 142)   PH 566, 575, 576; PS 173
The New Jerusalem (p. 146)   PS 177

PRAYERS OF THANKSGIVING AND INTERCESSION

Prayer concluding thanksgiving and intercession

Lord Jesus, unconquered light,
your power has dawned upon the world
    with transforming love.
Grant that we, who greet you on this joyful morning,
may be found faithful at the day's end,
and in that final day be gathered with all your children,
to that city whose light is the radiance of your face,
for you reign in splendor now and forever.   [480]

Amen.

LITANY FOR EPIPHANY

All the ends of the earth
have seen the salvation of our God, Alleluia!

Shout to the Lord, all the earth, Alleluia!

With joy let us pray to our Savior,
the Son of God who became one of us, saying:
The grace of God be with us all.

O Christ,
let your gospel shine in every place
where the Word of life is not yet received.
Draw the whole creation to yourself
that your salvation may be known through all the earth.

The grace of God be with us all.   ▼

O Christ, Savior and Lord,
extend your church to every place.
Make it a place of welcome for people of every race
and tongue.

The grace of God be with us all.

O Christ, Ruler of rulers,
direct the work and thoughts of the leaders of nations
that they may seek justice,
and further peace and freedom for all.

The grace of God be with us all.

O Christ, Master of all,
support of the weak and comfort of the afflicted,
strengthen the tempted and raise the fallen.
Watch over the lonely and those in danger.
Give hope to the despairing
and sustain the faith of the persecuted.

The grace of God be with us all.   Amen.   [170]

After a brief silence, the leader concludes the litany:

O Christ, light made manifest as the true light of God,
gladden our hearts on the joyful morning of your glory;
call us by our name on the great Day of your coming;
and give us grace to offer,
with all the hosts of heaven,
unending praise to God
in whom all things find their ending,
now and ever.   **Amen.**   [171]

EVENING PRAYER

OPENING SENTENCES

1

This is a holy day adorned with three mysteries:
Today a star leads the magi to the manger;

today water is made wine at the wedding;
today Christ is baptized by John in the Jordan to save us.
Alleluia!

2   *Mal. 1:11*

From the rising of the sun to its setting
my name is great among the nations,
and in every place incense is offered to my name,
and a pure offering;
for my name is great among the nations,
says the Lord of hosts.

EVENING HYMN

Seasonal alternatives to "Hymn to Christ the Light"
(Phos Hilaron):

Let All Mortal Flesh Keep Silence	PH 5
What Star Is This, with Beams So Bright	PH 68

CANTICLE

Alternatives to Canticle of Mary:

Christ, the Head of All Creation (p. 155)	PS 185
Jesus Christ Is Lord (p. 156)	PS 186
The Mystery of Our Religion (p. 156)	

PRAYERS OF THANKSGIVING AND INTERCESSION

Prayer concluding thanksgiving and intercession

1

Eternal Light,
you have shown us your glory in Christ,
    the Word made flesh.
Your light is strong,
your love is near.
Draw us beyond the limits which this world imposes,
to the life where the Spirit makes all life complete,
through Jesus Christ our Lord.   [481]

Amen.

Almighty God,
who anointed Jesus at his baptism with the Holy Spirit,
and revealed him as your beloved Son:
Keep us, your children born of water and the Spirit,
faithful in your service,
that we may rejoice to be called children of God,
through the same Jesus Christ our Lord.   [482]

Amen.

Litany for Baptism of the Lord

O Christ,
by your epiphany your light shines upon us,
giving us the fullness of salvation.
Help us show your light to all we meet today.

Lord, have mercy.

O Christ of glory,
you humbled yourself to be baptized,
showing us the way of humility.
Strengthen us to serve you in humility all the days of our life.

Lord, have mercy.

O Christ,
by your baptism you cleansed us from our sin,
making us children of your Father.
Give the grace of being a child of God to all who seek you.

Lord, have mercy.

O Christ,
by your baptism you sanctified creation
and opened the door of repentance
to all who are baptized.
Make us servants of your gospel in the world.

Lord, have mercy.

O Christ,
by your baptism you revealed to us the glorious Trinity
when the voice from heaven proclaimed,
  "This is my beloved Son,"
and the Holy Spirit descended upon you like a dove.
Renew a heart of worship within all the baptized.

Lord, have mercy.   [177]

  After a brief silence, the leader concludes the litany:

Almighty God,
you anointed Jesus at his baptism with the Holy Spirit,
and revealed him as your beloved Son.
Keep us, your children born of water and the Spirit,
faithful in your service,
that we may rejoice to be called children of God;
through the same Jesus Christ our Lord,
who lives and reigns with you and the Holy Spirit,
one God, now and forever.   **Amen.**   [178]

LENT

In daily prayer there is a tradition of using the Great
Litany (pp. 393–398) as an alternative service on all
Wednesdays and Fridays of Lent, beginning the Friday
after Ash Wednesday and continuing until the Friday
before Passion/Palm Sunday.

MORNING PRAYER

OPENING SENTENCES

1   *Ps. 86:5–6*

  O Lord, you are kind and forgiving,
  full of love to all who call on you.
  Listen to my prayer, O Lord;
  hear the cries of my pleading.

2   *Ps. 86:11–12*

Show me your way, O Lord,
that I may follow in your truth.
Teach me to revere your name,
and my whole heart will praise you.

3   *Matt. 16:24*

Jesus told his disciples:
If any want to become my followers,
let them deny themselves
and take up their cross and follow me.

4   *Ps. 51:10*

Create in me a clean heart, O God,
and renew a right spirit within me.

5

For Holy Week   *1 Peter 2:24*

Christ himself bore our sins in his body on the cross,
so that, free from sins, we might live to righteousness;
by his wounds we have been healed.

MORNING HYMN

Seasonal hymn, alternative to the morning psalm:

There's a Wideness in God's Mercy	PH 298
Holy Week: Ah, Holy Jesus	PH 93

CANTICLE

Alternatives to Canticle of Zechariah:

Seek the Lord (pp. 145–146)	PS 176
A Canticle of Penitence (pp. 151–152)	PS 183
We Praise You, O God (pp. 141–142)	PH 460; PS 170, 171
Glory to God (p. 142)	PH 566, 575, 576; PS 173
The New Jerusalem (p. 146)	PS 177

PRAYERS OF THANKSGIVING AND INTERCESSION

Prayer concluding thanksgiving and intercession

1

God of all joy,
fill our souls to overflowing
with the fullness of your grace.
In this season,
remind us of your triumph over the tragedy of the cross,
and your victory for us over the powers of sin and death,
so that we may reflect your glory
as disciples of Jesus Christ,
our risen Lord.   [483]

Amen.

2

God of love,
as you have given your life to us,
so may we live according to your holy will
revealed in Jesus Christ.
Make us bold to share your life,
and show your love,
in the power of your Holy Spirit.
Grant this through Jesus Christ
    our Redeemer and Lord.   [484]

Amen.

3

Take all our doubts and uncertainties, O God,
and fill us with such faith
that we may be confident of your love
and loyal in the service of him
who died and yet lives for us,
Jesus Christ the Lord.   [485]

Amen.

LITANY FOR LENT

O Christ,
out of your fullness we have all received grace upon grace.
You are our eternal hope;
you are patient and full of mercy;
you are generous to all who call upon you.

Save us, Lord.

O Christ, fountain of life and holiness,
you have taken away our sins.
On the cross you were wounded for our transgressions
and were bruised for our iniquities.

Save us, Lord.

O Christ, obedient unto death,
source of all comfort,
our life and our resurrection,
our peace and reconciliation:

Save us, Lord.

O Christ, Savior of all who trust you,
hope of all who die for you,
and joy of all the saints:

Save us, Lord.

Jesus, Lamb of God,

have mercy on us.

Jesus, bearer of our sins,

have mercy on us.

Jesus, redeemer of the world,

grant us peace. [213]

After a brief silence, the leader concludes the litany:

God of love,
as in Jesus Christ you gave yourself to us,
so may we give ourselves to you,
living according to your holy will.
Keep our feet firmly in the way
where Christ leads us;
make our mouths speak the truth
that Christ teaches us;
fill our bodies with the life
that is Christ within us.
In his holy name we pray. **Amen.** [214]

INTERCESSION FOR LENT

Jesus, remember us when you come into your kingdom.
Hear our intercessions.

For your church around the world,

we ask new life.

For all who carry out ministries in your church,

we ask grace and wisdom.

For people who have accepted spiritual disciplines,

we ask inspired discipleship.

For Christians of every land,

we ask new unity in your name.

For Jews and Muslims and people of other faiths,

we ask your divine blessing.

For those who cannot believe,

we ask your faithful love.

For governors and rulers in every land,

we ask your guidance.

For people who suffer and sorrow,

we ask your healing peace. [216]

After a brief silence, the leader concludes the litany:

Holy God,
your Word, Jesus Christ, spoke peace to a sinful world
and brought humanity the gift of reconciliation
by the suffering and death he endured.
Teach those who bear his name
to follow the example he gave us.
May our faith, hope, and charity
turn hatred to love, conflict to peace, and death to eternal life;
through Christ our Lord.   **Amen.**   [217]

RESPONSIVE PRAYER ON CHRIST'S PASSION

This litany is appropriate for use on Passion/Palm
Sunday, Good Friday, or Holy Saturday.

Our Redeemer suffered death,
was buried and rose again for our sake.
With love let us adore him, aware of our needs.

Christ our teacher,
for us you were obedient, even to death:

Teach us to obey God's will in all things.

Christ our life,
by dying on the cross
you destroyed the power of evil and death:

Enable us to die with you, and to rise with you in glory.

Christ our strength,
you were despised,
and humiliated as a condemned criminal:

Teach us the humility by which you saved the world.

Christ our salvation,
you gave your life out of love for us:

Help us to love one another.

Christ our Savior,
on the cross you embraced all time
with your outstretched arms:

Gather all the scattered children of God into your realm.

Jesus, Lamb of God,

have mercy on us.

Jesus, bearer of our sins,

have mercy on us.

Jesus, redeemer of the world,

grant us peace.　[243]

After a brief silence, the leader concludes the prayer:

Eternal God,
as we are baptized into the death of Jesus Christ,
so give us the grace of repentance
that we may pass through the grave with him
and be born again to eternal life.
For he is the One
who was crucified, dead, and buried,
and rose again for us,
Jesus our Savior.　**Amen.**　[244]

LITANY FOR GOOD FRIDAY

O crucified Jesus,
Son of the Father,
conceived by the Holy Spirit,
born of the Virgin Mary,
eternal Word of God,

we worship you.　▼

O crucified Jesus,
holy temple of God,
dwelling place of the Most High
gate of heaven,
burning flame of love,

we worship you.

O crucified Jesus,
sanctuary of justice and love,
full of kindness,
source of all faithfulness,

we worship you.

O crucified Jesus,
ruler of every heart,
in you are all the treasures of wisdom and knowledge,
in you dwells all the fullness of the Godhead,

we worship you.

Jesus, Lamb of God,

have mercy on us.

Jesus, bearer of our sins,

have mercy on us.

Jesus, redeemer of the world,

grant us peace. [253]

After a brief silence, the leader concludes the litany:

Almighty God,
look with mercy on your family
for whom our Lord Jesus Christ was willing to be betrayed
and to be given over to the hands of sinners
and to suffer death on the cross;
who now lives and reigns with you and the Holy Spirit,
one God, forever and ever. **Amen.** [251]

Evening Prayer

Opening Sentences

1 *Ps. 51:17*

The sacrifice acceptable to God is a humble spirit;
a broken and contrite heart, O God,
you will not despise.

2 *Ps. 143:10*

Teach me to do your will,
for you are my God.

3 *Ps. 103:8*

You, O Lord, are full of compassion and mercy,
slow to anger, and rich in kindness.

4 *Rom. 5:8*

God shows such love for us
in that while we still were sinners
Christ died for us.

Evening Hymn

Seasonal alternatives to "Hymn to Christ the Light"
(Phos Hilaron):

Jesus, Thou Joy of Loving Hearts	PH 510, 511
O Sacred Head, Now Wounded	PH 98

Canticle

Alternatives to Canticle of Mary:

A Canticle of the Redeemed (pp. 152–153)	PS 184
Jesus Christ Is Lord (p. 156)	PS 186
The Beatitudes (p. 157)	PS 188
Christ the Servant (pp. 157–158)	PS 189
Maundy Thursday: A Canticle of Love (pp. 154–155)	PS 187

PRAYERS OF THANKSGIVING AND INTERCESSION

The litany appointed for use for morning prayer during
Lent (pp. 84–85), the Intercession for Lent (pp. 85–86),
the Responsive Prayer on Christ's Passion (pp. 86–87),
or the Litany for Good Friday (pp. 87–88) may be used.

Prayer concluding thanksgiving and intercession

1

Eternal God,
as we are baptized into the death of Jesus Christ,
so give us the grace of repentance
that we may pass through the grave with him
and be born again to eternal life,
for he is the One who was crucified, dead, and buried,
and rose again for us,
Jesus our Savior.   [486]

Amen.

2

Eternal God,
source and goal of all life,
lead us to life eternal
by the mighty love of Jesus Christ,
who suffered on the cross,
was raised from the dead,
and lifted into glory
where with outstretched arms
he welcomes the world in his strong and loving embrace.
In his holy name we pray,
now and forever.   [487]

Amen.

3

Lord Jesus Christ,
who stretched out your arms of love on the hard wood
    of the cross
that everyone might come within the reach

of your saving embrace:
So clothe us in your Spirit
that we, reaching forth our hands in love,
may bring those who do not know you
to the knowledge and love of you;
for the honor of your name.   [488]

Amen.

EASTER

MORNING PRAYER

OPENING SENTENCES

1

Alleluia! Christ is risen!

Christ is risen indeed, Alleluia!

2   *1 Cor. 15:20*

Christ has been raised from the dead,
the first fruits of those who have fallen asleep.

3

Ascension   *Heb. 2:9*

We see Jesus,
who for a little while was made lower than the angels.
He is crowned with glory and honor. Alleluia!

MORNING HYMN

Seasonal hymn, alternative to the morning psalm:

Come, Ye Faithful, Raise the Strain   PH 114, 115
Ascension: At the Name of Jesus   PH 148

CANTICLE

Alternatives to Canticle of Zechariah:

We Praise You, O God (pp. 141–142)	PH 460; PS 170, 171
Glory to God (p. 142)	PS 173
Canticle of Miriam and Moses (p. 143)	PS 174
Canticle of David (p. 148)	
A Canticle of Creation (pp. 149–151)	PS 180, 181
A Canticle of Praise	PS 182

PRAYERS OF THANKSGIVING AND INTERCESSION

Prayer concluding thanksgiving and intercession

1

God of mercy,
we no longer look for Jesus among the dead,
for he is alive and has become the Lord of life.
From the waters of death you raise us with him
and renew your gift of life within us.
Increase in our hearts and minds
the risen life we share with Christ,
and help us to grow as your people
toward the fullness of eternal life with you,
through Christ our Lord.   [268]

Amen.

2

God of grace,
you cause the sun to rise
and chase away the shadows of death.
Each day you promise resurrection,
that we may be born again to new life
and overcome all that would hurt or destroy.
Fill us with the Holy Spirit,
that we may be alive again
with the power and the peace of Jesus Christ,
our risen Lord.   [490]

Amen.

RESPONSIVE PRAYER FOR EASTER

O Christ, in your resurrection,
the heavens and the earth rejoice. Alleluia!

By your resurrection you broke open the gates of hell,
and destroyed sin and death.

Keep us victorious over sin.

By your resurrection you raised the dead,
and brought us from death to life.

Guide us in the way of eternal life.

By your resurrection you confounded your guards
    and executioners,
and filled the disciples with joy.

Give us joy in your service.

By your resurrection you proclaimed good news
    to the women and apostles,
and brought salvation to the whole world.

Direct our lives as your new creation. [267]

After a brief silence, the leader concludes the prayer:

God of mercy,
we no longer look for Jesus among the dead,
for he is alive and has become the Lord of life.
From the waters of death you raise us with him
and renew your gift of life within us.
Increase in our minds and hearts
the risen life we share with Christ,
and help us to grow as your people
toward the fullness of eternal life with you,
through Christ our Lord,
who lives and reigns with you and the Holy Spirit,
one God, now and forever.   **Amen.** [268]

Arise, O Lord, in your strength.

We will praise you for your glory!

Let us pray with joy to Christ at the right hand of God, saying:
You are the king of glory!

You have raised the weakness of our flesh.
Heal us from our sins,
and restore to us the full dignity of life.

You are the king of glory!

May our faith lead us to the Father
as we follow the road you trod.

You are the king of glory!

You have promised to draw all people to yourself;
let no one of us be separate from your body.

You are the king of glory!

Grant that by our longing we may join you
    in your kingdom
where your humanity and ours is glorified.

You are the king of glory!

You are true God, and you will be our judge,
so lead us to contemplate your tender mercy.

You are the king of glory!   [300]

After a brief silence, the leader concludes the litany:

O King of glory and Lord of hosts,
who ascended triumphantly above the heavens,
do not abandon us,
but send us the promised one,
the Spirit of truth.
Blessed be the holy and undivided Trinity,
now and forever.   [301]

Evening Prayer

Opening Sentences

1   *See Rom. 6:4–11*

In baptism, we were buried with Christ;
in baptism we were also raised with Christ.
Once we were spiritually dead;
now God has brought us life with Christ. Alleluia!

2   *1 Peter 1:3*

By God's great mercy
we have been born anew to a living hope
through the resurrection of Jesus Christ from the dead.
Blessed be God the Father of our Lord Jesus Christ.

3   *Heb. 4:14, 16*
Ascension

We have a great high priest who has passed
    through the heavens,
Jesus, the Son of God.
Let us with boldness approach the throne of grace.

Evening Hymn

Seasonal alternatives to "Hymn to Christ the Light"
(Phos Hilaron):

The Strife Is O'er	PH 119
Ascension: The Head That Once Was Crowned	PH 149

Canticle

Alternatives to Canticle of Mary:

A Canticle to the Lamb (p. 152)	PS 191
Canticle of the Redeemed (pp. 152–153)	PS 184
Christ, the Head of All Creation (p. 155)	PS 185
Jesus Christ Is Lord (p. 156)	PS 186
Christ Our Passover (p. 158)	PS 190

PRAYERS OF THANKSGIVING AND INTERCESSION

Prayer concluding thanksgiving and intercession

1

Stay with us, Lord Jesus,
for evening draws near.
Be our companion on the way
to set our hearts on fire with new hope.
Help us to recognize your presence among us
in the scriptures we read
and in the breaking of bread,
that our lives may worship you now and forever.   [491]
Amen.

2

Sovereign God,
the whole universe is within your reach,
and all things are ordered by your hand.
You have claimed us to be your people
and appointed us disciples of Jesus Christ, our risen Lord.
As you have protected our lives,
so preserve our souls
and keep before us always
the vision of our Redeemer
that we may see and follow
and give him glory forever and ever.   [492]
Amen.

3

You have shown your glory, O God,
in raising Jesus from the dead.
Raise us to new life in him,
and empower us to serve you.
May your words be in our mouths,
your strength in our arms,
and your love in our hearts,
that we may be worthy disciples
of Jesus Christ the living Lord.   [493]
Amen.

Litany for Easter

Or, the Litany for Ascension (p. 94) may be used.

O Christ,
after your resurrection you appeared to your disciples;
you breathed on them,
that they might receive the Holy Spirit.
You gave joy and exultation to the whole creation.
Through your victory, we pray to you:

Hear us, Lord of glory.

O Christ,
after your resurrection you sent out your disciples
to teach all nations
and to baptize them
in the name of the Father and of the Son and
    of the Holy Spirit;
you promised to be with them
and us until the end of the world.
Through your victory, we pray to you:

Hear us, Lord of glory.

O Christ,
through your resurrection you lifted us up,
and filled us with rejoicing.
Through your salvation you enrich us with your gifts.
Renew our lives and fill our hearts with joy.
Through your victory, we pray to you:

Hear us, Lord of glory.

O Christ,
you are glorified by angels in heaven,
    and worshiped on earth.
On the glorious feast of your resurrection,
we pray to you:

Hear us, Lord of glory.   ▼

Save us, O Christ our Lord, in your goodness,
extend your mercy to your people who await the resurrection,
and have mercy on us.

Hear us, Lord of glory.

O merciful God, you raised your beloved Son,
and in your love you established him as head of your church,
and ruler of the universe.
By your goodness we pray:

Hear us, Lord of glory.   [269]

After a brief silence, the leader concludes the litany:

O God,
you gave your only Son
to suffer death on the cross for our redemption,
and by his glorious resurrection
you delivered us from the power of death.
Grant us so to die daily to sin,
that we may evermore live with him
    in the joy of his resurrection;
through Jesus Christ our Lord,
who lives and reigns with you and the Holy Spirit,
one God, now and forever.   **Amen.**   [270]

PENTECOST

MORNING PRAYER

OPENING SENTENCES
Acts 1:8

You shall receive power
when the Holy Spirit has come upon you,
and you shall be my witnesses.

MORNING HYMN

Seasonal hymn, alternative to the morning psalm:

Pentecost: Come, Holy Spirit, Heavenly Dove   PH 126

CANTICLE

Alternatives to Canticle of Zechariah:

We Praise You, O God (pp. 141–142) PH 460; PS 170, 171
Glory to God (p. 142)   PS 173
Canticle of Miriam and Moses (p. 143)   PS 174
God's Chosen One (pp. 143–144)
The Spirit of the Lord (p. 147)

PRAYERS OF THANKSGIVING AND INTERCESSION

Prayer concluding thanksgiving and intercession

1

True and only Light,
from whom comes every good gift,
send your Spirit into our lives
with the power of a mighty wind.
Open the horizons of our minds
by the flame of your wisdom.
Loosen our tongues to sing your praise,
for only in your Spirit
can we tell of your glory
and acclaim Jesus as Lord.   [314]

Amen.

2

God, our creator,
as in the beginning you formed us out of the dust of the earth
and breathed us into life,
so now, by your Spirit, breathe into us new life.
As at Pentecost your Spirit fell upon waiting disciples,
and empowered them as your faithful witnesses,
now, by your Spirit, fill us with joy and boldness.
May the power of your Spirit transform us,
the prompting of your Spirit lead us,
and the gifts of your Spirit mark our lives,
now and forever.   [494]

Amen.

Holy Spirit, Creator,
in the beginning you moved over the waters.
From your breath all creation drew life.
Without you, life turns to dust.

Come, Holy Spirit!

Holy Spirit, Counselor,
by your inspiration, the prophets spoke and acted in faith.
You clothed them in power to be bearers of your Word.

Come, Holy Spirit!

Holy Spirit, Power,
you came as fire to Jesus' disciples;
you gave them voice before the rulers of this world.

Come, Holy Spirit!

Holy Spirit, Sanctifier,
you created us children of God;
you make us the living temple of your presence;
you intercede within us with sighs too deep for words.

Come, Holy Spirit!

Holy Spirit, Giver of life,
you guide and make holy the church you create;
you give gifts—
    the spirit of wisdom and understanding,
    the spirit of counsel and fortitude,
    the spirit of knowledge and piety,
    the spirit of the fear of the Lord,
    that the whole creation may become what you want it
      to be.

Come, Holy Spirit!   [313]

After a brief silence, the leader concludes the litany:

True and only Light,
from whom comes every good gift:

Send your Spirit into our lives
with the power of a mighty wind.
Open the horizons of our minds
by the flame of your wisdom.
Loosen our tongues to show your praise,
for only in your Spirit can we voice your words of peace
and acclaim Jesus as Lord.   **Amen.**   [314]

LITANY FOR PENTECOST: B

Christ has gathered the church in unity through the Spirit.
With sure hope, let us pray: Lord, hear our prayer.

Maker of all things,
in the beginning, you created heaven and earth.
In the fullness of time, you restored all things in Christ.
Renew our world, in this day, with your grace and mercy.

Lord, hear our prayer.

Life of the world,
you breathed life into the flesh you created.
Now, by your Spirit, breathe new life
    into the children of earth.
Turn hatred into love, sorrow into joy, and war into peace.

Lord, hear our prayer.

Lover of concord,
you desire the unity of all Christians.
Set aflame the whole church with the fire of your Spirit.
Unite us to stand in the world as a sign of your love.

Lord, hear our prayer.

God of compassion,
through your Spirit you supply every human need.
Heal the sick, and comfort the distressed.
Befriend the friendless, and help the helpless.

Lord, hear our prayer.   ▼

Source of peace,
your Spirit restores our anxious spirits.
In our labor, give us rest;
in our temptation, strength;
in our sadness, consolation.

Lord, hear our prayer.   [315]

> After a brief silence, the leader concludes the litany:

God eternal,
as you sent upon the disciples
the promised gift of the Holy Spirit,
look upon your church
and open our hearts to the power of the Holy Spirit.
Kindle in us the fire of your love,
and strengthen our lives for service in your kingdom;
through your Son, Jesus Christ our Lord,
who lives and reigns with you in the unity
   of the Holy Spirit,
one God, now and forever.   **Amen.**   [316]

EVENING PRAYER

OPENING SENTENCES

Rom. 5:5

God's love has been poured into our hearts
through the Holy Spirit that has been given to us.

EVENING HYMN

> Seasonal alternative to "Hymn to Christ the Light"
> (Phos Hilaron):

> *Pentecost:*   Come, Holy Spirit, Our Souls Inspire   PH 125

CANTICLE

> Alternatives to Canticle of Mary:

> Canticle of the Redeemed (pp. 152–153)   PS 184
> A Canticle for Pentecost (pp. 153–154)

Prayers of Thanksgiving and Intercession

Prayer concluding thanksgiving and intercession

Holy God,
who suddenly appeared upon your children
    like the flaring of fire
and illumined a multitude with a common mind:
so fill us, and all your faithful,
with the Holy Spirit,
that in a blaze of truth
we may know that we are your sons and daughters,
one family of faith,
one body given life through Christ our Head,
who reigns with you and the Holy Spirit
forever and ever.   [495]

Amen.

Litany for Pentecost: C

God's Spirit joins with our spirits, Alleluia,

to declare that we are children of God. Alleluia!

Come, Spirit of wisdom,
and teach us to value the highest gifts.

Come, Holy Spirit.

Come, Spirit of understanding,
and show us all things in the light of eternity.

Come, Holy Spirit.

Come, Spirit of counsel,
and guide us along the straight and narrow path
    to our heavenly home.

Come, Holy Spirit.

Come, Spirit of might,
and strengthen us against every evil spirit and interest
which would separate us from you.   ▼

Come, Holy Spirit.

Come, Spirit of knowledge,
and teach us the shortness of life and the length of eternity.

Come, Holy Spirit.

Come, Spirit of godliness,
and stir up our minds and hearts
to love and serve the Lord our God all our days.

Come, Holy Spirit.

Come, Spirit of fear of the Lord,
and make us tremble with awe and reverence
before your divine majesty.

Come, Holy Spirit.   [317]

After a brief silence, the leader concludes the litany:

Come, Holy Spirit!
Rain upon our dry and dusty lives.
Wash away our sin
and heal our wounded spirits.
Kindle within us the fire of your love
to burn away our apathy.
With your warmth bend our rigidity,
and guide our wandering feet.   **Amen.**   [318]

An Outline of Midday Prayer

Opening Sentences
[Hymn]
    Psalm
    Psalm
    Silent Prayer
    Psalm Prayer
Scripture Reading
    Silent Reflection
Prayers of the People
    Individual Prayers
    Concluding Prayer
    Lord's Prayer
[Hymn or Canticle]
Dismissal
    [Sign of Peace]

When a person is worshiping alone, or in a family group, or when circumstances call for an abbreviated order, the following is suggested:

Psalm
Scripture Reading
    Silent Reflection
Prayers of Thanksgiving and Intercession

MIDDAY PRAYER

OPENING SENTENCES

All may stand.

Our help is in the name of the Lord,

who made heaven and earth.   *Ps. 124:8*

And one of the following:

1   *Mal. 1:11*

From the rising of the sun to its setting
my name is great among the nations,
says the Lord of hosts.

Praise the Lord.

The name of the Lord be praised.

2   *Deut. 32:11*

Like an eagle teaching her young to fly,
catching them safely on her spreading wings,
the Lord kept Israel from falling.

Praise the Lord.

The Lord's name be praised.

3   *Isa. 40:31*

Those who trust in the Lord for help
will find their strength renewed.

They will rise on wings like eagles;
they will run and not get weary;
they will walk and not grow weak.

Praise the Lord.

The Lord's name be praised.

[HYMN]

Following the hymn, all may sit.

PSALM

One of the following, or another psalm, is sung or said:

Psalm 19:1–6	PH 166	PS 12
Psalm 67	PH 202	PS 59, 60
Psalm 113	PH 225, 226	PS 113
Psalm 119:97–104		PS 123
Psalm 119:129–136		PS 124
Psalm 121	PH 234	PS 125
Psalm 122	PH 235	PS 126
Psalm 124	PH 236	PS 128
Psalm 126	PH 237	PS 130, 131
Psalm 127	PH 238	PS 132
Psalm 128	PH 239	PS 133
Psalm 130	PH 240	PS 134

Silence for reflection follows each psalm. A psalm prayer may follow the silence.

SCRIPTURE READING

At the conclusion of the reading from scripture (pp. 459–506), the reader may say:

The Word of the Lord.

Thanks be to God.

Silence may follow for reflection on the meaning of the scripture.

Prayers of the People

All may stand.

Individual Prayers

There may be a brief time of prayer, spoken and silent, in which the promises of God are claimed for individual and corporate needs and concerns.

Concluding Prayer

The leader concludes with one of the following or a similar prayer:

1

Eternal God,
send your Holy Spirit into our hearts,
to direct and rule us according to your will,
to comfort us in all our afflictions,
to defend us from all error,
and to lead us into all truth;
through Jesus Christ our Lord.　　[496]

Amen.

2

God, our creator,
you have given us work to do
and call us to use our talents for the good of all.
Guide us as we work,
and teach us to live
in the Spirit who made us your sons and daughters,
in the love that made us sisters and brothers,
through Jesus Christ our Lord.　　[497]

Amen.

3

Enable us, O God,
to do all things as unto you;

that small things may be filled with greatness,
and great things may be crowned with humility;
through Jesus Christ our Lord. [498]

Amen.

4

Eternal God,
your hand shaped our lives by grace
and your hand rescued us from sin by love.
May your hand guide us through this day,
shielding us from all evil,
strengthening us to do justice and love,
in Jesus Christ our Lord. [499]

Amen.

5

New every morning is your love,
great God of light,
and all day long you are working for good in the world.
Stir up in us the desire to serve you,
to live peacefully with our neighbors,
and to devote each day to your Son,
our Savior, Jesus Christ the Lord. [500]

Amen.

6

Noon

Blessed Savior,
at this hour you hung upon the cross,
stretching out your loving arms.
Grant that all the peoples of the earth
may be drawn to your redeeming love;
for your kingdom's sake. [501]

Amen.

7

Noon

God of mercy,
this midday moment of rest is your welcome gift.
Bless the work we have begun,
make good its defects,
and let us finish it in a way that pleases you.
Grant this through Christ our Lord.   [502]

Amen.

LORD'S PRAYER

All sing (musical settings: PH 571, 589, 590; PS 192–
195) or say:

Or

Our Father in heaven,
hallowed be your name,
your kingdom come,
your will be done,
on earth as in heaven.
Give us today
    our daily bread.
Forgive us our sins
as we forgive those
    who sin against us.
Save us from
    the time of trial
and deliver us from evil.
For the kingdom,
    the power,
    and the glory are yours
now and forever.   Amen.

Our Father,
    who art in heaven,
hallowed be thy name,
thy kingdom come,
thy will be done,
on earth as it is in heaven.
Give us this day
    our daily bread;
and forgive us our debts,
as we forgive our debtors;
and lead us not
    into temptation,
but deliver us from evil.
For thine is the kingdom,
    and the power,
    and the glory,
forever.   Amen.

[HYMN OR CANTICLE]

DISMISSAL

The leader concludes:

Phil. 4:9

The God of peace be with us.

Amen.

Bless the Lord.

The Lord's name be praised.

A sign of peace may be exchanged by all.

AN OUTLINE OF PRAYER AT THE CLOSE OF DAY

Opening Sentences
Hymn
Prayer of Confession
Psalm
    Psalm
    Silent Prayer
    [Psalm Prayer]
Scripture Reading
    Silent Reflection
Prayer
    Prayers
    Lord's Prayer
Canticle of Simeon
Dismissal
    [Sign of Peace]

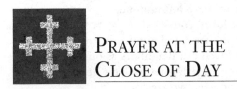

Prayer at the Close of Day

Opening Sentences

All may stand.

See Ps. 70:11

O God, come to our assistance.

O Lord, hasten to help us.

The Lord grant us a restful night and peace at the last.

Amen.

Hymn

A hymn appropriate to the end of the day may be sung.

Prayer of Confession

Almighty God, Maker of all things,

have mercy on us.

Jesus Christ, Redeemer of the world,

have mercy on us.

Holy Spirit, Giver of life,

have mercy on us.

After a brief silence for self-examination, one of the following prayers is said:

1

Merciful God,
we confess that we have sinned against you
in thought, word, and deed,
by what we have done,
and by what we have left undone.
We have not loved you
with our whole heart and mind and strength;
we have not loved our neighbors as ourselves.
In your mercy forgive what we have been,
help us amend what we are,
and direct what we shall be,
so that we may delight in your will
and walk in your ways
to the glory of your holy name.   [49]

2

Eternal God,
in whom we live and move and have our being,
whose face is hidden from us by our sins,
and whose mercy we forget in the blindness of our
    hearts:
Cleanse us from all our offenses,
and deliver us from proud thoughts and vain desires,
that with reverent and humble hearts
we may draw near to you,
confessing our faults,
confiding in your grace,
and finding in you our refuge and strength;
through Jesus Christ your Son.   [67]

3

Leader:
I confess to God Almighty,
before the whole company of heaven,
and to you, my brothers and sisters,
that I have sinned by my own fault,
in thought, word, and deed;

wherefore I pray God Almighty to have mercy on me,
forgive me all my sins,
and bring me to everlasting life. [503]

All:
**May Almighty God have mercy on you,
pardon and deliver you from all your sins
and give you time to amend your life.**

Leader:
Amen.

All:
**I confess to God Almighty,
before the whole company of heaven,
and to you, my brothers and sisters,
that I have sinned by my own fault,
in thought, word, and deed;
wherefore I pray God Almighty to have mercy on me,
forgive me all my sins,
and bring me to everlasting life.** [503]

Leader:
May Almighty God have mercy on you,
pardon and deliver you from all your sins
and give you time to amend your life.

All:

Amen.

All may sit.

PSALM

One of the following psalms is sung or said:

Psalm 4	PH 160	PS 3
Psalm 23	PH 170–175	PS 18–20
Psalm 33:1–12 or 33:13–22	PH 185	PS 30, 31
Psalm 34:1–10 or 34:11–22		PS 32, 33
Psalm 91:1–2, 4, 9–16	PH 212	PS 85

Psalm 121	PH 234	PS 125
Psalm 134	PH 242	PS 138
Psalm 136:1–9, 23–26	PH 243	PS 139
Psalm 139:1–12	PH 248	PS 142, 143

Silence for reflection follows each psalm.

A psalm prayer may follow the silence.

SCRIPTURE READING

One of the following is read:

1   *Matt. 11:28–30*
[Jesus said:] Come to me, all you that are weary and are carrying heavy burdens, and I will give you rest. Take my yoke
upon you, and learn from me; for I am gentle and humble
in heart, and you will find rest for your souls. For my yoke
is easy, and my burden is light.

2   *1 Thess. 5:23*
May the God of peace . . . sanctify you entirely; and may
your spirit and soul and body be kept sound and blameless
at the coming of our Lord Jesus Christ.

3   *Matt. 6:31–34*
Do not worry, saying, "What will we eat?" or "What will
we drink?" or "What will we wear?" For it is the Gentiles
who strive for all these things. But strive first for the kingdom of God and his righteousness, and all these things will
be given to you as well.

4   *2 Cor. 4:6–10*
It is the God who said, "Let light shine out of darkness,"
who has shone in our hearts to give the light of the knowledge of the glory of God in the face of Jesus Christ.

5   *1 John 4:18–20*
There is no fear in love, but perfect love casts out fear; for
fear has to do with punishment, and whoever fears has not
reached perfection in love. We love because he first loved

us. Those who say, "I love God," and hate their brothers or sisters, are liars; for those who do not love a brother or sister whom they have seen, cannot love God whom they have not seen.

6   Rev. 22:3c–5

[The servants of the Lamb] will worship him; they will see his face, and his name will be on their foreheads. And there will be no more night; they need no light of lamp or sun, for the Lord God shall be their light, and they will reign forever and ever.

7   John 14:27

[Jesus said:] Peace I leave with you; my peace I give to you. I do not give to you as the world gives. Do not let your hearts be troubled, and do not let them be afraid.

8   Rom. 8:38–39

I am convinced that neither death, nor life, nor angels, nor rulers, nor things present, nor things to come, nor powers, nor height, nor depth, nor anything else in all creation, will be able to separate us from the love of God in Christ Jesus our Lord.

9   Deut. 6:4–7

Hear, O Israel: The Lord is our God, the Lord alone. You shall love the Lord your God with all your heart, and with all your soul, and with all your might. Keep these words that I am commanding you today in your heart. Recite them to your children and talk about them when you are at home and when you are away, when you lie down and when you rise.

At the conclusion of the reading the leader may add:

The Word of the Lord.

Thanks be to God.

Silent reflection.

PRAYER

All may stand. A or B is sung or said:

A   *See Ps. 31:5; 17:8, 15*

Into your hands, O Lord, I commend my spirit;

for you have redeemed me, O Lord, O God of truth.

Keep us, O Lord, as the apple of your eye;

hide us under the shadow of your wings.

In righteousness I shall see you;

when I awake your presence shall give me joy.

Or

B   *Ps. 4:8*

I will lie down in peace and take my rest,

for in God alone I dwell unafraid.

One of the following prayers is then said:

1

O Lord, support us all the day long
until the shadows lengthen
and the evening comes,
and the busy world is hushed,
and the fever of life is over,
and our work is done.
Then, in your mercy,
grant us a safe lodging,
and a holy rest,
and peace at the last;
through Jesus Christ our Lord.   [504]

Amen.

2

O God,
you have designed this wonderful world,

and know all things good for us.
Give us such faith
that, by day and by night,
at all times and in all places,
we may without fear
entrust those who are dear to us
to your never-failing love,
in this life
and in the life to come;
through Jesus Christ our Lord.   [505]

Amen.

3

Keep watch, dear Lord,
with those who work or watch
or weep this night,
and give your angels charge over those who sleep.
Tend the sick, Lord Christ;
give rest to the weary,
bless the dying,
soothe the suffering,
pity the afflicted,
shield the joyous;
and all for your love's sake.   [506]

Amen.

4

O God,   ·
who appointed the day for labor
and the night for rest:
Grant that we may rest in peace and quietness
during the coming night
so that tomorrow
we may go forth to our appointed labors.
Take us into your holy keeping,
that no evil may befall us   ▼

nor any ill come near our home.
When at last our days are ended
and our work is finished,
grant that we may depart in your peace,
in the sure hope of that glorious kingdom
where there is day without night,
light without darkness,
and life without shadow of death forever;
through Jesus Christ,
the Light of the world. [507]

Amen.

5

Visit this place, O Lord,
and drive from it all snares of the enemy;
let your holy angels dwell with us
to preserve us in peace;
and let your blessing be upon us always,
through Jesus Christ our Lord. [508]

Amen.

6

Eternal God,
the hours of both day and night are yours,
and to you the darkness is no threat.
Be present, we pray,
with those who labor in these hours of night,
especially those who watch and work on behalf of others.
Grant them diligence in their watching,
faithfulness in their service,
courage in danger,
and competence in emergencies.
Help them to meet the needs of others
with confidence and compassion;
through Jesus Christ our Lord. [509]

Amen.

7

O God our Creator,
by whose mercy and might
the world turns safely into darkness
and returns again to light:
We give into your hands our unfinished tasks,
our unsolved problems,
and our unfulfilled hopes,
knowing that only those things which you bless will prosper.
To your great love and protection
we commit each other
and all for whom we have prayed,
knowing that you alone are our sure defender,
through Jesus Christ our Lord.   [510]

Amen.

8

Send your peace into our hearts, O Lord,
at the evening hour,
that we may be contented with your mercies of this day,
and confident of your protection for this night;
and now, having forgiven others,
even as you forgive us,
may we have a pure comfort
and a healthful rest
within the shelter of this home;
through Jesus Christ our Savior.   [511]

Amen.

9

Be our light in the darkness, O Lord,
and in your great mercy
defend us from all perils and dangers of this night;
for the love of your only Son,
our Savior Jesus Christ.   [512]

Amen.

10

> Be present, merciful God,
> and protect us through the silent hours of this night,
> so that we who are wearied
> by the changes and chances of this fleeting world
> may rest in your eternal changelessness;
> through Jesus Christ our Lord.   [513]

Amen.

11

> Merciful God,
> give our bodies restful sleep
> and let the work we have done today
> bear fruit in eternal life.
> We ask this through Christ our Lord.   [514]

Amen.

12

> Eternal and everlasting God,
> in the growing quietness of the evening
> and the deepening shadows of the night,
> grant us sleep and rest.
> With the stilling of the day's doings,
> and the end of coming and going about us,
> make us to be sleepy with heavy eyes and tired limbs.
> As your creatures are lying down in the wood,
> as the bird is quiet in its nest
> and the wild thing in its hole,
> as the stream is still in its bed
> reflecting the great expanse of stars above,
> may we in our sleep reflect our confidence in you,
> and our assurance in your constant peace.
> In our sleep give us that deeper communion of our souls
> with you who restores unto health.
> For your name's sake.   [515]

Amen.

All sing (musical settings: PH 571, 589, 590; PS 192–195) or say:

Or

Our Father in heaven,	Our Father,
hallowed be your name,	who art in heaven,
your kingdom come,	hallowed be thy name,
your will be done,	thy kingdom come,
on earth as in heaven.	thy will be done,
Give us today	on earth as it is in heaven.
our daily bread.	Give us this day
Forgive us our sins	our daily bread;
as we forgive those	and forgive us our debts,
who sin against us.	as we forgive our debtors;
Save us from	and lead us not
the time of trial	into temptation,
and deliver us from evil.	but deliver us from evil.
For the kingdom,	For thine is the kingdom,
the power,	and the power,
and the glory are yours	and the glory,
now and forever. Amen.	forever. Amen.

CANTICLE

The Canticle of Simeon (Nunc Dimittis) may be sung or said.

Canticle of Simeon   *Nunc Dimittis; Luke 2:29–32*
                                 PH 603–605; PS 164–166

Refrain: **Guide us waking, O Lord,**
              and guard us sleeping; *
              that awake we may watch with Christ,
              and asleep rest in his peace.

R

Now, Lord, you let your servant go in peace: *
   your word has been fulfilled.
My own eyes have seen the salvation *   ▼

which you have prepared in the sight of every people:
a light to reveal you to the nations *
and the glory of your people Israel.   **R**

DISMISSAL

May Almighty God bless, preserve, and keep us,
this night and forevermore.

Amen.

Bless the Lord.

The Lord's name be praised.

A sign of peace may be exchanged.

An Outline of Vigil of the Resurrection

For Saturday evening, the Eve of the Lord's Day

Opening Sentences
Evening Hymn: Hymn to Christ the Light (Phos Hilaron)
Thanksgiving for Light
Psalm 118
    Silent Prayer
    Psalm Prayer
The Resurrection Gospel
    Psalm 150
    Reading of a Gospel account of the resurrection
Thanksgiving for Our Baptism
Canticle
    Canticle of Miriam and Moses
        or
    We Praise You, O God
Prayer
Dismissal
    [Sign of Peace]

VIGIL OF THE RESURRECTION

For Saturday evening, the Eve of the Lord's Day

This service is for use late Saturday evening, as an alternative to Evening Prayer.

It takes place at the font, which should be filled with water, or around a container of water.

The room should be dimly lit. The paschal candle or another suitable candle or lamp may be lit.

Since the service is brief, all may stand throughout the service.

OPENING SENTENCES

One of the following is sung or said:

1   *See John 8:12; 1:5*

Jesus Christ is the light of the world

the light no darkness can overcome.

Or

2

Light and peace in Jesus Christ our Lord.

Thanks be to God.

EVENING HYMN

Hymn to Christ the Light

Phos Hilaron
PH 548, 549; PS 167–169

As the hymn is sung, additional candles may be lighted
from the flame of the paschal candle.

O radiant Light, O Sun divine,
of God the Father's deathless face,
O image of the Light sublime,
that fills the heavenly dwelling place.

O Son of God, the source of life,
praise is your due by night and day.
Our happy lips must raise the strain
of your esteemed and splendid name.

Lord Jesus Christ, as daylight fades,
as shine the lights of eventide,
we praise the Father with the Son,
the Spirit blest and with them one.

THANKSGIVING FOR LIGHT

The Lord be with you.

And also with you.

Let us give thanks to the Lord our God.

It is right to give our thanks and praise.

The leader continues:

We praise and thank you, O God,
through your Son, Jesus Christ our Lord.
Through him you have enlightened us
by revealing the Light that never fades,
for death has been destroyed
and radiant life is everywhere restored.
What was promised is fulfilled;   ▼

we have been joined to God
through renewed life in the Spirit of the risen Lord.

Glory and praise to you, through Jesus your Son,
who lives and reigns with you and the Holy Spirit,
in the kingdom of light eternal,
forever and ever.   [516]

Amen.

Or

We praise and glorify you, Lord God,
for Christ, our life, is risen
and has conquered sin and death.
He has broken the chains that bind us
and freed us to live in his kingdom of light.

May Christ enlighten the hearts of all who believe.
May Christ transform this world that longs to see him,
enlightening the hearts of all who believe,
and restore all creation to its rightful place.

Glory, praise, thanksgiving, and blessing to you, O God,
victor over sin and death,
now and forever.   [517]

Amen.

PSALM 118

Psalm 118:1–4, 14–21; or Psalm 118:22–29 is sung or said:

Psalm 118:1–4, 14–21   Tone 3; PH 231; PS 118–120

Refrain: **Give thanks to God, ***
            whose love endures forever.

R

1 Give thanks to the LORD, who is good, *
  whose mercy endures forever.

2 **Let Israel now proclaim,** *
  "The mercy of the LORD endures forever."

3 Let the house of Aaron now proclaim, *
  "The mercy of the LORD endures forever."

4 **Let those who fear the LORD now proclaim,** *
  "The mercy of the LORD endures forever."   **R**

14 The LORD is my strength and my song *
  and has become my salvation.

15 **There is a sound of exultation and victory** *
  in the tents of the righteous:

16 "The right hand of the LORD has triumphed! *
  the right hand of the LORD is exalted!
  the right hand of the LORD has triumphed!"

17 **I shall not die, but live,** *
  and declare the works of the LORD.

18 The LORD has punished me sorely *
  but did not hand me over to death.   **R**

19 **Open for me the gates of righteousness;** *
  I will enter them;
  I will offer thanks to the LORD.

20 "This is the gate of the LORD; *
  those who are righteous may enter."

21 **I will give thanks to you, for you answered me** *
  and have become my salvation.   **R**

Or

Refrain: **This is the day the Lord has made. ***
Alleluia! Alleluia!

22 The same stone which the builders rejected *
has become the chief cornerstone.

23 **This is the Lord's doing, ***
and it is marvelous in our eyes.

24 On this day the Lord has acted; *
we will rejoice and be glad in it.   **R**

25 **Hosanna, Lord, hosanna! ***
Lord, send us now success.

26 Blessed is the one who comes in the name of the Lord; *
we bless you from the house of the Lord.

27 **God is the Lord, who has shined upon us; ***
form a procession with branches up to the horns
of the altar.

28 "You are my God, and I will thank you; *
you are my God, and I will exalt you."

29 **Give thanks to the Lord, who is good; ***
whose mercy endures forever.   R

After the psalm, the leader says:

Let us pray.

Pause for silent prayer.

Almighty God,
by raising Christ your Son,
you conquered the power of death
and opened for us the way to eternal life.
Let our celebration this night
raise us up and renew our lives
by the Spirit who lives within us.
Grant this through our Lord Jesus Christ, your Son,

who lives and reigns with you and the Holy Spirit,
one God, forever and ever.   [518]

Amen.

THE RESURRECTION GOSPEL

Psalm 150   Tone 1 or 3; PH 258; PS 157

Refrain: **Praise the Lord. Praise the Lord.**[*]
            Praise the name of the Lord.

R

1 Hallelujah!
  Praise God in the holy temple; [*]
      give praise in the firmament of heaven.

2 **Praise God who is mighty in deed;** [*]
      give praise for God's excellent greatness.   **R**

3 Praise God with the blast of the ram's-horn; [*]
      give praise with lyre and harp.

4 **Praise God with timbrel and dance;** [*]
      give praise with strings and pipe.

5 Praise God with resounding cymbals; [*]
      give praise with loud-clanging cymbals.

6 **Let everything that has breath** [*]
      praise the LORD.
      Hallelujah!   **R**

One of the following accounts of the resurrection is
then read:

Matt. 28:1–10, 16–20	Luke 24:13–35	John 20:19–31
Mark 16:1–7	Luke 24:36–53	John 21:1–14
Mark 16:9–20	John 20:1–10	
Luke 23:55–24:9	John 20:11–18	

At the conclusion of the reading of scripture, the reader may say:

The gospel of the Lord.

Praise to you, O Christ.

Silence follows for reflection on the meaning of the scripture.

The scripture may be briefly interpreted.

THANKSGIVING FOR OUR BAPTISM

The congregation may gather at the font or around a container of water where thanks may be offered in these or similar words.

The Lord be with you.

And also with you.

Let us give thanks to the Lord our God.

It is right to give our thanks and praise.

We give you thanks, Eternal God,
for you nourish and sustain all living things
by the gift of water.
In the beginning of time,
your Spirit moved over the watery chaos,
calling forth order and life.

In the time of Noah,
you destroyed evil by the waters of the flood,
giving righteousness a new beginning.

You led Israel out of slavery,
through the waters of the sea,
into the freedom of the promised land.

In the waters of Jordan
Jesus was baptized by John
and anointed with your Spirit.
By the baptism of his own death and resurrection,

Christ set us free from sin and death,
and opened the way to eternal life.

We thank you, O God, for the water of baptism.
In it we were buried with Christ in his death.
From it we were raised to share in his resurrection.
Through it we were reborn by the power of
     the Holy Spirit.

Therefore in joyful obedience to your Son,
we celebrate our fellowship in him in faith.
We pray that all who have passed through the water
     of baptism
may continue forever in the risen life
of Jesus Christ our Savior.
To him, to you, and to the Holy Spirit,
be all honor and glory, now and forever.   [426]

Amen.

One of the following may be used:

1

The leader may place his or her hand into the water, lift
up some water, let it fall back into the font (or container
of water), and then make the sign of the cross over the
people, while saying:

Remember your baptism and be thankful.
In the name of the Father and of the Son
     and of the Holy Spirit.

Amen.

2

All approach the water. Each person dips a hand into the
water and may make the sign of the cross, remembering
his or her baptism.

During the ritual the Canticle of Miriam and Moses (A)
or "We Praise You, O God" (Te Deum Laudamus) (B)
is sung.

CANTICLE

A

Canticle of Miriam and Moses   *Ex. 15:1, 2, 11, 13, 17–18*
PS 174

Refrain: **Strong and unfailing is your love.** *
Alleluia! Alleluia!

R

I will sing to the LORD, for the LORD has triumphed
    gloriously; *
    the horse and its rider have been thrown into the sea.
The LORD is my strength and my song; *
    and has become my salvation.   **R**

You are my God, I will praise you, *
    the God of my people, I exalt you.
Who among the gods, O LORD, is like you; *
    who is like you, majestic in holiness,
Who among the gods, O LORD, is like you; *
    awesome in splendor, doing wonders?   **R**

With unfailing love you led the people you redeemed; *
    in your strength, you guided them
     to your holy dwelling.
You brought them in and planted them on your mountain, *
    the place, O LORD, you chose for your dwelling,
the sanctuary, O LORD, your hands established. *
    You, LORD, will reign forever and ever.   **R**

B

We Praise You, O God   *Te Deum Laudamus*
PH 460; PS 170, 171

We praise you, O God,
we acclaim you as Lord,
all creation worships you,
Father everlasting.

To you, all angels, all the powers of heaven,
the cherubim and seraphim, sing in endless praise:
Holy, holy, holy Lord, God of power and might,
heaven and earth are full of your glory.

The glorious company of apostles praise you.
The noble fellowship of prophets praise you.
The white-robed army of martyrs praise you.

Throughout the world the holy church acclaims you;
Father, of majesty unbounded,
your true and only Son, worthy of all praise,
the Holy Spirit, advocate and guide.

You, Christ, are the king of glory,
the eternal Son of the Father.
When you took our flesh to set us free
you humbly chose the Virgin's womb.

You overcame the sting of death
and opened the kingdom of heaven to all believers.

You are seated at God's right hand in glory.
We believe that you will come, and be our judge.

Come then, Lord, and help your people,
bought with the price of your own blood,
and bring us with your saints
to glory everlasting.

PRAYER

To our God belong victory, glory, and power,

for right and justice are God's judgments.

Praise our God, all you who serve God.

You who revere God, great and small.

Let us rejoice and triumph and give God praise.

The time has come for the wedding feast of the Lamb! ▼

O God who brought your people out of slavery
    with a mighty hand,
strengthen us to take our stand with you
beside the oppressed of the world,
that in the victory of Christ
every fetter of body, mind, and spirit may be broken,
and the whole human family, restored to your image,
may sing your praise in joy, freedom and peace;
through the same Jesus Christ our Lord.   [519]

Amen. Alleluia!

May God the Father, who raised Christ Jesus
    from the dead,
continually show us loving kindness.

Amen.

May God the Son, victor over sin and death,
grant us a share in the joy of his resurrection.

Amen.

May God the Spirit, giver of light and peace,
renew our hearts in love.

Amen.

May almighty God, the Father, the Son,
    and the Holy Spirit,
continue to bless us.

Amen. Alleluia!

A sign of peace may be exchanged.

CANTICLES AND
ANCIENT HYMNS: TEXTS

The texts of the canticles which are pointed may be sung to psalm tone B on pages 170–177. The refrains displayed with the canticles may also be sung to the tone selected. See page 169 for a description of singing with pointed texts.

1

Canticle of Zechariah   *Benedictus; Luke 1:68–79*
                              PH 601, 602; PS 158–160

Refrain: **You have come to your people ***
            and set them free.

        Or

            In the tender compassion of our God *
            the dawn from on high shall break upon us.

R

Blessed are you, Lord, the God of Israel; *
    you have come to your people and set them free.
You have raised up for us a mighty Savior, *
    born of the house of your servant David.   **R**

Through your holy prophets, you promised of old
to save us from our enemies, *
    from the hands of all who hate us,
to show mercy to our forebears, *
    and to remember your holy covenant.   **R**   ▼

This was the oath you swore to our father Abraham: *
    to set us free from the hands of our enemies,
free to worship you without fear, *
    holy and righteous before you,
    all the days of our life.   **R**

And you, child, shall be called the prophet
    of the Most High, *
    for you will go before the Lord to prepare the way,
to give God's people knowledge of salvation *
    by the forgiveness of their sins.   **R**

In the tender compassion of our God *
    the dawn from on high shall break upon us,
to shine on those who dwell in darkness
    and the shadow of death, *
    and to guide our feet into the way of peace.   **R**

Alternative seasonal refrains:

1

For Advent

The Lord proclaims: Repent, *
the kingdom of God is upon you. Alleluia!

2

For Christmas–Epiphany

You have raised up for us a mighty Savior, *
born of the house of David. Alleluia!

3

For Lent

God has given us knowledge of salvation *
by the forgiveness of our sins.

4

For Easter

The Lord, the God of Israel, has set us free. *
Alleluia! Alleluia!

Canticle of Mary

Magnificat; Luke 1:46–55
PH 600; PS 161–163

Refrain: **My soul proclaims the greatness
of the Lord;***
my spirit rejoices in God my Savior.

R

My soul proclaims the greatness of the Lord,
my spirit rejoices in God my Savior,*
    for you, Lord, have looked with favor
        on your lowly servant.
From this day all generations will call me blessed: *
    you, the Almighty, have done great things for me
    and holy is your name.
You have mercy on those who fear you, *
    from generation to generation.   **R**

You have shown strength with your arm, *
    and scattered the proud in their conceit,
casting down the mighty from their thrones *
    and lifting up the lowly.
You have filled the hungry with good things, *
    and sent the rich away empty.   **R**

You have come to the aid of your servant Israel, *
    to remember the promise of mercy,
the promise made to our forebears, *
    to Abraham and his children for ever.   **R**

Alternative seasonal refrains:

1   *Luke 1:30, 31*

For Advent

Fear not, Mary, you have found favor with the Lord;*
Behold, you shall conceive and bear a Son. Alleluia!

2   *John 1:14*

For Christmas–Epiphany

The Word was made flesh and dwelt among us, *
and we beheld his glory. Alleluia!

3   *Amos 5:24*

For Lent

Let justice roll down like waters, *
and righteousness like an everflowing stream.

4   *Ps. 118:24*

For Easter

This is the day the Lord has made. Alleluia! *
Let us rejoice and be glad in it.

3

Canticle of Simeon   *Nunc Dimittis; Luke 2:29–32*
                                           PH 603–605; PS 164–166

Refrain for Prayer at the Close of Day

> Guide us waking, O Lord,
> and guard us sleeping; *
> that awake we may watch with Christ,
> and asleep rest in his peace.

R

Now, Lord, you let your servant go in peace: *
    your word has been fulfilled.
My own eyes have seen the salvation *
    which you have prepared in the sight of every people:
a light to reveal you to the nations *
    and the glory of your people Israel.   **R**

4

Hymn to Christ the Light

Phos Hilaron
PH 548, 549; PS 167–169

O radiant Light, O Sun divine,
of God the Father's deathless face,
O image of the Light sublime,
that fills the heavenly dwelling place.

O Son of God, the source of life,
praise is your due by night and day.
Our happy lips must raise the strain
of your esteemed and splendid name.

Lord Jesus Christ, as daylight fades,
as shine the lights of eventide,
we praise the Father with the Son,
the Spirit blest and with them one.

5

We Praise You, O God

Te Deum Laudamus
PH 460; PS 170–171

We praise you, O God,
we acclaim you as Lord,
all creation worships you,
Father everlasting.

To you, all angels, all the powers of heaven,
the cherubim and seraphim, sing in endless praise:
Holy, holy, holy Lord, God of power and might,
heaven and earth are full of your glory.

The glorious company of apostles praise you.
The noble fellowship of prophets praise you.
The white-robed army of martyrs praise you.

Throughout the world the holy church acclaims you;
Father, of majesty unbounded,
your true and only Son, worthy of all praise,
the Holy Spirit, advocate and guide. ▼

You, Christ, are the king of glory,
the eternal Son of the Father.
When you took our flesh to set us free
you humbly chose the Virgin's womb.

You overcame the sting of death
and opened the kingdom of heaven to all believers.

You are seated at God's right hand in glory.
We believe that you will come, and be our judge.

Come then, Lord, and help your people,
bought with the price of your own blood,
and bring us with your saints
to glory everlasting.

6

Glory to God

Gloria in Excelsis
PH 566, 575, 576; PS 173

Glory to God in the highest,
and peace to God's people on earth.

Lord God, heavenly King,
almighty God and Father,
we worship you, we give you thanks,
we praise you for your glory.

Lord Jesus Christ, only Son of the Father,
Lord God, Lamb of God,
you take away the sin of the world:
have mercy on us;
you are seated at the right hand of the Father:
receive our prayer.

For you alone are the Holy One,
you alone are the Lord,
you alone are the Most High,
Jesus Christ,
with the Holy Spirit,
in the glory of God the Father.   Amen.

7

Canticle of Miriam and Moses   Ex. 15:1, 2, 11, 13, 17–18
PS 174

Refrain: **Strong and unfailing is your love, ***
Alleluia! Alleluia!

R

I will sing to the L ORD, for the L ORD has triumphed
    gloriously; *
      the horse and its rider have been thrown into the sea.
The L ORD is my strength and my song; *
    and has become my salvation.   **R**

You are my God, I will praise you, *
    the God of my people, I exalt you.
Who among the gods, O L ORD, is like you; *
    who is like you, majestic in holiness,
Who among the gods, O L ORD, is like you; *
    awesome in splendor, doing wonders?   **R**

With unfailing love you led the people you redeemed; *
    in your strength, you guided them to your
      holy dwelling.
You brought them in and planted them on your mountain, *
    the place, O L ORD, you chose for your dwelling,
the sanctuary, O L ORD, your hands established. *
    You, L ORD, will reign forever and ever.   **R**

8

God's Chosen One   Isa. 11:1–4, 6, 9

A shoot shall come out from the stump of Jesse, *
    and a branch shall grow out of its roots,
The Spirit of the L ORD shall rest on him, *
    the spirit of wisdom and understanding,
the spirit of counsel and might, *
    the spirit of knowledge and the fear of the L ORD.   ▼

He shall not judge by what his eyes see, *
    or decide by what his ears hear,
but with righteousness he shall judge the poor, *
    and decide with equity for the meek of the earth.

The wolf shall live with the lamb, *
    the leopard shall lie down with the kid,
the calf and the lion cub together, *
    and a little child shall lead them.
They shall not hurt or destroy on all my holy mountain, *
    for the earth shall be full of the knowledge of the LORD
    as the waters cover the sea.

9

The Desert Shall Blossom

Isa. 35:1, 2, 5, 6, 10
PH 18

The desert shall rejoice and blossom, *
    it shall rejoice with gladness and singing.
The glory of the LORD shall be revealed, *
    and the majesty of our God.

Then shall the eyes of the blind be opened, *
    and the ears of the deaf unstopped,
then shall the lame leap like the deer, *
    and the tongue of the speechless shall sing for joy.

For waters shall break forth in the wilderness, *
    and streams in the desert.
The ransomed of the LORD shall return, *
    and come with singing, with everlasting joy
        upon their heads.
They shall obtain joy and gladness, *
    and sorrow and sighing shall flee away.

10

Canticle of Thanksgiving   *First Song of Isaiah; Isa. 12:2–6*
PS 175

**Refrain: Sing praises, for the Lord has done
great things. ***
Let this be known in all the earth.

R

Surely God is my salvation; *
  I will trust, and will not be afraid,
for the L ORD G OD is my stronghold and my song, *
  and has become my Savior.   **R**

With joy you will draw water from the wells of salvation. *
  And in that day you will say:
Give thanks and call upon the name of the L ORD. *
  Make known among the nations what the L ORD has done;
  proclaim that the name of the L ORD is exalted.   **R**

Sing praises, for the L ORD has done great things; *
  let this be known in all the earth.
Shout, and sing for joy, O people of God, *
  for great in your midst is the Holy One.   **R**

11

Seek the Lord   *Second Song of Isaiah; Isa. 55:6–11*
PS 176

Refrain: You are full of mercy, O Lord, *
for you will abundantly pardon.

R

Seek the L ORD who is still to be found; *
  call upon God who is yet at hand.
Let the wicked forsake their way, *
  and the unrighteous their thoughts;
let them return to the L ORD, who will have mercy, *
  to our God, who will abundantly pardon.   **R**

For my thoughts are not your thoughts; *
  nor are your ways my ways, says the L ORD.   ▼

For as the heavens are higher than the earth; *
    so are my ways higher than your ways
and my thoughts than your thoughts.   **R**

For as the rain and snow fall from the heavens; *
    and return not again but water the earth,
bringing forth life and giving growth; *
    giving seed to the sower and bread to the hungry;
so is my word that goes forth from my mouth; *
    it shall not return to me empty,
but it shall accomplish that which I desire; *
    and achieve the purpose for which I sent it.   **R**

12

The New Jerusalem   *Third Song of Isaiah;*
                                        Isa. 60:1–3, 18, 19
                                        PS 177

Refrain: **The Lord will be our everlasting light; ***
            and God will be our glory.

R

Arise, shine, for your light has come; *
    and the glory of the LORD has risen upon you,
though darkness covers the earth *
    and dark night is over the nations.   **R**

But upon you the LORD will rise, *
    and the glory of the LORD will appear over you.
Nations shall come to your light; *
    and rulers to the brightness of your dawn.   **R**

No longer will violence be heard in your land, *
    nor ruin or destruction within your borders.
You will name your walls Salvation, *
    and all your gates Praise.   **R**

No more will the sun be your light by day, *
    nor by night will you need the brightness of the moon,
for the LORD will be your everlasting light, *
    and your God will be your glory.   **R**

13

The Spirit of the Lord

Isa. 61:1–3, 10, 11

The Spirit of the Lord GOD is upon me, *
    because the LORD has anointed me
    to bring good news to the oppressed.

The LORD has sent me to bind up the broken-hearted, *
    to proclaim liberty to the captives,
    and release for those in prison,
to comfort all who mourn, *
    to give them a garland instead of ashes,
the oil of gladness instead of mourning, *
    a garment of splendor for the heavy heart.
They shall be called trees of righteousness, *
    planted for the glory of the LORD.

Therefore I will greatly rejoice in the Lord, *
    my whole being shall exult in my God,
for God has robed me with salvation as a garment, *
    and clothed me with integrity as a cloak.
For the Lord GOD will cause righteousness and praise, *
    to spring up before all the nations.

14

Canticle of Hannah

1 Sam. 2:1–4, 7, 8

My heart exults in the LORD; *
    my strength is exalted in my God.
There is none holy like the LORD; *
    there is none beside you, no rock like our God.
For you, O LORD, are a God of knowledge; *
    and by you our actions are weighed.
The bows of the mighty are broken; *
    but the feeble gird on strength.

You, LORD, make poor and make rich; *
    you bring low and you also exalt.
You raise up the poor from the dust, *
    and lift the needy from the ash-heap.   ▼

You make them sit with princes, *
  and inherit a seat of honor.
For yours, O LORD, are the pillars of the earth; *
  and on them you have set the world.

15

Canticle of David
1 *Chron. 29:10–13*

Blessed are you, O LORD, *
  God of our ancestor Israel, forever and ever.
Yours, O LORD, are grandeur and power, *
  majesty, splendor, and glory.
For all in the heavens and on the earth is yours; *
  yours, O LORD, is the kingdom;
  you are exalted as head above all.

Riches and honor come from you, *
  and you rule over all.
In your hand are power and might; *
  it is yours to make great and to give strength to all.
And now we thank you, our God, *
  and praise your glorious name.

16

The Steadfast Love of the Lord
Lam. 3:22–26

PS 179

The steadfast love of the LORD never ceases, *
  God's mercies never come to an end;
they are new every morning; *
  your faithfulness, O LORD, is great.
You are all that I have, *
  and therefore I will wait for you.
You, O LORD, are good to those who wait for you, *
  to all those who seek you.
It is good to wait in patience *
  for the salvation of the LORD.

17

Canticle of Judith
Judith 16:13–15

I will sing a new song to my God: *
    Lord, you are great and glorious,
    wonderful in strength, invincible.
Let the whole creation serve you, *
    for you spoke, and all things came into being.
You sent out your breath and it formed them; *
    no one is able to resist your voice.
Mountains and seas are stirred to their depths; *
    rocks melt like wax at your presence.
But to those who revere you, *
    you will continue to show mercy.

18

A Canticle of Creation
Song of the Three Young Men
35–65, 34

PS 180, 181

Invocation
Let the whole creation bless the Lord.*

Praise and exalt our God forever.

I. *The Cosmic Order*
O let the heavens bless the Lord.
Bless the Lord, you angels of the Lord; *
    bless the Lord, all the heavenly hosts.

Praise and exalt our God forever.

Bless the Lord, you waters above the heavens; *
    bless the Lord, sun and moon and stars of the sky.

Praise and exalt our God forever.

Bless the Lord, every shower of rain and fall of dew; *
    bless the Lord, every breeze and gusty wind.

Praise and exalt our God forever. ▼

Bless the Lord, fire and heat; *
   bless the Lord, scorching wind and bitter cold.

Praise and exalt our God forever.

Bless the Lord, each drop of dew and flake of snow; *
   bless the Lord, nights and days, light and darkness.

Praise and exalt our God forever.

Bless the Lord, frost and cold, ice and sleet; *
   bless the Lord, thunderclouds and lightning flashes.

Praise and exalt our God forever.

II. *The Earth and Its Creatures*
O let the earth bless the Lord.
Bless the Lord, mountains and hills; *
   bless the Lord, all that grows from the earth.

Praise and exalt our God forever.

Bless the Lord, O springs of water; *
   bless the Lord, seas and rivers.

Praise and exalt our God forever.

Bless the Lord, you whales; *
   bless the Lord, all that swim in the depths of the seas.

Praise and exalt our God forever.

Bless the Lord, all birds of the air; *
   bless the Lord, beasts of the wild, flocks and herds.

Praise and exalt our God forever.

III. *The People of God*
O let all who dwell on the earth, bless the Lord.
Bless the Lord, men and women, children and youth; *
   bless the Lord, all people everywhere.

Praise and exalt our God forever.

Bless the Lord, you people of God; *
  bless the Lord, priests and all who serve the Lord.

Praise and exalt our God forever.

Bless the Lord, all who are upright in spirit; *
  bless the Lord, all who are holy and humble in heart.

Praise and exalt our God forever.

Doxology
Let us bless the Lord: Father, Son and Holy Spirit. *
  Blessed are you, O Lord, in the vast expanse of heaven.
  Praise and exalt our God forever.

19

A Canticle of Penitence   *Prayer of Manasseh*
Prayer of Manasseh 1–2, 4, 6–7a, 11, 13c–15

PS 183

Refrain: **O Lord, you are full of compassion,***
           long-suffering, and abounding in mercy.

R

O Lord almighty and God of our ancestors, *
  you made the heavens and the earth,
    in their glorious array.
All things quake with fear at your presence; *
  they tremble because of your power.
But your merciful promise is beyond all measure; *
  it surpasses all that our minds can fathom.   **R**
Lord, you are full of compassion, *
  long-suffering, and abounding in mercy.
And now, O Lord, I humble my heart, *
  and make my appeal, sure of your gracious goodness.
For you, O Lord, are the God of the penitent, *
  and in me you will show forth your goodness.   **R**   ▼

Unworthy as I am, you will save me, *
    and so I will praise you continually, all the days of my life.
For all the host of heaven sing your praises, *
    and your glory is forever and ever.   **R**

20

A Canticle to the Lamb   *Rev. 4:11; 5:9–10, 12, 13*
                                          PS 191

Refrain: **Worthy is the Lamb that was slain ***
             to receive glory and honor.

R

You are worthy, O Lord our God, *
    to receive glory and honor and power,
for you created all things, *
    and by your will they were created
        and have their being.   **R**

You are worthy, O Christ, for you were slain, *
    and by your blood have ransomed us for God,
from every tribe and people and nation, *
    a royal house of priests to our God.   **R**

Worthy is the Lamb who was slain, *
    to receive power and wealth, wisdom and might,
    honor and glory and blessing.
To the one seated upon the throne,
    and to Christ the Lamb, *
    be blessing and honor, glory and might,
        forever and ever.   **R**

21

Canticle of the Redeemed   *Rev. 15:3–4*
                                          PS 184

Refrain: **Your ways are just and true,***
             O Sovereign of all the ages.

R

> O Ruler of the universe, Lord God,
> great and wonderful are your deeds, *
> > surpassing human understanding.
> Your ways are just and true, *
> > O Sovereign of all the ages.   **R**

> Who can fail to do you homage, Lord,
> and sing the praises of your name, *
> > for you alone are holy.
> All nations will come and worship in your presence, *
> > for your just and holy works have been revealed.   **R**

22

A Canticle for Pentecost

John 14:16; 16:13a; 14:26
Acts 2:2, 4a; Rom. 8:26;
Joel 2:28

Refrain: **I will pour out my Spirit on all flesh.** *
Your sons and your daughters shall prophesy,
your old shall dream dreams *
and your young shall see visions.

R

> I will ask the Father,
> who will give you another Advocate, *
> > to be with you for ever.
> The Spirit of truth, having come, *
> > will guide you into all truth.   **R**

> The Advocate, the Holy Spirit *
> > whom the Father will send in my name,
> will teach you all things, *
> > and remind you of all that I have said to you.   **R**

> And suddenly from heaven there came a sound *
> > like the rush of a violent wind,
> and it filled the entire house where they were sitting. *
> > All were filled with the Holy Spirit.   **R**   ▼

The Spirit helps us in our weakness; *
　　for we do not know how we ought to pray,
but the Spirit pleads for us *
　　with sighs too deep for words.　　**R**

23

A Canticle of Love　　　　　　　　*1 John 4:7, 8;*
　　　　　　　　　　　　　　1 Cor. 13:4–10, 12–13
　　　　　　　　　　　　　　　　PS 187

Refrain:　　**Faith, hope and love abide, ***
　　　　　and the greatest of these is love.

R
　Beloved, let us love one another, *
　　for love is of God.
　All who love are born of God and know God; *
　　all who do not love do not know God.　　**R**

　Love does not insist on its own way, *
　　is not quick to take offense;
　it does not rejoice at wrong, *
　　but rejoices in the right.　　**R**

　Love is patient and kind; *
　　love is not envious or boastful;
　it is not arrogant or rude. *
　　Love bears all things and believes all things,
　Love hopes all things and endures all things. *
　　Love will never come to an end.　　**R**

　Prophecies will vanish; tongues will cease; *
　　and knowledge will pass away.
　For our knowledge and our prophecy are imperfect, *
　　but when the perfect comes,
　　　the imperfect will pass away.　　**R**

Now I know in part, *
    then I will know fully,
    even as I have been fully known.
Now abide faith, hope, and love, these three; *
    and the greatest of these is love.   **R**

24

Christ, the Head of All Creation   *Col. 1:15–20*
                                        PS 185

Refrain: **Glory to you, ***
               the firstborn of all creation!

R

Christ is the image of the invisible God, *
    the firstborn of all creation.
In him all things in heaven and on earth were created, *
    all that is seen and all that is unseen,
thrones and dominions, rulers and powers, *
    through him and for him all things were created.   **R**

Christ is before all things, *
    the one in whom all things hold together.
Christ is head of the body, the church; *
    he is its beginning, the firstborn from the dead,
    to be in all things alone supreme.   **R**

For in Christ, O God, you were pleased to have all your
       fullness dwell, *
    and through him to reconcile all things to yourself.
You made peace by the blood of his cross, *
    and brought back to yourself all things in heaven and
       on earth.   **R**

25

Jesus Christ Is Lord   *Phil. 2:5c–11*

PS 186

Christ Jesus, though he was in the form of God, *
  did not regard equality with God a thing to be grasped,
but emptied himself, taking the form of a slave, *
  being born in human likeness.
And being found in human form, he humbled himself, *
  and became obedient unto death, even death on a cross.

Therefore God has highly exalted him *
  and bestowed on him the name above every name,
that at the name of Jesus every knee should bend, *
  in heaven and on earth and under the earth,
and every tongue confess to the glory of God: *
  Jesus Christ is Lord!

26

The Mystery of Our Religion   *1 Tim. 3:16; 6:15, 16*

Christ Jesus our Lord was revealed in flesh, *
  and was vindicated in the Spirit,
he was seen by angels, *
  and proclaimed among the nations;
he was believed in throughout the world, *
  and was taken up in glory.

He will be revealed in due time by God, *
  the blessed and only ruler, the sovereign Lord of all,
who alone has immortality, *
  and dwells in unapproachable light,
whom no one has ever seen or can see, *
  to whom alone be honor and might forever and ever.

27

The Beatitudes

Matt. 5:3–12
PS 188

Blessed are the poor in spirit, *
    for the kingdom of heaven is theirs.
Blessed are the sorrowful, *
    for they will be comforted.
Blessed are those of a gentle spirit, *
    for they will inherit the earth.
Blessed are those who hunger and thirst to see right prevail, *
    for they will be filled.
Blessed are those who show mercy, *
    for mercy will be shown to them.
Blessed are those whose hearts are pure, *
    for they will see God.
Blessed are the peacemakers, *
    for they will be called children of God.
Blessed are those who are persecuted for the cause of right, *
    for theirs is the kingdom of heaven.
Blessed are you when you are reviled, and persecuted *
    and all kinds of evil are uttered against you on my account.
Rejoice and be glad, *
    for your reward is great in heaven.

28

Christ the Servant

1 Peter 2:21–25
PS 189

Refrain: **Christ bore our sins on the cross; ***
                 by his wounds we are healed.

R

Jesus Christ suffered for you, leaving you an example: *
    that you should follow in his steps.
Christ committed no sin, no deceit was found on his lips. *
    When he was abused, he did not return abuse;
when suffering, he did not threaten; *
    but he trusted the one who judges justly.   **R**   ▼

Christ bore our sins in his body on the cross, *
>so that, free from sins, we might live for righteousness.
By his wounds you have been healed. *
>For you were straying like sheep,
but have now returned *
>to the shepherd and guardian of your souls.*   **R**

29

Christ Our Passover   *1 Cor. 5:7–8; Rom. 6:9–11;*
                                        1 Cor. 15:20–22
                                        PS 190

Alleluia! Christ our paschal lamb has been sacrificed. *
>Therefore, let us keep the feast,
not with the old leaven, the leaven of malice and evil, *
>but with the unleavened bread of sincerity and truth.
>Alleluia!

Christ, being raised from the dead, will never die again; *
>death no longer has dominion over him.
The death that he died, he died to sin, once for all; *
>but the life he lives, he lives to God.
So also consider yourselves dead to sin *
>and alive to God in Christ Jesus. Alleluia!

Christ has been raised from the dead, *
>the first fruits of those who have died.
For since by one human being came death, *
>by one human being has also come
>>the resurrection of the dead.
For as in Adam all die, *
>so also in Christ will all be made alive. Alleluia!

PRAYERS AT MEALTIME

As a sign of reverence, some fold hands for prayer before the meal. Others, standing about the table, lift hands as a sign of praise. Others join hands around the table as a sign of peace and unity. Still others make the sign of the cross after the prayer.

1

Blessed are you, O Lord our God,
ruler of the universe,
for you give us food to sustain our lives
and make our hearts glad.   [520]
Amen.

2

Blessed are you, Lord.
You have fed us from our earliest days;
you give food to every living creature.
Fill our hearts with joy and delight.
Give us what we need
and enough to spare for works of mercy
in honor of Christ Jesus, our Lord.
Through him may glory, honor
    and power be yours for ever.   [521]
Amen.

3

Blessed are you, Lord, God of all creation,
for you feed the whole world with your goodness,
with grace, with loving kindness and tender mercy.
You give food to all creatures,
and your loving kindness endures forever.
Because of your great goodness, food has never failed us;
O may it not fail us forever and ever
for the sake of your great name.
You nourish and sustain all creatures
and do good to all.
Blessed are you, O Lord, for you give food to all.   [522]

Amen.

4

Creator of the universe,
you give us this gift of food to nourish us and give us life.
Bless this food that you have made
and human hands have prepared.
May it satisfy our hunger,
and in sharing it together
may we come closer to one another.   [523]

Amen.

5

Bless us, O Lord, and these your gifts
which we are about to receive from your goodness,
through Christ our Lord.   [524]

Amen.

6

Come, Lord Jesus, be our guest,
and let these gifts to us be blessed.   [525]

Amen.

7

All good gifts around us
are sent from heaven above,
then thank the Lord, O thank the Lord,
for all God's love. [526]

Amen.

8

For health and strength and daily food,
we praise your name, O Lord. [527]

Amen.

9

The eyes of all wait upon you, O Lord,
and you give them their food in due season.
You open wide your hand,
and satisfy the needs of every living thing.
Thanks be to you. [528]

Amen.

10

God of grace,
sustain our bodies with this food,
our hearts with true friendship,
and our souls with your truth,
for Christ's sake. [529]

Amen.

11

Lord Jesus, be our holy guest,
our morning joy, our evening rest;
and with our daily bread impart
your love and peace to every heart. [530]

Amen.

12

Give us grateful hearts, O God, for all your mercies,
and make us mindful of the needs of others;
through Jesus Christ our Lord.   [531]
Amen.

> The following (13–17) are taken from psalms and may
> be said in unison by all at the table. They may be used
> before the meal or after all have eaten.

13   *See Ps. 19:1, 2*

The heavens are telling the glory of God;
and the firmament proclaims God's handiwork.
In the day we give glory to God,
and at night we remember God's love.

14   *Ps. 24:1*

The earth is the Lord's and all that is in it,
the world, and those who live in it.

15   *Ps. 100:1, 2, 4b*

Make a joyful noise to the Lord, all the earth.
Worship the Lord with gladness;
come into God's presence with singing.
Give thanks, and bless God's name.

16   *Ps. 103:1, 2*

Bless the Lord, O my soul,
and all that is within me, bless God's holy name.
Bless the Lord, O my soul,
and do not forget all God's benefits.

17   *Ps. 121:1, 2*

I lift up my eyes to the hills—
from where will my help come?
My help comes from the Lord
who made heaven and earth.

The following grace is based upon Jewish and Christian table blessings. The actions are signs of gratitude to God for the joy of food and drink and for the presence of those about the table. If circumstances do not allow for blessings over both wine and bread, a blessing may be said over either.

A person at the table takes a glass of wine, or appropriate beverage, lifts it, and says:

Blessed are you, O Lord our God,
Ruler of all creation,
for you give us the fruit of the vine.   [532]

Amen.

The glass is passed and each person at the table drinks from it.

The same person, or another, takes bread, holds it up for all to see, and says:

Blessed are you, O Lord our God,
Ruler of all creation,
for you bring forth bread from the earth.   [533]

Amen.

The bread is broken and passed to those about the table for each one to eat of it.

THE PSALMS

Psalms in
Corporate Worship

The PSALMS THAT FOLLOW ARE for use in corporate worship.
One hundred twenty-seven psalms are represented, including all
the psalms displayed in the Daily Lectionary (pp. 459–506).
They are presented in a form that invites a variety of uses.

Singing the Psalms

It is preferable that the psalms be sung. *The Psalter—Psalms
and Canticles for Singing* provides a rich and varied collection of
responsorial settings for singing the psalms. *The Presbyterian
Hymnal* contains a large collection of metrical psalms and a
few responsorial settings.

The psalm texts that follow are pointed to enable the
psalms to be sung to simple psalm tones such as those provided in *The Psalter—Psalms and Canticles for Singing*, and on
pages 170–179 of this book.

Eight refrains with a choice of tones are provided in this
book. The pointing system displayed in the psalm texts and
tones is the system most commonly used. This enables these
psalm texts to be sung to many tones found in other resources.

The most common practice in singing the psalms to psalm
tones is to sing them responsorially. In singing the psalms
responsorially, a choir or cantor (soloist) sings the psalm to a
tone, with the congregation singing a metrical refrain. The

refrains, used together with either of the tones (A and B) that follow, provide for responsorial psalmody.

Some groups, however (for example, groups meeting regularly for daily prayer), may choose to sing the psalm in a responsive pattern. The group is divided into two sections. The singing of the psalm alternates between the two sections, one section singing one verse, the other section singing the next verse. Or the entire psalm may be sung in unison. In either instance, the refrain is not ordinarily used. Or the refrain may be used only at the beginning and at the end of the psalm. Tone B is then used, since it may be used with or without the refrain.

Tone B may also be used in singing the canticles on pages 137–158, and therefore provides additional resources for use with the canticle settings in *The Psalter—Psalms and Canticles for Singing.*

READING THE PSALMS

Some congregations will choose to read the psalms. The psalms that follow are presented in a form that will assist in reading the psalms responsively, antiphonally, or in unison.

In reading the psalms responsively, a leader reads the lightface type, the congregation reads the boldface type.

In reading the psalms antiphonally, the group is divided into two parts, such as the right and left sections of a congregation. One part of the group reads the lightface type, the other reads the boldface type.

PSALM PRAYERS

Psalm prayers are provided for each of the psalms in this book. Each psalm prayer captures some theme or image from the psalm and often adds Christian implications drawn from the psalm. The prayer helps us to pray the psalm and to see Christ in the psalm as we pray. Psalm prayers may also be composed that capture images in the psalms that address the immediate needs of the worshipers. The psalm prayer is spoken by the leader after the psalm is sung or read. Ordinarily, the leader upon completion of the singing or reading of the psalm will say, "Let us pray." Silence follows for silent prayer and reflection on the psalm. After the silence, the leader offers the prayer.

INSTRUCTIONS FOR SINGING PSALM TONES

1. A suggested psalm tone is noted with each psalm. The suggested tones match the spirit and theme of the psalm.

2. In presenting the psalm, the refrain is first played by the organist, pianist, or other instrumentalist, then is sung by the cantor or choir, and then is sung by all. The cantor sings the verses of the psalm, with the congregation singing the refrain wherever noted in the psalm text (**R**).

3. In singing the text of the psalm, each measure of the psalm tone is sung to a psalm half-verse, noted by an asterisk (*). Begin singing on the first note of the measure, then move to the second note on the syllable with a dot (·) above it. The third and fourth notes of the tone accommodate the remainder of each phrase of the text. When there are more than three syllables in a half-verse ending, the additional syllables are sung on the last note. When two syllables are joined by a tie (‿) they are sung on the one note.

Congregations are free to reproduce the melody line of the refrains and tones in a church bulletin. See pages 178–179 for refrains that may be reproduced.

THE PSALM REFRAINS AND TONES

Two tones appear with each refrain. Either tone A or tone B may be used when the refrain is sung. When the whole group sings the text of the psalm (instead of a cantor or choir) the refrain is not used, or is used only at the beginning and end of the psalm. Tone B is then used.

1: ALLELUIA

REFRAIN

TONE 1 (A)

TONE 1 (B)

Text: Hal H. Hopson
Music: Hal H. Hopson

2: PRAISE

REFRAIN

Let the peo-ple praise you, O God;____ let all the peo-ple praise you.

TONE 2 (A)

TONE 2 (B)

Text: Hal H. Hopson
Music: Hal H. Hopson

Text and music of refrain Copyright © 1986 Hope Publishing Company, Carol Stream, IL 60188. All rights reserved. Used by permission.
Music of (A) tone © 1987 The Westminster Press.
Music of (B) tone © 1993 Westminster/John Knox Press.

3: LORDSHIP

Psalm 135:1

REFRAIN

TONE 3 (A)

TONE 3 (B)

Text: Hal H. Hopson
Music: Hal H. Hopson

4: SALVATION HISTORY

Psalm 78:4

REFRAIN

Tell out the deeds of the Lord;___ tell out the won-ders God has wrought.

TONE 4 (A)

TONE 4 (B)

Text: Hal H. Hopson
Music: Hal H. Hopson

5: GOD'S LAW

Psalm 119:174

REFRAIN

O Lord, my de-light,_____ my de - light is in your law.

TONE 5 (A)

TONE 5 (B)

Text: Hal H. Hopson
Music: Hal H. Hopson

6: TRUST

Psalm 46:1

REFRAIN

God is our ref - uge; God is our strength.

TONE 6 (A)

TONE 6 (B)

Text: Hal H. Hopson
Music: Hal H. Hopson

Text and music of refrain Copyright © 1986 Hope Publishing Company, Carol Stream, IL 60188. All rights
reserved. Used by permission.
Music of (A) tone © 1987 The Westminster Press.
Music of (B) tone © 1993 Westminster/John Knox Press.

7: PENITENTIAL

Psalm 130:1–2

REFRAIN

TONE 7 (A)

TONE 7 (B)

Text: Hal H. Hopson
Music: Hal H. Hopson

8: LAMENT

Psalm 22:19

REFRAIN

Lord, you are my strength;_____ has-ten to help____ me.

TONE 8 (A)

TONE 8 (B)

Text: Hal H. Hopson
Music: Hal H. Hopson

REFRAINS FOR THE CONGREGATION

Free permission is granted by the publisher to reproduce the refrains that follow in church bulletins for congregational participation.

Hal H. Hopson

1

Al - le - lu - ia! Al - le - lu - ia! Al - le - lu - ia!

© 1988 Hope Publishing Company

Hal H. Hopson

2

Let the peo-ple praise you, O God; ___ Let all the peo-ple praise you.

© 1988 Hope Publishing Company

Hal H. Hopson

3

Praise the Lord. Praise the Lord. Praise the name of the Lord.

© 1988 Hope Publishing Company

Hal H. Hopson

4

Tell out the deeds of the Lord; ___ Tell out the won-ders God has wrought.

© 1988 Hope Publishing Company

Hal H. Hopsor

5

O Lord, my de-light, _____ my de - light is in your law.

© 1988 Hope Publishing Company

Hal H. Hopson

6

God is our ref - uge; God is our strength.

© 1988 Hope Publishing Company

Hal H. Hops

7

Lord, I call to you; O hear _____ my cry.

© 1988 Hope Publishing Company

Hal H. Hopson

8

Lord, you are my strength, has - ten to help me.

© 1988 Hope Publishing Company

THE PSALMS / 179

THE PSALMS

PSALM 1　　　　　　　　　　Tone 5 or 6; PH 158; PS 1

R

1　Happy are they who have not walked in the counsel
　　　of the wicked, *
　　　nor lingered in the way of sinners,
　　　nor sat in the seats of the scornful!

2　**Their delight is in the law of the LORD, ***
　　and on this law they meditate day and night.　　R

3　They are like trees planted by streams of water,
　　bearing fruit in due season, with leaves that do not wither; *
　　　everything they do shall prosper.

4　**It is not so with the wicked; ***
　　they are like chaff which the wind blows away.　　R

5　Therefore the wicked shall not stand upright
　　　when judgment comes, *
　　　nor the sinner in the council of the righteous.

6　**For the LORD knows the way of the righteous, ***
　　but the way of the wicked is doomed.　　R

Eternal God,
in your loving wisdom you set us beside the fountain of life,
like a tree planted by running streams.
Fill us with a love of your wisdom,
that we may bear fruit in the beauty of holiness;
through Christ, the way, the truth, and the life.　**Amen.**　[534]

R

1 Why are the nations in an uproar? *
      Why do the peoples mutter empty threats?

2 **Why do the kings of the earth rise up in revolt,**
   and the rulers plot together, *
      against the LORD and against the LORD's anointed?

3 "Let us break their yoke," they say; *
      "let us cast off their bonds from us."   **R**

4 **The One enthroned in heaven is laughing; ***
      the LORD has them in derision.

5 Then in wrath the LORD speaks to them, *
      and divine rage fills them with terror.

6 **"I myself have set my king ***
      upon my holy hill of Zion."   R

7 Let me announce the decree of the LORD: *
      the LORD said to me, "You are my Son;
      this day have I begotten you.

8 **Ask of me, and I will give you the nations**
         for your inheritance *
      and the ends of the earth for your possession.

9 You shall crush them with an iron rod *
      and shatter them like a piece of pottery."   **R**

10 **And now, you kings, be wise; ***
       be warned, you rulers of the earth.

11 Submit to the LORD with fear, *
       and with trembling bow down in worship;

12 **lest the LORD be angry and you perish; ***
       for divine wrath is quickly kindled.

[Unison]

13 **Happy are they all** *
      who take refuge in the LORD!   R

Sovereign God,
you gave us your only begotten to be the Savior of the world,
and you crowned him with grace to rule over all.
Give us humility
that we may faithfully serve him,
and so know the joy
given to all who take refuge in Christ our Lord.   **Amen.**   [535]

PSALM 4   Tone 8 or 6; PH 160; PS 3

R

1   Answer me when I call, O God, defender of my cause; *
      you set me free when I am hard-pressed;
      have mercy on me and hear my prayer.

2   **"You mortals, how long will you dishonor my glory;** *
      how long will you worship dumb idols
      and run after false gods?"

3   Know that the LORD does wonders for the faithful; *
      when I cry out, the LORD will hear me.   R

4   **Tremble, then, and do not sin;** *
      speak to your heart in silence upon your bed.

5   Offer the appointed sacrifices *
      and put your trust in the LORD.   R

6   **Many are saying, "Oh, that we might see better times!"** *
      Lift up the light of your countenance upon us,
        O LORD.

7   You have put gladness in my heart, *
      more than when grain and wine and oil increase.   ▼

8 **I lie down in peace; at once I fall asleep; ***
      for only you, LORD, make me dwell in safety.   R

O God, source of deliverance and help,
do not let our hearts be troubled,
but fill us with such confidence and joy
that we may sleep in your peace and rise in your light;
through Jesus Christ our Lord.   **Amen.**   [536]

PSALM 5   Tone 8; PH 161; PS 4

R

1 Give ear to my words, O LORD; *
     consider my meditation.

2 **Hearken to my cry for help, my Sovereign and my God, ***
     for I make my prayer to you.

3 In the morning, LORD, you hear my voice; *
     early in the morning I make my appeal
         and watch for you.   R

4 **For you are not a God who takes pleasure**
         in wickedness, *
     and evil cannot dwell with you.

5 Braggarts cannot stand in your sight; *
     you hate all those who work wickedness.

6 **You destroy those who speak lies; ***
     the bloodthirsty and deceitful, O LORD, you abhor.   R

7 But as for me, through the greatness of your mercy
         I will go into your house; *
     I will bow down toward your holy temple in awe of you.

8 **Lead me, O LORD, in your righteousness,**
     because of those who lie in wait for me; *
     make your way straight before me.   R

9 For there is no truth in their mouth; *
    there is destruction in their heart;

their throat is an open grave; *
    they flatter with their tongue.

10 Declare them guilty, O God; *
    let them fall, because of their schemes.

Because of their many transgressions cast them out, *
    for they have rebelled against you.   **R**

11 But all who take refuge in you will be glad; *
    they will sing out their joy forever.

You will shelter them, *
    so that those who love your name may exult in you.

[Unison]

12 **For you, O Lord, will bless the righteous; ***
    you will defend them with your favor
        as with a shield.   **R**

You alone, O God, are holy and righteous,
and we praise you for protecting us in times of trial.
Keep us safe from all evil
and lead us in paths of justice
that we may know the joy of trusting Jesus Christ
our shield and defender.   **Amen.**   [537]

Psalm 6   Tone 7

R

1 Lord, do not rebuke me in your anger; *
    do not punish me in your wrath.

2 **Have pity on me, Lord, for I am weak; ***
    heal me, Lord, for my bones are racked.   ▼

3   My spirit shakes with terror; *
      how long, O LORD, how long?   **R**

4   **Turn, O LORD, and deliver me; ***
      save me for your mercy's sake.

5   For in death no one remembers you; *
      and who will give you thanks in the grave?   **R**

6   **I grow weary because of my groaning; ***
      every night I drench my bed
      and flood my couch with tears.

7   My eyes are wasted with grief *
      and worn away because of all my enemies.   **R**

8   **Depart from me, all evildoers, ***
      for the LORD has heard the sound of my weeping.

9   The LORD has heard my supplication; *
      the LORD accepts my prayer.

10   **All my enemies shall be confounded and quake with fear; ***
      they shall turn back and suddenly be put to shame.   R

Merciful God,
you know our anguish, not from afar,
but in the suffering of Jesus Christ.
Take all our grieving and sorrow,
all our pain and tears,
and heal us according to your promises
in Jesus Christ our Lord.   **Amen.**   [538]

PSALM 7   Tone 8 or 6

R

1   O LORD my God, I take refuge in you; *
      save and deliver me from all who pursue me;

2 **lest like a lion they tear me in pieces ***
  and snatch me away with none to deliver me.

3 O LORD my God, if I have done these things: *
  if there is any wickedness in my hands,

4 **if I have repaid my friend with evil, ***
  or plundered anyone who without cause is my enemy;

5 then let my enemy pursue and overtake me, *
  trample my life into the ground,
  and lay my honor in the dust.   **R**

6 **Stand up, O LORD, in your wrath; ***
  rise up against the fury of my enemies.

Awake, O my God, decree justice; *
  7 let the assembly of the peoples gather round you.

Be seated on your lofty throne, O Most High; *
  8 O LORD, judge the nations.

Give judgment for me according to my righteousness,
    O LORD, *
  and according to my innocence, O Most High.   **R**

9 **Let the malice of the wicked come to an end,**
  but establish the righteous; *
  for you test the mind and heart, O righteous God.

10 God is my shield and defense, *
  the savior of the true in heart.

11 **God is a righteous judge; ***
  God sits in judgment every day.   **R**

12 If they will not repent, God will whet a sword, *
  bending a bow and making it ready.

13 **God has prepared weapons of death, ***
  making arrows into shafts of fire.   ▼

14 Look at those who are in labor with wickedness, *
   who conceive evil, and give birth to a lie.

15 **They dig a pit and make it deep** *
   and fall into the hole that they have made.

16 Their malice turns back upon their own head; *
   their violence falls on their own scalp. **R**

17 **I will bear witness that the LORD is righteous;** *
   I will praise the name of the LORD Most High. **R**

O God, our judge and redeemer,
by the light of your truth
let the righteous know your goodness
and sinners know your mercy,
that together they may give you grateful praise;
through Jesus Christ our Lord. **Amen.** [539]

PSALM 8   Tone 3; PH 162, 163; PS 5

R

1 O LORD our Lord, *
   how exalted is your name in all the world!

2 **Out of the mouths of infants and children** *
   your majesty is praised above the heavens.

   You have set up a stronghold against your adversaries, *
      to quell the enemy and the avenger. **R**

3 **When I consider your heavens, the work of your fingers,** *
   the moon and the stars you have set in their courses,

4 what are human beings that you should be mindful of them? *
   mortals that you should seek them out? **R**

5 **You have made them but little lower than the angels;** *
   you adorn them with glory and honor;

6 you give them mastery over the works of your hands; *
      you put all things under their feet: **R**

7 **All sheep and oxen, ***
      even the wild beasts of the field,

8 the birds of the air, the fish of the sea, *
      and whatsoever walks in the paths of the sea.

9 **O Lord our Lord, ***
      how exalted is your name in all the world!   R

God of glory,
despite the majesty of your creation
you sought us out,
and through Christ
you crowned us with dignity and honor,
giving us dominion over your works.
Enable us so to care for the earth
that all creation may radiate the splendor
of Jesus Christ our Lord.   **Amen.**   [540]

Psalm 9   Tone 8; PS 6

R

1 I will give thanks to you, O Lord, with my whole heart; *
      I will tell of all your marvelous works.

2 **I will be glad and rejoice in you; ***
      I will sing to your name, O Most High.   R

3 When my enemies are driven back, *
      they will stumble and perish at your presence.

4 **For you have maintained my right and my cause; ***
      you sit upon your throne judging right.   R

5 You have rebuked the ungodly and destroyed the wicked; *
      you have blotted out their name forever and ever.   ▼

6 **As for the enemy, they are finished, in perpetual ruin, ***
  their cities ploughed under,
      the memory of them perished; R

7 but you, O LORD, are enthroned forever; *
    you have set up your throne for judgment.

8 **It is you who rule the world with righteousness; ***
    you judge the peoples with equity.

9 The LORD will be a refuge for the oppressed, *
    a refuge in time of trouble.

10 **Those who know your name will put their trust in you, ***
    for you never forsake those who seek you,
        O LORD. R

11 Sing praise to the LORD who dwells in Zion; *
    proclaim to the peoples the things the LORD has done.

12 **The Avenger of blood will remember them, ***
    and will not forget the cry of the afflicted.

13 Have pity on me, O LORD; *
    see the misery I suffer from those who hate me,
    O you who lift me up from the gate of death;

14 **so that I may tell of all your praises**
    and rejoice in your salvation *
        in the gates of the city of Zion. R

15 The ungodly have fallen into the pit they dug, *
    and in the snare they set is their own foot caught.

16 **The LORD is known by divine acts of justice; ***
    the wicked are trapped in the works
        of their own hands. R

17 The wicked shall be given over to the grave, *
    and also all the peoples that forget God.

18 **For the needy shall not always be forgotten, ***
    and the hope of the poor shall not perish forever.

19 Rise up, O LORD, let not the ungodly have the upper hand; *
    let them be judged before you.

20 **Put fear upon them, O LORD; ***
    let the ungodly know they are but mortal.   **R**

God Most High,
in Jesus Christ you rule the world with righteousness
and judge the nations with equity.
Cast down the haughty and lift up the lowly.
Make us compassionate to the needy
that we may be close to Jesus Christ,
our servant Lord. **Amen.** [541]

PSALM 10   Tone 8

R

1 Why do you stand so far off, O LORD, *
    and hide yourself in time of trouble?

2 **The wicked arrogantly persecute the poor, ***
    but they are trapped in the schemes they have devised.

3 The wicked boast of their heart's desire; *
    the covetous curse and revile the LORD.

4 **The wicked are so proud that they care not for God; ***
    their only thought is, "God does not matter."   **R**

5 Their ways are devious at all times;
your judgments are far above out of their sight; *
    they defy all their enemies.

6 **They say in their heart, "I shall not be shaken; ***
    no harm shall happen to me ever."

7 Their mouth is full of cursing, deceit, and oppression; *
    under their tongue are mischief and wrong.   ▼

8 **They lurk in ambush in public squares**
   and in secret places they murder the innocent; *
        they spy out the helpless.   R

9 They lie in wait, like a lion in a covert;
   they lie in wait to seize upon the lowly; *
        they seize the lowly and drag them away in their net.

10 **The innocent are broken and humbled before them;** *
   the helpless fall before their power.

11 They say in their heart, "God has forgotten; *
   God's face is hidden; God will never notice."   R

12 **Rise up, O LORD;**
   lift up your hand, O God; *
        do not forget the afflicted.

13 Why should the wicked revile God? *
   why should they say in their heart that you do not care?

14 **Surely, you behold trouble and misery;** *
   you see it and take it into your own hand.

   The helpless commit themselves to you, *
   for you are the helper of orphans.   R

15 **Break the power of the wicked and evil;** *
   search out their wickedness until you find none.

16 The LORD is Sovereign forever and ever; *
   the ungodly shall perish from your land.

17 **The LORD will hear the desire of the humble;** *
   you will strengthen their heart
        and your ears shall hear;

   [Unison]

18 to give justice to the orphan and oppressed, *
   so that mere mortals may strike terror no more.   R

O Lord,
you are the hope of the weak,
the orphaned, and the oppressed.
You subvert the wicked and their plans
and strengthen the hearts of the helpless.
Blessed are you, Lord God,
Sovereign of the universe.   **Amen.**   [542]

PSALM 12 Tone 8

R

1 Help me, LORD, for there is no godly one left; *
   the faithful have vanished from among us.

2 **All speak falsely with their neighbor; ***
   with a smooth tongue they speak from a
      double heart.

3 Oh, that the LORD would cut off all smooth tongues, *
   and close the lips that utter proud boasts!

4 **Those who say, "With our tongue will we prevail; ***
   our lips are our own; who is lord over us?"   R

5 "Because the needy are oppressed,
   and the poor cry out in misery, *
      I will rise up," says the LORD,
      "and give them the help they long for."

6 **The words of the LORD are pure words, ***
   like silver refined from ore
      and purified seven times in the fire.   R

7 O LORD, watch over us *
   and save us from this generation forever.

8 **The wicked prowl on every side, ***
   and that which is worthless is highly prized
      by everyone.   R

God of justice,
in Jesus Christ you championed the weak
and befriended outcasts.
Through the shining light of his goodness
you expose hypocrisy.
Give us courage to follow his example,
that we may be faithful disciples
of our Lord, Jesus Christ.   **Amen.**   [543]

PSALM 13   Tone 8 or 7; PS 7

R
1 How long, O LORD?
   Will you forget me forever? *
      how long will you hide your face from me?

2 **How long shall I have perplexity in my mind,
   and grief in my heart, day after day? ***
      how long shall my enemy triumph over me?   R

3 Look upon me and answer me, O LORD my God; *
      give light to my eyes, lest I sleep in death;

4 **lest my enemy say, "I have prevailed," ***
      and my foes rejoice that I have fallen.   R

5 But I put my trust in your mercy; *
      my heart is joyful because of your saving help.

6 **I will sing to you, O LORD,
   for you have dealt with me richly; ***
      I will praise the name of the Lord Most High.   R

Loving and merciful God,
hear the prayers of those who cry to you,
and shine with the light of your presence
on those who live in the shadow of death.
May we rejoice in your saving help
and sing you songs of praise
in the name of our risen Savior, Jesus Christ.   **Amen.**   [544]

R

1 Fools say in their heart, "There is no God." *
       All are corrupt and commit abominable acts;
       there is none who does any good.

2 **The LORD looks down from heaven upon us all, ***
       to see if there is any who is wise,
       if there is one who seeks after God.

3 Every one has proved faithless;
   all alike have turned bad; *
       there is none who does good; no, not one.   R

4 **Have they no knowledge, all those evildoers ***
       who eat up my people like bread
       and do not call upon the LORD?

5 See how they tremble with fear, *
       because God is in the company of the righteous.

6 **Their aim is to confound the plans of the afflicted, ***
       but the LORD is their refuge.

   [Unison]

7 **Oh, that Israel's deliverance would come out of Zion! ***
       when the LORD restores the fortunes of the chosen
           people,
       Jacob will rejoice and Israel be glad.   R

God of wisdom and justice,
deliver us from the foolishness of ignoring you.
Teach us your wisdom through Jesus Christ,
that we may seek your goodness
and embody your love to all your people,
for the sake of Jesus Christ our Lord.   **Amen.**   [545]

PSALM 15

R

1 LORD, who may dwell in your tabernacle? *
    who may abide upon your holy hill?

2 **Those who lead a blameless life and do what is right, ***
    who speak the truth from their heart.   R

3 There is no guile upon their tongue;
    they do no evil to their friend; *
        they do not heap contempt upon their neighbor.

4 **In their sight the wicked are rejected, ***
    but they honor those who fear the LORD.   R

They have sworn to do no wrong *
    and do not take back their word.

5 **They do not give their money in hope of gain, ***
    nor do they take a bribe against the innocent.

[Unison]

Those who do these things *
    shall never be overthrown.   R

God of love,
you adopted us as your children.
Grant that we may pass through this world with such integrity
that no one will have just complaint against us.
At the end,
may we inherit what has been prepared for us in heaven;
through our Savior, Jesus Christ. **Amen.**   [546]

PSALM 16

R

1 Protect me, O God, for I take refuge in you; *
    I have said to the LORD, "You are my Lord,
        my good above all other."

2 **All my delight is upon the godly that are in the land, ***
upon those who are noble among the people. R

3 But those who run after other gods *
shall have their troubles multiplied.

4 **Their libations of blood I will not offer, ***
nor take the names of their gods upon my lips. R

5 O LORD, you are my portion and my cup; *
it is you who uphold my lot.

6 **My boundaries enclose a pleasant land; ***
indeed, I have a goodly heritage. R

7 I will bless the LORD who gives me counsel; *
my heart teaches me, night after night.

8 **I have set the LORD always before me; ***
because you are at my right hand I shall not fall. R

9 My heart, therefore, is glad, and my spirit rejoices; *
my body also shall rest in hope.

10 **For you will not abandon me to the grave, ***
nor let your holy one see the pit. R

[Unison]

11 **You will show me the path of life; ***
in your presence there is fullness of joy,
and in your right hand are pleasures forevermore. R

Gracious God,
in whom all hearts are glad
and all souls rejoice:
Show us the path of your presence,
that we may follow it in hope
and be filled with resurrection joy;
through Jesus Christ, our risen Savior. **Amen.** [547]

R

1 Hear my plea of innocence, O LORD;
give heed to my cry; *
  listen to my prayer, which does not come from lying lips.

2 **Let my vindication come forth from your presence; ***
  let your eyes be fixed on justice.   R

3 Weigh my heart, summon me by night, *
  melt me down; you will find no impurity in me.

4 **I give no offense with my mouth as others do; ***
  I have heeded the words of your lips.

5 My footsteps hold fast to the ways of your law; *
  in your paths my feet shall not stumble.   **R**

6 **I call upon you, O God, for you will answer me; ***
  incline your ear to me and hear my words.

7 Show me your marvelous loving-kindness, *
  O Savior of those who take refuge at your right hand
  from those who rise up against them.   **R**

8 **Keep me as the apple of your eye; ***
  hide me under the shadow of your wings,

9 from the wicked who assault me, *
  from my deadly enemies who surround me.

10 **They have closed their heart to pity, ***
  and their mouth speaks proud things.

11 They press me hard,
now they surround me, *
  watching how they may cast me to the ground,

12 **like a lion, greedy for its prey, ***
  and like a young lion lurking in secret places.   R

13 Arise, O LORD; confront them and bring them down; *
   deliver me from the wicked by your sword.

14 **Deliver me, O LORD, by your hand ***
   from those whose portion in life is this world;

   whose bellies you fill with your treasure, *
      who are well supplied with children
      and leave their wealth to their little ones.

15 **But at my vindication I shall see your face; ***
   when I awake, I shall be satisfied, beholding
      your likeness. R

Good Lord, you are the searcher of human hearts.
When we are surrounded by dangers,
show us your favor,
without which we would perish.
Let not our hearts be earthbound,
but may we follow your commandments
and aspire to heaven's joy,
which is won for us in Jesus Christ our Savior. **Amen.** [548]

PSALM 18   Tone 3

R

1 I love you, O LORD my strength, *
   O LORD my stronghold, my crag, and my haven.

2 **My God, my rock in whom I put my trust, ***
   my shield, the horn of my salvation, and my refuge;
   you are worthy of praise.

3 I will call upon the LORD, *
   and so shall I be saved from my enemies. R

4 **The breakers of death rolled over me, ***
   and the torrents of oblivion made me afraid. ▼

5 The cords of hell entangled me, *
    and the snares of death were set for me.

6 **I called upon the LORD in my distress ***
    and cried out to my God for help. R

You heard my voice from your heavenly dwelling; *
    my cry of anguish came to your ears.

7 **The earth reeled and rocked; ***
    the roots of the mountains shook;
    they reeled because of your anger.

8 Smoke rose from your nostrils
    and a consuming fire out of your mouth; *
    hot burning coals blazed forth from you.

9 **You parted the heavens and came down ***
    with a storm cloud under your feet.

10 You mounted on cherubim and flew; *
    you swooped on the wings of the wind.   R

11 **You wrapped darkness about you; ***
    you made dark waters and thick clouds your pavilion.

12 From the brightness of your presence, through the clouds, *
    burst hailstones and coals of fire.

13 **O LORD, you thundered out of heaven; ***
    O Most High, you uttered your voice.

14 You loosed your arrows and scattered them; *
    you hurled thunderbolts and routed them.

15 **The beds of the seas were uncovered,**
    and the foundations of the world laid bare, *
    at your battle cry, O LORD,
    at the blast of the breath of your nostrils.   R

16 You reached down from on high and grasped me; *
    you drew me out of great waters.

17 **You delivered me from my strong enemies**
    and from those who hated me; *
        for they were too mighty for me.

18 They confronted me in the day of my disaster; *
        but the LORD was my support.

19 **You brought me out into an open place;** *
    you rescued me because you delighted in me.   R

20 The LORD rewarded me because of my righteous dealing; *
        because my hands were clean God rewarded me;

21 **for I have kept the ways of the LORD** *
    and have not offended against my God;

22 for all God's judgments are before my eyes, *
        and the decrees of the LORD I have not put away
            from me;

23 **for I have been blameless with the LORD** *
    and have kept myself from iniquity;

24 Therefore the LORD rewarded me according
        to my righteous dealing, *
        seeing the cleanness of my hands.   R

25 **With the faithful you show yourself faithful, O God;** *
    with the forthright you show yourself forthright.

26 With the pure you show yourself pure, *
        but with the crooked you are wily.

27 **You will save a lowly people,** *
    but you will humble the haughty eyes.

28 You, O LORD, are my lamp; *
        my God, you make my darkness bright.

29 **With you I will break down an enclosure;** *
    with the help of my God I will scale any wall.   R ▼

30 As for you, O God, your ways are perfect;
   the words of the LORD are tried in the fire; *
   you are a shield to all who trust in you.

31 **For who is God, but the LORD? ***
   who is the Rock, except our God?

32 It is God who girds me about with strength *
   and makes my way secure.   **R**

33 **You make me sure-footed like a deer ***
   and let me stand firm on the heights.

34 You train my hands for battle *
   and my arms for bending even a bow of bronze.

35 **You have given me your shield of victory; ***
   your right hand also sustains me;
   your loving care makes me great.

36 You lengthen my stride beneath me, *
   and my ankles do not give way.   **R**

37 **I pursue my enemies and overtake them; ***
   I will not turn back till I have destroyed them.

38 I strike them down, and they cannot rise; *
   they fall defeated at my feet.

39 **You have girded me with strength for the battle; ***
   you have cast down my adversaries beneath me;
   40 you have put my enemies to flight.

   I destroy those who hate me;
41 they cry out, but there is none to help them; *
   they cry to the LORD, who does not answer.

42 **I beat them small like dust before the wind; ***
   I trample them like mud in the streets.   R

43 You deliver me from the strife of the peoples; *
   you put me at the head of the nations.

44 **A people I have not known shall serve me;**
   no sooner shall they hear than they shall obey me; *
   strangers will cringe before me.

45 The foreign peoples will lose heart; *
   they shall come trembling out of their strongholds.   R

46 **The LORD lives! Blessed is my Rock! ***
   Exalted is the God of my salvation!

47 The LORD is the God who gave me victory *
   and cast down the peoples beneath me.

48 **You rescued me from the fury of my enemies;**
   you exalted me above those who rose against me; *
   you saved me from my deadly foe.   R

49 Therefore will I extol you among the nations, O LORD, *
   and sing praises to your name.

50 **You multiply the victories of your king; ***
   you show loving-kindness to your anointed,
   to David and his descendants forever.   R

Praise to you, God of our salvation.
You come to our help and set us free.
May your strength be our shield
and your word, our lamp,
that we may serve you with pure hearts
and find deliverance in Jesus Christ, our Savior.   **Amen.**   [549]

PSALM 19   Tone 6 or 5; PH 166, 167; PS 12, 13

R

1 The heavens declare the glory of God, *
   and the firmament shows forth the work of God's hands.

2 **One day tells its tale to another, ***
   and one night imparts knowledge to another.   ▼

3 Although they have no words or language, *
   and their voices are not heard,

4 **their sound has gone out into all lands, ***
   and their message to the ends of the world. R

In the deep has God set a pavilion for the sun; *
   5 it comes forth like a bridegroom out of his chamber;
   it rejoices like a champion to run its course.

6 **It goes forth from the uttermost edge of the heavens**
   and runs about to the end of it again; *
   nothing is hidden from its burning heat. R

7 The law of the LORD is perfect and revives the soul; *
   the testimony of the LORD is sure
      and gives wisdom to the innocent.

8 **The statutes of the LORD are just and rejoice the heart; ***
   the commandment of the LORD is clear
      and gives light to the eyes. R

9 The fear of the LORD is clean and endures forever; *
   the judgments of the LORD are true
      and righteous altogether.

10 **More to be desired are they than gold,**
      more than much fine gold, *
   sweeter far than honey, than honey in the comb. R

11 By them also is your servant enlightened, *
   and in keeping them there is great reward.

12 **Can people tell how often they offend? ***
   cleanse me from my secret faults.

13 Above all, keep your servant from presumptuous sins;
   let them not get dominion over me; *
      then shall I be whole and sound,
      and innocent of a great offense. R

^{14} **Let the words of my mouth and the meditation**
of my heart be acceptable in your sight, *
O LORD, my strength and my redeemer.   R

Faithful God,
you sent us your Word as the sun of truth and justice
to shine upon all the world.
Open our eyes to see your glory in all your works,
that, rejoicing in your whole creation,
we may learn to serve you with gladness,
for the sake of him through whom all things were made,
Jesus Christ our Lord.   **Amen.**   [550]

PSALM 20   Tone 6; PH 169; PS 14

R

^{1} May the LORD answer you in the day of trouble, *
    the name of the God of Jacob defend you.

^{2} **From God's holy place may you receive help; ***
    may God strengthen you out of Zion.

^{3} May God remember all your offerings *
    and accept your burnt sacrifice;   R

^{4} **grant you your heart's desire ***
    and prosper all your plans.

^{5} We will shout for joy at your victory

    and triumph in the name of our God; *
    may the LORD grant all your requests.   R

^{6} **Now I know that the LORD gives victory to the**
        anointed one; *
    out of God's holy heaven will come an answer;
    the right hand of the LORD works victorious
        strength.   ▼

7 Some put their trust in chariots and some in horses, *
    but we will call upon the name of the LORD our God.

8 **They collapse and fall down, ***
    but we will arise and stand upright.

[Unison]

9 **O LORD, give victory to the king ***
    and answer us when we call.   R

Almighty God,
you have given victory to Christ, your anointed one.
Keep us from stumbling into lesser loyalties,
and give us strength to stand firm,
trusting in the grace and peace
of Jesus Christ our Lord. **Amen.**   [551]

PSALM 22   Tone 8; PH 168; PS 15–17

R

1 My God, my God, why have you forsaken me? *
    and are so far from my cry
    and from the words of my distress?

2 **O my God, I cry in the daytime, but you do not answer; ***
    by night as well, but I find no rest.   R

3 Yet you are the Holy One, *
    enthroned upon the praises of Israel.

4 **Our ancestors put their trust in you; ***
    they trusted, and you delivered them.

5 They cried out to you and were delivered; *
    they trusted in you and were not put to shame.   R

6 **But as for me, I am a worm and not a man, ***
    scorned by all and despised by the people.

7 All who see me laugh me to scorn; *
   they curl their lips and wag their heads, saying,

8 "He trusted in the LORD; let the LORD deliver him; *
   let God rescue him, if God delights in him."   R

9 Yet you are the one who took me out of the womb, *
   and kept me safe upon my mother's breast.

10 **I have been entrusted to you ever since I was born; ***
   you were my God when I was still in my mother's
      womb.

11 Be not far from me, for trouble is near, *
   and there is none to help.   R

12 **Many young bulls encircle me; ***
   strong bulls of Bashan surround me.

13 They open wide their jaws at me, *
   like a ravening and a roaring lion.

14 **I am poured out like water;**
   all my bones are out of joint; *
   my heart within my breast is melting wax.

15 My mouth is dried out like a pot-sherd;
   my tongue sticks to the roof of my mouth; *
      and you have laid me in the dust of the grave.   R

16 **Packs of dogs close me in,**
   and gangs of evildoers circle around me; *
   17 **they pierce my hands and my feet;**
   I can count all my bones.

   They stare and gloat over me; *
   18 they divide my garments among them;
      they cast lots for my clothing.   R

19 **Be not far away, O LORD; ***
   you are my strength; hasten to help me.   ▼

20 Save me from the sword, *
    my life from the power of the dog.

21 Save me from the lion's mouth, *
    my wretched body from the horns of wild bulls.   R

22 I will declare your name to the community; *
    in the midst of the congregation I will praise you.

23 Praise the LORD, you that are God-fearing; *
    stand in awe of the LORD, O offspring of Israel;
    all you of Jacob's line, give glory.

24 For the LORD does not despise nor abhor the poor
    in their poverty;
    neither is the LORD's face hidden from them; *
    but when they cry out, the LORD hears them.   R

25 My praise is of God in the great assembly; *
    I will perform my vows in the presence
    of those who worship the LORD.

26 The poor shall eat and be satisfied,
    and those who seek the LORD shall give praise: *
    "May your heart live forever!"

27 All the ends of the earth shall remember
    and turn to God, *
    and all the families of the nations
    shall bow before the LORD.

28 For sovereignty belongs to the LORD, *
    who rules over the nations.   R

29 To the LORD alone all who sleep in the earth
    bow down in worship; *
    all who go down to the dust fall before the LORD.

30 My soul shall live for God;
   my descendants shall serve the LORD; *
      they shall be known as the LORD's forever.

31 **They shall come and make known
         to a people yet unborn** *
      the saving deeds that God has done. R

Eternal God,
your tortured Son felt abandoned,
and cried out in anguish from the cross,
yet you delivered him.
He overcame the bonds of death
and rose in triumph from the grave.
Do not hide your face from those who cry out to you.
Feed the hungry, strengthen the weak,
and break the chains of the oppressed,
that your people may rejoice in your saving deeds.
This we ask in the name of Jesus Christ our Savior.   **Amen.** [552]

PSALM 23   Tone 6; PH 170–175; PS 18–20

R

1 The LORD is my shepherd; *
   I shall not be in want.

2 **You make me lie down in green pastures** *
   and lead me beside still waters. R

3 You revive my soul *
   and guide me along right pathways for your name's sake.

4 **Though I walk through the valley of the shadow of
         death,**
   I shall fear no evil; *
      for you are with me;
      your rod and your staff, they comfort me. R ▼

5 You spread a table before me in the presence of those who
       trouble me; *
    you have anointed my head with oil,
    and my cup is running over.

**6 Surely your goodness and mercy shall follow me all
       the days of my life, ***
    and I will dwell in the house of the LORD forever.   R

Lord Jesus Christ, our good shepherd,
in the waters of Baptism you give us birth,
and at your table you nourish us with heavenly food.
In your goodness and mercy,
lead us along safe paths,
beyond the terrors of evil and death,
to the house of the Lord
where we may rest securely in you forever.   **Amen.**   [553]

PSALM 24   Tone 3; PH 176, 177; PS 21, 22

R

1 The earth is the LORD's and all that is in it, *
    the world and all who dwell therein.

2 For it is the LORD who founded it upon the seas *
    and made it firm upon the rivers of the deep.   R

3 "Who can ascend the hill of the LORD? *
    and who can stand in God's holy place?"

4 "Those who have clean hands and a pure heart, *
    who have not pledged themselves to falsehood,
    nor sworn by what is a fraud.

5 They shall receive a blessing from the LORD *
    and a just reward from the God of their salvation."

6 Such is the generation of those who seek the LORD, *
    of those who seek your face, O God of Jacob.   R

7 Lift up your heads, O gates;
lift them high, O everlasting doors; *
   and the glorious Sovereign shall come in.

8 **"Who is this glorious Sovereign?"** *
"The LORD, strong and mighty,
   the LORD, mighty in battle."

9 Lift up your heads, O gates;
lift them high, O everlasting doors; *
   and the glorious Sovereign shall come in.

10 **"And who is this glorious Sovereign?"** *
"The LORD,
   the LORD of hosts is the glorious Sovereign."   **R**

God of all creation,
open our hearts
that Christ, the King of glory, may enter and rule our lives.
Give us clean hands and pure hearts,
that we may stand in your presence and receive your blessing
through the same, Jesus Christ our Lord. **Amen.** [554]

PSALM 25   Tone 8 or 7; PH 178; PS 23

R

1 To you, O LORD, I lift up my soul;
  2my God, I put my trust in you; *
   let me not be humiliated,
   nor let my enemies triumph over me.

3 **Let none who look to you be put to shame;** *
   let the treacherous be disappointed
     in their schemes.   **R**

4 Show me your ways, O LORD, *
   and teach me your paths.

5 **Lead me in your truth and teach me,** *   ▼

for you are the God of my salvation;
in you have I trusted all the day long.   **R**

6 Remember, O LORD, your compassion and love, *
for they are from everlasting.

7 **Remember not the sins of my youth and my**
       transgressions; *
   remember me according to your love
   and for the sake of your goodness, O LORD.   **R**

8 Gracious and upright are you, O LORD; *
therefore you teach sinners in your way.

9 **You guide the humble in doing right** *
   and teach your way to the lowly.

10 All your paths, O LORD, are love and faithfulness *
to those who keep your covenant and your testimonies.   **R**

11 **For your name's sake, O LORD,** *
    forgive my sin, for it is great.

12 Who are they who fear the LORD? *
the LORD will teach them the way that they should
choose.   **R**

13 **They shall dwell in prosperity,** *
    and their offspring shall inherit the land.

14 The LORD is a friend to the God-fearing *
and will show them the holy covenant.

15 **My eyes are ever looking to the LORD,** *
    who shall pluck my feet out of the net.   **R**

16 Turn to me and have pity on me, *
for I am left alone and in misery.

17 **The sorrows of my heart have increased;** *
    bring me out of my troubles.

¹⁸ Look upon my adversity and misery *
    and forgive me all my sin.   **R**

¹⁹ **Look upon my enemies, for they are many, ***
    and they bear a violent hatred against me.

²⁰ Protect my life and deliver me; *
    let me not be put to shame, for I have trusted in you.

²¹ **Let integrity and uprightness preserve me, ***
    for my hope has been in you.

[Unison]

²² **Deliver Israel, O God, ***
    out of all their troubles.   **R**

Covenant Friend,
remember not our sins,
but recall your compassion to your children.
We turn to you for guidance and life,
turn also to us and be gracious,
that we may always follow in the way
of Jesus Christ our Redeemer. **Amen.** [555]

Psalm 26

Tone 8; PS 24

R

¹ Give judgment for me, O Lord,
    for I have lived with integrity; *
      I have trusted in the Lord and have not faltered.

² **Test me, O Lord, and try me; ***
    examine my heart and my mind.

³ For your love is before my eyes; *
    I have walked faithfully with you.   **R**

⁴ **I have not sat with the worthless, ***
    nor do I consort with the deceitful.   ▼

5 I have hated the company of evildoers; *
    I will not sit down with the wicked.

6 **I will wash my hands in innocence, O LORD, ***
    that I may go in procession round your altar,

7 singing aloud a song of thanksgiving *
    and recounting all your wonderful deeds.   **R**

8 **LORD, I love the house in which you dwell ***
    and the place where your glory abides.

9 Do not sweep me away with sinners, *
    nor my life with those who thirst for blood,

10 **whose hands are full of evil plots, ***
    and their right hand full of bribes.   R

11 As for me, I will live with integrity; *
    redeem me, O LORD, and have pity on me.

12 **My foot stands on level ground; ***
    in the full assembly I will bless the LORD.   R

Eternal God,
you know what is in our hearts and minds;
you test us to strengthen our faith.
Keep your love always before us,
and direct our steps,
that we may be steadfast in your way
and join with all your saints
to give you praise, now and forever.   **Amen.**   [556]

PSALM 27   Tone 6 (27:1–6), Tone 7 (27:7–14);
                                          PH 179; PS 25

R

1 The LORD is my light and my salvation;
    whom then shall I fear? *

the LORD is the strength of my life;
of whom then shall I be afraid?

2 **When evildoers came upon me to eat up my flesh, ***
it was they, my foes and my adversaries, who
stumbled and fell.

3 Though an army should encamp against me, *
yet my heart shall not be afraid;

and though war should rise up against me, *
yet will I put my trust in the LORD.

4 One thing have I asked of the LORD;
one thing I seek; *
that I may dwell in the house of the LORD all the days
of my life;

to behold the fair beauty of the LORD, *
to seek God in the temple. R

5 For on the day of trouble the LORD shall shelter me
in safety; *
the LORD shall hide me in the secrecy of the holy place
and set me high upon a rock.

6 **Even now the LORD lifts up my head ***
above my enemies round about me.

Therefore I will offer in the holy place an oblation
with sounds of great gladness; *
I will sing and make music to the LORD. R

7 **Hearken to my voice, O LORD, when I call; ***
have mercy on me and answer me.

8 You speak in my heart and say, "Seek my face." *
Your face, LORD, will I seek.

9 **Hide not your face from me, ***
nor turn away your servant in displeasure. ▼

You have been my helper;
cast me not away; *
  do not forsake me, O God of my salvation.

10 **Though my father and my mother forsake me, ***
  the LORD will sustain me. R

11 Show me your way, O LORD; *
  lead me on a level path, because of my enemies.

12 **Deliver me not into the hand of my adversaries, ***
  for false witnesses have risen up against me,
  and also those who speak malice.

13 What if I had not believed
  that I should see the goodness of the LORD *
  in the land of the living!

14 **O tarry and await the LORD's pleasure;**
  be strong, and the LORD shall comfort your heart; *
  wait patiently for the LORD. R

O God, guardian and guide of all your people,
protect and lead us through times of trouble,
establishing our faith on the rock of Jesus Christ,
who is the way, the truth, and the life. **Amen.** [557]

PSALM 28   Tone 8

R

1 O LORD, I call to you;
  my Rock, do not be deaf to my cry; *
    lest, if you do not hear me,
    I become like those who go down to the pit.

2 **Hear the voice of my prayer when I cry out to you, ***
  when I lift up my hands to your holy of holies. R

3   Do not snatch me away with the wicked or with the
        evildoers, *
     who speak peaceably with their neighbors,
     while strife is in their hearts.

4   **Repay them according to their deeds, ***
     and according to the wickedness of their actions.

    According to the work of their hands repay them, *
     and give them their just deserts.

5   **O Lord, they have no understanding of your doings,**
  nor of the works of your hands; *
     therefore you will break them down and not build
        them up.   **R**

6   Blessed is the Lord! *
     for you have heard the voice of my prayer.

7   **The Lord is my strength and my shield; ***
     my heart trusts in you, and I have been helped;

    therefore my heart dances for joy, *
     and in my song will I praise you.   **R**

8   **You, O Lord, are the strength of your people, ***
     a safe refuge for your anointed.

    [Unison]

9   **Save your people and bless your inheritance; ***
     shepherd them and carry them forever.   **R**

Strong Shepherd of your people,
you hear us when we lift our hands in prayer to you.
Strengthen us to offer you thanks
for the mighty works that you have done,
and make our hearts leap for joy;
through Jesus Christ our Lord.   **Amen.**   [558]

R

1 Ascribe to the LORD, you gods, *
    ascribe to the LORD glory and strength.

2 **Ascribe to the LORD the glory that is due the holy name;***
    worship the LORD in the beauty of holiness.   R

3 The voice of the LORD is upon the waters;
    the God of glory thunders; *
      the LORD is upon the mighty waters.

4 **The voice of the LORD is a powerful voice; ***
    the voice of the LORD is a voice of splendor.   R

5 The voice of the LORD breaks the cedar trees; *
    the LORD breaks the cedars of Lebanon;

6 **the LORD makes Lebanon skip like a calf, ***
    and Mount Hermon like a young wild ox.   R

7 The voice of the LORD splits the flames of fire;
    the voice of the LORD shakes the wilderness; *
      the LORD shakes the wilderness of Kadesh.

8 **The voice of the LORD makes the oak trees writhe ***
    and strips the forests bare.

9 And in the temple of the LORD *
    all are crying, "Glory!"   R

10 **The LORD sits enthroned above the flood; ***
    the LORD sits enthroned as Sovereign forevermore.

   [Unison]

11 **The LORD shall give strength to the chosen people; ***
    the LORD shall give the people the blessing
      of peace.   R

God of mystery and power,
open our eyes to the fire of your love,
and open our ears to the thunder of your justice,
that we may receive your gifts of blessing and peace,
to the glory of your name;
through Jesus Christ our Lord.   **Amen.**   [559]

PSALM 30   Tone 3; PH 181; PS 27

R

1 I will exalt you, O LORD,
   because you have lifted me up *
       and have not let my enemies triumph over me.

2 **O LORD my God, I cried out to you, ***
       and you restored me to health.

3 You brought me up, O LORD, from the dead; *
       you restored my life as I was going down to the grave.   **R**

4 **Sing to the LORD, you faithful servants; ***
       give thanks for the remembrance of God's holiness.

5 For God's wrath lasts but the twinkling of an eye, *
       God's favor endures for a lifetime.

   Weeping may spend the night, *
       but joy comes in the morning.

6 While I felt secure, I said,
   "I shall never be disturbed. *
       7You, LORD, with your favor, made me as strong as the
           mountains."

   Then you hid your face, *
       and I was filled with fear.   **R**

8 I cried to you, O LORD; *
       I pleaded with the Lord, saying,   ▼

9   **"What profit is there in my blood,**
        if I go down to the pit? *
        will the dust praise you or declare your faithfulness?

10 Hear, O LORD, and have mercy upon me; *
      O LORD, be my helper."   **R**

11 **You have turned my wailing into dancing; ***
       you have put off my sack-cloth and clothed me
         with joy.

    [Unison]

12 **Therefore my heart sings to you without ceasing; ***
       O LORD my God, I will give you thanks forever.   **R**

Loving God,
glorious in giving and restoring life,
do not hide your face from your people overcome with
    loneliness and fear.
Turn our weeping into dancing,
our despair into joy,
and raise us up with Christ,
that we may rejoice in your presence forever.   **Amen.**   [560]

PSALM 31   Tone 6 or 8; PH 182, 183; PS 28

R
1 In you, O LORD, have I taken refuge;
    let me never be put to shame; *
       deliver me in your righteousness.

2 **Incline your ear to me; ***
       make haste to deliver me.   **R**

3 Be my strong rock, a castle to keep me safe,
    for you are my crag and my stronghold; *
       for the sake of your name, lead me and guide me.

4 **Take me out of the net**
        that they have secretly set for me, *
    for you are my tower of strength.

5 Into your hands I commend my spirit, *
        for you have redeemed me,
        O LORD, O God of truth.   R

6 **I hate those who cling to worthless idols,** *
        and I put my trust in the LORD.

7 I will rejoice and be glad because of your mercy; *
        for you have seen my affliction;
        you know my distress.

8 **You have not shut me up in the power of the enemy;** *
        you have set my feet in an open place.   R

9 Have mercy on me, O LORD, for I am in trouble; *
        my eye is consumed with sorrow,
        and also my throat and my belly.

10 **For my life is wasted with grief,**
    and my years with sighing; *
        my strength fails me because of affliction,
        and my bones are consumed.   R

11 I have become a reproach to all my enemies and even to
            my neighbors,
    a dismay to those of my acquaintance; *
        when they see me in the street they avoid me.

12 **I am forgotten, out of mind, as if I were dead;** *
        I am as useless as a broken pot.

13 For I have heard the whispering of the crowd;
    fear is all around; *
        they put their heads together against me;
        they plot to take my life.   R   ▼

14 But as for me, I have trusted in you, O LORD. *
   I have said, "You are my God.

15 My times are in your hand; *
   rescue me from the hand of my enemies,
   and from those who persecute me.

16 Make your face to shine upon your servant, *
   and in your loving-kindness save me."   R

17 LORD, let me not be ashamed for having called upon you; *
   rather, let the wicked be put to shame;
   let them be silent in the grave.

18 Let the lying lips be silenced which speak against the
      righteous, *
   haughtily, disdainfully, and with contempt.   R

19 How great is your goodness, O LORD!
   which you have laid up for those who fear you; *
   which you have done in the sight of all
   for those who put their trust in you.

20 You hide them in the covert of your presence
      from those who slander them; *
   you keep them in your shelter from the strife of
      tongues.   R

21 Blessed be the LORD! *
   for you have shown me the wonders of your love in a
      besieged city.

22 Yet I said in my alarm,
   "I have been cut off from the sight of your eyes." *
   Nevertheless, you heard the sound of my entreaty
      when I cried out to you.   R

23 Love the LORD, all you who are faithful; *
   the LORD protects the pious,
   but repays to the full those who act haughtily.

24 **Be strong and let your heart take courage, ***
    all you who wait for the LORD.   **R**

Helper of the helpless,
comforter of the afflicted,
may your servants who stand in the midst of evil
find strength in the knowledge of your presence,
and praise you for the wonders of your love;
through Jesus Christ our Redeemer.   **Amen.**   [561]

PSALM 32   Tone 6; PH 184; PS 29

R

1   Happy are they whose transgressions are forgiven, ***
    and whose sin is put away!

2   **Happy are they to whom the LORD imputes no guilt, ***
    and in whose spirit there is no guile!   **R**

3   While I held my tongue, my bones withered away, ***
    because of my groaning all day long.

4   **For your hand was heavy upon me day and night; ***
    my moisture was dried up as in the heat of summer.

5   Then I acknowledged my sin to you, ***
    and did not conceal my guilt.   **R**

    I said, "I will confess my transgressions to the LORD." *
    Then you forgave me the guilt of my sin.

6   Therefore all the faithful will make their prayers to you
         in time of trouble; ***
    when the great waters overflow, they shall not reach them.

7   **You are my hiding-place;**
  you preserve me from trouble; *
    you surround me with shouts of deliverance.   **R** ▼

8 "I will instruct you and teach you in the way that you
    should go; *
  I will guide you with my eye.

9 **Do not be like horse or mule, which have no
    understanding; ***
  who must be fitted with bit and bridle,
  or else they will not stay near you."

10 Great are the tribulations of the wicked; *
  but mercy embraces those who trust in the LORD.

11 **Be glad, you righteous, and rejoice in the LORD; ***
  shout for joy, all who are true of heart.   R

Merciful God,
we confess that we have squandered your blessings
and turned our backs on your love.
Help us to repent and return to you,
confident that you will welcome us as your sons and daughters
in Jesus Christ. **Amen.**   [562]

PSALM 33   Tone 6; PH 185; PS 30, 31

R

1 Rejoice in the LORD, you righteous; *
  it is good for the just to sing praises.

2 **Praise the LORD with the harp; ***
  play upon the psaltery and lyre.

3 Sing for the LORD a new song; *
  sound a fanfare with all your skill upon the trumpet.   R

4 **For your word, O LORD, is right, ***
  and all your works are sure.

5 You love righteousness and justice; *
  your loving-kindness, O LORD, fills the whole earth.

6 **By your word, O LORD, were the heavens made, ***
   by the breath of your mouth all the heavenly hosts.

7 You gather up the waters of the ocean as in a water-skin *
   and store up the depths of the sea.　　**R**

8 **Let all the earth fear the LORD; ***
   let all who dwell in the world stand in reverence.

9 For the LORD spoke, and it came to pass; *
   the LORD commanded, and it stood fast.　　**R**

10 **The LORD brings the will of the nations to naught ***
   and thwarts the designs of the peoples.

11 But the LORD's will stands fast forever, *
   and the designs of the LORD's heart from age to age.

12 **Happy is the nation whose God is the LORD! ***
   happy the people you have chosen to be your own!　**R**

13 O LORD, you look down from heaven *
   and behold all the people in the world.

14 **From where you sit enthroned you turn your gaze ***
   on all who dwell on the earth.

15 You fashion all the hearts of them *
   and understand all their works.

16 **There is no ruler that can be saved by a mighty army; ***
   a warrior is not delivered by great strength.

17 The horse is a vain hope for deliverance; *
   for all its strength it cannot save.　　**R**

18 **Behold, your eye, O LORD, is upon those who fear you, ***
   on those who wait upon your love,

19 to pluck their lives from death, *
   and to feed them in time of famine.　　**R**　▼

20 **Our soul waits for you, O LORD; ***
   you are our help and our shield.

21 Indeed, our heart rejoices in you, *
   for in your holy name we put our trust.

22 **Let your loving-kindness, O LORD, be upon us, ***
   as we have put our trust in you.   R

Lord God,
with your Son you made heaven and earth,
and through him you continue to accomplish your purpose
   for creation.
Make us witnesses to your truth and instruments of your peace,
that all may know you are the God of justice,
and trust your holy name;
through Jesus Christ our Savior.   **Amen.**   [563]

PSALM 34   Tone 6; PH 187; PS 32, 33

R

1   At all times I will bless the LORD, *
    whose praise shall ever be in my mouth.

2   **I will glory in the LORD; ***
    let the humble hear and rejoice.

3   Proclaim with me the greatness of the LORD; *
    let us exalt the name of the LORD together.   **R**

4   **I sought the LORD, who answered me ***
    and delivered me out of all my terror.

5   Look upon the LORD and be radiant, *
    and let not your faces be ashamed.   **R**

6   **I called in my affliction and the LORD heard me ***
    and saved me from all my troubles.

7 The angel of the LORD encompasses the God-fearing, *
   and the LORD will deliver them.

8 **Taste and see that the LORD is good; ***
   happy are they who trust in the LORD!   R

9 Fear the LORD, you holy ones, *
   for those who are God-fearing lack nothing.

10 **The young lions lack and suffer hunger, ***
   but those who seek the LORD lack nothing that is
   good.   R

11 Come, children, and listen to me; *
   I will teach you the fear of the LORD.

12 **Who among you loves life ***
   and desires long life to enjoy prosperity?

13 Keep your tongue from evil-speaking *
   and your lips from lying words.

14 **Turn from evil and do good; ***
   seek peace and pursue it.   R

15 The eyes of the LORD are upon the righteous, *
   and the ears of the LORD are open to their cry.

16 **The face of the LORD is against those who do evil, ***
   to root out the remembrance of them from the
   earth.

17 The righteous cry, and the LORD hears them *
   and delivers them from all their troubles.

18 **The LORD is near to the brokenhearted ***
   and will save those whose spirits are crushed.   R

19 Many are the troubles of the righteous, *
   but the LORD will deliver the just out of them all.   ▼

20 **The LORD will keep safe the bones of the righteous; ***
   not one of them shall be broken.

21 Evil shall slay the wicked, *
   and those who hate the righteous will be punished.

22 **The LORD ransoms the life of those chosen to serve, ***
   and none will be punished who trust in the LORD.   R

Graciously hear us, Lord, for you alone we seek.
Quiet us with the peace which passes understanding,
and make us radiant with the knowledge of your goodness;
through Jesus Christ our Lord.   **Amen.**   [564]

PSALM 35   Tone 8

R

1 Fight those who fight me, O LORD; *
   attack those who are attacking me.

2 **Take up shield and armor ***
   and rise up to help me.

3 Draw the sword and bar the way against those
         who pursue me; *
   say to my soul, "I am your salvation."   **R**

4 **Let those who seek after my life be shamed and**
         humbled, *
   let those who plot my ruin fall back and be dismayed.

5 Let them be like chaff before the wind, *
   and let the angel of the LORD drive them away.

6 **Let their way be dark and slippery, ***
   and let the angel of the LORD pursue them.   R

7 For they have secretly spread a net for me without a cause; *
   without a cause they have dug a pit to take me alive.

8 **Let ruin come upon them unawares; ***
   let them be caught in the net they hid;
   let them fall into the pit they dug.

9 Then I will be joyful in you, O LORD; *
   I will glory in your victory.

10 **My very bones will say, "LORD, who is like you? ***
   You deliver the poor from those who are too strong
       for them,
   the poor and needy from those who rob them."   R

11 Malicious witnesses rise up against me; *
   they charge me with matters I know nothing about.

12 **They pay me evil in exchange for good; ***
   my soul is full of despair.

13 But when they were sick I dressed in sack-cloth *
   and humbled myself by fasting;

14 **I prayed with my whole heart,**
   as one would for a friend or a brother; *
   I behaved like one who mourns for a mother,
   bowed down and grieving.   R

15 But when I stumbled, they were glad and gathered together;
   they gathered against me; *
   strangers whom I did not know tore me to pieces and
       would not stop.

16 **They put me to the test and mocked me; ***
   they gnashed at me with their teeth.   R

17 O Lord, how long will you look on? *
   rescue me from the roaring beasts,
   and my life from the young lions.

18 **I will give you thanks in the great congregation; ***
   I will praise you in the mighty throng.   R   ▼

19 Do not let my treacherous foes rejoice over me, *
nor let those who hate me without a cause wink at each
other.

20 **For they do not plan for peace, ***
but invent deceitful schemes against the quiet in the
land.

21 They opened their mouths at me and said, *
"Aha! we saw it with our own eyes."   **R**

22 **You saw it, O LORD; do not be silent; ***
O Lord, be not far from me.

23 Awake, arise, to my cause! *
to my defense, my God and my Lord!

24 **Give me justice, O LORD my God,**
according to your righteousness; *
do not let them triumph over me.

25 Do not let them say in their hearts,
"Aha! just what we want!" *
Do not let them say, "We have swallowed you up."   **R**

26 **Let all who rejoice at my ruin be ashamed and**
disgraced; *
let those who boast against me be clothed with
dismay and shame.

27 Let those who favor my cause sing out with joy and be glad; *
let them say always, "Great are you, O LORD;
you desire the prosperity of your servant."

28 **And my tongue shall be talking of your righteousness ***
and of your praise all the day long.   **R**

God of our salvation,
come quickly to free the poor from their oppressors,
and establish your reign of justice on earth,

that your people may sing out with joy;
through Jesus Christ our Lord.   **Amen.**   [565]

PSALM 36   Tone 6; PH 186; PS 34

R

1 There is a voice of rebellion deep in the heart of the wicked; *
    there is no fear of God before their eyes.

2 **They flatter themselves in their own eyes ***
    that their hateful sin will not be found out.

3 The words of their mouth are wicked and deceitful; *
    they have left off acting wisely and doing good.

4 **They think up wickedness upon their beds**
    and have set themselves in no good way; *
    they do not abhor that which is evil.   R

5 Your love, O LORD, reaches to the heavens, *
    and your faithfulness to the clouds.

6 **Your righteousness is like the strong mountains,**
    your justice like the great deep; *
    you save humans and beasts alike, O LORD.   R

7 How priceless is your love, O God! *
    your people take refuge under the shadow of your wings.

8 **They feast upon the abundance of your house; ***
    you give them drink from the river of your delights.

9 For with you is the well of life, *
    and in your light we see light.   R

10 **Continue your loving-kindness to those who know you, ***
    and your favor to those who are true of heart.

11 Let not the foot of the proud come near me, *
    nor the hand of the wicked push me aside.   ▼

¹² See how they are fallen, those who work wickedness! *
   they are cast down and shall not be able to rise.   **R**

Eternal God,
you satisfy our hunger
by feeding us with the bread of life,
and you quench our thirst for righteousness
by your mighty acts.
Nourish us always by your Spirit,
that we may grow into the stature of Jesus Christ.   **Amen.**   [566]

PSALM 37   Tone 6; PH 188; PS 35

R

¹ Do not fret yourself because of evildoers; *
   do not be jealous of those who do wrong.

² **For they shall soon wither like the grass, ***
   and like the green grass fade away.   **R**

³ Put your trust in the LORD and do good; *
   dwell in the land and feed on its riches.

⁴ **Take delight in the LORD, ***
   who shall give you your heart's desire.   **R**

⁵ Commit your way to the LORD; put your trust in the LORD, *
   who will bring it to pass.

⁶ **The LORD will make your righteousness as clear as**
      the light *
   and your just dealing as the noonday.

⁷ Be still before the LORD; *
   wait patiently for the LORD.

Do not fret yourself over the one who prospers, *
   the one who succeeds in evil schemes.   **R**

8 Refrain from anger, leave rage alone; *
   do not fret yourself; it leads only to evil.

9 **For evildoers shall be cut off, ***
   but those who wait upon the Lord
      shall possess the land.   R

10 In a little while the wicked shall be no more; *
    you shall search out their place, but they will not be there.

11 **But the lowly shall possess the land; ***
    they will delight in abundance of peace.   R

      *   *   *

39 But the deliverance of the righteous comes from the Lord, *
    who is their stronghold in time of trouble.

40 **The Lord will help them and rescue them; ***
    the Lord will rescue them from the wicked and
       deliver them,
    because in the Lord they seek refuge.   R

God our strength,
give us the humility to trust in your loving care,
and the patience to be faithful in seeking your kingdom,
that we may come to share in the inheritance of your saints;
through Jesus Christ our Savior.   **Amen.**   [567]

Psalm 38   Tone 7

R

1 O Lord, do not rebuke me in your anger; *
   do not punish me in your wrath.

2 **For your arrows have already pierced me, ***
   and your hand presses hard upon me.   R   ▼

3 There is no health in my flesh,
  because of your indignation; *
      there is no soundness in my body, because of my sin.

4 **For my iniquities overwhelm me; ***
  like a heavy burden they are too much for me to
      bear.   R

5 My wounds stink and fester *
  by reason of my foolishness.

6 **I am utterly bowed down and prostrate; ***
  I go about in mourning all the day long.

7 Searing pain fills my innards; *
  there is no health in my body.

8 **I am utterly numb and crushed; ***
  I wail, because of the groaning of my heart.   R

9 O Lord, you know all my desires, *
  and my sighing is not hidden from you.

10 **My heart is pounding, my strength has failed me, ***
   and the brightness of my eyes is gone from me.

11 My friends and companions draw back from my affliction; *
   my neighbors stand afar off.   **R**

12 **Those who seek after my life lay snares for me; ***
   those who strive to hurt me speak of my ruin
       and plot treachery all the day long.

13 But I am like the deaf who do not hear, *
   like those who are mute and do not open their mouth.

14 **I have become like one who does not hear ***
   and from whose mouth comes no defense.   R

15 For in you, O LORD, have I fixed my hope; *
   you will answer me, O Lord my God.

16 **For I said, "Do not let them rejoice at my expense, ***
   those who gloat over me when my foot slips."   R

17 Truly, I am on the verge of falling, *
   and my pain is always with me.

18 **I will confess my iniquity ***
   and be sorry for my sin.

19 Those who are my enemies without cause are mighty, *
   and many in number are those who wrongfully hate me.

20 **Those who repay evil for good slander me, ***
   because I follow the course that is right.   R

21 O LORD, do not forsake me; *
   be not far from me, O my God.

22 **Make haste to help me, ***
   O Lord of my salvation.   R

God of compassion,
when we are weighed down by the burden of our sins,
help us to remember that you do not forsake us,
but show mercy through Jesus Christ our Savior.   **Amen.**   [568]

PSALM 39   Tone 8

R

1 I said, "I will keep watch upon my ways, *
   so that I do not offend with my tongue.

   I will put a muzzle on my mouth *
   while the wicked are in my presence."

2 So I held my tongue and said nothing; *
   I refrained from rash words;
   but my pain became unbearable.   ▼

3 **My heart was hot within me;**
   while I pondered, the fire burst into flame; *
      I spoke out with my tongue: R

4 LORD, let me know my end and the number of my days, *
   so that I may know how short my life is.

5 **You have given me a mere handful of days,**
   and my lifetime is as nothing in your sight; *
      truly, even those who stand erect are but a
         puff of wind.

6 We walk about like a shadow,
   and in vain we are in turmoil; *
      we heap up riches and cannot tell who will gather them. R

7 **And now, what is my hope? ***
   O Lord, my hope is in you.

8 Deliver me from all my transgressions *
   and do not make me the taunt of the fool.

9 **I fell silent and did not open my mouth, ***
   for surely it was you that did it.

10 Take your affliction from me; *
   I am worn down by the blows of your hand.   R

11 **With rebukes for sin you punish us;**
   like a moth you eat away all that is dear to us; *
      truly, everyone is but a puff of wind.   R

12 Hear my prayer, O LORD,
   and give ear to my cry; *
      hold not your peace at my tears.

   For I am but a sojourner with you, *
      a wayfarer, as all my ancestors were.

13 **Turn your gaze from me, that I may be glad again, ***
   before I go my way and am no more.   R

God of hope,
when we are troubled by fear and uncertainty,
teach us to commit our lives to your care,
and to trust in the knowledge of your love and forgiveness,
that we may find peace in Jesus Christ our Redeemer.
Amen.   [569]

PSALM 40   Tone 6; PS 36

R

1 I waited patiently upon you, O LORD; *
      you stooped to me and heard my cry.

2 **You lifted me out of the desolate pit, out of the**
         mire and clay; *
      you set my feet upon a high cliff and made my
         footing sure.

3 You put a new song in my mouth,
   a song of praise to our God; *
      many shall see, and stand in awe,
      and put their trust in the LORD.   **R**

4 **Happy are they who trust in the LORD! ***
      they do not resort to evil spirits or turn to false gods.

5 Great things are they that you have done, O LORD my God!
   how great your wonders and your plans for us! *
      there is none who can be compared with you.

   Oh, that I could make them known and tell them! *
      but they are more than I can count.   R   ▼

6 In sacrifice and offering you take no pleasure *
    (you have given me ears to hear you);

burnt-offering and sin-offering you have not required, *
    7 and so I said, "Behold, I come.

In the roll of the book it is written concerning me: *
    8 'I love to do your will, O my God;
    your law is deep in my heart.'"   **R**

9 **I proclaimed righteousness in the great congregation; ***
    behold, I did not restrain my lips;
    and that, O LORD, you know.

10 Your righteousness have I not hidden in my heart;
    I have spoken of your faithfulness and your deliverance; *
    I have not concealed your love and faithfulness from the
        great congregation.

11 **You are the LORD;**
    do not withhold your compassion from me; *
    let your love and your faithfulness keep me safe
        forever,   R

12 for innumerable troubles have crowded upon me;
    my sins have overtaken me, and I cannot see; *
    they are more in number than the hairs of my head,
    and my heart fails me.   **R**

13 **Be pleased, O LORD, to deliver me; ***
    O LORD, make haste to help me.

14 Let them be ashamed and altogether dismayed
    who seek after my life to destroy it; *
    let them draw back and be disgraced
    who take pleasure in my misfortune.

15 **Let those who say "Aha!" and gloat over me be**
        confounded, *
    because they are ashamed.   R

16 Let all who seek you rejoice in you and be glad; *
   let those who love your salvation continually say,
   "Great is the LORD!"

17 **Though I am poor and afflicted, ***
   the Lord will have regard for me.

   [Unison]

   You are my helper and my deliverer; *
   do not tarry, O my God.   R

O God,
none can compare with you,
for your wondrous deeds for our salvation are without number.
Make us bold witnesses to your faithfulness
that all the earth may rejoice in your love toward us
in Jesus Christ our Redeemer.   **Amen.**   [570]

PSALM 41   Tone 8

R

1 Happy are they who consider the poor and needy! *
   the LORD will deliver them in the time of trouble.

2 **The LORD preserves them and keeps them alive,**
   so that they may be happy in the land; *
      the LORD does not hand them over to the will of
         their enemies.

3 The LORD sustains them on their sickbed *
   and ministers to them in their illness.   **R**

4 **I said, "LORD, be merciful to me; ***
   heal me, for I have sinned against you."

5 My enemies are saying wicked things about me, *
   asking when I will die, and when my name will perish.   ▼

6 **Even if they come to see me, they speak empty words; ***
   their heart collects false rumors;
   they go outside and spread them.

7 All my enemies whisper together about me *
   and devise evil against me.   R

8 **They say that a deadly thing has fastened on me, ***
   that I have taken to my bed and will never
         get up again.

9 Even my best friend, whom I trusted,
   who broke bread with me, *
      has scorned me and turned against me.

10 **But you, O LORD, be merciful to me and raise me up, ***
   and I shall repay them.   R

11 By this I know you are pleased with me, *
      that my enemy does not triumph over me.

12 **In my integrity you hold me fast, ***
   and shall set me before your face forever.

   [Unison]

13 **Blessed be the LORD God of Israel, ***
   from age to age. Amen. Amen.   R

Remember us, gracious God,
when we are lonely and depressed,
and support us in the night of grief and despair,
for you are faithful
and you do not abandon your broken ones.
We ask this in the name of Jesus Christ our Lord.   **Amen.**   [571]

PSALM 42   Tone 8; PH 189, 190; PS 37

R

1 As the deer longs for the water-brooks, *
      so longs my soul for you, O God.

2 **My soul is athirst for God, athirst for the living God; ***
when shall I come to appear before the presence
of God?

3 My tears have been my food day and night, *
while all day long they say to me,
"Where now is your God?"   R

4 **I pour out my soul when I think on these things: ***
how I went with the multitude and led them into
the house of God,

with the voice of praise and thanksgiving, *
among those who keep holy-day.

5 **Why are you so full of heaviness, O my soul? ***
and why are you so disquieted within me?   R

Put your trust in God; *
for I will yet give thanks to the One
who is the help of my countenance, 6 and my God.

My soul is heavy within me; *
therefore I will remember you from the land of
Jordan,
and from the peak of Mizar among the heights of
Hermon.

7 One deep calls to another in the noise of your cataracts; *
all your rapids and floods have gone over me.

8 **The LORD grants loving-kindness in the daytime; ***
in the night season the song of the LORD is with me,
a prayer to the God of my life.   R

9 I will say to the God of my strength,
"Why have you forgotten me? *
and why do I go so heavily while the enemy oppresses
me?"   ▼

10 **While my bones are being broken,** *
    my enemies mock me to my face;

   all day long they mock me *
   and say to me, "Where now is your God?"   **R**

11 **Why are you so full of heaviness, O my soul?** *
    and why are you so disquieted within me?

   [Unison]

   Put your trust in God; *
      for I will yet give thanks to the One
      who is the help of my countenance, and my God.   **R**

Gracious God,
in the night of distress we forget the days of sun and joy.
When we do not know your presence,
preserve us from the deep torrent of despair.
We ask this in the name of Jesus Christ our Lord.   **Amen.**   [572]

PSALM 43   Tone 8; PS 38

R

1   Give judgment for me, O God,
    and defend my cause against an ungodly people; *
       deliver me from the deceitful and the wicked.

2   **For you are the God of my strength;**
    why have you put me from you? *
       and why do I go so heavily while the enemy
          oppresses me?   **R**

3   Send out your light and your truth, that they may lead me, *
       and bring me to your holy hill
       and to your dwelling;

4   **that I may go to the altar of God,**

to the God of my joy and gladness; *
   and on the harp I will give thanks to you, O God
      my God.   R

5 Why are you so full of heaviness, O my soul? *
   and why are you so disquieted within me?

Put your trust in God; *
   for I will yet give thanks to the One
   who is the help of my countenance, and my God.   R

Eternal God, source of everlasting light,
send forth your truth into our hearts,
and bring us into your presence with joy and gladness
in the name of Jesus Christ the Lord.   Amen.   [573]

PSALM 45   Tone 3; PS 39

R

1 My heart is stirring with a noble song;
   let me recite what I have fashioned for the king; *
      my tongue shall be the pen of a skilled writer.

2 You are the fairest of men; *
      grace flows from your lips,
      because God has blessed you forever.

3 Strap your sword upon your thigh, O mighty warrior, *
      in your pride and in your majesty.   R

4 Ride out and conquer in the cause of truth *
      and for the sake of justice.

5 Your right hand will show you marvelous things; *
      your arrows are very sharp, O mighty warrior.

The peoples are falling at your feet, *
      and the king's enemies are losing heart.   R   ▼

6 Your throne, O God, endures forever and ever, *
    a scepter of righteousness is the scepter of your reign;
  7 you love righteousness and hate iniquity.

Therefore God, your God, has anointed you *
with the oil of gladness above your fellows.

8 All your garments are fragrant with myrrh, aloes, and cassia, *
    and the music of strings from ivory palaces makes you
      glad.

9 **Kings' daughters stand among the noble women of the**
      court; *
    on your right hand is the queen,
      adorned with the gold of Ophir.   R

10 "Hear, O daughter; consider and listen closely; *
    forget your people and your father's house.

11 **The king will have pleasure in your beauty; ***
    he is your master; therefore do him honor.

12 The people of Tyre are here with a gift; *
    the rich among the people seek your favor."   R

13 **All glorious is the princess as she enters; ***
    her gown is cloth-of-gold.

14 In embroidered apparel she is brought to the king; *
    after her the bridesmaids follow in procession.

15 **With joy and gladness they are brought, ***
    and enter into the palace of the king.   R

16 "In place of fathers, O king, you shall have sons; *
    you shall make them princes over all the earth.

17 **I will make your name to be remembered**
    from one generation to another; *
    therefore nations will praise you forever and ever."   R

God of majesty,
you exalted Jesus, the Anointed One,
that every knee on earth might bow before him.
Strengthen us to confess him as our Sovereign,
and to serve him with joy,
that we might be led even to the marriage supper of the Lamb,
Christ Jesus our Lord.   **Amen.**   [574]

PSALM 46   Tone 6; PH 191–193; PS 40, 41

R

1   God is our refuge and strength, *
        a very present help in trouble.

2   **Therefore we will not fear, though the earth be
        moved, ***
        **and though the mountains be toppled into the
        depths of the sea;**

3   though its waters rage and foam, *
        and though the mountains tremble at its tumult.

    The Lord of hosts is with us; *
        the God of Jacob is our stronghold.   R

4   There is a river whose streams make glad the city of God, *
        the holy habitation of the Most High.

5   **God is in the midst of the city;**
    it shall not be overthrown; *
        God shall help it at the break of day.

6   The nations make much ado, and the realms are shaken; *
        God has spoken, and the earth shall melt away.

7   **The Lord of hosts is with us; ***
        the God of Jacob is our stronghold.   R

8   Come now and look upon the works of the Lord, *
        what awesome things God has done on earth.   ▼

9 It is the LORD who makes war to cease in all the world, *
    who breaks the bow, and shatters the spear,
    and burns the shields with fire.

10 "Be still, then, and know that I am God; *
    I will be exalted among the nations;
    I will be exalted in the earth."

11 The LORD of hosts is with us; *
    the God of Jacob is our stronghold.   R

God our strength,
you are the only refuge of all who trust you.
Fortify us with your goodness to live in quietness of spirit,
that we may serve you all our days;
through Jesus Christ, your Son. **Amen.** [575]

PSALM 47   Tone 2; PH 194; PS 42

R

1 Clap your hands, all you peoples; *
    shout to God with a cry of joy.

2 For the LORD Most High is to be feared, *
    the great Sovereign over all the earth.

3 The LORD subdues the peoples under us, *
    and the nations under our feet.

4 The LORD chooses our inheritance for us, *
    the pride of the beloved Jacob.   R

5 God has gone up with a shout, *
    the LORD with the sound of the ram's-horn.

6 Sing praises to God, sing praises; *
    sing praises to our Sovereign, sing praises.

7 For God is Sovereign of all the earth; *
    sing praises with all your skill.   R

8 **God reigns over the nations; ***
   God sits upon heaven's holy throne.

9 The nobles of the peoples have gathered together *
   with the people of the God of Abraham.

10 **The rulers of the earth belong to God, ***
   and God is highly exalted.   R

God of power and righteousness,
you stand in power over all authorities,
and you rule over all governments.
Let the peoples of the earth rejoice
and the leaders of nations follow the way of Jesus Christ,
the Prince of Peace. **Amen.**   [576]

PSALM 48   Tone 3; PS 43

R

1 Great is the LORD, and highly to be praised; *
   in the city of our God is the LORD's holy hill.

2 **Beautiful and lofty, the joy of all the earth, is the hill of**
      Zion, *
      the city of the great Sovereign and the very center
      of the world.

3 God is in the citadels of Zion; *
   God is known to be its sure refuge.   **R**

4 **Behold, the rulers of the earth assembled ***
   and marched forward together.

5 They looked and were astounded; *
   they retreated and fled in terror.

6 **Trembling seized them there; ***
      7**they writhed like a woman in childbirth,**
      like ships of the sea when the east wind shatters
      them.   ▼

8   As we have heard, so have we seen,
    in the city of the LORD of hosts, in the city of our God; *
       God has established it forever.   **R**

9   **We have waited in silence on your loving-kindness,
    O God, ***
    in the midst of your temple.

10   Your praise, like your name, O God, reaches to the
       world's end; *
    your right hand is full of justice.

11   **Let Mount Zion be glad
    and the cities of Judah rejoice, ***
    because of your judgments.   **R**

12   Make the circuit of Zion;
    walk round about it; *
       count the number of its towers.

13   **Consider well its bulwarks;
    examine its strongholds; ***
    that you may tell those who come after.

[Unison]

This God is our God forever and ever; *
    God shall be our guide forevermore.   **R**

Gracious God,
you have made us fellow citizens
with the saints in the city of your eternal light.
In the time of upheaval, when the foundations shake,
teach us to wait in silence on your steadfast and
    transforming love,
made known to us in Jesus Christ our Lord.   **Amen.**   [577]

R

1 Hear this, all you peoples;
    hearken, all you who dwell in the world, *
      2 you of high degree and low, rich and poor together.

3 **My mouth shall speak of wisdom, ***
      and my heart shall meditate on understanding.

4 I will incline my ear to a proverb *
    and set forth my riddle upon the harp.   R

5 **Why should I be afraid in evil days, ***
      when the wickedness of those at my heels surrounds
    me,

6 the wickedness of those who put their trust in their goods, *
    and boast of their great riches?

7 **We can never ransom ourselves, ***
      or deliver to God the price of our life;

8 for the ransom of our life is so great, *
    that we should never have enough to pay it,

9 **in order to live forever and ever, ***
      and never see the grave.   R

10 For we see that the wise die also;
    like the dull and stupid they perish *
      and leave their wealth to those who come after them.

11 **Their graves shall be their homes forever,**
    their dwelling places from generation to generation, *
      though they call the lands after their own names.

12 Even though honored, they cannot live forever; *
    they are like the beasts that perish.   R   ▼

13 **Such is the way of those who foolishly trust**
  in themselves, *
  and the end of those who delight in their own words.

14 Like a flock of sheep they are destined to die;
  death is their shepherd; *
    they go down straightway to the grave.

  Their form shall waste away, *
  and the land of the dead shall be their home.

15 But God will ransom my life *
    and snatch me from the grasp of death.   **R**

16 **Do not be envious when some become rich, ***
  or when the grandeur of their house increases;

17 for they will carry nothing away at their death, *
    nor will their grandeur follow them.

18 **Though they thought highly of themselves while they**
      lived, *
  and were praised for their success,

19 they shall join the company of their ancestors, *
    who will never see the light again.

20 **Those who are honored, but have no understanding, ***
  are like the beasts that perish.   **R**

Giver of all wisdom,
deliver us from the folly of betraying our eternal birthright
for temporal gain.
Teach us to hold firmly to you
so that we may not treasure things,
but show the imperishable riches of your love
in Jesus Christ.   **Amen.**   [578]

R

1 The LORD, the God of gods, has spoken *
    and has called the earth from the rising of the sun to its
      setting.

2 **Out of Zion, perfect in its beauty, ***
    God shines forth in glory.   R

3 Our God will come and will not keep silence; *
    before God there is a consuming flame,
    and round about a raging storm.

4 **God calls the heavens and the earth from above ***
    to witness the judgment of the chosen people.

5 "Gather before me my loyal followers, *
    those who have made a covenant with me
    and sealed it with sacrifice."

6 **Let the heavens declare the rightness of God's cause; ***
    for it is God who is judge.   R

7 Hear, O my people, and I will speak:
    "O Israel, I will bear witness against you; *
    for I am God, your God.

8 **I do not accuse you because of your sacrifices; ***
    your offerings are always before me.

9 I will take no bull-calf from your stalls, *
    nor he-goats out of your pens;

10 **for all the beasts of the forest are mine, ***
    the herds in their thousands upon the hills.

11 I know every bird in the sky, *
    and the creatures of the fields are in my sight.   R

12 **If I were hungry, I would not tell you, ***
    for the whole world is mine and all that is in it. ▼

13 Do you think I eat the flesh of bulls, *
    or drink the blood of goats?

14 **Offer to God a sacrifice of thanksgiving ***
    and make good your vows to the Most High.

15 Call upon me in the day of trouble; *
    I will deliver you, and you shall honor me."   **R**

16 **But to the wicked God says: ***
    "Why do you recite my statutes,
    and take my covenant upon your lips;

17 since you refuse discipline, *
    and toss my words behind your back?

18 **When you see thieves, you make them your friends, ***
    and you cast in your lot with adulterers.   R

19 You have loosed your lips for evil, *
    and harnessed your tongue to a lie.

20 **You are always speaking evil of your kin ***
    and slandering your own flesh and blood.

21 These things you have done, and I kept still, *
    and you thought that I am like you.   **R**

   I have made my accusation; *
   I have put my case in order before your eyes.

22 Consider this well, you who forget God, *
    lest I rend you and there be none to deliver you.

23 **Whoever offers me the sacrifice of thanksgiving honors**
    me; *
    but to those who keep in my way will I show the
    salvation of God."   R

Almighty God,
because Jesus your servant became obedient to death,

his sacrifice was greater than all the sacrifices of old.
Accept our offering of praise,
and help us to do your will,
until our whole life becomes worship in spirit and truth;
through Jesus Christ our Lord.   **Amen.**   [579]

PSALM 51   Tone 7; PH 195, 196; PS 47–49

R

1   Have mercy on me, O God, according to your
         loving-kindness; *
      in your great compassion blot out my offenses.

2   **Wash me through and through from my wickedness ***
      and cleanse me from my sin.   **R**

3   For I know my transgressions, *
      and my sin is ever before me.

4   **Against you only have I sinned ***
      and done what is evil in your sight.

    And so you are justified when you speak *
      and upright in your judgment.

5   **Indeed, I have been wicked from my birth, ***
      a sinner from my mother's womb.   **R**

6   For behold, you look for truth deep within me, *
      and will make me understand wisdom secretly.

7   **Purge me from my sin, and I shall be pure; ***
      wash me, and I shall be clean indeed.

8   Make me hear of joy and gladness, *
      that the body you have broken may rejoice.

9   **Hide your face from my sins ***
      and blot out all my iniquities.   **R**   ▼

10 Create in me a clean heart, O God, *
    and renew a right spirit within me.

11 **Cast me not away from your presence ***
    and take not your holy Spirit from me.

12 Give me the joy of your saving help again *
    and sustain me with your bountiful Spirit.   **R**

13 **I shall teach your ways to the wicked, ***
    and sinners shall return to you.

14 Deliver me from death, O God, *
    and my tongue shall sing of your righteousness,
    O God of my salvation.   **R**

15 **Open my lips, O Lord, ***
    and my mouth shall proclaim your praise.

16 Had you desired it, I would have offered sacrifice, *
    but you take no delight in burnt-offerings.

17 **The sacrifice of God is a troubled spirit; ***
    a broken and contrite heart, O God, you will not
        despise.   R

18 Be favorable and gracious to Zion, *
    and rebuild the walls of Jerusalem.

19 **Then you will be pleased with the appointed sacrifices,**
    with burnt-offerings and oblations; *
        then shall they offer young bullocks upon your
            altar.   R

God of mercy,
you know us better than we know ourselves,
and still you love us.
Wash us from all our sins,
create in us clean hearts,

and strengthen us by your Holy Spirit
that we may give you praise;
through Jesus Christ our Savior.   **Amen.**   [580]

PSALM 52   Tone 8; PS 50

R

1 You tyrant, why do you boast of wickedness *
      against the godly all day long?

2 **You plot ruin;**
   your tongue is like a sharpened razor, *
      O worker of deception.

3 You love evil more than good *
      and lying more than speaking the truth.

4 **You love all words that hurt, ***
      O you deceitful tongue.   R

5 Oh, that God would demolish you utterly, *
      topple you, and snatch you from your dwelling,
      and root you out of the land of the living!

6 **The righteous shall see and tremble, ***
      and they shall laugh at you, saying,

7 "This is the one who did not take God for a refuge, *
      but trusted in great wealth
      and relied upon wickedness."   **R**

8 **But I am like a green olive tree in the house of God; ***
      I trust in the mercy of God forever and ever.

   [Unison]

9 **I will give you thanks for what you have done ***
      and declare the goodness of your name in the
         presence of the godly.   R

Sovereign God,
you cut down trees that bear no fruit,
and prune fruitful trees that they may bear more.
Make us grow like rich olive trees in your kingdom,
firmly rooted in the power and mercy
of Jesus Christ our Lord.   **Amen.**   [581]

PSALM 53   Tone 8

R

1 Fools say in their heart, "There is no God." *
   All are corrupt and commit abominable acts;
      there is none who does any good.

2 **God looks down from heaven upon us all,** *
   to see if there is any who is wise,
      if there is one who seeks after God.

3 Every one has proved faithless;
   all alike have turned bad; *
      there is none who does good; no, not one.   **R**

4 **Have they no knowledge, those evildoers** *
   who eat up my people like bread
      and do not call upon God?

5 See how greatly they tremble,
   such trembling as never was; *
      for God has scattered the bones of the enemy;
         they are put to shame, because God has rejected them.

6 **Oh, that Israel's deliverance would come out of Zion!** *
   when God restores the fortunes of the chosen people
      Jacob will rejoice and Israel be glad.   **R**

Holy God,
apart from you nothing is true, nothing is holy.

Deliver us from evil
and strengthen us when we are weak,
so that all who believe in Christ
may rejoice in his glory now and forever. **Amen.** [582]

PSALM 54

R

1 Save me, O God, by your name; *
     in your might, defend my cause.

2 **Hear my prayer, O God;** *
     give ear to the words of my mouth.

3 For the arrogant have risen up against me,
     and the ruthless have sought my life, *
       those who have no regard for God.   R

4 **Behold, God is my helper;** *
     it is the Lord who sustains my life.

5 Render evil to those who spy on me; *
     in your faithfulness, destroy them.

6 **I will offer you a freewill sacrifice** *
     and praise your name, O LORD, for it is good.

   [Unison]

7 **For you have rescued me from every trouble,** *
     and my eye has seen the ruin of my foes.   R

God our helper, hear our prayer
and uphold your church in times of testing.
Deliver us from evil,
so that from the rising of the sun to its setting
we may offer you our sacrifice of praise;
through Jesus Christ our Lord.   **Amen.**   [583]

R

1 Hear my prayer, O God; *
   do not hide yourself from my petition.

2 **Listen to me and answer me;** *
   I have no peace, because of my cares.

   I am shaken by the ³ noise of the enemy *
   and by the pressure of the wicked;

   for they have cast an evil spell upon me *
   and are set against me in fury.   R

4 My heart quakes within me, *
   and the terrors of death have fallen upon me.

5 **Fear and trembling have come over me,** *
   and horror overwhelms me.

6 And I said, "Oh, that I had wings like a dove! *
   I would fly away and be at rest.

7 **I would flee to a far-off place** *
   and make my lodging in the wilderness.

8 I would hasten to escape *
   from the stormy wind and tempest."   R

9 **Swallow them up, O Lord;**
   confound their speech; *
   for I have seen violence and strife in the city.

10 Day and night the sentries make their rounds upon its walls, *
   but trouble and misery are in the midst of it.

11 **There is corruption at its heart;** *
   its streets are never free of oppression and deceit.   R

12 For had it been an adversary who taunted me,
   then I could have borne it; *

or had it been enemies who vaunted themselves against me,
  then I could have hidden from them.

13 **But it was you, my companion,** *
  my own familiar friend, dear to my own heart.

14 We took sweet counsel together, *
  and walked with the throng in the house of God.

15 **Let death come upon them suddenly;**
  let them go down alive into the grave; *
    for wickedness is in their dwellings,
      in their very midst.   **R**

16 But I will call upon God, *
  and the LORD will deliver me.

17 **In the evening, in the morning, and at noonday,**
  I will complain and lament, *
    and the LORD will hear my voice.

18 God will bring me safely back from the battle waged
      against me; *
  for there are many who fight me.

19 **God, who is enthroned of old, will hear me and bring**
      them down; *
    they never change; they do not fear God.   **R**

20 My companion stretched forth a hand against a comrade *
  and broke a covenant.

21 **The speech of my companion is softer than butter,** *
  but with war at heart.

  The words of my comrade are smoother than oil, *
    but they are drawn swords.   **R**

22 **Cast your burden upon the LORD,**
  who will sustain you; *
    the LORD will never let the righteous stumble.   ▼

²³ For you will bring the bloodthirsty and deceitful *
　　down to the pit of destruction, O God.

They shall not live out half their days, *
but I will put my trust in you. R

God of grace,
when we are frightened and alone,
help us to trust you and cast our burdens upon you,
that we may be upheld by your saving strength.
We ask this in the name of Jesus Christ. **Amen.** [584]

PSALM 56　　　　　　　　　　　　　　　　Tone 8

R

¹ Have mercy on me, O God,
　　for my enemies are hounding me; *
　　　　all day long they assault and oppress me.

² **They hound me all the day long; ***
truly there are many who fight against me,
O Most High.

³ Whenever I am afraid, *
　　I will put my trust in you.

⁴ **In God, whose word I praise,**
in God I trust and will not be afraid, *
for what can flesh do to me? R

⁵ All day long they damage my cause; *
　　their only thought is to do me evil.

⁶ **They band together; they lie in wait; ***
they spy upon my footsteps;
because they seek my life.

⁷ Shall they escape despite their wickedness? *
　　O God, in your anger, cast down the peoples. R

8 **You have noted my lamentation;**
put my tears into your bottle; *
   are they not recorded in your book?

9 Whenever I call upon you, my enemies will be put to flight; *
   this I know, for God is on my side.

10 **In God the LORD, whose word I praise,**
in God I trust and will not be afraid, *
   11 **for what can mortals do to me?**   R

12 I am bound by the vow I made to you, O God; *
   I will present to you thank-offerings;

13 **for you have rescued my soul from death and my feet**
      from stumbling, *
   that I may walk before God in the light of
      the living.   R

O God,
when our path is hard and dangerous,
give us the grace of quiet confidence.
Remind us that we belong to you in baptism,
for you have claimed us in Jesus Christ,
the way, the truth, and the life.   **Amen.**

PSALM 57   Tone 8

R

1 Be merciful to me, O God, be merciful,
   for I have taken refuge in you; *
      in the shadow of your wings will I take refuge
      until this time of trouble has gone by.

2 **I will call upon you, O Most High God,** *
      the God who maintains my cause.

3 You will send from heaven and save me;
   you will confound those who trample upon me; *   ▼

O God, you will send forth your love and your
    faithfulness.   **R**

4 **I lie in the midst of lions that devour the people; ***
    their teeth are spears and arrows,
    their tongue a sharp sword.

6 They have laid a net for my feet,
and I am bowed low; *
    they have dug a pit before me,
    but have fallen into it themselves.

5 **Exalt yourself above the heavens, O God, ***
    and your glory over all the earth.

7 My heart is firmly fixed, O God, my heart is fixed; *
    I will sing and make melody.   **R**

8 **Wake up, my spirit;**
awake, lute and harp; *
    I myself will waken the dawn.

9 I will confess you among the peoples, O LORD; *
    I will sing praise to you among the nations.

10 **For your loving-kindness is greater than the heavens, ***
    and your faithfulness reaches to the clouds.

[Unison]

11 **Exalt yourself above the heavens, O God, ***
    and your glory over all the earth.   **R**

Merciful God,
refuge in times of trouble,
our only hope in living,
and our only salvation in dying,
keep us in your care
that we may always praise you
and faithfully proclaim your name before the nations;
in Jesus Christ our Lord.   **Amen.** [586]

R

1 Rescue me from my enemies, O God; *
    protect me from those who rise up against me.

2 **Rescue me from evildoers ***
    and save me from those who thirst for my blood.   R

3 See how they lie in wait for my life,
    how the mighty gather together against me; *
        not for any offense or fault of mine, O LORD.

4 **Not because of any guilt of mine ***
    they run and prepare themselves for battle.   R

Rouse yourself, come to my side, and see; *
    5 for you, LORD God of hosts, are Israel's God.

Awake, and punish all the ungodly; *
    show no mercy to those who are faithless and evil.

6 They go to and fro in the evening; *
    they snarl like dogs and run about the city.

7 **Behold, they boast with their mouths,**
    and taunts are on their lips; *
        "For who," they say, "will hear us?"   R

8 But you, O LORD, you laugh at them; *
    you laugh all the ungodly to scorn.

9 **My eyes are fixed on you, O my Strength; ***
    for you, O God, are my stronghold.

10 My merciful God comes to meet me; *
    God will let me look in triumph on my enemies.   R

11 **Slay them, O God, lest my people forget; ***
    send them reeling by your might
        and put them down, O Lord our shield.   ▼

12 For the sins of their mouths, for the words of their lips,
 for the cursing and lies that they utter, *
  let them be caught in their pride.

13 Make an end of them in your wrath; *
 make an end of them, and they shall be no more.

Let everyone know that God rules in Jacob, *
 and to the ends of the earth. **R**

14 They go to and fro in the evening; *
 they snarl like dogs and run about the city.

15 They forage for food, *
 and if they are not filled, they howl.

16 For my part, I will sing of your strength; *
 I will celebrate your love in the morning;

for you have become my stronghold, *
 a refuge in the day of my trouble.

17 To you, O my Strength, will I sing; *
 for you, O God, are my stronghold and my merciful
  God. **R**

God of power,
deliver us from evil
and confirm our trust in you,
that at dusk we may sing of your justice
and at dawn exult in your mercy;
through Jesus Christ our Lord. **Amen.** [587]

PSALM 62   Tone 6; PH 197; PS 52

R

1 For God alone my soul in silence waits; *
 from God comes my salvation.

2 **God alone is my rock and my salvation,** *
my stronghold, so that I shall not be greatly
shaken.   R

3 How long will you assail me to crush me,
all of you together, *
as if you were a leaning fence, a toppling wall?

4 **They seek only to bring me down from my place**
of honor; *
lies are their chief delight.

They bless with their lips, *
but in their hearts they curse.   R

5 **For God alone my soul in silence waits;** *
truly, my hope is in God.

6 God alone is my rock and my salvation, *
my stronghold, so that I shall not be shaken.

7 **In God is my safety and my honor;** *
God is my strong rock and my refuge.   R

8 Put your trust in God always, O people, *
pour out your hearts before God, who is our refuge.

9 **Those of high degree are but a fleeting breath,** *
even those of low estate cannot be trusted.

On the scales they are lighter than a breath, *
all of them together.

10 **Put no trust in extortion;**
in robbery take no empty pride; *
though wealth increase, set not your heart
upon it.   R

11 God has spoken once, twice have I heard it, *
that power belongs to God.   ▼

12 **Steadfast love is yours, O Lord,** *
    for you repay all people according to their deeds.   **R**

Lord God,
in a threatening world we look to you as our rock of hope.
Hear us as we pour out our hearts to you,
and give us your grace and protection;
through Jesus Christ our Lord.   **Amen.** [588]

PSALM 63   Tone 6 or 8; PH 198, 199; PS 53, 54

R

1 O God, you are my God; eagerly I seek you; *
    my soul thirsts for you, my flesh faints for you,
    as in a barren and dry land where there is no water.

2 **Therefore I have gazed upon you in your holy place,** *
    that I might behold your power and your glory.

3 For your loving-kindness is better than life itself; *
    my lips shall give you praise.

4 **So will I bless you as long as I live** *
    and lift up my hands in your name.   **R**

5 My soul is content, as with marrow and fatness, *
    and my mouth praises you with joyful lips,

6 **when I remember you upon my bed,** *
    and meditate on you in the night watches.

7 For you have been my helper, *
    and under the shadow of your wings I will rejoice.

8 **My soul clings to you;** *
    your right hand holds me fast.   **R**

9 May those who seek my life to destroy it *
    go down into the depths of the earth;

10 let them fall upon the edge of the sword, *
      and let them be food for jackals.

   [Unison]

11 But I will rejoice in God;
      all those who swear by God will be glad; *
         for the mouth of those who speak lies shall be
            stopped.   **R**

Creating God,
deep within our hearts we yearn for your presence,
and hunger and thirst for your righteousness.
Satisfy us by the power of your Spirit,
yet keep us restless to seek your will
as we follow where Christ may lead.   **Amen.**   [589]

PSALM 65   Tone 6; PH 200, 201; PS 55, 56

R

1 You are to be praised, O God, in Zion; *
      to you shall vows be performed in Jerusalem.

2 **To you that hear prayer shall all flesh come, ***
      because of their transgressions.   R

3 Our sins are stronger than we are, *
      but you will blot them out.

4 **Happy are they whom you choose**
   and draw to your courts to dwell there! *
         they will be satisfied by the beauty of your house,
         by the holiness of your temple.   R

5 Awesome things will you show us in your righteousness,
   O God of our salvation, *
         O Hope of all the ends of the earth
         and of the seas that are far away.   ▼

6 **You make fast the mountains by your power; ***
   they are girded about with might.   R

7 You still the roaring of the seas, *
   the roaring of their waves,
   and the clamor of the peoples.

8 **Those who dwell at the ends of the earth will tremble**
   at your marvelous signs; *
   you make the dawn and the dusk to sing for joy.   R

9 You visit the earth and water it abundantly;
   you make it very plenteous; *
   the river of God is full of water.

   You prepare the grain, *
   for so you provide for the earth.   R

10 You drench the furrows and smooth out the ridges; *
    with heavy rain you soften the ground and bless its
       increase.

11 **You crown the year with your goodness, ***
    and your paths overflow with plenty.   R

12 May the fields of the wilderness be rich for grazing, *
    and the hills be clothed with joy.

13 **May the meadows cover themselves with flocks,**
    and the valleys cloak themselves with grain; *
    let them shout for joy and sing.   R

Lord God, joy is your gift;
beauty, abundance, and peace
are tokens of your work in all creation.
Work also in our lives,
that by these signs we may see the splendor of your love
and praise you through Jesus Christ our Lord.   **Amen.**   [590]

R

1 Be joyful in God, all you lands; *
     2 sing the glory of God's name;
       sing the glory of God's praise.

3 **Say to God, "How awesome are your deeds! ***
     because of your great strength your enemies cringe
       before you.

4 All the earth bows down before you, *
     sings to you, sings out your name."   R

5 **Come now and see the works of God, ***
     how wonderful God's actions toward all people.

6 God turned the sea into dry land,
     so that they went through the water on foot, *
       and there we rejoiced in God.

7 **In might God rules forever**
   and keeps watch over the nations; *
       let no rebel rise up against God.   R

8 Bless our God, you peoples; *
     make the voice of praise to be heard.

9 **God holds our souls in life, ***
     and will not allow our feet to slip.

10 For you, O God, have proved us; *
     you have tried us just as silver is tried.

11 **You brought us into the snare; ***
     you laid heavy burdens upon our backs.

12 You let enemies ride over our heads;
     we went through fire and water; *
       but you brought us out into a place of refreshment. **R** ▼

13 **I will enter your house with burnt-offerings**
  and will pay you my vows, *
    14 **which I promised with my lips**
      and spoke with my mouth when I was in trouble.

15 I will offer you sacrifices of fat beasts
  with the smoke of rams; *
    I will give you oxen and goats.   **R**

16 **Come and listen, all you who fear God,** *
    and I will tell you what God has done for me.

17 I cried out with my mouth, *
    and God's praise was on my tongue.

18 **If I had found evil in my heart,** *
    the Lord would not have heard me;

19 but in truth God has heard me *
    and attended to the voice of my prayer.   **R**

20 **Blessed be God, who has not rejected my prayer,** *
    nor withheld steadfast love from me.   R

God of power and might,
you bring your people out of darkness and slavery
into light and freedom
through the waters of salvation.
Receive our sacrifice of praise and thanksgiving,
and keep us always in your steadfast love;
through Jesus Christ our Lord.   **Amen.**   [591]

PSALM 67   Tone 2; PH 202, 203; PS 59, 60

R

1 O God, be merciful to us and bless us; *
    show us the light of your countenance and come to us.

2 **Let your ways be known upon earth,** *
    your saving health among all nations.

3 Let the peoples praise you, O God; *
   let all the peoples praise you.   **R**

4 **Let the nations be glad and sing for joy, ***
   for you judge the peoples with equity
   and guide all the nations upon earth.

5 Let the peoples praise you, O God; *
   let all the peoples praise you.   **R**

6 **The earth has brought forth its increase; ***
   may God, our own God, bless us.

[Unison]

7 **O God, give us your blessing; ***
   may all the ends of the earth stand in awe of you.   **R**

Light of the world,
you have come into the world's darkness
and the darkness cannot overwhelm the light.
Let your holy name be known through all the earth,
that all people and nations may praise you
and walk in your ways;
through Jesus Christ our Lord. **Amen.** [592]

PSALM 68   Tone 6; PS 61

R

1 O God, arise, and let your enemies be scattered; *
   let those who hate you flee before you.

2 **Let them vanish like smoke when the wind drives**
      it away; *
   as the wax melts at the fire,
   so let the wicked perish at the presence of God.

3 But let the righteous be glad and rejoice before God; *
   let them also be merry and joyful.   **R**   ▼

⁴ **Sing to God, sing praises to God's name;**
 exalt the One who rides upon the heavens;*
  the name of our God is the LORD; rejoice before
   the LORD!

⁵ Defender of widows, father of orphans,*
  God in heaven's holy habitation!

⁶ **God gives the solitary a home and brings forth**
   prisoners into freedom;*
  but the rebels shall live in dry places.   R

⁷ O God, when you went forth before your people,*
  when you marched through the wilderness,

⁸ **the earth shook, and the skies poured down rain,**
 at the presence of God, the God of Sinai,*
 at the presence of God, the God of Israel.

⁹ You sent a gracious rain, O God, upon your inheritance;*
  you refreshed the land when it was weary.

¹⁰ **Your people found their home in it;***
  in your goodness, O God, you have made provision for
   the poor.   R

¹¹ The Lord gave the word;*
  great was the company of women who bore the tidings:

¹² **"Kings with their armies are fleeing away;***
  the women at home are dividing the spoils."

¹³ Though you lingered among the sheepfolds,*
  you shall be like a dove whose wings are covered
   with silver,
  whose feathers are like green gold.

¹⁴ **When the Almighty scattered kings,***
  it was like snow falling in Zalmon.   R

¹⁵ O mighty mountain, O hill of Bashan!*
  O rugged mountain, O hill of Bashan!

16 **Why do you look with envy, O rugged mountain,**
   at the hill on which God chose to rest? *
   truly, the LORD will dwell there forever.   R

17 The chariots of God are twenty thousand,
   even thousands of thousands; *
   the Lord comes in holiness from Sinai.

18 **You have gone up on high and led captivity captive;**
   you have received gifts even from your enemies, *
   that the LORD God might dwell among them.

19 Blessed be the Lord day by day, *
   the God of our salvation, who bears our burdens.

20 **You are our God, the God of our salvation;** *
   God is the LORD, by whom we escape death.   R

21 You, O God, shall crush the heads of your enemies, *
   and the hairy scalp of those who go on still in their
      wickedness.

22 **The Lord has said, "I will bring them back from**
      Bashan; *
   I will bring them back from the depths of the sea;

23 that your foot may be dipped in blood, *
   the tongues of your dogs in the blood of your enemies." R

24 **They see your procession, O God,** *
   your procession into the sanctuary, my Sovereign
      and my God.

25 The singers go before, musicians follow after, *
   in the midst of young women playing upon the
      hand-drums.

26 **Bless God in the congregation;** *
   bless the LORD, you that are of the fountain
      of Israel.   ▼

27 There is Benjamin, least of the tribes, at the head;
   the princes of Judah in a company; *
      and the princes of Zebulon and Naphtali.   R

28 Send forth your strength, O God; *
   establish, O God, what you have wrought for us.

29 Rulers shall bring gifts to you, *
   for your temple's sake at Jerusalem.

30 Rebuke the wild beast of the reeds, *
   and the peoples, a herd of wild bulls with its calves.

   Trample down those who lust after silver; *
   scatter the peoples that delight in war.

31 Let tribute be brought out of Egypt; *
   let Ethiopia stretch out its hands to God.   R

32 Sing to God, O realms of the earth; *
   sing praises to the Lord.

33 God rides in the heavens, the ancient heavens; *
   God's voice thunders forth, a mighty voice.

34 Ascribe power to God, *
   whose majesty is over Israel,
   whose strength is in the skies.

35 How wonderful is God in the holy places! *
   the God of Israel giving strength and power to the
      chosen people!
   Blessed be God!   R

Lord Jesus,
you came to us in our bondage,
and led us to freedom by the cross and resurrection.
May our lives praise you,
and our lips proclaim your mighty power to all people
that they may find their hope in you,
and live to your honor and glory,
now and forever.   **Amen.**   [593]

R

1 Save me, O God, *
    for the waters have risen up to my neck.

2 **I am sinking in deep mire, ***
    and there is no firm ground for my feet.

  I have come into deep waters, *
    and the torrent washes over me.   R

3 **I have grown weary with my crying;**
  my throat is inflamed; *
    my eyes have failed from looking for my God.

4 Those who hate me without a cause are more than the
        hairs of my head;
  my lying foes who would destroy me are mighty. *
    Must I then give back what I never stole?

5 **O God, you know my foolishness, ***
    and my faults are not hidden from you.

6 Let not those who hope in you be put to shame through me,
        Lord GOD of hosts; *
    let not those who seek you be disgraced because of me,
        O God of Israel.   R

7 **Surely, for your sake have I suffered reproach, ***
    and shame has covered my face.

8 I have become a stranger to my own kindred, *
    an alien to my mother's children.

9 **Zeal for your house has eaten me up; ***
    the scorn of those who scorn you has fallen upon me.

10 I humbled myself with fasting, *
    but that was turned to my reproach.   R   ▼

11 **I put on sack-cloth also, ***
   and became a byword among them.

12 Those who sit at the gate murmur against me, *
   and the drunkards make songs about me.   R

13 **But as for me, this is my prayer to you, ***
   at the time you have set, O LORD:

   "In your great mercy, O God, *
   answer me with your unfailing help.

14 **Save me from the mire; do not let me sink; ***
   let me be rescued from those who hate me
   and out of the deep waters.

15 Let not the torrent of waters wash over me,
   neither let the deep swallow me up; *
   do not let the pit shut its mouth upon me.   R

16 **Answer me, O LORD, for your love is kind; ***
   in your great compassion, turn to me.

17 Hide not your face from your servant; *
   be swift and answer me, for I am in distress.

18 **Draw near to me and redeem me; ***
   because of my enemies deliver me.   R

19 You know my reproach, my shame, and my dishonor; *
   my adversaries are all in your sight."

20 **Reproach has broken my heart, and it cannot**
   be healed; *
   I looked for sympathy, but there was none,
   for comforters, but I could find no one.

21 They gave me gall to eat, *
   and when I was thirsty, they gave me vinegar to drink.   R

22 **Let the table before them be a trap** *
   and their sacred feasts a snare.

23 Let their eyes be darkened, that they may not see, *
   and give them continual trembling in their inner parts.

24 **Pour out your indignation upon them,** *
   and let the fierceness of your anger overtake them.

25 Let their camp be desolate, *
   and let there be none to dwell in their tents.

26 **For they persecute the one whom you have stricken** *
   and add to the pain of those whom you have pierced.

27 Lay to their charge guilt upon guilt, *
   and let them not receive your vindication.

28 **Let them be wiped out of the book of the living** *
   and not be written among the righteous.   R

29 As for me, I am afflicted and in pain; *
   your help, O God, will lift me up on high.

30 **I will praise the name of God in song;** *
   I will proclaim the greatness of the LORD with
      thanksgiving.

31 This will please the LORD more than an offering of oxen, *
   more than bullocks with horns and hoofs.

32 **The afflicted shall see and be glad;** *
   you who seek God, your heart shall live.

33 For the Lord listens to the needy *
   and does not despise those who are in prison.   R

34 **Let the heavens and the earth give praise,** *
   the seas and all that moves in them;

35 for God will save Zion and rebuild the cities of Judah; *
   they shall live there and have it in possession.   ▼

36 **The servants of the LORD will inherit it,** *
    and those who love the name of God
        will dwell therein.   **R**

Blessed are you, God of hope;
you restore the fallen
and rebuild the broken walls.
Teach us the song of thanksgiving,
for you are the strength of your people;
through Jesus Christ our Lord.   **Amen.**   [594]

PSALM 70   Tone 8; PS 62

R

1   Be pleased, O God, to deliver me; *
        O LORD, make haste to help me.

2   **Let those who seek my life be ashamed**
    and altogether dismayed; *
        let those who take pleasure in my misfortune
        draw back and be disgraced.

3   Let those who say to me "Aha!" and gloat over me
            turn back, *
        because they are ashamed.   **R**

4   **Let all who seek you rejoice and be glad in you;** *
        let those who love your salvation say forever,
        "Great is the LORD!"

5   But as for me, I am poor and needy; *
        come to me speedily, O God.

    You are my helper and my deliverer; *
        O LORD, do not tarry.   R

God, our help and deliverer,
do not abandon us
among the many temptations of life,

but deliver us from evil
and turn our tears and struggles into joy;
through Jesus Christ our Lord.   **Amen.**   [595]

PSALM 71   Tone 8; PS 63

R

1 In you, O LORD, have I taken refuge; *
   let me never be ashamed.

2 **In your righteousness, deliver me and set me free; ***
   incline your ear to me and save me.

3 Be my strong rock, a castle to keep me safe; *
   you are my crag and my stronghold.   **R**

4 **Deliver me, my God, from the hand of the wicked, ***
   from the clutches of the evildoer and the oppressor.

5 For you are my hope, O Lord GOD, *
   my confidence since I was young.

6 **I have been sustained by you ever since I was born;**
   from my mother's womb you have been my strength; *
   my praise shall be always of you.   R

7 I have become a portent to many; *
   but you are my refuge and my strength.

8 **Let my mouth be full of your praise ***
   and your glory all the day long.

9 Do not cast me off in my old age; *
   forsake me not when my strength fails.

10 **For my enemies are talking against me, ***
   and those who lie in wait for my life take counsel
   together.

11 They say that God has forsaken me,
   that they will come after me and seize me; *
   because there is none who will save.   **R**   ▼

12 **O God, be not far from me; ***
   come quickly to help me, O my God.

13 Let those who set themselves against me be put to shame
      and be disgraced; *
      let those who seek to do me evil be covered with scorn
      and reproach.

14 **But I shall always wait in patience, ***
   and shall praise you more and more. R

15 My mouth shall recount your mighty acts
   and saving deeds all day long; *
      though I cannot know the number of them.

16 **I will begin with the mighty works of the Lord GOD; ***
   I will recall your righteousness, yours alone. R

17 O God, you have taught me since I was young, *
      and to this day I tell of your wonderful works.

18 **And now that I am old and gray-headed, O God, do not**
      forsake me, *
      till I make known your strength to this generation
      and your power to all who are to come.

19 Your righteousness, O God, reaches to the heavens; *
      you have done great things;
      who is like you, O God?

20 **You have showed me great troubles and adversities, ***
      but you will restore my life
      and bring me up again from the deep places
         of the earth.

21 You strengthen me more and more; *
      you enfold and comfort me, R

22 **therefore I will praise you upon the lyre for your**
      faithfulness, O my God; *
      I will sing to you with the harp, O Holy One of Israel.

23 My lips will sing with joy when I play to you, *
    and so will my soul, which you have redeemed.

**24 My tongue will proclaim your righteousness all day
    long, ***
    **for they are ashamed and disgraced who sought to
    do me harm.   R**

God our strong fortress,
do not desert us in old age.
Help us to follow your will
through all our years
and under all circumstances,
that forever we may praise your faithfulness;
through your Son, Jesus Christ our Lord. **Amen.** [596]

PSALM 72   Tone 3; PH 204, 205; PS 64, 65

R

1 Give the king your justice, O God, *
    and your righteousness to the king's son;

2 that he may rule your people righteously *
    and the poor with justice;

3 that the mountains may bring prosperity to the people, *
    and the little hills bring righteousness.

4 He shall defend the needy among the people *
    and shall rescue the poor and crush the oppressor. R

5 He shall live as long as the sun and moon endure, *
    from one generation to another.

6 He shall come down like rain upon the mown field, *
    like showers that water the earth.

7 In his time shall the righteous flourish; *
    there shall be abundance of peace till the moon
    shall be no more. **R** ▼

8 He shall rule from sea to sea, *
      and from the river to the ends of the earth.

9 His foes shall bow down before him, *
      and his enemies lick the dust.

10 The kings of Tarshish and of the isles shall pay tribute, *
      and the rulers of Arabia and Saba offer gifts.

11 All kings shall bow down before him, *
      and all the nations do him service.

12 For he shall deliver the poor who cries out in distress, *
      and the oppressed who has no helper.

13 He shall have pity on the lowly and poor *
      and shall preserve the lives of the needy.

14 He shall redeem their lives from oppression
         and violence, *
      and dear shall their blood be in his sight.   R

15 Long may he live!
   and may there be given to him gold from Arabia; *
      may prayer be made for him always,
      and may they bless him all the day long.

16 May there be abundance of grain on the earth,
   growing thick even on the hilltops; *
      may its fruit flourish like Lebanon,
      and its grain like grass upon the earth.

17 May his name remain forever
   and be established as long as the sun endures; *
      may all the nations bless themselves in him and call him
         blessed.   R

18 Blessed be the Lord GOD, the God of Israel, *
      who alone does wondrous deeds!

   [Unison]

19 And blessed be God's glorious name forever! *

**and may all the earth be filled with the glory
of the Lord.
Amen. Amen.   R**

O God, bring our nation and all nations
to uphold justice and equity,
that poverty, oppression, and violence may vanish
and all may know peace and plenty;
in the name of Jesus Christ, the ruler of all.   **Amen.**   [597]

Psalm 73   Tone 6

R

1   Truly, God is good to Israel, *
    to those who are pure in heart.

2   **But as for me, my feet had nearly slipped; *
    I had almost tripped and fallen;**

3   because I envied the proud *
    and saw the prosperity of the wicked: **R**

4   **For they suffer no pain, *
    and their bodies are sleek and sound;**

5   in the misfortunes of others they have no share; *
    they are not afflicted as others are;

6   **therefore they wear their pride like a necklace *
    and wrap their violence about them like a cloak.**

7   Their iniquity comes from gross minds, *
    and their hearts overflow with wicked thoughts.

8   **They scoff and speak maliciously; *
    out of their haughtiness they plan oppression.**

9   They set their mouths against the heavens, *
    and their evil speech runs through the world.   **R**   ▼

10 **And so the people turn to them ***
   and find in them no fault.

11 They say, "How should God know? *
   is there knowledge in the Most High?"

12 **So then, these are the wicked; ***
   always at ease, they increase their wealth.

13 In vain have I kept my heart clean, *
   and washed my hands in innocence.

14 **I have been afflicted all day long, ***
   and punished every morning.   R

15 Had I gone on speaking this way, *
   I should have betrayed the generation of your children.

16 **When I tried to understand these things, ***
   it was too hard for me;

17 until I entered the sanctuary of God *
   and discerned the end of the wicked.

18 **Surely, you set them in slippery places; ***
   you cast them down in ruin.

19 Oh, how suddenly do they come to destruction, *
   come to an end, and perish from terror!

20 **Like a dream when one awakens, O Lord, ***
   when you arise you will make their image vanish.   R

21 When my mind became embittered, *
   I was sorely wounded in my heart.

22 **I was stupid and had no understanding; ***
   I was like a brute beast in your presence.

23 Yet I am always with you; *
   you hold me by my right hand.

24 **You will guide me by your counsel,** *
　　and afterwards receive me with glory.

25 Whom have I in heaven but you? *
　　and having you I desire nothing upon earth.

26 **Though my flesh and my heart should waste away,** *
　　God is the strength of my heart and my portion
　　forever.　　R

27 Truly, those who forsake you will perish; *
　　you destroy all who are unfaithful.

28 **But it is good for me to be near God;** *
　　I have made the Lord GOD my refuge.

　　[Unison]

　　I will speak of all your works *
　　　　in the gates of the city of Zion.　　R

God our strength,
you give honor to the pure in heart
and uphold all who trust in you.
Deliver us from chasing after this world's illusions
that we may follow instead
the imperishable truth of your Word
in Jesus Christ our Lord.　**Amen.**　[598]

PSALM 77　　　　　　　　　　　　　　　　　Tone 8; PS 66

R

1　I will cry aloud to God; *
　　I will cry aloud, and God will hear me.

2　**In the day of my trouble I sought the Lord;** *
　　my hands were stretched out by night and did not tire;
　　I refused to be comforted.　　▼

3   I think of God, I am restless, *
        I ponder, and my spirit faints.   R

4   **You will not let my eyelids close; ***
        I am troubled and I cannot speak.

5   I consider the days of old; *
        I remember the years long past;

6   **I commune with my heart in the night; ***
        I ponder and search my mind.   R

7   Will the Lord cast me off forever *
        and show favor to me no more?

8   **Has the loving-kindness of the LORD come to an end? ***
        Has God's promise failed forevermore?

9   Has God forgotten to be gracious, *
        and in anger withheld compassion?

10 **And I said, "My grief is this: ***
        the right hand of the Most High
            has lost its power."   R

11 I will remember the works of the LORD, *
        and call to mind your wonders of old time.

12 **I will meditate on all your acts ***
        and ponder your mighty deeds.

13 Your way, O God, is holy; *
        who is so great a god as our God?

14 **You are the God who works wonders ***
        and have declared your power among the peoples.

15 By your strength you have redeemed your people, *
        the children of Jacob and Joseph.   R

16 **The waters saw you, O God;**
    the waters saw you and trembled; *
    the very depths were shaken.

17 The clouds poured out water;
    the skies thundered; *
    your arrows flashed to and fro;

18 **the sound of your thunder was in the whirlwind;**
    your lightnings lit up the world; *
    the earth trembled and shook.

19 Your way was in the sea,
    and your paths in the great waters, *
    yet your footsteps were not seen.

20 **You led your people like a flock ***
    by the hand of Moses and Aaron.   R

God of the ages,
by signs and wonders you established your ancient covenant,
and through the sacrifice of your Son
you confirmed the new covenant yet more wondrously.
Guide your church to the land of promise,
that there we may celebrate your name with lasting praise
through Jesus Christ our Lord.   **Amen.**   [599]

PSALM 78   Tone 4 or 6; PS 67, 68

R

1 Hear my teaching, O my people; *
    incline your ears to the words of my mouth.

2 **I will open my mouth in a parable; ***
    I will declare the mysteries of ancient times.

3 That which we have heard and known,
    and what our ancestors have told us, *
    we will not hide from their children.   **R**   ▼

4 **We will recount to generations to come**
the praiseworthy deeds and the power of the LORD**, ***
and the wonderful works God has done.

5 God set up decrees for Jacob
and established a law for Israel, *
commanding them to teach it to their children;

6 **that the generations to come might know,**
and the children yet unborn; *
that they in their turn might tell it to their children;

7 so that they might put their trust in God, *
and not forget the deeds of God,
but keep God's commandments;

8 **and not be like their ancestors,**
a stubborn and rebellious generation, *
a generation whose heart was not steadfast,
and whose spirit was not faithful to God. **R**

* * *

12 God worked marvels in the sight of their ancestors, *
in the land of Egypt, in the field of Zoan.

13 **God split open the sea and let them pass through, ***
making the waters stand up like walls.

14 God led them with a cloud by day, *
and all the night through with a glow of fire.

15 **God split the hard rocks in the wilderness ***
and gave them drink as from the great deep.

16 God brought streams out of the cliff, *
and the waters gushed out like rivers. **R**

* * *

34 **Whenever God slew them, they would repent, ***
and they would diligently search for God.

35 They would remember that God was their rock, *
    and the Most High God their redeemer.

36 **But they flattered God with their mouths ***
    and lied to God with their tongues.

37 Their heart was not steadfast toward God, *
    and they were not faithful to the covenant.

38 **But being so merciful, God forgave their sins**
    and did not destroy them; *
        many times God held back anger
        and did not permit divine wrath to be roused.   **R**

    *   *   *

God of pilgrims,
strengthen our faith, we pray.
Guide us through the uncertainties of our journey,
and hold before us the vision of your eternal kingdom,
made known to us in Jesus Christ our Lord.   **Amen.**   [600]

PSALM 79   Tone 8; PS 69

R

1 O God, the heathen have come into your inheritance;
    they have profaned your holy temple; *
        they have made Jerusalem a heap of rubble.

2 **They have given the bodies of your servants as food**
        for the birds of the air, *
    and the flesh of your faithful ones
        to the beasts of the field.

3 They have shed their blood like water on every side
        of Jerusalem, *
    and there was no one to bury them.

4 **We have become a reproach to our neighbors, ***
    an object of scorn and derision to those
        around us.   **R**   ▼

5 How long will you be angry, O LORD? *
    will your fury blaze like fire forever?

6 **Pour out your wrath upon the heathen who have not
    known you ***
    **and upon the realms that have not called upon your
    name.**

7 For they have devoured the people of Jacob *
    and made their dwelling a ruin.   **R**

8 **Remember not our past sins;
    let your compassion be swift to meet us; ***
    for we have been brought very low.

[Unison]

9 **Help us, O God our Savior, for the glory of your name; ***
    deliver us and forgive us our sins,
    for your name's sake.   **R**

Gracious God,
in times of sorrow and depression,
when hope itself seems lost,
help us to remember the transforming power
    of your steadfast love
and to give thanks for that new life we cannot now imagine.
We ask this in the name
    of Jesus Christ our Savior.   **Amen.**   [601]

PSALM 80   Tone 8; PH 206; PS 70, 71

R

1 Hear, O Shepherd of Israel, leading Joseph like a flock; *
    shine forth, you that are enthroned upon the cherubim.

2 **In the presence of Ephraim, Benjamin, and Manasseh, ***
    stir up your strength and come to help us.

3 Restore us, O God of hosts; *
    show the light of your countenance, and we shall
      be saved. **R**

4 **O Lord God of hosts, ***
    how long will you be angered
    despite the prayers of your people?

5 You have fed them with the bread of tears; *
    you have given them bowls of tears to drink.

6 **You have made us the derision of our neighbors, ***
    and our enemies laugh us to scorn.

7 Restore us, O God of hosts; *
    show the light of your countenance, and we shall
      be saved. **R**

8 **You have brought a vine out of Egypt; ***
    you cast out the nations and planted it.

9 You prepared the ground for it; *
    it took root and filled the land.

10 **The mountains were covered by its shadow ***
    and the towering cedar trees by its boughs.

11 You stretched out its tendrils to the sea *
    and its branches to the river.

12 **Why have you broken down its wall, ***
    so that all who pass by pluck off its grapes?

13 The wild boar of the forest has ravaged it, *
    and the beasts of the field have grazed upon it. **R**

14 **Turn now, O God of hosts, look down from heaven;**
behold and tend this vine; *
    15preserve what your right hand has planted.

16 They burn it with fire like rubbish; *
    at the rebuke of your countenance let them perish. ▼

17 **Let your hand be upon the one at your right hand,** *
     the one you have made so strong for yourself.

18 And so will we never turn away from you; *
     give us life, that we may call upon your name.

19 **Restore us, O LORD God of hosts;** *
     **show the light of your countenance, and we shall
     be saved.   R**

Lord God,
you so tend the vine you planted
that now it extends its branches throughout the world.
Keep us in Christ as branches on the vine,
that grafted firmly in your love,
we may show the whole world your great power
and bear the fruit of righteousness;
through Jesus Christ our Lord.   **Amen.**   [602]

PSALM 81   Tone 2; PS 72

R

1 Sing with joy to God our strength *
     and raise a loud shout to the God of Jacob.

2 **Raise a song and sound the timbrel,** *
     the merry harp, and the lyre.

3 Blow the ram's-horn at the new moon, *
     and at the full moon, the day of our feast.

4 **For this is a statute for Israel,** *
     a law of the God of Jacob.

5 God laid it as a solemn charge upon Joseph, *
     when the people came out of the land of Egypt.   **R**

     I heard an unfamiliar voice saying, *
       6 **"I eased their shoulder from the burden;**
         their hands were set free from bearing the load.

7 You called on me in trouble, and I saved you; *
  I answered you from the secret place of thunder
  and tested you at the waters of Meribah.

8 Hear, O my people, and I will admonish you: *
  O Israel, if you would but listen to me!

9 There shall be no strange god among you; *
  you shall not worship a foreign god.

10 I am the LORD your God,
  who brought you out of the land of Egypt and said, *
    'Open your mouth wide, and I will fill it.'   R

11 And yet my people did not hear my voice, *
  and Israel would not obey me.

12 So I gave them over to the stubbornness of their hearts, *
  to follow their own devices.

13 Oh, that my people would listen to me! *
  that Israel would walk in my ways!

14 I should soon subdue their enemies *
  and turn my hand against their foes.

15 Those who hate the LORD would cringe before me, *
  and their punishment would last forever.

16 But Israel would I feed with the finest wheat *
  and satisfy them with honey from the rock."   R

God our strength,
you rescue us in times of trouble
and set us in places of safety.
Help us to listen always to your voice
and feed us always with that living bread
given for the life of the world,
your Son, Jesus Christ our Lord.   **Amen.**   [603]

PSALM 82   Tone 8; PS 73

R

1 God arises in the council of heaven *
    and gives judgment in the midst of the gods:

2 **"How long will you judge unjustly, ***
    and show favor to the wicked?

3 Save the weak and the orphan; *
    defend the humble and needy;

4 **rescue the weak and the poor; ***
    deliver them from the power of the wicked.   R

5 They do not know, neither do they understand;
    they go about in darkness; *
    all the foundations of the earth are shaken.

6 **Now I say to you, 'You are gods, ***
    and all of you children of the Most High;

7 nevertheless, you shall die like mortals, *
    and fall like any leader' "

8 **Arise, O God, and rule the earth, ***
    for you shall take all nations for your own.   R

Strength of the weak,
defender of the needy,
rescuer of the poor,
deliver us from the power of wickedness,
that we may rejoice in your justice now and forever;
through Jesus Christ our Lord.   **Amen.**   [604]

PSALM 84   Tone 6; PH 207, 208; PS 74, 75

R

1   How dear to me is your dwelling, O LORD of hosts! *

²My soul has a desire and longing for the courts
　　of the LORD;
　　my heart and my flesh rejoice in the living God.

3　**The sparrow has found her a house
　　and the swallow a nest where she may lay her young; ***
　　**by the side of your altars, O LORD of hosts,
　　my Sovereign and my God.**

4　Happy are they who dwell in your house! *
　　they will always be praising you.　　**R**

5　**Happy are the people whose strength is in you! ***
　　whose hearts are set on the pilgrims' way.

6　Those who go through the desolate valley will find it a
　　　　place of springs, *
　　for the early rains have covered it with pools of water.

7　**They will climb from height to height, ***
　　and the God of gods will appear in Zion.　　R

8　LORD God of hosts, hear my prayer; *
　　hearken, O God of Jacob.

9　**Behold our defender, O God; ***
　　and look upon the face of your anointed.　　R

10　For one day in your courts is better than a thousand in my
　　　　own room, *
　　and to stand at the threshold of the house of my God
　　than to dwell in the tents of the wicked.

11　**For the LORD God is both sun and shield; ***
　　the LORD will give grace and glory;

　　no good thing will the LORD withhold *
　　from those who walk with integrity.

12　**O LORD of hosts, ***
　　happy are they who put their trust in you!　　R

Lord, your presence is better than life itself.
You are strength to all in need,
and hope to those who travel through sorrow.
As the sparrow and the swallow entrust their young to you,
so we place our lives before you.
Receive them in the name and for the sake of
Jesus Christ our Lord. **Amen.** [605]

PSALM 85 Tone 8; PS 76–78

R

1 You have been gracious to your land, O LORD, *
   you have restored the good fortune of Jacob.

2 **You have forgiven the iniquity of your people ***
   and blotted out all their sins.

3 You have withdrawn all your fury *
   and turned yourself from your wrathful indignation. **R**

4 **Restore us then, O God our Savior; ***
   let your anger depart from us.

5 Will you be displeased with us forever? *
   will you prolong your anger from age to age?

6 **Will you not give us life again, ***
   that your people may rejoice in you?

7 Show us your mercy, O LORD, *
   and grant us your salvation. **R**

8 **I will listen, O LORD God, to what you are saying, ***
   for you are speaking peace to your faithful people
   and to those who turn their hearts to you.

9 Truly, your salvation is very near to those who fear you, *
   that your glory may dwell in our land. **R**

¹⁰ **Mercy and truth have met together; ***
    righteousness and peace have kissed each other.

¹¹ Truth shall spring up from the earth, *
    and righteousness shall look down from heaven.

¹² **O LORD, you will indeed grant prosperity, ***
    and our land will yield its increase.

[Unison]

¹³ **Righteousness shall go before you, ***
    and peace shall be a pathway for your feet.   **R**

God of grace,
you loved the world so much
that you gave your only Son to be our Savior.
Help us to rejoice in your redeeming grace
by showing mercy,
and by walking in the way of justice and peace,
for the sake of Jesus Christ,
    redeemer of the world.   **Amen.**   [606]

PSALM 86   Tone 8; PS 79

R

¹ Bow down your ear, O LORD, and answer me, *
    for I am poor and in misery.

² **Keep watch over my life, for I am faithful; ***
    save your servant, for I put my trust in you.

³ Be merciful to me, O LORD, for you are my God; *
    I call upon you all the day long.   **R**

⁴ **Gladden the soul of your servant, ***
    for to you, O LORD, I lift up my soul.

⁵ For you, O LORD, are good and forgiving, *
    and great is your love toward all who call upon you.   ▼

6 **Give ear, O LORD, to my prayer, ***
    and attend to the voice of my supplications.

7 In the time of my trouble I will call upon you, *
    for you will answer me.   **R**

8 **Among the gods there is none like you, O LORD, ***
    nor anything like your works.

9 All nations you have made will come and worship you,
        O LORD, *
    and glorify your name.

10 **For you are great;**
    you do wondrous things; *
        and you alone are God.   R

11 Teach me your way, O LORD,
    and I will walk in your truth; *
        knit my heart to you that I may fear your name.

12 **I will thank you, O LORD my God, with all my heart, ***
    and glorify your name forevermore.

13 For great is your love toward me; *
    you have delivered me from the nethermost pit.   **R**

14 **The arrogant rise up against me, O God,**
    and a violent mob seeks my life; *
        they have not set you before their eyes.

15 But you, O LORD, are gracious and full of compassion, *
    slow to anger, and full of kindness and truth.

16 **Turn to me and have mercy upon me; ***
    give your strength to your servant;
    and save the child of your handmaid.

    [Unison]

17 **Show me a sign of your favor,**
    so that those who hate me may see it and be ashamed; *

because you, O LORD, have helped me and
   comforted me.   **R**

Eternal God,
in every time and place and circumstance your people call on you,
rejoicing in your love and cherishing your truth.
Hear the prayers of our hearts
that we may be protected from sin
and delivered from evil;
through Jesus Christ our Lord.   **Amen.** [607]

PSALM 88   Tone 8

R

1 O LORD, my God, my Savior, *
    by day and night I cry to you.

2 **Let my prayer enter into your presence; ***
    incline your ear to my lamentation.   R

3 For I am full of trouble; *
    my life is at the brink of the grave.

4 **I am counted among those who go down to the pit; ***
    I have become like one who has no strength;

5 lost among the dead, *
    like the slain who lie in the grave,

    Whom you remember no more, *
    for they are cut off from your hand.

6 You have laid me in the depths of the pit, *
    in dark places, and in the abyss.

7 **Your anger weighs upon me heavily, ***
    and all your great waves overwhelm me.   R

8 You have put my friends far from me;
    you have made me to be abhorred by them; *
       I am in prison and cannot get free.   ▼

9 My sight has failed me because of trouble; *
       LORD, I have called upon you daily;
       I have stretched out my hands to you.

10 Do you work wonders for the dead? *
       will those who have died stand up and give you thanks?

11 Will your loving-kindness be declared in the grave? *
       your faithfulness in the land of destruction?

12 Will your wonders be known in the dark? *
       or your righteousness in the country where all is
           forgotten?   R

13 But as for me, O LORD, I cry to you for help; *
       in the morning my prayer comes before you.

14 LORD, why have you rejected me? *
       why have you hidden your face from me?

15 Ever since my youth, I have been wretched and at the
       point of death; *
       I have borne your terrors with a troubled mind.

16 Your blazing anger has swept over me; *
       your terrors have destroyed me;

17 they surround me all day long like a flood; *
       they encompass me on every side.

   [Unison]

18 My friend and my neighbor you have put away from
       me, *
       and darkness is my only companion.   R

O Lord,
where we are plunged into the darkness of despair,
make known to us the wonders of your grace,
for you alone are God
and from you comes all our help and strength.
We ask this in the name of Jesus Christ.   **Amen.**   [608]

R

1 Your love, O LORD, forever will I sing; *
     from age to age my mouth will proclaim your faithfulness.

2 **For I am persuaded that your love is established forever;***
     you have set your faithfulness firmly in the heavens.

3 "I have made a covenant with my chosen one; *
     I have sworn an oath to David my servant:

4 **'I will establish your line forever, ***
     and preserve your throne for all generations.'"   R

5 The heavens bear witness to your wonders, O LORD, *
     and to your faithfulness in the assembly of the holy ones;

6 **for who in the skies can be compared to the LORD? ***
     who is like the LORD among the gods?

7 God is much to be feared in the council of the holy ones, *
     great and terrible to all those circled around.   R

8 **Who is like you, LORD God of hosts? ***
     O mighty LORD, your faithfulness is all around you.

9 You rule the raging of the sea *
     and still the surging of its waves.

10 **You have crushed Rahab of the deep with a deadly**
        wound; *
     you have scattered your enemies with your mighty
        arm.   R

11 Yours are the heavens; the earth also is yours; *
     you laid the foundations of the world and all that is in it.

12 **You have made the north and the south; ***
     Tabor and Hermon rejoice in your name.   ▼

13 You have a mighty arm; *
    strong is your hand and high is your right hand.

14 **Righteousness and justice are the foundations of your throne; ***
    love and truth go before your face.   R

15 Happy are the people who know the festal shout! *
    they walk, O LORD, in the light of your presence.

16 **They rejoice daily in your name; ***
    they are jubilant in your righteousness.

17 For you are the glory of their strength, *
    and by your favor our might is exalted.

18 **Truly, the LORD is our ruler; ***
    the Holy One of Israel is our Sovereign.   R

19 You spoke once in a vision and said to your faithful people: *
    "I have set the crown upon a warrior
    and have exalted one chosen out of the people.

20 **I have found David my servant; ***
    with my holy oil have I anointed him.

21 My hand will hold him fast *
    and my arm will make him strong.

22 **No enemy shall deceive him, ***
    nor any wicked man bring him down.

23 I will crush his foes before him *
    and strike down those who hate him.   R

24 **My faithfulness and love shall be with him, ***
    and he shall be victorious through my name.

25 I shall make his dominion extend *
    from the great sea to the river.

26 **He will say to me, 'You are my father, ***
my God, and the rock of my salvation.'

27 I will make him my firstborn *
and higher than the rulers of the earth.

28 **I will keep my love for him forever, ***
and my covenant will stand firm for him.

29 I will establish his line forever *
and his throne as the days of heaven.   **R**

30 **If his children forsake my law ***
and do not walk according to my judgments;

31 if they break my statutes *
and do not keep my commandments;

32 **I will punish their transgressions with a rod ***
and their iniquities with the lash;

33 But I will not take my love from him, *
nor let my faithfulness prove false.

34 **I will not break my covenant, ***
nor change what has gone out of my lips.   R

35 Once for all I have sworn by my holiness: *
'I will not lie to David.

36 **His line shall endure forever ***
and his throne as the sun before me;

37 it shall stand fast forevermore like the moon, *
the abiding witness in the sky.'"   **R**

38 **But you have cast off and rejected your anointed; ***
you have become enraged at him.

39 You have broken your covenant with your servant, *
defiled his crown, and hurled it to the ground.   ▼

⁴⁰ **You have breached all his walls ***
  and laid his strongholds in ruins.

⁴¹ All who pass by despoil him; *
  he has become the scorn of his neighbors.

⁴² **You have exalted the right hand of his foes ***
  and made all his enemies rejoice.

⁴³ You have turned back the edge of his sword *
  and have not sustained him in battle.

⁴⁴ **You have put an end to his splendor ***
  and cast his throne to the ground.

⁴⁵ You have cut short the days of his youth *
  and have covered him with shame.   **R**

⁴⁶ **How long will you hide yourself, O LORD?**
  will you hide yourself forever? *
  how long will your anger burn like fire?

⁴⁷ Remember, LORD, how short life is, *
  how frail you have made all flesh.

⁴⁸ **Who can live and not see death? ***
  who can escape from the power of the grave?   **R**

⁴⁹ Where, Lord, are your loving-kindnesses of old, *
  which you promised David in your faithfulness?

⁵⁰ **Remember, Lord, how your servant is mocked, ***
  how I carry in my bosom the taunts of many
    peoples,

⁵¹ the taunts your enemies have hurled, O LORD, *
  which they hurled at the heels of your anointed.

⁵² **Blessed be the LORD forevermore! ***
  Amen, I say, Amen.   **R**

Remember us, gracious God,
when we cannot see your way and purpose,
and renew in us the joy of your kingdom of light and life.
We ask this in the name of Jesus Christ the Lord.   **Amen.**   [609]

Psalm 90   Tone 8; PH 210, 211; PS 83, 84

R

1 Lord, you have been our refuge *
     from one generation to another.

2 **Before the mountains were brought forth,**
   or the land and the earth were born, *
        from age to age you are God.   R

3 You turn us back to the dust and say, *
     "Go back, O child of earth."

4 **For a thousand years in your sight are like yesterday**
           when it is past *
        and like a watch in the night.   R

5 You sweep us away like a dream; *
     we fade away suddenly like the grass.

6 **In the morning it is green and flourishes; ***
     in the evening it is dried up and withered.   R

7 For we consume away in your displeasure; *
     we are afraid because of your wrathful indignation.

8 **Our iniquities you have set before you, ***
     and our secret sins in the light of your
        countenance.   R

9 When you are angry, all our days are gone; *
     we bring our years to an end like a sigh.   ▼

10 **The span of our life is seventy years,**
   perhaps in strength even eighty; *
      yet the sum of them is but labor and sorrow,
      for they pass away quickly and we are gone.   R

11 Who regards the power of your wrath? *
   who rightly fears your indignation?

12 **So teach us to number our days ***
   that we may apply our hearts to wisdom.   R

13 Return, O LORD; how long will you tarry? *
   be gracious to your servants.

14 **Satisfy us by your loving-kindness in the morning; ***
   so shall we rejoice and be glad all the days of our
      life.   R

15 Make us glad by the measure of the days that you
      afflicted us *
   and the years in which we suffered adversity.

16 **Show your servants your works ***
   and your splendor to their children.

[Unison]

17 **May the graciousness of the LORD our God be**
      upon us; *
   prosper the work of our hands;
   prosper our handiwork.   R

Eternal God,
you alone are constant in this changing world.
Grant us true wisdom of heart
and guide us in serving you all the days of our life;
through Jesus Christ our Lord. **Amen.** [610]

R

1 You who dwell in the shelter of the Most High, *
       abide under the shadow of the Almighty.

2 **You shall say to the LORD,**
   "You are my refuge and my stronghold, *
       my God in whom I put my trust."

3 God shall deliver you from the snare of the hunter *
       and from the deadly pestilence.

4 **God's pinions will cover you,**
   and you shall find refuge under the wings of the LORD, *
       whose faithfulness shall be a shield and buckler.   R

5 You shall not be afraid of any terror by night, *
       nor of the arrow that flies by day;

6 **Of the plague that stalks in the darkness, ***
       nor of the sickness that lays waste at mid-day.

7 A thousand shall fall at your side
   and ten thousand at your right hand, *
       but it shall not come near you.

8 **Your eyes have only to behold ***
       to see the reward of the wicked.   R

9 Because you have made the LORD your refuge, *
       and the Most High your habitation,

10 **there shall no evil happen to you, ***
       neither shall any plague come near your dwelling.   R

11 For God shall give the holy angels charge over you, *
       to keep you in all your ways.

12 **They shall bear you in their hands, ***
       lest you dash your foot against a stone.   ▼

13 You shall tread upon the lion and adder; *
    you shall trample the young lion and the serpent
        under your feet.   R

14 **Because they are bound to me in love,**
    therefore will I deliver them; *
    I will protect them, because they know my name.

15 They shall call upon me, and I will answer them; *
    I am with them in trouble;
    I will rescue them and bring them to honor.

16 **With long life will I satisfy them, ***
    and show them my salvation.   R

O God,
to know you is to live,
to serve you is to reign.
Defend us from every enemy,
that, trusting in your protective care,
we may have no fear;
through the power of Jesus Christ our Lord. **Amen.** [611]

PSALM 92

Tone 6; PS 86

R

1 It is a good thing to give thanks to the LORD, *
    and to sing praises to your name, O Most High;

2 **to tell of your loving-kindness early in the morning ***
    and of your faithfulness in the night season;

3 on the psaltery, and on the lyre, *
    and to the melody of the harp.

4 **For you have made me glad by your acts, O LORD; ***
    and I shout for joy because of the works of your
        hands.   R

5 LORD, how great are your works! *
  your thoughts are very deep.

6 **The dullard does not know,**
  nor does the fool understand, *
     7 **that though the wicked grow like weeds,**
     and all the workers of iniquity flourish,

they flourish only to be destroyed forever; *
     8 but you, O LORD, are exalted forevermore.

9 **For lo, your enemies, O LORD,**
  lo, your enemies shall perish, *
     and all the workers of iniquity shall be scattered.   R

10 But my horn you have exalted like the horns of wild bulls; *
   I am anointed with fresh oil.

11 **My eyes also gloat over my enemies, ***
   and my ears rejoice to hear the doom of the wicked
       who rise up against me.   R

12 The righteous shall flourish like a palm tree, *
   and shall spread abroad like a cedar of Lebanon.

13 **Those who are planted in the house of the LORD ***
   shall flourish in the courts of our God;

14 they shall still bear fruit in old age; *
   they shall be green and succulent;

15 **that they may show how upright the LORD is, ***
   my Rock, in whom there is no fault.   R

Creator God,
you have planted your Word in our hearts
that you might harvest forth justice.
So root us in your love,
that we may always flourish,
yielding all the fruits of the Spirit
from youth to old age;
through Christ our Lord.   **Amen.**   [612]

R

1 You, O LORD, are Sovereign;
   you have put on splendid apparel; *
       you, O LORD, have put on your apparel
       and girded yourself with strength.

You have made the whole world so sure *
   that it cannot be moved;

2 ever since the world began, your throne has been
           established; *
       you are from everlasting.   **R**

3 **The waters have lifted up, O LORD,**
   the waters have lifted up their voice; *
       the waters have lifted up their pounding waves.

4 Mightier than the sound of many waters,
   mightier than the breakers of the sea, *
       mightier is the LORD who dwells on high.

5 **Your testimonies are very sure, ***
       and holiness adorns your house, O LORD,
       forever and forevermore.   R

Omnipotent God,
your glory is incomprehensible,
your majesty infinite,
and your power incomparable.
Found us on the certainty of your promises,
that no matter what happens,
we may be firm in faith
and live uprightly in your church,
bought by the blood of Jesus Christ.   **Amen.**   [613]

R

1 O Lord God of vengeance, *
      O God of vengeance, show yourself.

2 **Rise up, O Judge of the world; ***
      give the arrogant their just deserts.

3 How long shall the wicked, O Lord, *
      how long shall the wicked triumph?   R

4 **They bluster in their insolence; ***
      all evildoers are full of boasting.

5 They crush your people, O Lord, *
      and afflict your chosen nation.

6 **They murder the widow and the stranger ***
      and put the orphans to death.

7 Yet they say, "The Lord does not see, *
      the God of Jacob takes no notice."   R

8 **Consider well, you dullards among the people; ***
      when will you fools understand?

9 Does the One who planted the ear not hear? *
      does the One who formed the eye not see?

10 **Does the One who admonishes the nations not punish? ***
      does the One who teaches all the world have no
         knowledge?

11 The Lord knows our human thoughts; *
      how like a puff of wind they are.   R

12 **Happy are they whom you instruct, O Lord! ***
      whom you teach out of your law;   ▼

13 to give them rest in evil days, *
  until a pit is dug for the wicked.

14 **For you, O LORD, will not abandon your people, ***
  nor will you forsake your own.

15 For judgment will again be just, *
  and all the true of heart will follow it.   R

16 **Who rose up for me against the wicked? ***
  who took my part against the evildoers?

17 If the LORD had not come to my help, *
  I should soon have dwelt in the land of silence.

18 **As often as I said, "My foot has slipped," ***
  your love, O LORD, upheld me.

19 When many cares fill my mind, *
  your consolations cheer my soul.   R

20 **Can a corrupt tribunal have any part with you, ***
  one which frames evil into law?

21 They conspire against the life of the just *
  and condemn the innocent to death.

22 **But the LORD has become my stronghold, ***
  and my God the rock of my trust.

  [Unison]

23 **The LORD will turn their wickedness back upon them**
  and destroy them in their own malice; *
    the LORD our God will destroy them.   R

Faithful God,
you do not abandon your people to the power of evil.
Grant that those who suffer for the sake of justice
may find strength in the cross of Jesus
and be filled with your peace now and forever. **Amen.**   [614]

R

1 Come, let us sing to the LORD; *
    let us shout for joy to the Rock of our salvation.

2 **Let us come before God's presence with thanksgiving ***
    and raise a loud shout to the LORD with psalms.   R

3 For the LORD is a great God, *
    and a great Sovereign above all gods.

4 **The LORD holds the caverns of the earth, ***
    and sustains the heights of the hills.

5 The sea belongs to God, who made it, *
    whose hands have molded the dry land.   R

6 **Come, let us bow down, and bend the knee, ***
    and kneel before the LORD our Maker.

7 For the LORD is our God,
    and we are the people of God's pasture and the sheep
        of God's hand. *
    Oh, that today you would hearken to God's voice!   R

8 **Harden not your hearts,**
 as your ancestors did in the wilderness, *
    at Meribah, and on that day at Massah,
    when they tempted me.

9 They put me to the test, *
    though they had seen my works.

10 **Forty years long I detested that generation and said, ***
    "This people are wayward in their hearts;
    they do not know my ways."

   [Unison]

11 **So I swore in my wrath, ***
    "They shall not enter into my rest."   R

O Lord, our protector and our strength,
you guide us as the sheep of your fold.
In your goodness sustain us,
that our hearts may never be hardened
through unbelief of your holy Word,
but that we may serve you in true and living faith
and so enter into your heavenly rest;
through Jesus Christ our Lord.   **Amen.**   [615]

PSALM 96   Tone 3; PH 216, 217; PS 91, 92

R

1 Sing to the LORD a new song; *
     sing to the LORD, all the whole earth.

2 **Sing to the LORD and bless the LORD's name; ***
     proclaim the good news of salvation from day to day.

3 Declare the glory of the LORD among the nations *
     and the wonders of the LORD among all peoples.   **R**

4 **For great is the LORD and greatly to be praised, ***
     more to be feared than all gods.

5 As for all the gods of the nations, they are but idols; *
     but it is the LORD who made the heavens.

6 **Oh, the majesty and magnificence of the presence**
        of the LORD! *
     Oh, the power and the splendor of the sanctuary
        of our God!   **R**

7 Ascribe to the LORD, you families of the peoples; *
     ascribe to the LORD honor and power.

8 **Ascribe to the LORD the honor due the divine name; ***
     come to the holy courts with your offerings.

9 Worship the LORD in the beauty of holiness; *
     let the whole earth tremble in awe.   **R**

10 **Tell it out among the nations: "The Lord is Sovereign! ***
the Lord has made the world so firm that it cannot
be moved
and will judge the peoples with equity."

11 Let the heavens rejoice, and let the earth be glad;
let the sea thunder and all that is in it; *
12 let the field be joyful and all that is therein.

Then shall all the trees of the wood shout for joy
13 **before the Lord who is coming, ***
who is coming to judge the earth.

[Unison]

The Lord will judge the world with righteousness *
and the peoples with truth.   R

Ever-living God,
the heavens were glad and the earth rejoiced
when you sent your Son, the incarnate Word,
to dwell with us.
Help us to proclaim your glory to those who do not know you,
until the whole earth sings a new song to you
now and forever.   **Amen.**   [616]

Psalm 97   Tone 2; PS 93

R

1   The Lord is Sovereign;
let the earth rejoice; *
let the multitude of the isles be glad.

2   **Clouds and darkness are round about you, ***
righteousness and justice are the foundations of
your throne.

3   A fire goes before you *
and burns up your enemies on every side.   ▼

4 **Your lightnings light up the world; ***
   the earth sees it and is afraid.

5 The mountains melt like wax at the presence of the LORD, *
   at the presence of the Lord of the whole earth.   **R**

6 **The heavens declare your righteousness, O LORD, ***
   and all the peoples see your glory.

7 Confounded be all who worship carved images
   and delight in false gods! *
      Bow down before the LORD, all you gods.

8 **Zion hears and is glad, and the cities of Judah rejoice, ***
   because of your judgments, O LORD.

9 For you are the LORD,
   most high over all the earth; *
      you are exalted far above all gods.   **R**

10 **The LORD loves those who hate evil; ***
    the LORD preserves the lives of the faithful
    and delivers them from the hand of the wicked.

11 Light has sprung up for the righteous, *
    and joyful gladness for those who are truehearted.

12 **Rejoice in the LORD, you righteous, ***
    and to the holy name of the LORD give your
       praise.   R

O God,
you clothe the sky with light, and ocean depths with darkness.
You work your mighty wonders among us.
Claim us for your purposes,
that we may be among those who see your glory and give you
   praise,
for you live and reign, now and forever.   **Amen.**   [617]

R

1 Sing to the LORD a new song, *
   for the LORD has done marvelous things.

   The right hand and the holy arm of the LORD *
   have secured the victory.

2 The LORD has made known this victory *
   and has openly showed righteousness in the sight of the
   nations.

3 **The LORD remembers mercy and faithfulness to the**
   house of Israel, *
   and all the ends of the earth have seen the victory of
   our God.   R

4 Shout with joy to the LORD, all you lands; *
   lift up your voice, rejoice, and sing.

5 **Sing to the LORD with the harp, ***
   with the harp and the voice of song.

6 With trumpets and the sound of the horn *
   shout with joy before the Sovereign, the LORD.   **R**

7 **Let the sea make a noise and all that is in it, ***
   the lands and those who dwell therein.

8 Let the rivers clap their hands, *
   and let the hills ring out with joy before the LORD,
   who is coming to judge the earth.

9 **In righteousness shall the LORD judge the world ***
   and the peoples with equity.   R

Eternal God,
you redeemed humanity by sending your only Son
in fulfillment of your promises of old.
Let the truth and power of your salvation
be known in all places of the earth,
that all nations may give you praise, honor, and glory;
through Jesus Christ your Son. **Amen.** [618]

PSALM 99   Tone 3; PS 96

R

1 The LORD is Sovereign;
     let the people tremble; *
          the LORD is enthroned upon the cherubim;
          let the earth shake.

2 **The LORD is great in Zion ***
     and is high above all peoples.   R

3 Let them confess the name of the LORD,
     which is great and awesome; *
          the LORD is the Holy One.

4 **"O mighty Sovereign, lover of justice,**
     you have established equity; *
          you have executed justice and righteousness in
               Jacob."

5 Proclaim the greatness of the LORD our God, *
     and fall down before the footstool of the Holy One.   R

6 **Moses and Aaron among your priests,**
     and Samuel among those who call upon your name, *
          they called upon you, O LORD, and you answered
               them.

7 You spoke to them out of the pillar of cloud; *
     they kept your testimonies and the decree that you gave
          them.   R

8 **O LORD our God, you answered them indeed;** *
   you were a God who forgave them,
   yet punished them for their evil deeds.

[Unison]

9 **Proclaim the greatness of the LORD our God**
   and worship upon God's holy hill; *
   for the LORD our God is the Holy One. R

Holy God,
you are exalted over all the nations,
and just in all your ways.
Strengthen us to worship you with our deeds
and to proclaim your greatness with our lips,
for the glory of Jesus Christ our Lord. **Amen.** [619]

PSALM 100   Tone 3; PH 220; PS 97–101

R

1 Be joyful in the LORD, all you lands; *
   2 serve the LORD with gladness
      and come before God's presence with a song.

3 **Know this: The LORD alone is God;** *
   we belong to the LORD, who made us,
   we are God's people and the sheep of God's
      pasture. R

4 Enter God's gates with thanksgiving;
   go into the holy courts with praise; *
      give thanks and call upon the name of the LORD.

5 **For good is the LORD,**
   whose mercy is everlasting; *
      and whose faithfulness endures from age to age. R

Mighty God,
by your power you created us,
and by your goodness you call us to be your people. ▼

Accept the offering of our worship
that every race and nation may enter your courts,
praising you in song;
through Jesus Christ our Lord. **Amen.** [620]

PSALM 102   Tone 7 or 8

R

1 LORD, hear my prayer, and let my cry come before you; *
   2 hide not your face from me in the day of my trouble.

   Incline your ear to me; *
   when I call, make haste to answer me, R

3 for my days drift away like smoke, *
   and my bones are hot as burning coals.

4 **My heart is smitten like grass and withered, ***
   so that I forget to eat my bread.

5 Because of the voice of my groaning *
   I am but skin and bones.

6 **I have become like a vulture in the wilderness, ***
   like an owl among the ruins.

7 I lie awake and groan; *
   I am like a sparrow, lonely on a house-top.

8 **My enemies revile me all day long, ***
   and those who scoff at me have taken an oath
   against me.

9 For I have eaten ashes for bread *
   and mingled my drink with weeping.

10 **Because of your indignation and wrath ***
   you have lifted me up and thrown me away.

11 My days pass away like a shadow, *
   and I wither like the grass. R

12 **But you, O LORD, endure forever, ***
   and your name from age to age.

13 You will arise and have compassion on Zion,
   for it is time to have mercy upon it; *
      indeed, the appointed time has come.

14 **For your servants love its very rubble, ***
   and are moved to pity even for its dust.

15 The nations shall fear your name, O LORD, *
   and all the rulers of the earth your glory.

16 **For you, O LORD, will build up Zion, ***
   and your glory will appear.

17 You will look with favor on the prayer of the homeless; *
   you will not despise their plea.   R

18 **Let this be written for a future generation, ***
   so that a people yet unborn may praise the LORD.

19 For the LORD looked down from the holy place on high *
   and from the heavens beheld the earth;

20 **to hear the groan of the captive ***
   and to set free those condemned to die;

21 that they may declare in Zion the name of the LORD, *
   and the praise of our God in Jerusalem;

22 **when the peoples are gathered together, ***
   and the realms also, to serve the LORD.   R

23 The LORD has brought down my strength before my time *
   and shortened the number of my days;

24 **and I said, "O my God,**
   do not take me away in the midst of my days; *
   your years endure throughout all generations.   ▼

²⁵ In the beginning, O L_{ORD}, you laid the foundations of the
   earth, *
   and the heavens are the work of your hands;

²⁶ they shall perish, but you will endure;
   they all shall wear out like a garment; *
      as clothing you will change them,
      and they shall be changed;

²⁷ but you are always the same, *
   and your years will never end.

²⁸ The children of your servants shall continue, *
   and their offspring shall stand fast in your sight."   R

Lord, while our days vanish like shadows
and our lives wear out like a garment,
you are eternal.
Although our earthly lives come to an end,
help us to live in Christ's endless life
and at length attain our home,
the heavenly Jerusalem,
where he lives and reigns with you and the Holy Spirit,
now and forever.   **Amen.**   [621]

P_{SALM} 103   Tone 4; PH 222, 223; PS 102, 103

R

¹ Bless the L_{ORD}, O my soul, *
      and all that is within me, bless God's holy name.

² Bless the L_{ORD}, O my soul, *
      and forget not all the benefits of the L_{ORD},

³ who forgives all your sins *
      and heals all your infirmities;

⁴ who redeems your life from the grave *
      and crowns you with mercy and loving-kindness;

5 who satisfies you with good things, *
  and your youth is renewed like an eagle's. **R**

6 **The LORD executes righteousness ***
  and judgment for all who are oppressed.

7 To Moses were made known God's ways *
  and to the children of Israel the works of the LORD.

8 **The LORD is full of compassion and mercy, ***
  slow to anger and of great kindness.

9 The LORD will not always accuse us *
  nor remain angry forever.

10 **The LORD has not dealt with us according to our sins, ***
   nor rewarded us according to our wickedness.   R

11 For as the heavens are high above the earth, *
   so is the LORD's mercy great upon the God-fearing.

12 **As far as the east is from the west, ***
   so far has the LORD removed our sins from us.

13 As a father cares for his children, *
   so does the LORD care for the God-fearing.

14 **For the LORD knows whereof we are made ***
   and remembers that we are but dust.   R

15 Our days are like the grass; *
   we flourish like a flower of the field;

16 **when the wind goes over it, it is gone, ***
   and its place shall know it no more.

17 But the merciful goodness of the LORD endures forever on
       the God-fearing, *
   and the righteousness of the LORD on children's
       children;   ▼

¹⁸ **on those who keep the holy covenant ***
   and remember the commandments and do them.   R

¹⁹ The L<small>ORD</small> has set up a throne in heaven, *
   and the sovereignty of the L<small>ORD</small> has dominion over all.

²⁰ **Bless the L<small>ORD</small>, you holy angels,**
   you mighty ones who do God's bidding, *
   and hearken to the voice of God's word.

²¹ Bless the L<small>ORD</small>, all you holy hosts, *
   you holy ministers who do God's will.

²² **Bless the L<small>ORD</small>, all you works of God,**
   in all places of God's dominion; *
   bless the L<small>ORD</small>, O my soul.   R

God of might and mercy,
you bring us to new life each day,
and nurture us in your tender love.
Keep us far from all sinfulness,
that our lives may be a blessing to you;
in Jesus Christ our Lord.   **Amen.**   [622]

PSALM **104**   Tone 1 or 3; PH 224; PS 104, 105

R

¹ Bless the L<small>ORD</small>, O my soul; *
   O L<small>ORD</small> my God, how excellent is your greatness!
   you are clothed with majesty and splendor.

² **You wrap yourself with light as with a cloak ***
   and spread out the heavens like a curtain.

³ You lay the beams of your chambers in the waters above; *
   you make the clouds your chariot;
   you ride on the wings of the wind.

⁴ **You make the winds your messengers ***
   and flames of fire your servants.   R

5 You have set the earth upon its foundations, *
    so that it never shall move at any time.

6 **You covered it with the deep as with a mantle; ***
    the waters stood higher than the mountains.

7 At your rebuke they fled; *
    at the voice of your thunder they hastened away.

8 **They went up into the hills and down to the valleys**
        beneath, *
    to the places you had appointed for them.

9 You set the limits that they should not pass; *
    they shall not again cover the earth.   R

10 **You send the springs into the valleys; ***
     they flow between the mountains.

11 All the beasts of the field drink their fill from them, *
     and the wild asses quench their thirst.

12 **Beside them the birds of the air make their nests ***
     and sing among the branches.

13 You water the mountains from your dwelling on high; *
     the earth is fully satisfied by the fruit of your works.   R

14 **You make grass grow for flocks and herds ***
     and plants to serve humankind;

    that they may bring forth food from the earth, *
       15and wine to gladden our hearts,

    oil to make a cheerful countenance, *
     and bread to strengthen the heart.

16 The trees of the LORD are full of sap, *
     the cedars of Lebanon which the LORD planted,

17 **in which the birds build their nests, ***
     and in whose tops the stork makes its dwelling. R ▼

18 The high hills are a refuge for the mountain goats, *
      and the stony cliffs for the rock badgers.

19 **You appointed the moon to mark the seasons, ***
      and the sun knows the time of its setting.

20 You make darkness that it may be night, *
      in which all the beasts of the forest prowl.

21 **The lions roar after their prey ***
      and seek their food from God.

22 The sun rises, and they slip away *
      and lay themselves down in their dens.

23 **Mortals go forth to their work ***
      and to their labor until the evening.   R

24 O LORD, how manifold are your works! *
      in wisdom you have made them all;
      the earth is full of your creatures.

25 **Yonder is the great and wide sea**
      with its living things too many to number, *
      creatures both small and great.

26 There move the ships,
      and there is that Leviathan, *
      which you have made for the sport of it.   R

27 **All of them look to you ***
      to give them their food in due season.

28 You give it to them; they gather it; *
      you open your hand, and they are filled with good things.

29 **You hide your face, and they are terrified; ***
      you take away their breath,
      and they die and return to their dust.

30 You send forth your Spirit, and they are created; *
      and so you renew the face of the earth.   R

31 **May your glory, O Lord, endure forever; ***
   may you rejoice in all your works.

32 You look at the earth and it trembles; *
   you touch the mountains and they smoke.

33 **I will sing to the Lord as long as I live; ***
   I will praise my God while I have my being.

34 May these words of mine please you; *
   I will rejoice in the Lord.

35 **Let sinners be consumed out of the earth, ***
   and the wicked be no more.

   [Unison]

   Bless the Lord, O my soul. *
   Hallelujah!   R

God of majesty,
we are constantly surrounded by your gifts
and touched by your grace;
our words of praise do not approach the wonders of your love.
Send forth your Spirit,
that our lives may be refreshed
and the whole world may be renewed,
in Jesus Christ our Lord.   **Amen.**   [623]

Psalm 105   Tone 4; PS 106, 107

R

1 Give thanks to the Lord and call upon God's name; *
   make known the deeds of the Lord among the peoples.

2 **Sing to the Lord, sing praises, ***
   and speak of all God's marvelous works.

3 Glory in God's holy name; *
   let the hearts of those who seek the Lord rejoice.   ▼

⁴ **Search for the L<small>ORD</small> and the strength of the L<small>ORD</small>; ***
   continually seek the face of God.

⁵ Remember the marvels God has done, *
   the wonders and the judgments of God's mouth,

⁶ **O offspring of Abraham, God's servant, ***
   O children of Jacob, God's chosen.   R

⁷ The L<small>ORD</small> is our God, *
   whose judgments prevail in all the world.

⁸ **The L<small>ORD</small> has always been mindful of the covenant, ***
   the promise made for a thousand generations:

⁹ The covenant made with Abraham, *
   the oath sworn to Isaac,

¹⁰ **which God established as a statute for Jacob, ***
   an everlasting covenant for Israel,

¹¹ Saying, "To you will I give the land of Canaan *
   to be your allotted inheritance."   R

¹² **When they were few in number, ***
   of little account, and sojourners in the land,

¹³ wandering from nation to nation *
   and from one realm to another,

¹⁴ **God let no one oppress them ***
   and rebuked rulers for their sake,

¹⁵ saying, "Do not touch my anointed *
   and do my prophets no harm."   R

¹⁶ **Then the L<small>ORD</small> called for a famine in the land ***
   and destroyed the supply of bread.

¹⁷ The L<small>ORD</small> sent a man before them, *
   Joseph, who was sold as a slave.

18 **They bruised his feet in fetters; ***
   his neck they put in an iron collar.

19 Until his prediction came to pass, *
   the word of the LORD tested him.

20 **The king sent and released him; ***
   the ruler of the peoples set him free.

21 He set him as a master over his household, *
   as a ruler over all his possessions,

22 **to instruct his officials according to his will ***
   and to teach his elders wisdom.   R

23 Israel came into Egypt, *
   and Jacob became a sojourner in the land of Ham.

24 **The LORD made the chosen people exceedingly fruitful; ***
   the LORD made them stronger than their enemies;

25 whose heart God turned, so that they hated the chosen
      people, *
   and dealt unjustly with the servants of the LORD.   R

26 **There came Moses, the servant of the LORD, ***
   and Aaron whom God had chosen.

27 They worked signs from the LORD among them, *
   and portents in the land of Ham.

28 **God sent darkness, and it grew dark; ***
   but the Egyptians rebelled against the words of the
      LORD.

29 God turned their waters into blood *
   and caused their fish to die.

30 **Their land was overrun by frogs, ***
   in the very chambers of their rulers.   ▼

31 God spoke, and there came swarms of insects *
   and gnats within all their borders.

32 **God gave them hailstones instead of rain, ***
   and flames of fire throughout their land.

33 God blasted their vines and their fig trees *
   and shattered every tree in their country.

34 **God spoke, and the locust came, ***
   and young locusts without number,

35 which ate up all the green plants in their land *
   and devoured the fruit of their soil.

36 **God struck down the firstborn of their land, ***
   the first fruits of all their strength.   R

37 God led out the chosen people with silver and gold; *
   in all their tribes there was not one that stumbled.

38 **Egypt was glad of their going, ***
   because they were afraid of them.

39 God spread out a cloud for a covering *
   and a fire to give light in the night season.

40 **They asked, and quails appeared, ***
   and God satisfied them with bread from heaven.

41 God opened the rock, and water flowed, *
   so the river ran in the dry places.

42 **For God remembered the holy promise ***
   and Abraham, chosen to serve.   R

43 So God led forth the people with gladness, *
   the chosen ones with shouts of joy.

44 **God gave the chosen people the lands of the nations, ***
   and they took the fruit of others' toil,

[Unison]

45 **that they might keep God's statutes ***
   and observe the laws of the LORD.
   Hallelujah! R

God of our salvation,
through the death and resurrection of Jesus Christ,
you have fulfilled your promise to our ancestors in the faith
to redeem the world from slavery
and to lead us into the promised land.
Grant us living water from the rock
and bread from heaven,
that we may survive our desert pilgrimage
and praise you forever;
through Jesus Christ our Redeemer. **Amen.** [624]

PSALM 106   Tone 4; PS 108

R

1 Hallelujah!
   Give thanks to the LORD, who is good, *
      whose mercy endures forever.

2 **Can anyone declare the mighty acts of the LORD ***
   or show forth all God's praise?

3 Happy are those who act with justice *
      and always do what is right!   R

4 **Remember me, O LORD, with the favor you have**
         for your people, *
      and visit me with your saving help;

5 that I may see the prosperity of your elect
   and be glad with the gladness of your people, *
      that I may glory with your inheritance.   R   ▼

6 **We have sinned as our ancestors did; ***
   we have done wrong and dealt wickedly.

7 In Egypt they did not consider your marvelous works,
   nor remember the abundance of your love; *
      they defied the Most High at the Red Sea.

8 **But you saved them for your name's sake, ***
   to make your power known.

9 The LORD rebuked the Red Sea, and it dried up; *
   God led them through the deep as through a desert.

10 **The LORD saved them from the hand of those who**
      hated them *
   and redeemed them from the hand of the enemy.

11 The waters covered their oppressors; *
   not one of them was left.

12 **Then they believed the words of the LORD ***
   and sang out songs of praise.   R

13 But they soon forgot the deeds of the LORD *
   and did not await divine counsel.

14 **A craving seized them in the wilderness, ***
   and they put God to the test in the desert.

15 God gave them what they asked, *
   but sent leanness into their soul.

16 **They envied Moses in the camp, ***
   and Aaron, the holy one of the LORD.

17 The earth opened and swallowed Dathan *
   and covered the company of Abiram.

18 **Fire blazed up against their company, ***
   and flames devoured the wicked.   R

19 Israel made a bull-calf at Horeb *
   and worshiped a molten image;

20 **and so they exchanged their glory ***
   for the image of an ox that feeds on grass.

21 They forgot God their Savior, *
   who had done great things in Egypt,

22 **wonderful deeds in the land of Ham, ***
   and fearful things at the Red Sea.

23 So God would have destroyed them,
   had not Moses, the chosen one, stood before God
        in the breach, *
   to turn away divine wrath from consuming them.   R

24 **They refused the pleasant land ***
   and would not believe God's promise.

25 They grumbled in their tents *
   and would not listen to the voice of the LORD.

26 **So God's hand was lifted against them, ***
   to overthrow them in the wilderness,

27 to cast out their seed among the nations, *
   and to scatter them throughout the lands.   R

28 **They joined themselves to Baal-Peor ***
   and ate sacrifices offered to the dead.

29 They provoked the LORD to anger with their actions, *
   and a plague broke out among them.

30 **Then Phinehas stood up and interceded, ***
   and the plague came to an end.

31 This was reckoned to Phinehas as righteousness *
   throughout all generations forever.

32 **Again they provoked God's anger**
       at the waters of Meribah, *
   and the LORD punished Moses because of them;

33 for they so embittered his spirit *
   that he spoke rash words with his lips.   R   ▼

34 **They did not destroy the peoples ***
   as the LORD had commanded them.

35 They intermingled with the heathen *
   and learned their pagan ways,

36 **so that they worshiped their idols, ***
   which became a snare to them.

37 They sacrificed their sons *
   and their daughters to evil spirits.

38 **They shed innocent blood,**
   the blood of their sons and daughters, *
   which they offered to the idols of Canaan,
   and the land was defiled with blood.

39 Thus they were polluted by their actions *
   and went whoring in their evil deeds.   R

40 **Therefore the wrath of the LORD was kindled against**
       the people *
   and God abhorred the chosen inheritance.

41 God gave them over to the hand of the heathen, *
   and those who hated them ruled over them.

42 **Their enemies oppressed them, ***
   and they were humbled under their hand.

43 Many a time did God deliver them,
   but they rebelled through their own devices, *
   and were brought down in their iniquity.

44 **Nevertheless, the LORD saw their distress ***
   and heard their lamentation.

45 God remembered the covenant with them *
   and out of abundant mercy relented.   R

46 **God caused them to be pitied ***
   by those who held them captive.

47 Save us, O LORD our God,
    and gather us from among the nations, *
        that we may give thanks to your holy name
        and glory in your praise.

48 **Blessed be the LORD, the God of Israel,**
    from everlasting and to everlasting; *
        and let all the people say, "Amen!"
        Hallelujah!   R

Merciful God,
remembering your covenant,
you graciously pardoned those who rebelled against you.
Grant that, where sin abounds,
grace may abound more;
through Jesus Christ our Lord.   **Amen.**   [625]

PSALM 107   Tone 3; PS 109, 110

R

1   Give thanks to the LORD, who is good, *
        whose mercy endures forever.

2   **Let all those whom the LORD has redeemed proclaim ***
        that the LORD redeemed them from the hand of the
            foe.

3   God gathered them out of the lands; *
        from the east and from the west,
        from the north and from the south.   R

4   **Some wandered in desert wastes; ***
        they found no way to a city where they might dwell.

5   They were hungry and thirsty; *
        their spirits languished within them.

6   **Then in their trouble they cried to the LORD, ***
        who delivered them from their distress.   ▼

7 The LORD put their feet on a straight path *
   to go to a city where they might dwell.

8 **Let them give thanks for the mercy of God, ***
   for the wonders the LORD does for all people.

9 For God satisfies the thirsty *
   and fills the hungry with good things.   R

10 **Some sat in darkness and deep gloom, ***
    bound fast in misery and iron;

11 because they rebelled against the words of God *
    and despised the counsel of the Most High.

12 **So God humbled their spirits with hard labor; ***
    they stumbled, and there was none to help.

13 Then in their trouble they cried to the LORD, *
    who delivered them from their distress.

14 **The LORD led them out of darkness and deep gloom ***
    and broke their bonds asunder.

15 Let them give thanks for the mercy of God, *
    for the wonders the LORD does for all people.

16 **For God shatters the doors of bronze ***
    and breaks in two the iron bars.   R

17 Some were fools and took to rebellious ways; *
    they were afflicted because of their sins.

18 **They abhorred all manner of food ***
    and drew near to death's door.

19 Then in their trouble they cried to the LORD, *
    who delivered them from their distress.

20 **God sent forth a word to heal them ***
    and saved them from the grave.

21 Let them give thanks for the mercy of God, *
   for the wonders the LORD does for all people.

22 **Let them offer a sacrifice of thanksgiving ***
   and recount the deeds of God with shouts of joy.   R

23 Some went down to the sea in ships *
   and plied their trade in deep waters;

24 **they beheld the works of the LORD, ***
   whose wonders are in the deep.

25 Then the LORD spoke, and a stormy wind arose, *
   which tossed high the waves of the sea.

26 **They mounted up to the heavens and fell back**
   to the depths; *
   their hearts melted because of their peril.

27 They reeled and staggered like drunkards *
   and were at their wits' end.

28 **Then in their trouble they cried to the LORD, ***
   who delivered them from their distress.

29 God stilled the storm to a whisper *
   and quieted the waves of the sea.

30 **Then were they glad because of the calm, ***
   and God brought them to the harbor
   they were bound for.

31 Let them give thanks for the mercy of God, *
   for the wonders the LORD does for all people.

32 **Let them exalt the LORD in the congregation of the**
   people *
   and praise God in the council of the elders.   R

33 The LORD changed rivers into deserts, *
   and water-springs into thirsty ground,   ▼

³⁴ a fruitful land into salt flats, *
     because of the wickedness of those who dwell there.

³⁵ God changed deserts into pools of water *
     and dry land into water-springs.

³⁶ **God settled the hungry there, ***
     and they founded a city to dwell in.

³⁷ They sowed fields, and planted vineyards, *
     and brought in a fruitful harvest.   **R**

³⁸ **God blessed them, so that they increased greatly; ***
     God did not let their herds decrease.

³⁹ Yet when they were diminished and brought low, *
     through stress of adversity and sorrow,

⁴⁰ **(God pours contempt on nobles ***
     and makes them wander in trackless wastes)

⁴¹ God lifted up the poor out of misery *
     and multiplied their families like flocks of sheep.

⁴² **The upright will see this and rejoice, ***
     but all wickedness will shut its mouth.

[Unison]

Whoever is wise will ponder these things, *
     and consider well the mercies of the LORD.   **R**

O God,
you are light to the lost,
bread to the hungry,
deliverance to the captive,
healing to the sick,
eternal vision to the dying,
and harbor to every soul in peril.
Gather the wanderers from every corner of the world
into the community of your mercy and grace,
that we may eternally praise you
for our salvation in Jesus Christ our Lord.   **Amen.**   [626]

R

1 My heart is firmly fixed, O God, my heart is fixed; *
    I will sing and make melody.

2 **Wake up, my spirit;**
awake, lute and harp; *
    I myself will waken the dawn.

3 I will confess you among the peoples, O LORD; *
    I will sing praises to you among the nations.

4 **For your loving-kindness is greater than the heavens,** *
    and your faithfulness reaches to the clouds.   **R**

5 Exalt yourself above the heavens, O God, *
    and your glory over all the earth.

6 **So that those who are dear to you may be delivered,** *
    save with your right hand and answer me.   **R**

7 From God's holy place came a voice; *
    God said, "I will exult and parcel out Shechem;
    I will divide the valley of Succoth.

8 **Gilead is mine and Manasseh is mine;** *
    Ephraim is my helmet and Judah my scepter.

9 Moab is my washbasin,
on Edom I throw down my sandal to claim it, *
    and over Philistia will I shout in triumph."   **R**

10 **Who will lead me into the strong city?** *
    who will bring me into Edom?

11 Have you not cast us off, O God? *
    you no longer go out, O God, with our armies.

12 **Grant us your help against the enemy,** *
    for vain is the help of mortals.   ▼

13 **With God we will do valiant deeds, ***
　　and God shall tread our enemies under foot.　　R

O God,
your love is wider than all the universe
and your mercy greater than the heights of heaven.
When we are tempted to break faith with you,
put a new song of love on our lips,
that we may sing your praises to all nations on earth,
through your Son, our only hope and defense.　**Amen.**　[627]

PSALM 110　　　　　　　　　　　　　　　　　Tone 6

R

1　The LORD said to my lord, "Sit at my right hand, *
　　until I make your enemies your footstool."　　R

2　**The LORD will send the scepter of your power out of**
　　　　Zion, *
　　　saying, "Rule over your enemies round about you.

3　Nobility has been yours from the day of your birth; *
　　in the beauty of holiness have I begotten you,
　　like dew from the womb of the morning."

4　**The LORD has sworn and will not recant: ***
　　"You are a priest forever after the order of
　　　　Melchizedek."　　R

5　The lord who is at God's right hand
　　will smite rulers in the day of his wrath; *
　　he will rule over the nations.

6　**He will heap high the corpses ***
　　and will smash heads over the wide earth.

[Unison]

He will drink from the brook beside the road *
   and therefore will lift high his head.   R

Jesus Christ,
King of kings and Lord of lords,
born as one of us,
exalted now on high,
priest of the new covenant,
judge who will come at the end of time,
glory to you forever and ever.   **Amen.**   [628]

PSALM 111   Tone 3 or 4; PS 111

R

1 Hallelujah!
   I will give thanks to the LORD with my whole heart, *
      in the assembly of the upright, in the congregation.

2 **Great are the deeds of the LORD!** *
      they are studied by all who delight in them.

3 Full of majesty and splendor is the work of the LORD, *
      whose righteousness endures forever.

4 **Gracious and full of compassion is the LORD,** *
      whose marvelous works are to be remembered.

5 The LORD gives food to the God-fearing, *
      ever mindful of the covenant.   **R**

6 **The LORD has shown the chosen people works of**
         power *
      in giving them the lands of the nations.

7 The hands of the LORD work faithfulness and justice; *
      all the commandments of the LORD are sure.

8 **They stand fast forever and ever,** *
      because they are done in truth and equity.   ▼

9   The LORD sent redemption to the chosen people,
        commanding the covenant forever; *
            holy and awesome is the name of the LORD.

10 **The fear of the LORD is the beginning of wisdom; ***
        those who act accordingly have a good
            understanding;
            the praise of the LORD endures forever.   **R**

Faithful God,
you have nourished us in your holy covenant
with the food and drink of Christ's love.
Keep us firm in our faith
and loyal in our love,
that we may obediently serve as disciples of Jesus Christ,
our Lord and Savior.   **Amen.**   [629]

PSALM 112   Tone 3 or 6; PS 112

R

1   Hallelujah!
    Happy are they who fear the LORD *
        and have great delight in the LORD's commandments!

2   **Their descendants will be mighty in the land; ***
        the generation of the upright will be blessed.

3   Wealth and riches will be in their house, *
        and their righteousness will last forever.   **R**

4   **Light shines in the darkness for the upright; ***
        the righteous are merciful and full of compassion.

5   It is good for them to be generous in lending *
        and to manage their affairs with justice.

6   **For they will never be shaken; ***
        the righteous will be kept in everlasting
            remembrance.   **R**

7 They will not be afraid of any evil rumors; *
    their heart is right;
    they put their trust in the LORD.

8 **Their heart is established and will not shrink,** *
    until they see their desire upon their enemies.

9 They have given freely to the poor, *
    and their righteousness stands fast forever;
    they will hold up their head with honor.

10 **The wicked will see it and be angry;**
    they will gnash their teeth and pine away; *
    the desires of the wicked will perish.   **R**

Eternal God,
in the order of your creation
you have given righteousness, justice, peace, and love
for the enlightenment of all people.
Keep us always in that light
so that throughout our lives,
we may show forth the glory of Jesus Christ,
the light of the world.   **Amen.**   [630]

PSALM 113   Tone 1 or 3; PH 225, 226; PS 113

R

1 Hallelujah!
    Give praise, you servants of the LORD; *
    praise the name of the LORD.

2 **Let the name of the LORD be blessed,** *
    from this time forth forevermore.

3 From the rising of the sun to its going down *
    let the name of the LORD be praised.

4 **High above all nations is the LORD,** *
    whose glory is above the heavens.   **R**   ▼

5 Who is like the LORD our God, who sits enthroned on high *
   but stoops to behold the heavens and the earth?

6 **The LORD takes up the weak out of the dust ***
   and lifts up the poor from the ashes.

7 The LORD sets them with the nobles, *
   with the nobles of the chosen people.

8 **The LORD makes the woman of a childless house ***
   to be a joyful mother of children.   R

Sovereign God,
you subdue the arrogant
and raise the humble;
you feed the hungry
and reveal the poverty of wealth.
Help us to praise your name in all times and places,
that we may be faithful servants
of Jesus Christ our Lord.   **Amen.**   [631]

PSALM 114   Tone 4; PS 114

R

1 Hallelujah!
   When Israel came out of Egypt, *
     the house of Jacob from a people of strange speech,

2 **Judah became God's sanctuary ***
   and Israel God's dominion.

3 The sea beheld it and fled; *
   Jordan turned and went back.

4 **The mountains skipped like rams, ***
   and the little hills like young sheep.   R

5 What ailed you, O sea, that you fled? *
   O Jordan, that you turned back?

6 **You mountains, that you skipped like rams? ***
   you little hills like young sheep?

7 Tremble, O earth, at the presence of the Lord, *
   at the presence of the God of Jacob,

8 **who turned the hard rock into a pool of water ***
   and flint-stone into a flowing spring.   R

Mighty God,
by your power you led your people out of slavery in Egypt,
and raised the dead Christ to life.
Deliver us continually by your power
from slavery to freedom
and from death to life,
for the glory of Jesus Christ our Savior.   **Amen.**   [632]

PSALM 115   Tone 6; PH 227

R

1 Not to us, O LORD, not to us,
   but to your name give glory; *
      because of your love and because of your faithfulness.

2 **Why should the heathen say, ***
   "Where then is their God?"   R

3 Our God is in heaven; *
   whatever God wills to do, God does.

4 **Their idols are silver and gold, ***
   the work of human hands.

5 They have mouths, but they cannot speak; *
   eyes have they, but they cannot see;

6 **they have ears, but they cannot hear; ***
   noses, but they cannot smell;   ▼

7 they have hands, but they cannot feel;
feet, but they cannot walk; *
    they make no sound with their throat.

8 **Those who make them are like them, ***
    and so are all who put their trust in them. R

9 O Israel, trust in the LORD, *
    who is your help and your shield.

10 **O house of Aaron, trust in the LORD, ***
    who is your help and your shield.

11 You who fear the LORD, trust in the LORD, *
    who is your help and your shield. **R**

12 **The LORD has been mindful of us and will bless us; ***
    the LORD will bless the house of Israel
    and will bless the house of Aaron;

13 the LORD will bless the God-fearing, *
    both small and great together. **R**

14 **May the LORD increase you more and more, ***
    you and your children after you.

15 May you be blessed by the LORD, *
    the maker of heaven and earth. **R**

16 **The heaven of heavens is the LORD's, ***
    but the LORD entrusted the earth to its peoples.

17 The dead do not praise the LORD, *
    nor all those who go down into silence;

18 **but we will bless the LORD, ***
    from this time forth forevermore.
    Hallelujah! R

God, you delivered Israel from the worship of false gods.
Redeem your people in every age

from the pursuit of all that is worthless and untrue;
through Jesus our Savior,
who came to bring us life in all its fullness.   **Amen.**   [633]

PSALM 116   Tone 6; PH 228; PS 115, 116

R

1   I love the LORD, because the LORD has heard the voice of
        my supplication *
        2 and inclined an ear to me whenever I cried out.

3   **The cords of death entangled me;**
    the grip of the grave took hold of me; *
        I came to grief and sorrow.

4   Then I called upon the name of the LORD: *
        "O LORD, I pray you, save my life."   **R**

5   **Gracious is the LORD and righteous; ***
    our God is full of compassion.

6   The LORD watches over the innocent; *
        I was brought very low, and the LORD helped me.

7   **Turn again to your rest, O my soul, ***
    for the LORD has treated you well.   **R**

8   For you have rescued my life from death, *
        my eyes from tears, and my feet from stumbling.

9   **I will walk in the presence of the LORD ***
    in the land of the living.

10 I believed, even when I said,
    "I have been brought very low." *
        11 In my distress I said, "No one can be trusted."   **R**

12 **How shall I repay you, O LORD, ***
    for all the good things you have done for me?   ▼

¹³ I will lift up the cup of salvation *
    and call upon the name of the LORD.

¹⁴ I will fulfill my vows to the LORD *
    in the presence of all the chosen people.

¹⁵ Precious in your sight, O LORD, *
    is the death of your servants.   R

¹⁶ O LORD, I am your servant; *
    I am your servant and the child of your handmaid;
    you have freed me from my bonds.

¹⁷ I will offer you the sacrifice of thanksgiving *
    and call upon the name of the LORD.

¹⁸ I will fulfill my vows to the LORD *
    in the presence of all the people,

[Unison]

¹⁹ in the courts of the LORD's house, *
    in the midst of you, O Jerusalem.
    Hallelujah!   R

God our Redeemer,
you have delivered us from death
    in the resurrection of Jesus Christ
and brought us to new life by the power of your Spirit.
Give us grace to keep our promises
to praise and serve you all our days;
through Jesus Christ our Lord.   **Amen.**   [634]

PSALM 117   Tone 3; PH 229; PS 117

R

¹   Praise the LORD, all you nations; *
    give praise, all you peoples.

2 **For the loving-kindness of the L**ORD **toward us is great,** *
   and the faithfulness of the LORD **endures forever.**
   Hallelujah!   **R**

Lord God,
you have revealed your kindness to all peoples.
Gather all nations to yourself,
that in all the various tongues of the earth
one hymn of praise may rise to you;
through Jesus Christ our Lord.   **Amen.**   [635]

PSALM **118**   Tone 3; PH 230–232; PS 118–120

R

1 Give thanks to the L**ORD**, who is good, *
   whose mercy endures forever.

2 **Let Israel now proclaim,** *
   "The mercy of the LORD **endures forever."**

3 Let the house of Aaron now proclaim, *
   "The mercy of the L**ORD** endures forever."

4 **Let those who fear the L**ORD **now proclaim,** *
   "The mercy of the LORD **endures forever."**   **R**

5 I called to the L**ORD** in my distress; *
   the L**ORD** answered by setting me free.

6 **The L**ORD **is at my side, therefore I will not fear;** *
   what can anyone do to me?

7 The L**ORD** is at my side to help me; *
   I will triumph over those who hate me.

8 **It is better to rely on the L**ORD *
   than to put any trust in flesh.

9 It is better to rely on the L**ORD** *
   than to put any trust in rulers.   **R**   ▼

10 **All the ungodly encompass me;** *
   in the name of the LORD I will repel them.

11 They hem me in, they hem me in on every side; *
   in the name of the LORD I will repel them.

12 **They swarm about me like bees;**
   they blaze like a fire of thorns; *
   in the name of the LORD I will repel them.

13 I was pressed so hard that I almost fell, *
   but the LORD came to my help.   **R**

14 **The LORD is my strength and my song** *
   and has become my salvation.

15 There is a sound of exultation and victory *
   in the tents of the righteous:

16 **"The right hand of the LORD has triumphed!** *
   the right hand of the LORD is exalted!
   the right hand of the LORD has triumphed!"

17 I shall not die, but live, *
   and declare the works of the LORD.

18 **The LORD has punished me sorely** *
   but did not hand me over to death.   **R**

19 Open for me the gates of righteousness; *
   I will enter them;
   I will offer thanks to the LORD.

20 **"This is the gate of the LORD;** *
   those who are righteous may enter."   **R**

21 I will give thanks to you, for you answered me *
   and have become my salvation.

22 **The same stone which the builders rejected** *
   has become the chief cornerstone.

23 This is the LORD's doing, *
    and it is marvelous in our eyes.

24 On this day the LORD has acted; *
    we will rejoice and be glad in it.   **R**

25 Hosanna, LORD, hosanna! *
    LORD, send us now success.

26 Blessed is the one who comes in the name of the LORD; *
    we bless you from the house of the LORD.

27 God is the LORD, who has shined upon us; *
    form a procession with branches up to the horns of the
        altar.

28 "You are my God, and I will thank you; *
    you are my God, and I will exalt you."

[Unison]

29 Give thanks to the LORD, who is good; *
    whose mercy endures forever.   **R**

Holy and mighty God,
your Son's triumph over sin and death
has opened to us the gate of eternal life.
Purify our hearts
that we may follow him
and share in the radiance of his glory.
We ask this for the sake of our risen Lord.   **Amen.** [636]

PSALM 119   Tone 5; PH 233; PS 121–124

R

1 Happy are they whose way is blameless, *
    who walk in the law of the LORD!

2 **Happy are they who observe your decrees ***
    and seek you with all their hearts!   ▼

3 Who never do any wrong, *
    but always walk in your ways.

4 **You laid down your commandments, ***
    that we should fully keep them.

5 Oh, that my ways were made so direct *
    that I might keep your statutes!

6 **Then I should not be put to shame, ***
    when I regard all your commandments.

7 I will thank you with an unfeigned heart, *
    when I have learned your righteous judgments.

8 **I will keep your statutes; ***
    do not utterly forsake me. R

9 How shall the young cleanse their way? *
    By keeping to your words.

10 **With my whole heart I seek you; ***
    let me not stray from your commandments.

11 I treasure your promise in my heart, *
    that I may not sin against you.

12 **Blessed are you, O LORD; ***
    instruct me in your statutes.

13 With my lips will I recite *
    all the judgments of your mouth.

14 **I have taken greater delight in the way of your decrees ***
    than in all manner of riches.

15 I will meditate on your commandments *
    and give attention to your ways.

16 **My delight is in your statutes; ***
    I will not forget your word. R

17 Deal bountifully with your servant, *
    that I may live and keep your word.

18 **Open my eyes, that I may see** *
    the wonders of your law.

19 I am a stranger here on earth; *
    do not hide your commandments from me.

20 **My soul is consumed at all times** *
    with longing for your judgments.

21 You have rebuked the insolent; *
    cursed are they who stray from your commandments!

22 **Turn from me shame and rebuke,** *
    for I have kept your decrees.

23 Even though rulers sit and plot against me, *
    I will meditate on your statutes.

24 **For your decrees are my delight,** *
    and they are my counselors.   R

    *   *   *

33 Teach me, O LORD, the way of your statutes, *
    and I shall keep it to the end.

34 **Give me understanding, and I shall keep your law;** *
    I shall keep it with all my heart.

35 Make me go in the path of your commandments, *
    for that is my desire.

36 **Incline my heart to your decrees** *
    and not to unjust gain.

37 Turn my eyes from watching what is worthless; *
    give me life in your ways.

38 **Fulfill your promise to your servant,** *
    which you make to those who fear you.   ▼

39   Turn away the reproach which I dread, *
     because your judgments are good.

40   Behold, I long for your commandments; *
     in your righteousness preserve my life.   **R**

   *   *   *

73   Your hands have made me and fashioned me; *
     give me understanding, that I may learn your
      commandments.

74   Those who fear you will be glad when they see me, *
     because I trust in your word.

75   I know, O LORD, that your judgments are right *
     and that in faithfulness you have afflicted me.

76   Let your loving-kindness be my comfort, *
     as you have promised to your servant.

77   Let your compassion come to me, that I may live, *
     for your law is my delight.

**78   Let the arrogant be put to shame, for they wrong me
      with lies; ***
     but I will meditate on your commandments.

79   Let those who fear you turn to me, *
     and also those who know your decrees.

80   Let my heart be sound in your statutes, *
     that I may not be put to shame.   **R**

   *   *   *

97   Oh, how I love your law! *
     all the day long it is in my mind.

**98   Your commandment has made me wiser than my
      enemies, ***
     and it is always with me.

99 I have more understanding than all my teachers, *
  for your decrees are my study.

100 **I am wiser than the elders,** *
  because I observe your commandments.

101 I restrain my feet from every evil way, *
  that I may keep your word.

102 **I do not shrink from your judgments,** *
  because you yourself have taught me.

103 How sweet are your words to my taste! *
  they are sweeter than honey to my mouth.

104 **Through your commandments I gain understanding;** *
  therefore I hate every lying way.   R

105 Your word is a lantern to my feet *
  and a light upon my path.

106 **I have sworn and am determined** *
  to keep your righteous judgments.

107 I am deeply troubled; *
  preserve my life, O LORD, according to your word.

108 **Accept, O LORD, the willing tribute of my lips,** *
  and teach me your judgments.

109 My life is always in my hand, *
  yet I do not forget your law.

110 **The wicked have set a trap for me,** *
  but I have not strayed from your commandments.

111 Your decrees are my inheritance forever; *
  truly, they are the joy of my heart.

112 **I have applied my heart to fulfill your statutes** *
  forever and to the end.   R   ▼

    *   *   *

129 Your decrees are wonderful; *
    therefore I obey them with all my heart.

130 When your word goes forth it gives light; *
    it gives understanding to the simple.

131 I open my mouth and pant; *
    I long for your commandments.

132 Turn to me in mercy, *
    as you always do to those who love your name.

133 Steady my footsteps in your word; *
    let no iniquity have dominion over me.

134 Rescue me from those who oppress me, *
    and I will keep your commandments.

135 Let your countenance shine upon your servant *
    and teach me your statutes.

136 My eyes shed streams of tears, *
    because people do not keep your law.   R

137 You are righteous, O LORD, *
    and upright are your judgments.

138 You have issued your decrees *
    with justice and in perfect faithfulness.

139 My indignation has consumed me, *
    because my enemies forget your words.

140 Your word has been tested to the uttermost, *
    and your servant holds it dear.

141 I am small and of little account, *
    yet I do not forget your commandments.

142 Your justice is an everlasting justice *
    and your law is the truth.

143 Trouble and distress have come upon me, *
    yet your commandments are my delight.

¹⁴⁴ **The righteousness of your decrees is everlasting;** *
     grant me understanding, that I may live.   R

Holy God,
you are just in all your ways
and your commandments are the greatest of treasures.
Give us understanding of your law
and direct us according to your will
that we may be faithful in serving you
for the sake of Jesus our Lord.   **Amen.**   [637]

PSALM 121   Tone 6; PH 234; PS 125

R

¹ I lift up my eyes to the hills; *
     from where is my help to come?

² **My help comes from the LORD,** *
     the maker of heaven and earth.   R

³ The LORD will not let your foot be moved, *
     and the One who watches over you will not fall asleep.

⁴ **Behold, the One who keeps watch over Israel** *
     shall neither slumber nor sleep;   R

⁵ it is the LORD who watches over you; *
     the LORD is your shade at your right hand,

⁶ **so that the sun shall not strike you by day,** *
     nor the moon by night.   R

⁷ The LORD shall preserve you from all evil; *
     the LORD shall keep you safe.

⁸ **The LORD shall watch over your going out and your**
          coming in, *
     from this time forth forevermore.   R

God, our helper,
you are strength greater than the mountains;
you look to our needs and watch over us day and night.
Teach us to hold confidently to your grace
that in times of fear and danger
we may know you are near and depend on you,
our sure deliverer. **Amen.** [638]

PSALM 122   Tone 2; PH 235; PS 126

R

1 I was glad when they said to me, *
    "Let us go to the house of the LORD."

2 **Now our feet are standing ***
    within your gates, O Jerusalem.   **R**

3 Jerusalem is built as a city *
    that is at unity with itself;

4 **to which the tribes go up,**
  the tribes of the LORD, *
    the assembly of Israel,
      to praise the name of the LORD.

5 For there are the thrones of judgment, *
    the thrones of the house of David.   **R**

6 **Pray for the peace of Jerusalem: ***
    "May they prosper who love you.

7 Peace be within your walls *
    and quietness within your towers.

8 **For the sake of my kindred and companions, ***
    I pray for your prosperity.

  [Unison]

9 **Because of the house of the LORD our God, ***
    I will seek to do you good."   **R**

Lord Jesus,
because there was no peace in Jerusalem,
you wept hard tears.
Bring all nations under your rule
that they make peace
and, with thanksgiving
enter together the heavenly Jerusalem
where you live and reign with the Father
and the Holy Spirit, now and forever.   **Amen.**   [639]

PSALM 123   Tone 8; PS 127

R

1   To you I lift up my eyes, *
    to you enthroned in the heavens.

2   **As the eyes of servants look to the hand**
    of their masters, *
    and the eyes of a maid to the hand of her mistress,

    so our eyes look to you, O LORD our God, *
    until you show us your mercy.   **R**

3   **Have mercy upon us, O LORD, have mercy, ***
    for we have had more than enough of contempt,

    [Unison]

4   **too much of the scorn of the indolent rich, ***
    and of the derision of the proud.   **R**

Lord, our creator and redeemer,
we look to you for all that we need.
Look with favor on us, your servants,
and give us your grace;
for the sake of your Son, Jesus Christ our Lord.   **Amen.**   [640]

R

1   If the LORD had not been on our side, *
        let Israel now say;

2   **if the LORD had not been on our side, ***
        when enemies rose up against us;

3   then would they have swallowed us up alive *
        in their fierce anger toward us;

4   **then would the waters have overwhelmed us ***
        and the torrent gone over us;

5   then would the raging waters *
        have gone right over us.   **R**

6   **Blessed be the LORD, ***
        who has not given us over to be a prey for their teeth.

7   We have escaped like a bird from the snare of the fowler; *
        the snare is broken, and we have escaped.

8   **Our help is in the name of the LORD, ***
        the maker of heaven and earth.   R

Helper and defender of Israel,
rescue the peoples of the world from destructive anger,
and set us free to love and serve each other
in the peace of Christ our Lord.   **Amen.**   [641]

R

1   Those who trust in the LORD are like Mount Zion, *
        which cannot be moved, but stands fast forever.

2   **The hills stand about Jerusalem; ***
        so does the LORD stand round about the chosen

people,
from this time forth forevermore.

3 The scepter of the wicked shall not hold sway over the land
allotted to the just, *
so that the just shall not put their hands to evil.

4 **Show your goodness, O LORD, to those who are good ***
and to those who are true of heart.

[Unison]

5 **As for those who turn aside to crooked ways,**
the LORD will lead them away with the evildoers; *
but peace be upon Israel.   R

Almighty God,
surround us with your power
and defend us from the forces of evil.
Keep us standing on the solid rock of your Word,
that we may not fall,
but remain upright in your presence;
through the Lord Jesus Christ.   **Amen.**   [642]

PSALM 126   Tone 8; PH 237; PS 130, 131

R

1 When the LORD restored the fortunes of Zion, *
then were we like those who dream.

2 **Then was our mouth filled with laughter, ***
and our tongue with shouts of joy.

Then they said among the nations, *
"The LORD has done great things for them."

3 **The LORD has done great things for us, ***
and we are glad indeed.   R

4 Restore our fortunes, O LORD, *
like the watercourses of the Negev.   ▼

5 Those who sowed with tears *
    will reap with songs of joy.

    [Unison]

6 Those who go out weeping, carrying the seed, *
    will come again with joy,
        shouldering their sheaves.   **R**

Faithful God,
let the seeds of justice,
which we have sown in tears,
grow and increase in your sight.
May we reap in joy the harvest for which we patiently hope;
in Jesus Christ our Lord.   **Amen.**   [643]

PSALM 127   Tone 6; PH 238; PS 132

R

1 Unless the LORD builds the house, *
    their labor is in vain who build it.

    Unless the LORD watches over the city, *
    in vain the sentries keep vigil.

2 It is in vain that you rise so early and go to bed so late; *
    vain, too, to eat the bread of toil,
        for to the beloved the LORD gives sleep.   **R**

3 **Children are a heritage from the LORD, ***
    and the fruit of the womb is a gift.

4 Like arrows in the hand of a warrior *
    are the children of one's youth.

5 **Happy are the warriors with a quiver full of them! ***
    they shall not be put to shame
        when they contend with their enemies in the gate.   R

Lord God,
the land is brought to flower
not with human tears
but with the tears of your Son.
Grant that those who labor for you
may not trust in their own work
but in your help;
through Jesus Christ our Lord.   **Amen.**   [644]

Tone 6; PH 239; PS 133

R

1   Happy are they all who fear the LORD, *
        and who follow in the ways of the LORD!

2   **You, O man, shall eat the fruit of your labor; ***
        happiness and prosperity shall be yours.   R

3   Your wife shall be like a fruitful vine within your house, *
        your children like olive shoots round about your table.

4   **The husband who fears the LORD ***
        shall thus indeed be blessed.   R

5   The LORD bless you from Zion, *
        and may you see the prosperity of Jerusalem all the days
            of your life.

6   **May you live to see your children's children; ***
        may peace be upon Israel.   R

Gracious God,
giver of life in its fullness,
you take no pleasure in human want
but intend your bounty to be shared among your children.
Lead us in the ways of justice and peace,
for Jesus Christ's sake.   **Amen.**   [645]

R

1 Out of the depths have I called to you, O LORD;
  2 LORD, hear my voice; *
    let your ears consider well the voice
      of my supplication.   R

3 **If you, LORD, were to note what is done amiss, ***
  O Lord, who could stand?

4 For there is forgiveness with you; *
  therefore you shall be feared.   R

5 **I wait for you, O LORD; my soul waits for you; ***
  in your word is my hope.

6 My soul waits for the LORD,
  more than sentries for the morning, *
    more than sentries for the morning.   R

7 **O Israel, wait for the LORD, ***
  for with the LORD there is mercy;

[Unison]

8 **there is plenteous redemption with the LORD, ***
  who shall redeem Israel from all their sins.   R

O God,
you come to us in the depths of our darkest despair,
in the suffering of Jesus Christ.
By the rising of your Son,
give us new light to guide us,
that we may always praise your holy name;
through Jesus Christ our Lord. **Amen.** [646]

R

1   O LORD, I am not proud; *
      I have no haughty looks.

   I do not occupy myself with great matters, *
      or with things that are too hard for me.

2   But I still my soul and make it quiet,
      like a child upon its mother's breast; *
         my soul is quieted within me.

3   **O Israel, wait upon the LORD, ***
      from this time forth forevermore.   R

Lord Jesus, gentle and humble of heart,
you promised your kingdom to those who are like children.
Never let pride reign in our hearts.
In compassion embrace all who willingly bear your gentle yoke
now and forever.   **Amen.**   [647]

PSALM 132   Tone 4; PS 136

R

1   LORD, remember David, *
      and all the hardships he endured;

2   **how he swore an oath to the LORD ***
      and vowed a vow to the Mighty One of Jacob:

3   "I will not come under the roof of my house,*
      nor climb up into my bed;

4   **I will not allow my eyes to sleep, ***
      nor let my eyelids slumber;

5   until I find a place for the LORD, *
      a dwelling for the Mighty One of Jacob."   **R**   ▼

6 **"The ark! We heard it was in Ephratah; ***
 we found it in the fields of Jearim.

7 Let us go to God's dwelling place; *
 let us fall upon our knees before God's footstool."

8 **Arise, O LORD, into your resting-place, ***
 you and the ark of your strength.

9 Let your priests be clothed with righteousness; *
 let your faithful people sing with joy.

10 **For your servant David's sake, ***
 do not turn away the face of your anointed. R

11 The LORD has sworn an oath to David, *
 and in truth will not break it:

 "A son, the fruit of your body *
 will I set upon your throne.

12 If your children keep my covenant
 and my testimonies that I shall teach them, *
 their children will sit upon your throne forevermore." R

13 **For the LORD has chosen Zion ***
 and desired it for the holy habitation:

14 "This shall be my resting-place forever; *
 here will I dwell, for in Zion I delight.

15 **I will surely bless the provisions of Zion, ***
 and satisfy its poor with bread.

16 I will clothe its priests with salvation, *
 and its faithful people will rejoice and sing.

17 **There will I make the horn of David flourish; ***
 I have prepared a lamp for my anointed.

 [Unison]

18 **As for his enemies, I will clothe them with shame; ***
 but as for him, his crown will shine." R

Faithful God,
we remember your promises to David,
and how you kept them in Jesus Christ.
Come to dwell among us in Christ,
that we at last may come to dwell with you forever. **Amen.** [648]

PSALM 133   Tone 6; PS 137

R

1   Oh, how good and pleasant it is, *
        when the community lives together in unity!

2   **It is like fine oil upon the head ***
        that runs down upon the beard,

    upon the beard of Aaron, *
        and runs down upon the collar of his robe.

3   **It is like the dew of Hermon ***
        that falls upon the hills of Zion.

    [Unison]

    For there the LORD has ordained the blessing: *
        life forevermore.   R

Creator of the universe,
from whom all things come,
to whom all things return,
give your people such unity of heart and mind,
that all the world may grow in the life of your eternal kingdom;
through Jesus Christ our Lord. **Amen.** [649]

PSALM 134   Tone 2; PH 242; PS 138

R

1   Behold now, bless the LORD, all you servants of the LORD, *
        you that stand by night in the house of the LORD.   ▼

² **Lift up your hands in the holy place and bless the LORD;** *
  ³ **the LORD who made heaven and earth
    bless you out of Zion.**   R

Lord, where two or three gather in your name,
you promise to be with them.
Look upon your family gathered in your name,
and graciously pour out your blessing upon us;
for the sake of Jesus Christ our Lord.   **Amen.**   [650]

PSALM 135   Tone 1 or 3

R

¹ Hallelujah!
  Praise the name of the LORD; *
    give praise, you servants of the LORD,

² **you who stand in the house of the LORD,** *
    in the courts of the house of our God.

³ Praise the LORD, for the LORD is good; *
    sing praises to the name of God, for it is lovely.

⁴ **For the LORD has chosen Jacob** *
    and taken Israel as a possession.   R

⁵ For I know that the LORD is great, *
    and that our Lord is above all gods.

⁶ **The LORD does whatever the LORD wills, in heaven
      and on earth,** *
    in the seas and all the deeps.

⁷ The LORD brings up rain clouds from the ends of the earth, *
    sends out lightning with the rain,
    and brings the winds out of heaven's storehouse.   R

8 **It was the LORD who struck down the firstborn of**
   Egypt, *
   the firstborn both of humans and beasts.

9 The LORD sent signs and wonders into the midst of you,
      O Egypt, *
   against Pharaoh and all his servants.

10 **The LORD overthrew many nations ***
   and put mighty rulers to death:

11 Sihon, king of the Amorites,
   and Og, the king of Bashan, *
   and all the realms of Canaan.

12 **The LORD gave their land to be an inheritance, ***
   an inheritance for Israel, the chosen people.   R

13 O LORD, your name is everlasting; *
   your renown, O LORD, endures from age to age.

14 **For you, O LORD, give your people justice ***
   and show compassion to your servants.   R

15 The idols of the heathen are silver and gold, *
   the work of human hands.

16 **They have mouths, but they cannot speak; ***
   eyes have they, but they cannot see.

17 They have ears, but they cannot hear; *
   neither is there any breath in their mouth.

18 **Those who make them are like them, ***
   and so are all who put their trust in them.   R

19 Bless the LORD, O house of Israel; *
   O house of Aaron, bless the LORD.

20 **Bless the LORD, O house of Levi; ***
   you who fear the LORD, bless the LORD.   ▼

[Unison]

21 **Blessed be the LORD out of Zion, ***
   who dwells in Jerusalem.
   Hallelujah!   R

Deliver us, O God,
from the tyranny of idols;
they cannot give happiness or life;
they bind us to the ways of death.
Claim us as your own
and lead us in the way, the truth, and the life,
Jesus Christ our Lord.   **Amen.**   [651]

PSALM 136   Tone 4; PH 243, 244; PS 139

R

1 Give thanks to the LORD, who is good, *
     for the mercy of God endures forever.

2 **Give thanks to the God of gods, ***
     for the mercy of God endures forever.

3 Give thanks to the Lord of lords, *
     for the mercy of God endures forever.   R

4 **Who only does great wonders, ***
     for the mercy of God endures forever;

5 who by wisdom made the heavens, *
     for the mercy of God endures forever;

6 **who spread out the earth upon the waters, ***
     for the mercy of God endures forever;

7 who created great lights, *
     for the mercy of God endures forever;

8 **the sun to rule the day, ***
     for the mercy of God endures forever;

9 the moon and the stars to govern the night, *
  for the mercy of God endures forever.   R

10 **Who struck down the firstborn of Egypt, ***
   for the mercy of God endures forever;

11 and brought out Israel from among them, *
   for the mercy of God endures forever;

12 **with a mighty hand and a stretched-out arm, ***
   for the mercy of God endures forever;

13 who divided the Red Sea in two, *
   for the mercy of God endures forever;

14 **and made Israel to pass through the midst of it, ***
   for the mercy of God endures forever;

15 but swept Pharaoh and his army into the Red Sea, *
   for the mercy of God endures forever;

16 **who led the chosen people through the wilderness, ***
   for the mercy of God endures forever.   R

17 Who struck down great rulers, *
   for the mercy of God endures forever;

18 **and slew mighty kings, ***
   for the mercy of God endures forever;

19 Sihon, king of the Amorites, *
   for the mercy of God endures forever;

20 **and Og, the king of Bashan, ***
   for the mercy of God endures forever;

21 and gave away their lands for an inheritance, *
   for the mercy of God endures forever;

22 **an inheritance for Israel, the chosen servant, ***
   for the mercy of God endures forever.   R   ▼

23 Who remembered us in our low estate, *
  for the mercy of God endures forever;

24 **and delivered us from our enemies, ***
  for the mercy of God endures forever;

25 who gives food to all creatures, *
  for the mercy of God endures forever.

26 **Give thanks to the God of heaven, ***
  for the mercy of God endures forever.   R

God of everlasting love,
through your Word you made all things
in heaven and on earth;
you have opened to us the path from death to life.
Listen to the song of the universe,
the hymn of resurrection sung by your church,
and give us your blessing;
through Jesus Christ our Lord.   **Amen.**   [652]

PSALM 137   Tone 8; PH 245, 246; PS 140

R

1 By the waters of Babylon we sat down and wept, *
  when we remembered you, O Zion.

2 **As for our harps, we hung them up ***
  on the trees in the midst of that land.

3 For those who led us away captive asked us for a song,
  and our oppressors called for mirth: *
    "Sing us one of the songs of Zion."   **R**

4 **How shall we sing the LORD's song ***
  upon an alien soil.

5 If I forget you, O Jerusalem, *
  let my right hand forget its skill.

6 **Let my tongue cleave to the roof of my mouth**
if I do not remember you, *
   if I do not set Jerusalem above my highest joy.   R

7 Remember the day of Jerusalem, O LORD,
against the people of Edom, *
   who said, "Down with it! down with it!
   even to the ground!"

8 **O city of Babylon, doomed to destruction, ***
   happy the one who pays you back
   for what you have done to us!

[Unison]

9 **Happy shall they be who take your little ones, ***
   and dash them against the rock!   R

God of courage and compassion,
comfort the exiled and oppressed,
strengthen the faith of your people,
and bring us all to our true home,
the kingdom of our Lord and Savior Jesus Christ. **Amen.** [653]

PSALM 138   Tone 3; PH 247; PS 141

R

1 I will give thanks to you, O LORD, with my whole heart; *
   before the gods I will sing your praise.

2 **I will bow down toward your holy temple**
and praise your name, *
   because of your love and faithfulness;

for you have glorified your name *
   and your word above all things.

3 **When I called, you answered me; ***
   you increased my strength within me.   R   ▼

4 All the rulers of the earth will praise you, O LORD, *
    when they have heard the words of your mouth.

5 **They will sing of the ways of the LORD, ***
    that great is the glory of the LORD.

6 The LORD is high, yet the LORD cares for the lowly *
    and perceives the haughty from afar.   **R**

7 **Though I walk in the midst of trouble, you keep me**
    safe; *
    you stretch forth your hand against the fury of my
    enemies;
    your right hand shall save me.

[Unison]

8 **O LORD, you will make good your purpose for me; ***
    O LORD, your love endures forever;
    do not abandon the works of your hands.   **R**

God of creation and fulfillment,
help us to seek and discover your purposes,
that we may become willing instruments of your grace,
and that all the world may come to love and praise your name,
in the kingdom of your Son,
    Jesus Christ our Lord. **Amen.**   [654]

PSALM 139   Tone 6; PH 248; PS 142, 143

R

1 LORD, you have searched me out and known me; *
   2 you know my sitting down and my rising up;
    you discern my thoughts from afar.

3 **You trace my journeys and my resting-places ***
    and are acquainted with all my ways.

4 Indeed, there is not a word on my lips, *
    but you, O LORD, know it altogether.

5 **You press upon me behind and before ***
   and lay your hand upon me.

6 Such knowledge is too wonderful for me; *
   it is so high that I cannot attain to it.   R

7 **Where can I go then from your Spirit? ***
   where can I flee from your presence?

8 If I climb up to heaven, you are there; *
   if I make the grave my bed, you are there also.

9 **If I take the wings of the morning ***
   and dwell in the uttermost parts of the sea,

10 even there your hand will lead me *
   and your right hand hold me fast.

11 **If I say, "Surely the darkness will cover me, ***
   and the light around me turn to night,"

12 darkness is not dark to you;
   the night is as bright as the day; *
      darkness and light to you are both alike.   R

13 **For you yourself created my inmost parts; ***
   you knit me together in my mother's womb.

14 I will thank you because I am marvelously made; *
   your works are wonderful, and I know it well.

15 **My body was not hidden from you, ***
   while I was being made in secret
   and woven in the depths of the earth.

16 Your eyes beheld my limbs, yet unfinished in the womb;
   all of them were written in your book; *
      they were fashioned day by day,
      when as yet there was none of them.

17 **How deep I find your thoughts, O God! ***
   how great is the sum of them!   ▼

18 If I were to count them, they would be more in number
   than the sand; *
      to count them all, my life span would need to be like
      yours.   **R**

19 **Oh, that you would slay the wicked, O God!** *
      You that thirst for blood, depart from me.

20 They speak despitefully against you; *
      your enemies take your name in vain.

21 **Do I not hate those, O LORD, who hate you?** *
      and do I not loathe those who rise up against you?

22 I hate them with a perfect hatred; *
      they have become my own enemies.

23 **Search me out, O God, and know my heart;** *
      try me and know my restless thoughts.

   [Unison]

24 **Look well whether there be any wickedness in me** *
      and lead me in the way that is everlasting.   R

Almighty God, creator of the universe,
we are awed by your wondrous works
and overwhelmed by your infinite wisdom.
For all your majesty we praise you;
yet even more
we rejoice that you do not forget us,
that you want to know us,
that you come to care for us,
sisters and brothers of Jesus Christ, your Son.   **Amen.**   [655]

PSALM 141   Tone 8; PH 249; PS 144, 145

R

1 O LORD, I call to you; come to me quickly; *
      hear my voice when I cry to you.

2 **Let my prayer be set forth in your sight as incense, ***
   the lifting up of my hands as the evening sacrifice.

3 Set a watch before my mouth, O LORD,
   and guard the door of my lips; *
      4 let not my heart incline to any evil thing.

Let me not be occupied in wickedness with evildoers, *
nor eat of their choice foods.   R

5 Let the righteous smite me in friendly rebuke;
   let not the oil of the unrighteous anoint my head; *
      for my prayer is continually against their wicked deeds.

6 **Let their rulers be overthrown in stony places, ***
   that they may know my words are true.

7 As when a plower turns over the earth in furrows, *
   let their bones be scattered at the mouth of the grave.

8 **But my eyes are turned to you, Lord GOD; ***
   in you I take refuge;
   do not strip me of my life.

9 Protect me from the snare which they have laid for me *
   and from the traps of the evildoers.

10 **Let the wicked fall into their own nets, ***
   while I myself escape.   R

Holy God,
let the incense of our prayer ascend before you,
and let your loving-kindness descend upon us,
that with devoted hearts we may sing your praises
with the church on earth and the whole heavenly host,
and glorify you forever and ever.   **Amen.**   [456]

PSALM 142   Tone 8

R

1 I cry to the LORD with my voice; *
   to the LORD I make loud supplication.   ▼

2 **I pour out my complaint before you, O LORD, ***
    and tell you all my trouble.

3 When my spirit languishes within me, you know my path; *
    in the way wherein I walk they have hidden a trap for me.

4 **I look to my right hand and find no one who knows me; ***
    I have no place to flee to, and no one cares for me.   R

5 I cry out to you, O LORD; *
    I say, "You are my refuge,
    my portion in the land of the living."

6 **Listen to my cry for help,**
    for I have been brought very low; *
    save me from those who pursue me,
    for they are too strong for me.

[Unison]

7 **Bring me out of prison, that I may give thanks**
    to your name; *
    when you have dealt bountifully with me,
    the righteous will gather around me.   R

God our refuge,
when all friends have forsaken us
and enemies line all our paths,
come quickly to our aid.
Lead us out from captivity
into the light of your freedom,
secured for us in the sacrifice
of Jesus Christ our Lord. **Amen.**   [656]

PSALM 143   Tone 7; PH 250; PS 146

R

1 LORD, hear my prayer,
    and in your faithfulness heed my supplications; *
    answer me in your righteousness.

2 **Enter not into judgment with your servant, ***
    for in your sight shall no one living be justified.

3 For my enemy has sought my life,
   crushed me to the ground, *
     and made me live in dark places like those who are long
      dead.

4 **My spirit faints within me; ***
    my heart within me is desolate.   **R**

5 I remember the time past;
   I muse upon all your deeds; *
     I consider the works of your hands.

6 **I spread out my hands to you; ***
    my soul gasps to you like a thirsty land.

7 O LORD, make haste to answer me; my spirit fails me; *
     do not hide your face from me
     or I shall be like those who go down to the pit.

8 **Let me hear of your loving-kindness in the morning,**
   for I put my trust in you; *
    show me the road that I must walk,
    for I lift up my soul to you.   **R**

9 Deliver me from my enemies, O LORD, *
     for I flee to you for refuge.

10 **Teach me to do what pleases you, for you are my God; ***
    let your good Spirit lead me on level ground.

11 Revive me, O LORD, for your name's sake; *
     for your righteousness' sake, bring me out of trouble.

12 **Of your goodness, destroy my enemies**
   and bring all my foes to naught, *
    for truly I am your servant.   **R**

God of our hope,
when we are distracted by care and sickness,
help us to recognize your image in ourselves and others,
that we may be made whole
and the world become the kingdom of our Lord and Savior
    Jesus Christ. **Amen.** [657]

PSALM 144   Tone 6

R

1   Blessed be the LORD my rock! *
        who trains my hands to fight and my fingers to battle;

2   **my help and my fortress, my stronghold and my**
            deliverer, *
        my shield in whom I trust,
        who subdues the peoples under me.   R

3   O LORD, what are we that you should care for us? *
        mere mortals that you should think of us?

4   **We are like a puff of wind; ***
        our days are like a passing shadow. R

5   Bow your heavens, O LORD, and come down; *
        touch the mountains, and they shall smoke.

6   **Hurl the lightning and scatter them; ***
        shoot out your arrows and rout them.

7   Stretch out your hand from on high; *
        rescue me and deliver me from the great waters,
        from the hand of foreign peoples,

8   **whose mouths speak deceitfully ***
        and whose right hand is raised in falsehood.   R

9   O God, I will sing to you a new song; *
        I will play to you on a ten-stringed lyre.

10 **You give victory to rulers ***
   and have rescued David your servant.

11 Rescue me from the hurtful sword *
   and deliver me from the hand of foreign peoples,

   whose mouths speak deceitfully *
   and whose right hand is raised in falsehood.   R

12 May our sons be like plants well nurtured from their youth, *
   and our daughters like sculptured corners of a palace.

13 **May our barns be filled to overflowing with all manner**
       of crops; *
   may the flocks in our pastures increase by thousands
       and tens of thousands;
   14**may our cattle be fat and sleek.**

   May there be no breaching of the walls, no going into exile, *
       no wailing in the public squares.

15 **Happy are the people of whom this is so! ***
   happy are the people whose God is the LORD!   R

Generous and bountiful God,
give compassion to the prosperous
and comfort to the needy,
that all people may come to love and praise you;
through Jesus Christ our Lord.   **Amen.**   [658]

PSALM 145   Tone 3; PH 251, 252; PS 147–149

R

1   I will exalt you, O God my Sovereign, *
       and bless your name forever and ever.

2   **Every day will I bless you ***
       and praise your name forever and ever.   ▼

3 Great is the LORD and greatly to be praised; *
 there is no end to your greatness. **R**

4 **One generation shall praise your works to another ***
 and shall declare your power.

5 I will ponder the glorious splendor of your majesty *
 and all your marvelous works.

6 **They shall speak of the might of your wondrous acts, ***
 and I will tell of your greatness.

7 They shall publish the remembrance of your great
 goodness; *
 they shall sing of your righteous deeds.

8 **The LORD is gracious and full of compassion, ***
 slow to anger and of great kindness.

9 O LORD, you are loving to everyone, *
 and your compassion is over all your works. **R**

10 **All your works praise you, O LORD, ***
 and your faithful servants bless you.

11 They make known the glory of your reign *
 and speak of your power;

12 **that the peoples may know of your power ***
 and the glorious splendor of your reign.

13 Your reign is an everlasting reign; *
 your dominion endures throughout all ages.

 O LORD, you are faithful in all your words *
 and merciful in all your deeds. R

14 The LORD upholds all those who fall *
 and lifts up those who are bowed down.

15 **The eyes of all wait upon you, O LORD, ***
 and you give them their food in due season.

¹⁶ You open wide your hand *
  and satisfy the needs of every living creature.   **R**

¹⁷ **O LORD, you are righteous in all your ways ***
  and loving in all your works.

¹⁸ O LORD, you are near to those who call upon you, *
  to all who call upon you faithfully.

¹⁹ **You fulfill the desire of those who fear you; ***
  you hear their cry and help them.

²⁰ O LORD, you preserve all those who love you, *
  but you destroy all the wicked.

²¹ **My mouth shall speak the praise of the LORD; ***
  let all flesh bless your holy name forever and ever.   **R**

Merciful Lord,
you are faithful in all your promises,
and just in all your ways.
Govern us, for we are weak;
strengthen us, for we are failing;
refresh us, for we are famished;
abundantly bestow your gifts upon us.
Defend us from evil,
that we be not tempted from your way,
but may praise your name forever.   **Amen.**   [659]

PSALM 146   Tone 3; PH 253, 254; PS 150–152

R

¹ Hallelujah!
  Praise the LORD, O my soul! *
    ² I will praise the LORD as long as I live;
    I will sing praises to my God while I have my being.   **R**

³ **Put not your trust in rulers, nor in any child of earth, ***
  for there is no help in them.   ▼

4 When they breathe their last, they return to earth, *
       and in that day their thoughts perish.   R

5 **Happy are they who have the God of Jacob for their**
       help! *
       whose hope is in the LORD their God;

6 who made heaven and earth, the seas, and all that is in them; *
       who keeps faith forever;

7 **who gives justice to those who are oppressed,** *
       and food to those who hunger.   R

   The LORD sets the prisoners free;
8 the LORD opens the eyes of the blind; *
       the LORD lifts up those who are bowed down;

   the LORD loves the righteous
9 **and cares for the stranger;** *
       the LORD sustains the orphan and widow,
       but frustrates the way of the wicked.   R

   [Unison]

10 **The LORD shall reign forever,** *
       your God, O Zion, throughout all generations.
       Hallelujah!   R

Blessed are those who put their trust in you, O God,
our sure rock and refuge.
Guard us from giving to any other
the allegiance which belongs only to you.
Shine upon us with the brightness of your light,
that we may love you with a pure heart
and praise you forever;
through Jesus Christ our Lord.   **Amen.**   [660]

R

1 Hallelujah!
 How good it is to sing praises to our God! *
   how pleasant it is to honor the LORD with praise!

2 **The LORD rebuilds Jerusalem** *
   and gathers the exiles of Israel.

3 The LORD heals the brokenhearted *
   and binds up their wounds.

4 **The LORD counts the number of the stars** *
   and calls them all by their names.

5 Great is our Lord and mighty in power, *
   whose wisdom is beyond limit.

6 **The LORD lifts up the lowly,** *
   but casts the wicked to the ground.   R

7 Sing to the LORD with thanksgiving; *
   make music to our God upon the harp.

8 **God covers the heavens with clouds** *
   and prepares rain for the earth;

 God makes grass to grow upon the mountains *
   and green plants to serve humankind.

9 **God provides food for flocks and herds** *
   and for the young ravens when they cry.

10 The LORD is not impressed by the might of a horse *
   and has no pleasure in the strength of a man;

11 **but the LORD has pleasure in the God-fearing,** *
   in those who await God's gracious favor.   R

12 Worship the LORD, O Jerusalem; *
   praise your God, O Zion;   ▼

13 **for God has strengthened the bars of your gates ***
and blessed your children within you.

14 God has established peace on your borders *
and satisfies you with the finest wheat. **R**

15 **God's command is sent out to the earth, ***
and the word of the LORD runs very swiftly.

16 God gives snow like wool *
and scatters hoarfrost like ashes.

17 **God scatters hail like bread crumbs; ***
who can stand against the cold of the LORD?

18 God's word is sent forth and melts them; *
God's stormwinds blow, and the waters flow.

19 **God's word is declared to Jacob, ***
God's statutes and judgments to Israel.

[Unison]

20 **The LORD has not done so to any other nation; ***
to them God's judgments have not been revealed.
Hallelujah! R

Psalm 147:1–11

Loving God,
great builder of the heavenly Jerusalem,
you know the number of the stars
and call them by name.
Heal hearts that are broken,
gather those who have been scattered,
and enrich us all from the fullness of your eternal wisdom,
Jesus Christ our Lord. **Amen.** [661]

Psalm 147:12–20

O Lord,
marvelous is your might

by which you cast down the proud
and lift up the humble.
Restore and rebuild your church.
Gather your scattered sheep
and nourish us by your holy Word,
that we may follow your will
and come at last to the heritage
prepared for us in Christ Jesus.   **Amen.**   [662]

PSALM 148   Tone 1 or 3; PH 256; PS 155

R

1   Hallelujah!
    Praise the LORD from the heavens; *
        praise the LORD in the heights.

2   **Praise the LORD, all you holy angels; ***
        praise the LORD, all heavenly host.   R

3   Praise the LORD, sun and moon; *
        praise the LORD, all you shining stars.

4   **Praise the LORD, heaven of heavens, ***
        and you waters above the heavens.

5   Let them praise the name of the LORD, *
        who commanded, and they were created.

6   **The LORD made them stand fast forever and ever ***
        and gave them a law which shall not pass away.   R

7   Praise the LORD from the earth, *
        you sea-monsters and all deeps;

8   **fire and hail, snow and fog, ***
        tempestuous wind, obeying God's will;

9   mountains and all hills, *
        fruit trees and all cedars;   ▼

10 **wild beasts and all cattle,** *
   creeping things and winged birds;

11 kings of the earth and all peoples, *
   rulers and all judges of the world;

12 **young men and women,** *
   old and young together.   R

13 Let them praise the name of the LORD, *
   for the name of the LORD only is exalted,
   and the splendor of the LORD is over earth and heaven.

14 **The LORD has raised up strength for the chosen people**
   and praise for all loyal servants, *
   the children of Israel, a people who are near to the
      LORD.
   Hallelujah!   R

God Most High,
by your Word you created a wondrous universe,
and through your Spirit
you breathed into it the breath of life.
Accept creation's hymn of praise from our lips,
and let the praise that is sung in heaven
resound in the heart of every creature on earth,
to the glory of the Father, and the Son, and the Holy Spirit,
now and forever.   **Amen.**   [663]

PSALM 149   Tone 1 or 3; PH 257; PS 156

R

1 Hallelujah!
   Sing to the LORD a new song; *
      sing praise to God in the congregation of the faithful.

2 **Let Israel rejoice in their Maker;** *
   let the children of Zion be joyful in their Sovereign.

3 Let them praise God's name in the dance; *
   let them sing praise to the LORD with timbrel and harp.

4 **For the LORD takes pleasure in the chosen people ***
   and adorns the poor with victory.

5 Let the faithful rejoice in triumph; *
   let them be joyful on their beds.

6 **Let the praises of God be in their throat ***
   and a two-edged sword in their hand;   R

7 to wreak vengeance on the nations *
   and punishment on the peoples;

8 **to bind their rulers in chains ***
   and their nobles with links of iron;

   [Unison]

9 **to inflict on them the judgment decreed; ***
   this is glory for all God's faithful people.
   Hallelujah!   R

God our Maker,
you crown the humble with honor
and exalt the faithful who gather in your name.
Because you have favored us with life,
we dance before you in our joy
and praise you with unending song
for Jesus Christ our Lord.   **Amen.**   [664]

PSALM 150   Tone 1 or 3; PH 258; PS 157

R

1 Hallelujah!
   Praise God in the holy temple; *
      give praise in the firmament of heaven.   ▼

2 **Praise God who is mighty in deed; ***
   give praise for God's excellent greatness.   R

3 Praise God with the blast of the ram's-horn; *
   give praise with lyre and harp.

4 **Praise God with timbrel and dance; ***
   give praise with strings and pipe.

5 Praise God with resounding cymbals; *
   give praise with loud-clanging cymbals.

6 **Let everything that has breath ***
   praise the LORD.
   Hallelujah!   R

Great and glorious God,
in your wisdom you created us,
in Jesus Christ you came to redeem us,
and through your Holy Spirit you guide and sanctify us.
Give us breath to sing of your majesty,
and with all creation,
praise you as the true life of all;
through Jesus Christ,
who reigns with you and the Holy Spirit;
one God forever.   **Amen.**   [665]

Prayers
for Various
Occasions

THE GREAT LITANY

The Great Litany is appropriate for times of special petition or supplication. It may be sung or said. In daily prayer, there is a tradition that it is to be used as a separate service on all Wednesdays and Fridays of Lent beginning the Friday after Ash Wednesday until Palm Sunday. There is a long tradition of singing the Great Litany in procession on Sundays of Advent and Lent, and at penitential times. If the entire litany is not used, the Prayer of Approach to God and the Concluding Prayers are used, but a selection of appropriate petitions may be made from the remaining sections.

PRAYER OF APPROACH TO GOD

O God the Father, creator of heaven and earth,

Have mercy on us.

O God the Son, redeemer of the world,

Have mercy on us.

O God the Holy Spirit, advocate and guide,

Have mercy on us.

Holy, blessed, and glorious Trinity,
three persons and one God,

Have mercy on us. ▼

Remember not, Lord Christ, our offenses,
nor the offenses of our forebears.
Spare us, good Lord,
spare your people whom you have redeemed with your
  precious blood.

Spare us, good Lord.

From all spiritual blindness;
from pride, vainglory, and hypocrisy;
from envy, hatred, and malice;
and from all want of charity,

Good Lord, deliver us.

From all deadly sin;
and from the deceits of the world,
the flesh, and the devil,

Good Lord, deliver us.

From all false doctrine, heresy, and schism;
from hardness of heart,
and contempt for your Word and commandments,

Good Lord, deliver us.

From earthquake and tempest;
from drought, fire, and flood;
from civil strife and violence;
from war and murder;
and from dying suddenly and unprepared,

Good Lord, deliver us.

PRAYER RECALLING CHRIST'S SAVING WORK

By the mystery of your holy incarnation,
by your baptism, fasting, and temptation;
and by your proclamation of the kingdom,

Good Lord, deliver us.

By your bloody sweat and bitter grief;
by your cross and suffering;
and by your precious death and burial,

Good Lord, deliver us.

By your mighty resurrection;
by your glorious ascension;
and by the coming of the Holy Spirit,

Good Lord, deliver us.

In our times of trouble;
in our times of prosperity;
in the hour of death,
and on the day of judgment,

Good Lord, deliver us.

Prayers of Intercession

Receive our prayers, O Lord our God.

Hear us, good Lord.

For the church

Govern and direct your holy church;
fill it with love and truth;
and grant it that unity which is your will.

Hear us, good Lord.

Enlighten all ministers
with true knowledge and understanding of your Word,
that by their preaching and living
they may declare it clearly
and show its truth.

Hear us, good Lord.

Encourage and prosper your servants
who spread the gospel in all the world,
and send out laborers into the harvest.

Hear us, good Lord.   ▼

Bless and keep your people,
that all may find and follow their true vocation
  and ministry.

Hear us, good Lord.

Give us a heart to love and reverence you,
that we may diligently live according to your
  commandments.

Hear us, good Lord.

To all your people
give grace to hear and receive your Word,
and to bring forth the fruit of the Spirit.

Hear us, good Lord.

Strengthen those who stand firm in the faith,
encourage the fainthearted,
raise up those who fall,
and finally give us the victory.

Hear us, good Lord.

For our country

Rule the hearts of your servants,
the President of the United States (*or* of this nation),
and all others in authority,
that they may do justice, and love mercy,
and walk in the ways of truth.

Hear us, good Lord.

Bless and defend all who strive for our safety and protection,
and shield them in all dangers and adversities.

Hear us, good Lord.

Grant wisdom and insight to those who govern us,
and to judges and magistrates the grace to execute justice
  with mercy.

Hear us, good Lord.

For all people

To all nations grant unity, peace, and concord,
and to all people give dignity, food, and shelter.

Hear us, good Lord.

Grant us abundant harvests,
strength and skill to conserve the resources of the earth,
and wisdom to use them well.

Hear us, good Lord.

Enlighten with your Spirit all who teach
and all who learn.

Hear us, good Lord.

Come to the help of all who are in danger, necessity, and
    trouble;
protect all who travel by land, air, or water;
and show your pity on all prisoners and captives.

Hear us, good Lord.

Strengthen and preserve all women who are in childbirth,
and all young children,
and comfort the aged, the bereaved, and the lonely.

Hear us, good Lord.

Defend and provide for the widowed and the orphaned,
the refugees and the homeless,
the unemployed,
and all who are desolate and oppressed.

Hear us, good Lord.

Heal those who are sick in body or mind,
and give skill and compassion to all who care for them.

Hear us, good Lord.

Grant us true repentance,
forgive our sins,
and strengthen us by your Holy Spirit
to amend our lives according to your Holy Word.

Hear us, good Lord. ▼

Son of God, we ask you to hear us.

Son of God, we ask you to hear us.

Lamb of God, you take away the sin of the world,

have mercy on us.

Lamb of God, you take away the sin of the world,

have mercy on us.

Lamb of God, you take away the sin of the world,

grant us peace.

Lord, have mercy on us.

Christ, have mercy on us.

Lord, have mercy on us.   [666]

> The Lord's Prayer is said, unless the Lord's Supper is to follow.

> The Litany concludes with the following or some other collect.

Let us pray.

Almighty God,
you have given us grace at this time with one accord
to make our common supplication to you;
and you have promised through your beloved Son
that when two or three are gathered together in his name
you will be in the midst of them.
Fulfill now, O Lord, our desires and petitions
as may be best for us;
granting us in this world knowledge of your truth,
and in the age to come life everlasting.   **Amen.**   [96]

LITANIES AND PRAYERS
FOR VARIOUS OCCASIONS

LITANY

PRAYERS OF THE PEOPLE: E

This litany is based on litanies from the Eastern liturgies of St. Basil and St. John Chrysostom. It may be sung using the following musical setting.

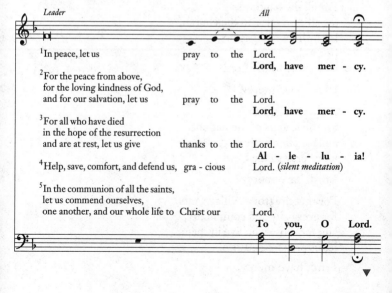

1 In peace, let us pray to the Lord.
Lord, have mer - cy.

2 For the peace from above,
for the loving kindness of God,
and for our salvation, let us pray to the Lord.
Lord, have mer - cy.

3 For all who have died
in the hope of the resurrection
and are at rest, let us give thanks to the Lord.
Al - le - lu - ia!

4 Help, save, comfort, and defend us, gra - cious Lord. (*silent meditation*)

5 In the communion of all the saints,
let us commend ourselves,
one another, and our whole life to Christ our Lord.
To you, O Lord.

[1]In peace, let us pray to the Lord.

Lord, have mercy.

[2]For the peace from above,
for the loving kindness of God,
and for our salvation,
let us pray to the Lord.

Lord, have mercy.

For the peace of the world,
for the unity of the church of God,
and for the well-being of all peoples,
let us pray to the Lord.

Lord, have mercy.

For this gathering of the faithful,
and for all who offer here their worship and praise,
let us pray to the Lord.

Lord, have mercy.

For all the baptized,
for all who serve in the church,
for bishops and pastors,
[for N.],
let us pray to the Lord.

Lord, have mercy.

For our president,
for the leaders of the nations,
and for all in authority,
let us pray to the Lord.

Lord, have mercy.

For this city (town, village, etc.),
for every city and community,
and for those who live in them,
let us pray to the Lord.

Lord, have mercy.

For seasonable weather,
and for abundant harvests for all to share,
let us pray to the Lord.

Lord, have mercy.

For the good earth which God has given us,
and for the wisdom and will to conserve it,
let us pray to the Lord.

Lord, have mercy.

For those who travel by land, water, or air
[or through outer space],
let us pray to the Lord.

Lord, have mercy.

For the aged and infirm,
for the widowed and orphaned,
and for the sick and the suffering,
let us pray to the Lord.

Lord, have mercy.

For the poor and the oppressed,
for those unemployed and the destitute,
for prisoners and captives,
and for all who remember and care for them,
let us pray to the Lord.

Lord, have mercy.

For deliverance in times of affliction,
strife, and need,
let us pray to the Lord.

Lord, have mercy.

Other petitions may be added.

For_____,
let us pray to the Lord.

Lord, have mercy. ▼

Here follows commemoration of those who have died in the faith:

³For all who have died in the hope of the resurrection
and are at rest,
let us give thanks to the Lord.

Alleluia! (*Lent:* **To you, O Lord.**)

⁴Help, save, comfort, and defend us, gracious Lord.

Pause for silent prayer.

⁵In the communion of all the saints,
let us commend ourselves,
one another,
and our whole life to Christ our Lord.   [95]

To you, O Lord.

After a brief silence, the leader concludes the prayers
with the following prayer. The prayer may be spoken,
even though the litany itself is sung.

Almighty God,
you have given us grace at this time with one accord
to make our common supplication to you;
and you have promised through your beloved Son
that when two or three are gathered together in his name
you will be in the midst of them.
Fulfill now, O Lord, our desires and petitions
as may be best for us,
granting us in this world knowledge of your truth,
and in the age to come life everlasting.   **Amen.**   [96]

A LITANY OF THANKSGIVING

Give thanks to the Lord who is good.

God's love is everlasting.

Come, let us praise God joyfully.

Let us come to God with thanksgiving.

For the good world;
for things great and small, beautiful and awesome;
for seen and unseen splendors;

Thank you, God.

For human life;
for talking and moving and thinking together;
for common hopes and hardships shared
    from birth until our dying;

Thank you, God.

For work to do and strength to work;
for the comradeship of labor;
for exchanges of good humor and encouragement;

Thank you, God.

For marriage;
for the mystery and joy of flesh made one;
for mutual forgiveness and burdens shared;
for secrets kept in love;

Thank you, God.

For family;
for living together and eating together;
for family amusements and family pleasures;

Thank you, God.

For children;
for their energy and curiosity;
for their brave play and startling frankness;
for their sudden sympathies;

Thank you, God.

For the young;
for their high hopes;
for their irreverence toward worn-out values;
for their search for freedom;
for their solemn vows;

Thank you, God. ▼

For growing up and growing old;
for wisdom deepened by experience;
for rest in leisure;
and for time made precious by its passing;

Thank you, God.

For your help in times of doubt and sorrow;
for healing our diseases;
for preserving us in temptation and danger;

Thank you, God.

For the church into which we have been called;
for the good news we receive by Word and Sacrament;
for our life together in the Lord;

We praise you, God.

For your Holy Spirit,
who guides our steps and brings us gifts of faith and love;
who prays in us and prompts our grateful worship;

We praise you, God.

Above all, O God, for your Son Jesus Christ,
who lived and died and lives again for our salvation;
for our hope in him;
and for the joy of serving him;

**We thank and praise you, Eternal God,
for all your goodness to us.**

Give thanks to the Lord, who is good.

God's love is everlasting.   [667]

A LITANY OF CONFESSION

Almighty God: you alone are good and holy.
Purify our lives and make us brave disciples.
We do not ask you to keep us safe,

but to keep us loyal,
so we may serve Jesus Christ,
who, tempted in every way as we are,
was faithful to you.

Amen.

From lack of reverence for truth and beauty;
from a calculating or sentimental mind;
from going along with mean and ugly things;

O God, deliver us.

From cowardice that dares not face truth;
laziness content with half-truth;
or arrogance that thinks we know it all;

O God, deliver us.

From artificial life and worship;
from all that is hollow or insincere;

O God, deliver us.

From trite ideals and cheap pleasures;
from mistaking hard vulgarity for humor;

O God, deliver us.

From being dull, pompous, or rude;
from putting down our neighbors;

O God, deliver us.

From cynicism about others;
from intolerance or cruel indifference;

O God, deliver us.

From being satisfied with things as they are,
in the church or in the world;
from failing to share your indignation about injustice;

O God, deliver us. ▼

From selfishness, self-indulgence, or self-pity;

O God, deliver us.

From token concern for the poor,
for lonely or loveless people;
from confusing faith with good feeling,
or love with wanting to be loved;

O God, deliver us.

For everything in us that may hide your light;

O God, light of life, forgive us. [668]

PRAYERS FOR THE WORLD

1

For Peace

Eternal God,
in your perfect realm no sword is drawn
but the sword of righteousness,
and there is no strength but the strength of love.
So mightily spread abroad your Spirit,
that all peoples may be gathered
under the banner of the Prince of Peace,
as your children;
to you be dominion and glory,
now and forever. **Amen.** [669]

2

For Peace   *Brother Roger of Taizé*

Lord Christ,
at times we are like strangers on this earth,
taken aback by all the violence, the harsh oppositions.
Like a gentle breeze, you breathe upon us the Spirit of peace.
Transfigure the deserts of our doubts,
and so prepare us to be bearers of reconciliation
wherever you place us,
until the day when a hope of peace
dawns in our world. **Amen.** [670]

3

For Racial Peace

Great God over us all,
destroy prejudice that turns us against one another.
Teach us that we are all children of your love,
whether we are black or red or white or yellow.
Encourage us to live together,
loving one another in peace,
so that someday a golden race of people
may have the world,
giving praise to Jesus Christ our Lord.   **Amen.**   [671]

4

For Racial and Cultural Diversity

O God,
you created all people in your image.
We thank you for the astonishing variety
of races and cultures in this world.
Enrich our lives by ever-widening circles of friendship,
and show us your presence in those who differ most from us,
until our knowledge of your love is made perfect
in our love for all your children;
through your Son, Jesus Christ our Lord.   **Amen.**   [672]

5

For Peace Among Nations

Almighty God,
guide the nations of the world into ways of justice and truth,
and establish among them that peace
which is the fruit of righteousness,
that they may become the kingdom
of our Lord and Savior Jesus Christ.   **Amen.**   [673]

6

For Hope   *A prayer of the Chippewa*

We pray that someday an arrow will be broken,
not in something or someone,   ▼

but by each of humankind,
to indicate peace, not violence.
Someday, oneness with creation,
rather than domination over creation,
will be the goal to be respected.
Someday fearlessness to love and make a difference
will be experienced by all people.
Then the eagle will carry our prayer for peace and love,
and the people of the red, white, yellow, brown,
and black communities
can sit in the same circle together to communicate in love
and experience the presence of the Great Mystery in their
    midst.
Someday can be today for you and me.   **Amen.**   [674]

7

For the Human Family

O God, you made us in your own image
and redeemed us through Jesus your Son.
Look with compassion on the whole human family,
take away the arrogance and hatred that infect our hearts,
break down the walls that separate us,
unite us in bonds of love,
and, through our struggle and confusion,
work to accomplish your purposes on earth;
that, in your good time,
all nations and races may serve you in harmony
around your heavenly throne;
through Jesus Christ our Lord.   **Amen.**   [675]

8

For World Community

Almighty God,
in Jesus Christ you have ordered us
to live as loving neighbors.
Though we are scattered in different places,

speak different words,
or descend from different races,
give us common concern,
so that we may be one people,
who share the governing of the world
under your guiding purpose.
May greed, war, and lust for power be curbed,
and all people enter the community of love
promised in Jesus Christ our Lord. **Amen.** [676]

9

For World Unity *A prayer from Zaire*

O God,
you love justice and you establish peace on earth.
We bring before you the disunity of today's world:
the absurd violence, and the many wars,
which are breaking the courage of the peoples of the world;
militarism and the armaments race,
which are threatening life on the planet;
human greed and injustice,
which breed hatred and strife.
Send your Spirit and renew the face of the earth;
teach us to be compassionate toward the whole human family;
strengthen the will of all those who fight for justice and for
    peace;
lead all nations into the path of peace,
and give us that peace which the world cannot give.
                         Amen. [677]

10

For World Religions

We thank you, God of the universe,
that you call all people to worship you
and to serve your purpose in this world.
We praise you for the gift of faith
we have received in Jesus Christ. ▼

We praise you also for diverse faith
among the peoples of the earth.
For you have bestowed your grace
that Christians, Jews, Muslims,
Buddhists, and others
may celebrate your goodness,
act upon your truth,
and demonstrate your righteousness.
In wonder and awe
we praise you great God.   **Amen.**   [678]

11

For International Organizations

From the Mainau Prayerbook

O God,
we pray for all international organizations of goodwill,
that their efforts may lead to a strengthening
of those influences which make for peace.
Great sacrifices have been made for war;
awaken in us and in all people, O God,
the willingness to make great sacrifices for peace,
so that the day may be hastened
when no nation shall draw the sword against another,
and people no longer shall learn to fight.
We ask in the name of him who is the Prince of Peace.
                                        Amen.   [679]

12

For Governments of the World

High God, holy God:
you rule the ways of peoples,
and govern every earthly government.
Work with those who work for peace.
Make every person in authority an agent of your
    reconciliation,

and every diplomat an ambassador of hope.
Bring peace and goodwill among all people,
fulfilling among us the promise made
in Jesus Christ, who was born to save the world.
Amen. [680]

13

In a Time of International Crisis

Eternal God, our only hope,
our help in times of trouble:
show nations ways to work out differences.
Do not let threats multiply
or power be used without compassion.
May your will overrule human willfulness,
so that people may agree and settle claims peacefully.
Hold back those who are impulsive,
lest desire for vengeance overwhelm our common welfare.
Bring peace to earth, through Jesus Christ,
the Prince of Peace and Savior of us all. **Amen.** [681]

PRAYERS FOR THE NATURAL ORDER

14

For Creation   *A prayer from Samoa*

Almighty God, your word of creation
caused the water to be filled
with many kinds of living beings
and the air to be filled with birds.
We rejoice in the richness of your creation,
and we pray for your wisdom
for all who live on this earth,
that we may wisely manage and not destroy what you have
  made
for us and for our descendants.
In Jesus' name we pray. **Amen.** [682]

15

For Creation   *"Canticle of the Sun"—Francis of Assisi*

O Most High, Almighty, good Lord God,
to you belong praise, glory, honor, and blessing!

Praised be my Lord God for all creatures,
and especially for our brother the sun,
who brings us the day and who brings us the light;
fair is he and shines with a very great splendor;
O Lord, he signifies you to us.

Praised be my Lord for our sister the moon,
and for the stars,
which you have set clear and lovely in heaven.

Praised be my Lord for our brother the wind,
and for air and cloud, calms and all weather,
by which you uphold life in all creatures.

Praised be my Lord for our sister water,
who is very useful to us and humble
and precious and clean.

Praised be my Lord for our brother fire,
through whom you give us light in the darkness
and he is very bright and pleasant
and very mighty and strong.

Praised be my Lord for our mother the earth,
which sustains and keeps us
and brings forth many diverse fruits
and flowers of many colors, and grass.

Praised be my Lord for all those
who pardon one another for love's sake,
and who endure weakness and tribulation;
blessed are those who endure peaceably,
for you, O Most High, will give them a crown.

Praised be my Lord for our sister,
the death of the body, from which no one can escape.
Woe to those who die in mortal sin!

Blessed are those who are found to be in your most holy will,
for the second death shall have no power to do them harm.

Praise and bless the Lord, and give thanks.
Serve the Lord with humility.   **Amen.**   [683]

16

For Fruits of the Earth

Almighty God,
we thank you for making the fruitful earth produce
what is needed for life.
Bless those who work in the fields;
give us favorable weather;
and grant that we may all share the fruits of the earth,
rejoicing in your goodness;
through your Son, Jesus Christ our Lord.   **Amen.**   [684]

17

For the Harvest

Most gracious God,
according to your wisdom
deep waters are opened up
and clouds drop gentle moisture.
We praise you for the return of planting and harvest seasons,
for the fertility of the soil,
for the harvesting of crops,
and for all other blessings
which you in your generosity pour on this nation and people.
Give us a full understanding of your mercy,
and lives which will be respectful,
holy, and obedient to you throughout all our days;
through Jesus Christ our Lord.   **Amen.**   [685]

18

When There Is a Natural Disaster

God of earthquake, wind, and fire,
tame natural forces that defy control,
or shock us by their fury.   ▼

Keep us from calling disaster your justice;
and help us, in good times or in calamity,
to trust your mercy which never ends,
and your power,
which in Jesus Christ stilled storms,
raised the dead,
and put down demonic powers.   **Amen.**   [686]

19

For Natural Resources

Almighty God,
in giving us dominion over things on earth,
you made us co-workers in your creation.
Give us wisdom and reverence
to use the resources of nature,
so that no one may suffer from our abuse of them,
and that generations yet to come
may continue to praise you for your bounty;
through your Son, Jesus Christ our Lord.   **Amen.**   [687]

20

For Nature

We give you thanks, most gracious God,
for the beauty of earth and sky and sea;
for the richness of mountains, plains, and rivers;
for the songs of birds
and the loveliness of flowers.
We praise you for these good gifts,
and pray that we may safeguard them for our posterity.
Grant that we may continue to grow
in our grateful enjoyment of your abundant creation,
to the honor and glory of your name,
now and forever.   **Amen.**   [688]

21

For Nature   *Fyodor Mikhailovich Dostoevsky (1821–1881)*

Lord, may we love all your creation,
all the earth and every grain of sand in it.
May we love every leaf, every ray of your light.

May we love the animals;
you have given them the rudiments of thought and joy
    untroubled.
Let us not trouble it;
let us not harass them,
let us not deprive them of their happiness,
let us not work against your intent.

For we acknowledge unto you that all is like an ocean,
all is flowing and blending,
and that to withhold any measure of love from anything in
    your universe
is to withhold that same measure from you.   **Amen.** [689]

22

For a Right Use of Nature's Power

Mighty God,
your power fills heaven and earth,
is hidden in atoms
and flung from the sun.
Control us
so that we may never turn natural forces to destruction,
or arm nations with cosmic energy;
but guide us with wisdom and love,
so that we may tame power to good purpose,
for the building of human community
and the betterment of our common lives;
through Jesus Christ our Lord.   **Amen.** [690]

PRAYERS FOR THE CHURCH
AND OTHER PEOPLE OF FAITH

23

For the Church

Almighty and ever-living God,
ruler of all things in heaven and earth,
hear our prayers for this congregation.
Strengthen the faithful,
arouse the careless,
and restore the penitent.
Grant us all things necessary for our common life,
and bring us all to be of one heart and mind
within your holy church;
through Jesus Christ our Lord.   **Amen.**   [691]

24

For the Proclamation of the Gospel

By your word, O God, your creation sprang forth,
and we were given the breath of life.
By your word, eternal God,
death is overcome,
Christ is raised from the tomb,
and we are given a new life in the power of your Spirit.
May we boldly proclaim this good news,
by the words of our mouths
and the deeds of our lives,
rejoicing always in your powerful presence;
through Jesus Christ our risen Lord.   **Amen.**   [692]

25

For a New Church Building

Eternal God, high and holy,
no building can contain your glory
or display the wonders of your love.

May this space be used as
a gathering place for people of goodwill.
When we worship, let us worship gladly;
when we study, let us learn your truth.
May every meeting held here
meet with your approval,
so that this building may stand
as a sign of your Spirit at work in the world,
and as a witness to our Lord and Savior,
Jesus Christ.   **Amen.**   [693]

26

For Founders and Previous Leaders of a Congregation

We thank you, Lord God,
for brave and believing people
who brought your message to this place.
Let us not forget them,
especially N., N.
By their energies this church was gathered,
given order, and continued.
Remembering all those Christians who have gone before us,
may we follow as they followed,
in the way, truth, and life of Jesus Christ,
the head of the church.   **Amen.**   [694]

27

For an Inclusive Church

How great is your love, Lord God,
how wide is your mercy!
Never let us board up the narrow gate that leads to life
with rules or doctrines that you dismiss;
but give us a Spirit to welcome all people with affection,
so that your church may never exclude secret friends of yours,
who are included in the love of Jesus Christ,
who came to save us all.   **Amen.**   [695]

28

For a Meeting of the General Assembly, Synod, or Presbytery

Almighty God,
in Jesus Christ you called disciples
and, by the Holy Spirit, made them one church to serve you.
Be with members of our *General Assembly/synod/presbytery*.
Help them to welcome new things you are doing in the
    world,
and to respect old things you keep and use.
Save them from empty slogans or senseless controversy.
In their deciding,
determine what is good for us and for all people.
As this *General Assembly/synod/presbytery* meets,
let your Spirit rule,
so that our church may be joined in love and service to
    Jesus Christ,
who, having gone before us,
is coming to meet us in the promise of your kingdom.
                                Amen.   [696]

29

For a Church Meeting

Eternal God, you called us to be a special people,
to preach the gospel and show mercy.
Keep your Spirit with us as we meet together,
so that in everything we may do your will.
Guide us lest we stumble
or be misguided by our own desires.
May all we do be done
for the reconciling of the world,
for the upbuilding of the church,
and for the greater glory
    of Jesus Christ our Lord.   **Amen.**   [697]

30

For New Church Members

Almighty God, by the love of Jesus Christ you draw people
    to faith,
and welcome them into the church family.
May we show your joy by embracing new brothers and
    sisters,
who with us believe
and with us will work to serve you.
Keep us close together in your Spirit,
breaking bread in faith and love,
one with Jesus Christ our Lord and Master. **Amen.** [698]

31

For the Mission of the Church

By your will, O God,
we go out into the world
with good news of your undying love,
and minister in the midst of human need
to show wonders of your grace.
We pray for men and women
who minister for you in _____.
May they be strengthened by our concern,
and supported by our gifts.
Do not let them be discouraged,
but make them brave and glad and hopeful in your word;
through Jesus Christ the Lord. **Amen.** [699]

32

For the Mission of the Church

Almighty God, you sent your Son Jesus Christ
to reconcile the world to yourself.
We praise and bless you
for those whom you have sent in the power of the Spirit
to preach the gospel to all nations. ▼

We thank you that in all parts of the earth
a community of love has been gathered together
by their prayers and labors,
and that in every place your servants call upon your name;
for the kingdom and the power and the glory
are yours forever. **Amen.** [700]

33

For Trust

Loving God,
you want us to give thanks for all things,
to fear nothing except losing you,
and to lay all our cares on you,
knowing that you care for us. ▼
Protect us from faithless fears and worldly anxieties,
and grant that no clouds in this mortal life
may hide from us the light of your immortal love
shown to us in your Son,
Jesus Christ our Lord. **Amen.** [701]

34

For Courage in Christ's Mission   *Toyohiko Kagawa*
(1888–1960)

O God, show us clearly the heart of the kingdom of God.
We do not protest
even if our life is destined to lead to the cross,
or if the way leads to our losing our lives.
We will march in the face of distress and contrary winds.
Teach us how to dispense with unnecessary things.
Let us go forward without fear of death
in order to fulfill our mission simply, surely, and steadily.
Reveal to us our station clearly,
and strengthen us to teach and guide, by our example, all
persons,
even those who are ruled by evil.
We pray that you may find us worthy to work through us.
Amen. [702]

35

For a Moderator

Almighty God,
you called us into the church,
and from among us chose leaders to direct us in your way.
We thank you for N., our Moderator.
Enlarge *his/her* gifts
and help *him/her* to obey you,
so that we may enjoy good work under *his/her* guidance,
loyally serving Jesus Christ the Lord.   **Amen.**   [703]

36

For Church Musicians and Artists

God of majesty,
whom saints and angels delight to worship in heaven:
Be with your servants who make art and music
    for your people,
that with joy we on earth may glimpse your beauty,
and bring us to the fulfillment of that hope of perfection
which will be ours as we stand before your unveiled glory.
We pray in the name of Jesus Christ our Lord.   **Amen.**   [704]

37

For Church Musicians and Artists

God of life,
you filled the world with beauty.
Thank you for artists who see clearly,
who with trained skill
can paint, shape, or sing your truth to us.
Keep them attentive
and ready to applaud the wonder of your works,
finding in the world signs of the love
revealed in Jesus Christ our Lord.   **Amen.**   [705]

38

For Deacons in the Church

God of love and compassion,
you poured out your life in service
in your Son, Jesus Christ.
By word and example he taught us
to find fulfillment in giving ourselves,
and greatness in serving others.
Bless those called to be deacons,
who lead us in service and caring.
Empower them by the grace of your Spirit,
that your whole church may give its life for the sake of the
    world,
in the name of Jesus Christ
who came not to be served, but to serve. **Amen.**   [706]

39

For Ministers of the Word and Sacrament

Almighty God,
through your Son Jesus Christ
you gave the holy apostles many gifts
and commanded them to feed your flock.
Inspire all pastors to preach your Word diligently
and your people to receive it willingly,
that finally we may receive the crown of eternal glory;
through Jesus Christ our Lord. **Amen.**   [707]

40

For Elders in the Church

God of righteousness and truth,
you brought us into your church
to show in our life together
something of the orderliness of your creation,
and the love of Jesus Christ.
Bless those called to be elders,
that they may govern wisely and fairly.

Give them full measure of your Spirit,
that they may refresh your people
along the journey of faith,
discerning, teaching, and sharing the Word of life,
Jesus Christ our Lord.   **Amen.**   [708]

41

At an Ordination   *Philip Melanchthon (1497–1560)*

Merciful God,
through the mouth of your beloved Son, our Lord Jesus
    Christ,
you said to us,
"The harvest is plentiful but the laborers are few;
pray therefore the Lord of the harvest
to send out laborers into his harvest."
We respond to your divine command, O Lord,
and sincerely beseech you
to richly bestow the Holy Spirit on these your servants
and on all of us who are called to your ministry
that we, with a great multitude,
may be your evangelists, true and steadfast against evil.
So may your name be hallowed,
your kingdom come,
and your will be done.
Hear this our prayer
through your beloved Son, Jesus Christ our Lord,
who, with you and the Holy Spirit,
lives and reigns throughout eternity.   **Amen.**   [709]

42

For Peace in the Church

God of our lives,
by the power of your Holy Spirit
we have been drawn together by one baptism into one faith,
serving one Lord and Savior.
Do not let us tear away from one another
through division or hard argument.   ▼

May your peace embrace our differences,
preserving us in unity,
as one body of Jesus Christ our Lord.   **Amen.**   [710]

43

For Church Secretaries

God of creation,
you bring order out of chaos
and set us in this world to do your will.
Bless those who serve your cause
as secretaries in church offices.
Confirm their dedication,
that their love for you may show in diligence.
Strengthen their compassion
that they may represent your love
to church members and strangers they encounter.
May their work be appreciated by all
as important to the ministry of Christ Jesus,
our Lord and Savior.   **Amen.**   [711]

44

For Stewardship in the Church

Righteous God,
you have taught us that the poor shall have your kingdom,
and that the gentle-minded shall inherit the earth.
Keep the church poor enough to preach to poor people,
and humble enough to walk with the despised.
Never weigh us down with property or accumulated funds.
Save your church from vain display or lavish comforts,
so that we may travel light
and move through the world
showing your generous love
made known in Jesus Christ our Lord.   **Amen.**   [712]

45

For Teachers in the Church

Almighty God,
you have given your law to guide us in a life of love,
and you have appointed teachers to interpret your will.
Create in those who instruct your people
a mind to study your Word,
and good understanding,
so that we may all learn your truth
and do it gladly;
for the sake of Jesus Christ our Master.   **Amen.**   [713]

46

For Seminaries

Almighty God,
in Jesus Christ you called ordinary people to be disciples
and sent them out to teach and preach your truth.
Bring to seminaries men and women
who are honest and eager to serve you.
Give them tender hearts to care for others,
and tough minds to wrestle with your Word,
so that, as they speak and act for you,
people may repent and return to love,
believing in Jesus Christ,
who is our Lord and Master.   **Amen.**   [714]

47

At the Time of a Minister's Retirement

God of grace,
we thank you for the gifts of Christian ministry
given in your servant, N.
We celebrate the years of *his/her* labor
in the fields of the Lord,
and rejoice in the blessings so many have received.
Give your servant a sense of fulfillment and completion,
a time of refreshment and rest, and new opportunities
for living the good news of your love in Jesus Christ.
                                    Amen.   [715]

48

For Church Unity

A prayer from Zaire

O God,
you are the giver of life.
We pray for the church in the whole world.
Sanctify her life, renew her worship,
give power to her witnessing,
restore her unity.
Give strength to those who are searching together
for that kind of obedience which creates unity.
Heal the divisions separating your children one from another,
so that they will make fast, with bonds of peace,
the unity which the Spirit gives. **Amen.**   [716]

49

For Church Unity

Holy God, giver of peace, author of truth,
we confess that we are divided and at odds with one another,
that a bad spirit has risen among us
and set us against your Holy Spirit of peace and love.
Take from us the mistrust, party spirit, contention,
and all evil that now divides us.
Work in us a desire for reconciliation,
so that, putting aside personal grievances,
we may go about your business with a single mind,
devoted to our Lord and Savior, Jesus Christ. **Amen.**   [717]

50

For Church Unity

Dionysius of Alexandria (d. 264)

God,
good beyond all that is good,
fair beyond all that is fair,
in you is calmness, peace, and concord.
Heal the dissensions that divide us from one another
and bring us back to a unity of love
bearing some likeness to your divine nature.

Through the embrace of love
and the bonds of godly affection,
make us one in the Spirit
by your peace which makes all things peaceful.
We ask this through the grace, mercy, and tenderness
of your Son, Jesus Christ our Lord.   **Amen.**   [718]

51

For Other Churches

Almighty God,
in Jesus Christ you called disciples
and prayed for them to be joined in faith.
We pray for Christian churches from which we are separated.
Let us never be so sure of ourselves
that we condemn the faith of others
or refuse reunion with them,
but make us ever ready to reach out for more truth,
so that your church may be one in the Spirit;
through Jesus Christ our Lord.   **Amen.**   [719]

52

For Candidates for Church Service

God of prophets and apostles,
you have chosen leaders to train your people
in the way of Jesus Christ.
We thank you that in our day
you are still claiming men and women
for special work within the church.
As N. has dedicated *himself/herself* to you,
let us pledge ourselves to *him/her*,
so that, surrounded by affection and hope,
he/she may grow in wisdom,
mature in love,
and become a faithful worker,
approved by Jesus Christ our Lord.   **Amen.**   [720]

53

For Enemies of the Church

Strong God of love:
your Son Jesus told us
that his church would be persecuted
as he was persecuted.
If we should suffer for righteousness' sake,
save us from self-righteousness.
Give us grace to pray for enemies,
and to forgive them,
even as you have forgiven us;
through Jesus Christ,
who was crucified but is risen,
whom we praise forever.   **Amen.**   [721]

54

Thanksgiving for Heroes and Heroines of the Faith

We give thanks to you, O Lord our God,
for all your servants and witnesses of time past:
for Abraham, the father of believers,
and for Sarah, his wife,
for Moses the lawgiver, and Aaron the priest,
for Miriam and Joshua,
Deborah and Gideon,
Samuel and Hannah, his mother;
for Isaiah and all the prophets;
for Mary, the mother of our Lord;
for Peter and Paul and all the apostles;
for Mary, Martha, and Mary Magdalene;
for Stephen, the first martyr,
and all the saints and martyrs
in every time and in every land.
In your mercy, give us, as you gave them,
the hope of salvation
and the promise of eternal life;
through the firstborn from the dead,
Jesus Christ our Lord.   **Amen.**   [722]

55
Thanksgiving for Heroes and Heroines of the Faith

Eternal and Almighty God,
we give you thanks for all your faithful people
who have followed your will in a grand procession of praise
throughout the world and down through the centuries,
into our own time and place.
We hear their stories in the pages of scripture,
in the records of history,
in the recollections of our families
and in our own childhood memories.
As we remember these people,
inspire us by your Spirit to join their ranks
and follow our Lord through life,
to be bold as they were, and brave as well,
witnessing to your righteous truth and generous love.
Give us grace, O God,
that we will leave a legacy of faithfulness
to encourage and challenge those who follow us
along the way of discipleship;
through Jesus Christ our Lord.   **Amen.**   [723]

56
Remembrance of Those Who Have Died

With reverence and affection
we remember before you, O everlasting God,
all our departed friends and relatives.
Keep us in union with them
here, through faith and love toward you,
that hereafter we may enter into your presence
and be numbered with those who serve you
and look upon your face in glory everlasting;
through your Son, Jesus Christ our Lord.   **Amen.**   [724]

57

For Jews

Almighty God, you are the one true God,
and have called forth people of faith
in every time and place.
Your promises are sure and true.
We bless you for your covenant given to Abraham and Sarah,
that you keep even now with the Jews.
We rejoice that you have brought us into covenant with you
by the coming of your Son, Jesus Christ,
himself a Jew, nurtured in the faith of Israel.
We praise you that you are faithful to covenants made
with us and Jewish brothers and sisters,
that together we may serve your will,
and come at last to your promised peace.   **Amen.**   [725]

58

For Muslims

Eternal God,
you are the one God to be worshiped by all,
the one called Allah by your Muslim children,
descendants of Abraham as we are.
Give us grace to hear your truth
in the teachings of Mohammed, the prophet,
and to show your love as disciples of Jesus Christ,
that Christians and Muslims together
may serve you in faith and friendship.   **Amen.**   [726]

PRAYERS FOR THE NATIONAL LIFE

59

For Our Nation   *Woodrow Wilson (1856–1924)*

Almighty God, ruler of all the peoples of the earth,
forgive, we pray, our shortcomings as a nation;
purify our hearts to see and love truth;
give wisdom to our counselors
and steadfastness to our people;

and bring us at last to the fair city of peace,
whose foundations are mercy, justice, and goodwill,
and whose builder and maker you are;
through your Son, Jesus Christ our Lord. **Amen.** [727]

60

For Our Country

Almighty God,
you have given us this good land as our heritage.
Make us always remember your generosity
and constantly do your will.
Bless our land with honest industry,
sound learning,
and an honorable way of life.
Save us from violence, discord, and confusion;
from pride and arrogance,
and from every evil way.
Make us who come from many nations
with many different languages
a united people.
Defend our liberties
and give those whom we have entrusted with the authority
    of government
the spirit of wisdom,
that there might be justice and peace in our land.
When times are prosperous, let our hearts be thankful;
and, in troubled times, do not let our trust in you fail.
We ask all this through Jesus Christ our Lord. **Amen.** [728]

61

For Government Leaders

O Lord, our governor,
your glory shines throughout the world.
We commend our nation to your merciful care,
that we may live securely in peace
and may be guided by your providence. ▼

Give all in authority the wisdom and strength
to know your will and to do it.
Help them remember that they are called to serve the people
as lovers of truth and justice;
through Jesus Christ our Lord.   **Amen.**   [729]

62

For the Courts of Justice

Almighty God,
you sit in judgment to declare what is just and right.
Bless the courts and the magistrates in our land.
Give them the spirit of wisdom and understanding,
that they may perceive the truth
and administer the law impartially
as instruments of your divine will.
We pray in the name of him who will come to be our judge,
your Son, Jesus Christ our Lord.   **Amen.**   [730]

63

For State and Local Governments

Almighty God,
bless those who hold office in the government
    of this *state/city/town*,
that they may do their work
in a spirit of wisdom, kindness, and justice.
Help them use their authority to serve faithfully
and to promote the general welfare;
through your Son, Jesus Christ our Lord.   **Amen.**   [731]

64

At the Time of an Election

Under your law we live, great God,
and by your will we govern ourselves.
Help us as good citizens
to respect neighbors whose views differ from ours,
so that without partisan anger,

we may work out issues that divide us,
and elect candidates to serve the common welfare;
through Jesus Christ the Lord. **Amen.** [732]

65

For Those in the Military

Righteous God, you rule the nations.
Guard brave men and women
who risk themselves in battle for their country.
Give them compassion for enemies
who also fight for patriotic causes.
Keep our sons and daughters from hate that hardens,
or from scorekeeping with human lives.
Though they must be at war,
let them live for peace,
as eager for agreement as for victory.
Encourage them as they encourage one another,
and never let hard duty separate them
from loyalty to your Son, our Lord, Jesus Christ.
Amen. [733]

66

During a National Crisis

God of ages,
in your sight nations rise and fall,
and pass through times of peril.
Now when our land is troubled,
be near to judge and save.
May leaders be led by your wisdom;
may they search your will and see it clearly.
If we have turned from your way,
help us to reverse our ways and repent.
Give us your light and your truth to guide us;
through Jesus Christ,
who is Lord of this world, and our Savior. **Amen.** [734]

67

For Social Justice

Grant, O God,
that your holy and life-giving Spirit
may so move every human heart,
that the barriers which divide us may crumble,
suspicions disappear,
and hatreds cease,
and that, with our divisions healed,
we might live in justice and peace;
through your Son, Jesus Christ our Lord.   **Amen.**   [735]

68

For Social Justice

You give us prophets, holy God,
to cry out for justice and mercy.
Open our ears to hear them,
and to follow the truth they speak,
lest we support injustice to secure our own well-being.
Give prophets the fire of your Word,
but love as well.
Though they speak for you,
may they know that they stand with us before you,
and have no Messiah other than your Son,
Jesus Christ, the Lord of all.   **Amen.**   [736]

69

For Social Justice   *Martin Luther King, Jr.*
                                                    (1929–1968)

Yes, Jesus,
I want to be on your right side
or your left side,
not for any selfish reason.

I want to be on your right or your best side,
not in terms of some political kingdom or ambition,
but I just want to be there
in love and in justice and in truth
and in commitment to others,
so we can make of this old world a new world.   **Amen.**   [737]

70

For Those Suffering from Addictions

O blessed Jesus,
you ministered to all who came to you.
Look with compassion upon all who through addiction
have lost their health and freedom.
Restore to them the assurance
of your unfailing mercy;
remove the fears that attack them;
strengthen them in the work of their recovery;
and to those who care for them,
give patient understanding and persevering love;
for your mercy's sake.   **Amen.**   [738]

71

For Those in Business

God of the covenant:
you give love without return,
and lavish gifts without looking for gain.
Watch over the ways of business,
so that those who buy or sell, get or lend,
may live justly and show mercy
and walk in your ways.
May profits be fair and contracts kept.
In our dealings with each other
may we display true charity;
through Jesus Christ,
who has loved us with mercy.   **Amen.**   [739]

72

For Those in Commerce and Industry

Almighty God,
your Son Jesus Christ dignified our labor
by sharing our toil.
Be with your people where they work;
make those who carry on the industries and commerce of
    this land
responsive to your will;
and to all of us,
give pride in what we do
and a just return for our labor;
through your Son, Jesus Christ our Lord.   **Amen.**   [740]

73

For Cities

God of heaven and earth,
in your Word you have given us a vision of that holy city
to which the nations of the world bring their glory.
Look upon and visit the cities of the earth.
Renew the ties of mutual regard that form our civic life.
Send us honest and able leaders.
Help us to eliminate poverty, prejudice, and oppression,
that peace may prevail with righteousness,
and justice with order,
and that men and women from various cultures
and with differing talents
may find with one another
the fulfillment of their humanity;
through Jesus Christ our Lord.   **Amen.**   [741]

74

For the Neighborhood

O Lord, our creator,
by your holy prophet you taught your ancient people
to seek the welfare of the cities in which they lived.
We commend our neighborhood to your care,

that it might be kept free from social strife and decay.
Give us strength of purpose and concern for others,
that we may create here a community of justice and peace
where your will may be done;
through your Son, Jesus Christ our Lord.   **Amen.**   [742]

75

For Students

Eternal God,
your wisdom is greater than our small minds can attain,
and your truth shows up our little learning.
To those who study,
give curiosity, imagination,
and patience enough to wait and work for insight.
Help them to doubt with courage,
but to hold all their doubts
in the larger faith of Jesus Christ our Lord.   **Amen.**   [743]

76

For Graduates

Eternal God,
in your will our lives are lived,
and by your wisdom truth is found.
We pray for graduates who finish a course of study,
and move on to something new.
Take away anxiety or confusion of purpose,
and give them confidence in the future you plan,
where energies may be gathered up
and given to neighbors in love;
for the sake of Jesus Christ our Lord.   **Amen.**   [744]

77

For Responsible Citizenship

Lord, keep this nation under your care.
Bless the leaders of our land,
that we may be a people at peace among ourselves
and a blessing to other nations of the earth.   ▼

Help us elect trustworthy leaders,
contribute to wise decisions for the general welfare,
and thus serve you faithfully in our generation,
to the honor of your holy name;
through Jesus Christ the Lord. **Amen.** [745]

78

For Those Who Suffer for the Sake of Conscience

God of love and strength,
your Son forgave his enemies
while he was suffering shame and death.
Strengthen those who suffer for the sake of conscience.
When they are accused, save them from speaking in hate;
when they are rejected, save them from bitterness;
when they are imprisoned, save them from despair.
To us, your servants,
give grace to respect their witness
and to discern the truth,
that our society may be cleansed and strengthened.
This we ask for the sake of our merciful and righteous judge,
Jesus Christ our Lord. **Amen.** [746]

PRAYERS FOR THE FAMILY
AND PERSONAL LIFE

79

For Those Engaged to Marry

Almighty God,
in the beginning you made man and woman
to join themselves in shared affection.
May those who engage to marry be filled with joy.
Let them be so sure of each other
that no fear or disrespect may shake their vows.
Though their eyes may be bright with love for each other,
keep in sight a wider world,

where neighbors want and strangers beg,
and where service is a joyful duty;
through Jesus Christ the Lord.   **Amen.**   [747]

80

For the Newly Married

God of grace,
in your wisdom you made man and woman
to be one flesh in love.
As in Jesus Christ you came to serve us,
let newlyweds serve each other,
putting aside selfishness and separate rights.
May they build homes where there is free welcome.
At work or in leisure,
let them enjoy each other,
forgive each other,
and embrace each other faithfully,
serving the Lord of love, Jesus Christ.   **Amen.**   [748]

81

For Families

Eternal God, our creator,
you set us to live in families.
We commend to your care
all the homes where your people live.
Keep them, we pray, free from bitterness,
from the thirst for personal victory,
and from pride in self.
Fill them with faith, virtue, knowledge,
moderation, patience, and godliness.
Knit together in enduring affection
those who have become one in marriage.
Let children and parents have full respect for one another;
and light the fire of kindliness among us all,
that we may show affection for each other;
through Jesus Christ our Lord.   **Amen.**   [749]

82

For a Family   *Robert Louis Stevenson (1850–1894)*

Lord, behold our family here assembled.
We thank you for this place in which we dwell,
for the love that unites us,
for the peace given us this day,
for the hope with which we expect the morrow;
for the health, the work, the food, and the bright skies
that make our lives delightful;
for our friends in all parts of the earth.

Give us courage and gaiety and the quiet mind.
Spare to us our friends, soften to us our enemies.
Bless us, if it may be, in all our innocent endeavors;
if it may not, give us the strength to endure that which is to
    come;
that we may be brave in peril,
constant in tribulation,
temperate in wrath and in all changes of fortune
and down to the gates of death,
loyal and loving to one another.

As the clay to the potter,
as the windmill to the wind,
as children of their parent,
we beseech of you this help and mercy
for Christ's sake.   **Amen.**   [750]

83

For Single People

Almighty God,
grant that those who live alone
may not be lonely in their solitude,
but may find fulfillment
in loving you and their neighbors
as they follow in the footsteps of Jesus Christ our Lord.
                                Amen.   [751]

84

For Parents

Almighty God, from whom we receive our life,
you have blessed us with the joy and care of children.
As we bring them up,
give us calm strength and patient wisdom,
that we may teach them to love
whatever is just and true and good,
following the example of our Savior Jesus Christ.
Amen. [752]

85

For Children

Great God,
guard the laughter of children.
Bring them safely through injury and illness,
so they may live the promises you give.
Do not let us be so preoccupied with our purposes
that we fail to hear their voices,
or pay attention to their special vision of the truth;
but keep us with them,
ready to listen and to love,
even as in Jesus Christ you have loved us,
your grown-up, wayward children. **Amen.** [753]

86

For Young People

Almighty God,
you see your children growing up
in an uncertain and confusing world.
Show them that your ways give more life
than the ways of the world,
and that following you
is better than chasing after selfish goals.
Help them to take failure,
not as a measure of their worth,
but as an opportunity for a new start. ▼

Give them strength to hold their faith in you
and to keep alive their joy in your creation;
through Jesus Christ our Lord.   **Amen.**   [754]

87

For Young People

Almighty God,
again and again you have called upon young people
to force change or fire human hopes.
Never let older people be so set in their ways
that they refuse to hear young voices,
or so firm in their grip on power
that they reject youth's contributions.
Let the young be candid, but not cruel.
Keep them dreaming dreams that you approve,
and living in the Spirit of the young man Jesus,
the crucified one who now rules the world.   **Amen.**   [755]

88

At the Birth of a Child

Mighty God,
by your love we are given children
through the miracle of birth.
May we greet each new son and daughter with joy,
and surround them all with faith,
so they may know who you are
and want to be your disciples.
Never let us neglect children,
but help us enjoy them,
showing them the welcome you have shown us all;
through Jesus Christ the Lord.   **Amen.**   [756]

89

At a Birthday

O God, our times are in your hand:
Look with favor, we pray, on your servant N.,
as *he/she* begins another year.

Grant that *he/she* may grow in wisdom and grace,
and strengthen *his/her* trust in your goodness
all the days of *his/her* life;
through Jesus Christ our Lord.   **Amen.**   [757]

90

For Parents

Almighty God, giver of life and love,
bless N. and N.
Grant them wisdom and devotion
in the ordering of their common life,
that each may be to the other
a strength in need,
a counselor in perplexity,
a comfort in sorrow,
and a companion in joy.
And so knit their wills together in your will
and their spirits in your Spirit,
that they may live together in love and peace
all the days of their life;
through Jesus Christ our Lord.   **Amen.**   [758]

91

For Families with One Parent

Gracious God,
we are never away from your care,
and what we lack you give in love.
Watch over families where, by death or separation,
a parent is left alone with children.
Lift bitterness and the burden of lonely obligation.
Show them that they live under your protection,
so they have not less love, but more;
through Jesus Christ,
your Son and our eternal brother.   **Amen.**   [759]

92

For Those Having Marital Difficulty

Lord God, you set us in families,
where we learn to live together in charity and truth.
Strengthen weak bonds of love.
Where separation threatens,
move in with forgiving power.
Melt hard hearts,
free fixed minds,
break the hold of stubborn pride.
Lay claim on us,
so that our separate claims may be set aside in love;
through Jesus Christ our Lord.   **Amen.**   [760]

93

For the Divorced or Separated

God of grace,
you are always working to hold us together,
to heal division,
and make love strong.
Help men and women whose marriages fail
to know that you are faithful.
Restore confidence,
bring understanding,
and ease the hurt of separation.
If they marry others,
instruct them in better love,
so that vows may be said and kept with new resolve;
through Jesus Christ our Lord.   **Amen.**   [761]

94

For Orphans

Gracious God,
you remember all your children,
especially those who are left alone,
innocent victims of the acts of others.

Remind us of the orphans of this world,
that we may show special care
and embrace them with your love.
Give them confidence in your parental guidance,
so they will find a home in your family of faith,
with brothers and sisters who follow Jesus Christ,
your Son, our Lord.   **Amen.**   [762]

95

In a Personal Crisis   *Attributed to Augustine of Hippo*
                                                          (354–430)

God of life,
there are days when the burdens we carry
are heavy on our shoulders and weigh us down,
when the road seems dreary and endless,
the skies gray and threatening,
when our lives have no music in them,
and our hearts are lonely,
and our souls have lost their courage.
Flood the path with light,
turn our eyes to where the skies are full of promise;
tune our hearts to brave music;
give us the sense of comradeship
with heroes and saints of every age;
and so quicken our spirits
that we may be able to encourage
the souls of all who journey with us on the road of life,
to your honor and glory.   **Amen.**   [763]

96

In a Personal Crisis   *Teresa of Lisieux (1873–1897)*

Just for today,
what does it matter, O Lord, if the future is dark?
To pray now for tomorrow I am not able.
Keep my heart only for today,
grant me your light—
just for today.   **Amen.**   [764]

97

In a Personal Crisis *Thomas à Kempis (c. 1380–1471)*

Write your blessed name, O Lord,
upon my heart,
there to remain so indelibly engraven,
that no prosperity,
no adversity,
shall ever move me from your love.
Be to me a strong tower of defense,
a comforter in tribulation,
a deliverer in distress,
a very present help in trouble,
and a guide to heaven
through the many temptations and dangers of this life.

Amen. [765]

98

Self-Dedication

Almighty God,
so draw our hearts to you,
so guide our minds,
so fill our imaginations,
so control our wills,
that we may be wholly yours,
utterly dedicated to you.
Use us as you will,
always to your glory and the welfare of your people;
through our Lord and Savior Jesus Christ.   **Amen.**   [766]

99

For Faithfulness *Thomas Aquinas (c. 1225–1274)*

Give me, O Lord, a steadfast heart,
which no unworthy affection may drag downward;
give me an unconquered heart,
which no tribulation can wear out;

give me an upright heart,
which no unworthy purpose may tempt aside.
Bestow on me also, O Lord my God,
understanding to know you,
diligence to seek you,
wisdom to find you,
and a faithfulness that may finally embrace you;
through Jesus Christ our Lord.   **Amen.**   [767]

100

For Guidance

Direct us, O Lord, in all our doings
with your most gracious favor
and further us with your continual help,
that in all our works,
begun, continued, and ended in you,
we may glorify your holy name,
and finally, by your mercy, obtain everlasting life;
through Jesus Christ our Lord.   **Amen.**   [768]

101

For Appreciation of Truth and Beauty

Give us, O Lord, a reverence for the truth,
the desire both to think and to speak truly.
Save us from all fear of truth.
Grant us all an appreciation of beauty
and things that are lovely.
Increase our reverence for them;
help us to see in them a part of your revelation of yourself,
that beauty becomes you no less than truth and righteousness;
through Jesus Christ our Lord,
who lives and reigns with you and the Holy Spirit,
one God, now and forever.   **Amen.**   [769]

102

For the Sick

O God,
the strength of the weak and the comfort of sufferers,
mercifully hear our prayers
and grant to your servant N.,
the help of your power,
that *his/her* sickness may be turned into health
and our sorrow into joy;
through Jesus Christ.   **Amen.**   [770]

103

During an Illness   *Ambrose of Milan (340–397)*

You are medicine for me when I am sick.
You are my strength when I need help.
You are life itself when I fear death.
You are the way when I long for heaven.
You are light when all is dark.
You are my food when I need nourishment!   **Amen.**   [771]

104

For Healing

Mighty and merciful God,
you sent Jesus Christ to heal broken lives.
We praise you that today
you send healing in doctors and nurses,
and bless us with technology in medicine.
We claim your promises of wholeness
as we pray for those who are ill in body or mind,
who long for your healing touch.
Make the weak strong,
the sick healthy,
the broken whole,
and confirm those who serve them
as agents of your love.

Then all shall be renewed in vigor
to point to the risen Christ,
who conquered death
    that we might live eternally.   **Amen.** [772]

105

For Health Restored

Almighty God,
we rejoice that, by the power of your Spirit,
you have given the gift of health and wholeness
to your servant N.
In thanksgiving we renew our commitment to you,
so that health regained
may provide opportunities for service
in the helping and healing work of Jesus Christ,
our Lord and Savior.   **Amen.** [773]

106

For Leisure

O God,
give us times of refreshment and peace
in the course of this busy life.
Grant that we may so use our leisure
to rebuild our bodies and renew our minds,
that our spirits may be opened to the goodness of your
    creation;
through Jesus Christ our Lord.   **Amen.** [774]

107

For Those Who Are Absent   *Henry van Dyke (1852–1933)*

Almighty God, we commend to your goodness
all who are near and dear to us,
wherever they may be today.
Watch over them;
provide for them;
bless them in body and soul; ▼

at last bring them and us
into the perfect and eternal joy of heaven;
through Jesus Christ our Lord.   **Amen.**   [775]

PRAYERS FOR THE HUMAN CONDITION

108

For the Afflicted

Almighty and everlasting God,
you are the comfort of the sad
and strength to those who suffer.
Let the prayers of your children who are in any trouble
rise to you.
To everyone in distress
grant mercy,
grant relief,
grant refreshment;
through Jesus Christ our Lord.   **Amen.**   [776]

109

For the Mentally Distressed

Mighty God,
in Jesus Christ you dealt with spirits that darken minds
or set people against themselves.
Give peace to those who are torn by conflict,
are cast down,
or dream deceiving dreams.
By your power,
drive from our minds
demons that shake confidence and wreck love.
Tame unruly forces in us,
and bring us to your truth,
so that we may accept ourselves
as good, glad children of your love,
known in Jesus Christ.   **Amen.**   [777]

110

For the Middle-Aged

Eternal God,
you have led us through our days and years,
made wisdom ripe and faith mature.
Show men and women your purpose for them,
so that, when youth is spent,
they may not find life empty or labor stale,
but may devote themselves to dear loves and worthy tasks,
with undiminished strength;
for the sake of Jesus Christ the Lord.   **Amen.**   [778]

111

For the Aged

O Lord God,
look with mercy on all whose increasing years bring them
isolation, distress, or weakness.
Provide for them homes of dignity and peace;
give them understanding helpers
and the willingness to accept help;
and, as their strength diminishes,
increase their faith
and their assurance of your love.
We pray in the name
    of Jesus Christ our Lord.   **Amen.**   [779]

112

For the Bereaved

O merciful God,
you teach us in your Holy Word
that you do not willingly afflict or grieve your children.
Look with pity on the sorrows of N., your servant,
for whom we pray.
Remember *him/her*, O Lord, in mercy.   ▼

Strengthen *him/her* in patience,
comfort *him/her* with the memory of your goodness,
let your presence shine on *him/her*,
and give *him/her* peace;
through Jesus Christ our Lord.   **Amen.**   [780]

113
For the Lonely

God of comfort, companion of the lonely:
be with those who by neglect or willful separation are left
    alone.
Fill empty places with present love,
and long times of solitude with lively thoughts of you.
Encourage us to visit lonely men and women,
so they may be cheered by the Spirit of Jesus Christ,
who walked among us as a friend,
and is our Lord forever.   **Amen.**   [781]

114
For the Oppressed

Look with compassion, O God,
upon the people in this land
who live with injustice, terror, disease, and death
as their constant companions.
Have mercy upon us.
Help us to eliminate cruelty to these our neighbors.
Strengthen those who spend their lives
establishing equal protection of the law
and equal opportunities for all.
And grant that every one of us may enjoy
a fair portion of the abundance of this land;
through your Son, Jesus Christ our Lord.   **Amen.**   [782]

115
For the Outcast

God of grace,
no one is beyond the reach of your love,
or outside your limitless mercy.

Move us toward those the world despises and people reject,
so we may venture to follow Christ,
and risk showing his love.
Stand with those who are outcast;
strengthen them in peace;
encourage them by your presence;
and use them to build on the cornerstone of Christ,
until differences are honored and respected,
and all people together give you glory. **Amen.**   [783]

116

For the Poor and Neglected   *Mother Teresa of Calcutta*

Make us worthy, Lord,
to serve our fellow human beings throughout the world
who live and die in poverty and hunger.
Give them through our hands this day their daily bread,
and by our understanding love,
give peace and joy. **Amen.**   [784]

117

For the Retired

Your love for us never ends, eternal God,
even when by age or weakness we can no longer work.
When we retire,
keep us awake to your will for us.
Give us energy to enjoy the world,
to attend to neighbors busy people neglect,
and to contribute wisely to the life of the church.
If we can offer nothing but our prayers,
remind us that our prayers are a useful work you want,
so that we may live always serving Jesus Christ,
our hope and our true joy. **Amen.**   [785]

118

For the Sexually Confused

God of creation,
you made men and women to find in love
fulfillment as your creatures.   ▼

We pray for those who deny physical love,
who are repelled by flesh,
or frightened by their daydreams.
Straighten us all out, O Lord,
and show us who we are,
so that we may affirm each other bodily in covenants of love,
approved by Jesus Christ our Lord.   **Amen.**   [786]

119

For Those in Distress   *The Liturgy of St. Mark*

Almighty and everlasting God,
the comfort of the sad,
the strength of those who suffer,
let the prayers of your children who cry out of any tribulation
come to you.
To every soul that is distressed,
grant mercy, grant relief, grant refreshment;
through Jesus Christ our Lord.   **Amen.**   [787]

120

At a Time of Tragedy

God of compassion,
you watch our ways,
and weave out of terrible happenings
wonders of goodness and grace.
Surround those who have been shaken by tragedy
with a sense of your present love,
and hold them in faith.
Though they are lost in grief,
may they find you and be comforted;
through Jesus Christ who was dead, but lives
and rules this world with you.   **Amen.**   [788]

121
For Travelers

The world is yours, mighty God,
and all people live by your faithfulness.
Watch over those who are traveling,
who drive or fly,
or speed through space.
May they be careful, but not afraid,
and safely reach their destinations.
Wherever we wander in your spacious world,
teach us that we never journey beyond your loving care,
revealed in Jesus Christ the Lord.   **Amen.**   [789]

122
For the Unemployed

Gracious God,
we remember before you
those who suffer want and anxiety from lack of work.
Guide the people of this land
so to use our wealth and resources
that all persons may find suitable and fulfilling employment
and receive just payment for their labor;
through your Son, Jesus Christ our Lord.   **Amen.**   [790]

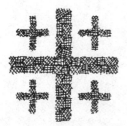

DAILY
LECTIONARY

Daily Lectionary

THE DAILY LECTIONARY that follows is arranged in a two-year cycle and provides for reading twice through the New Testament and once through the Old Testament during the two-year cycle. The readings reflect the seasons and festivals of the liturgical year. This lectionary is prepared for use at morning and evening prayer, rather than at the Service for the Lord's Day. The Table of Major Celebrations of the Liturgical Calendar (pp. 508–509) displays the schedule for using this lectionary.

The psalms follow a weekly cycle throughout each season, except for the period from Christmas to the Baptism of the Lord, when each day has its own appointed psalms, and Ordinary Time, which follows a four-week cycle of psalms. One of the laudate psalms (Ps. 145–150) is appointed for a particular day in each week for use in morning prayer throughout the year. If circumstances do not allow the singing or reading of both of the appointed psalms, one may be used.

Three readings are provided for each day, although only one or two are normally used in a single service. Ordinarily the Old Testament reading and one of the New Testament readings (Epistle—Year One; Gospel—Year Two) are read in the morning, and the remaining New Testament reading in the evening. Or one reading may be read in the morning and one in the evening. For example, the Old Testament reading may be read in the morning and the Gospel reading in the evening throughout a two-year cycle. In the following two years the epistle reading may be read in the morning and the Gospel reading in the evening.

At certain festivals, some readings are more appropriate for the morning or for the evening. An asterisk (*) indicates that the reading is intended for use in the morning. Two asterisks (**) indicate that the reading is intended for use in the evening. The Old Testament is traditionally read first. When a festival interrupts the sequence of readings (or if the readings in the Lectionary for Sundays and Festivals are used for daily prayer on Sundays and festivals), the daily readings may be reordered or modified to preserve continuity or avoid repetition. Readings for special days, for use in both years, are listed on page 506.

This lectionary includes some readings from the Apocrypha. Within the Reformed tradition, the Apocryphal books are not recognized as part of the canon of Holy Scripture and are not considered authoritative for doctrine. Nevertheless, the Apocryphal books may be instructive. Selections from the Old Testament are provided as alternatives to the readings from the Apocrypha for use when canonical readings are preferred or when the Apocrypha is not accessible.

Dec 19 – Nov 20 YR 2

DAILY LECTIONARY

DAY	PSALM	YEAR 1	YEAR 2
1st Week of Advent			
Sunday	*Morning:* Ps. 24; 150 *Evening:* Ps. 25; 110	Isa. 1:1-9 2 Peter 3:1-10 Matt. 25:1-13	Amos 1:1-5, 13–2:8 1 Thess. 5:1-11 Luke 21:5-19
Monday	*Morning:* Ps. 122; 145 *Evening:* Ps. 40; 67	Isa. 1:10-20 1 Thess. 1:1-10 Luke 20:1-8	Amos 2:6-16 2 Peter 1:1-11 Matt. 21:1-11
Tuesday	*Morning:* Ps. 33; 146 *Evening:* Ps. 85; 94	Isa. 1:21-31 1 Thess. 2:1-12 Luke 20:9-18	Amos 3:1-11 2 Peter 1:12-21 Matt. 21:12-22
Wednesday	*Morning:* Ps. 50; 147:1-11 *Evening:* Ps. 53; 17	Isa. 2:1-4 1 Thess. 2:13-20 Luke 20:19-26	Amos 3:12–4:5 2 Peter 3:1-10 Matt. 21:23-32
Thursday	*Morning:* Ps. 18:1-20; 147:12-20 *Evening:* Ps. 126; 62	Isa. 2:5-22 1 Thess. 3:1-13 Luke 20:27-40	Amos 4:6-13 2 Peter 3:11-18 Matt. 21:33-46
Friday	*Morning:* Ps. 102; 148 *Evening:* Ps. 130; 16	Isa. 3:1–4:1 1 Thess. 4:1-12 Luke 20:41–21:4	Amos 5:1-17 Jude 1-16 Matt. 22:1-14
Saturday	*Morning:* Ps. 90; 149 *Evening:* Ps. 80; 72	Isa. 4:2-6 1 Thess. 4:13-18 Luke 21:5-19	Amos 5:18-27 Jude 17-25 Matt. 22:15-22

Day	Psalm	Year 1	Year 2

2nd Week of Advent

Day	Psalm	Year 1	Year 2
Sunday	*Morning:* Ps. 24; 150	Isa. 5:1-7	Amos 6:1-14
	Evening: Ps. 25; 110	2 Peter 3:11-18	2 Thess. 1:5-12
		Luke 7:28-35	Luke 1:57-68
Monday	*Morning:* Ps. 122; 145	Isa. 5:8-17	Amos 7:1-9
	Evening: Ps. 40; 67	1 Thess. 5:1-11	Rev. 1:1-8
		Luke 21:20-28	Matt. 22:23-33
Tuesday	*Morning:* Ps. 33; 146	Isa. 5:18-25	Amos 7:10-17
	Evening: Ps. 85; 94	1 Thess. 5:12-28	Rev. 1:9-16
		Luke 21:29-38	Matt. 22:34-46
Wednesday	*Morning:* Ps. 50; 147:1-11	Isa. 6:1-13	Amos 8:1-14
		2 Thess. 1:1-12	Rev. 1:17–2:7
	Evening: Ps. 53; 17	John 7:53–8:11	Matt. 23:1-12
Thursday	*Morning:* Ps. 18:1-20; 147:12-20	Isa. 7:1-9	Amos 9:1-10
		2 Thess. 2:1-12	Rev. 2:8-17
	Evening: Ps. 126; 62	Luke 22:1-13	Matt. 23:13-26
Friday	*Morning:* Ps. 102; 148	Isa. 7:10-25	Hag. 1:1-15
	Evening: Ps. 130; 16	2 Thess. 2:13*–3:5	Rev. 2:18-29
		Luke 22:14-30	Matt. 23:27-39
Saturday	*Morning:* Ps. 90; 149	Isa. 8:1-15	Hag. 2:1-9
	Evening: Ps. 80; 72	2 Thess. 3:6-18	Rev. 3:1-6
		Luke 22:31-38	Matt. 24:1-14

3rd Week of Advent

Day	Psalm	Year 1	Year 2
Sunday	*Morning:* Ps. 24; 150	Isa. 13:1-13	Amos 9:11-15
	Evening: Ps. 25; 110	Heb. 12:18-29	2 Thess. 2:1-3, 13-17
		John 3:22-30	John 5:30-47

The readings below are interrupted after December 17 in favor of the readings identified by date in the 4th Week of Advent.

Day	Psalm	Year 1	Year 2
Monday	*Morning:* Ps. 122; 145	Isa. 8:16–9:1	Zech. 1:7-17
	Evening: Ps. 40; 67	2 Peter 1:1-11	Rev. 3:7-13
		Luke 22:39-53	Matt. 24:15-31

Day	Psalm	Year 1	Year 2
Tuesday	*Morning:* Ps. 33; 146 *Evening:* Ps. 85; 94	Isa. 9:2-7 2 Peter 1:12-21 Luke 22:54-69	Zech. 2:1-13 Rev. 3:14-22 Matt. 24:32-44
Wednesday	*Morning:* Ps. 50; 147:1-11 *Evening:* Ps. 53; 17	Isa. 9:8-17 2 Peter 2:1-10a Mark 1:1-8	Zech. 3:1-10 Rev. 4:1-8 Matt. 24:45-51
Thursday	*Morning:* Ps. 18:1-20; 147:12-20 *Evening:* Ps. 126; 62	Isa. 9:18-10:4 2 Peter 2:10b-16 Matt. 3:1-12	Zech. 4:1-14 Rev. 4:9-5:5 Matt. 25:1-13
Friday	*Morning:* Ps. 102; 148 *Evening:* Ps. 130; 16	Isa. 10:5-19 2 Peter 2:17-22 Matt. 11:2-15	Zech. 7:8-8:8 Rev. 5:6-14 Matt. 25:14-30
Saturday	*Morning:* Ps. 90; 149 *Evening:* Ps. 80; 72	Isa. 10:20-27 Jude 17-25 Luke 3:1-9	Zech. 8:9-17 Rev. 6:1-17 Matt. 25:31-46

4th Week of Advent

Day	Psalm	Year 1	Year 2
December 18	**Sunday** *Morning:* Ps. 24; 150 *Evening:* Ps. 25; 110	Isa. 11:1-9 Eph. 6:10-20 John 3:16-21	Gen. 3:8-15 Rev. 12:1-10 John 3:16-21
December 19	**Monday** *Morning:* Ps. 122; 145 *Evening:* Ps. 40; 67	Isa. 11:10-16 Rev. 20:1-10 John 5:30-47	Zeph. 3:14-20 Titus 1:1-16 Luke 1:1-25
December 20	**Tuesday** *Morning:* Ps. 33; 146 *Evening:* Ps. 85; 94	Isa. 28:9-22 Rev. 20:11-21:8 Luke 1:5-25	1 Sam. 2:1b-10 Titus 2:1-10 Luke 1:26-38
December 21	**Wednesday** *Morning:* Ps. 50; 147:1-11 *Evening:* Ps. 53; 17	Isa. 29:9-24 Rev. 21:9-21 Luke 1:26-38	2 Sam. 7:1-17 Titus 2:11-3:8a Luke 1:39-48a (48b-56)

DAY	PSALM	YEAR 1	YEAR 2
December 22	**Thursday** *Morning:* Ps. 18:1-20; 147:12-20 *Evening:* Ps. 126; 62	Isa. 31:1-9 Rev. 21:22–22:5 Luke 1:39-48a (48b-56)	2 Sam. 7:18-29 Gal. 3:1-14 Luke 1:57-66
December 23	**Friday** *Morning:* Ps. 102; 148 *Evening:* Ps. 130; 16	Isa. 33:17-22 Rev. 22:6-11, 18-20 Luke 1:57-66	Jer. 31:10-14 Gal. 3:15-22 Luke 1:67-80 *or* Matt. 1:1-17
December 24	**Saturday** *Morning:* Ps. 90; 149 *Evening:* Ps. 80; 72	Isa. 35:1-10 Rev. 22:12-17, 21 Luke 1:67-80	Isa. 60:1-6 Gal. 3:23–4:7 Matt. 1:18-25
Christmas Eve	Ps. 132; 114	Isa. 59:15b-21 Phil. 2:5-11	Isa. 59:15b-21 Phil. 2:5-11
Christmas Day	*Morning:* Ps. 2; Laudate Psalm* *Evening:* Ps. 98; 96	Zech. 2:10-13 1 John 4:7-16 John 3:31-36	Micah 4:1-5; 5:2-4 1 John 4:7-16 John 3:31-36
1st Sunday after *Christmas*	[Use psalms appointed for date.]	Isa. 62:6-7, 10-12 Heb. 2:10-18 Matt. 1:18-25	1 Sam. 1:1-2, 7b-28 Col. 1:9-20 Luke 2:22-40
December 26	*Morning:* Ps. 116; Laudate Psalm* *Evening:* Ps. 119:1- 24; Ps. 27	Wisd. of Sol. 4:7-15 *or* 2 Chron. 24:17- 22 Acts 6:1-7 Acts 7:59–8:8	Wisd. of Sol. 4:7-15 *or* 2 Chron. 24:17- 22 Acts 6:1-7 Acts 7:59–8:8
December 27	*Morning:* Ps. 34; Laudate Psalm* *Evening:* Ps. 19; 121	Prov. 8:22-30 1 John 5:1-12 John 13:20-35	Prov. 8:22-30 1 John 5:1-12 John 13:20-35
December 28	*Morning:* Ps. 2; Laudate Psalm* *Evening:* Ps. 110; 111	Isa. 49:13-23 Isa. 54:1-13 Matt. 18:1-14	Isa. 49:13-23 Isa. 54:1-13 Matt. 18:1-14

---

* *Laudate psalms: Sunday*—Ps. 150; *Monday*—Ps. 145; *Tuesday*—Ps. 146; *Wednesday*—Ps. 147:1-11;
Thursday—Ps. 147:12-20; *Friday*—Ps. 148; *Saturday*—Ps. 149

Day	Psalm	Year 1	Year 2
December 29	*Morning:* Ps. 96;	Isa. 12:1-6	2 Sam. 23:13-17b
	Laudate Psalm*	Rev. 1:1-8	2 John 1-13
	Evening: Ps. 132; 97	John 7:37-52	John 2:1-11
December 30	*Morning:* Ps. 93;	Isa. 25:1-9	1 Kings 17:17-24
	Laudate Psalm*	Rev. 1:19-20	3 John 1-15
	Evening: Ps. 89:1-18;	John 7:53–8:11	John 4:46-54
	39:19-52		
December 31	*Morning:* Ps. 98;	Isa. 26:1-6	1 Kings 3:5-14
	Laudate Psalm*	2 Cor. 5:16–6:2	James 4:13-17; 5:7-11
	Evening: Ps. 45; 96	John 8:12-19	John 5:1-15
January 1	*Morning:* Ps. 98;	Gen. 17:1-12a, 15-16	Isa. 62:1-5, 10-12
	Laudate Psalm*	Col. 2:6-12	Rev. 19:11-16
	Evening: Ps. 99; 8	John 16:23b-30	Matt. 1:18-25
2nd Sunday after Christmas	[Use psalms appointed for date.]	Ecclus. 3:3-9, 14-17 *or* Deut. 33:1-5 1 John 2:12-17 John 6:41-47	1 Kings 3:5-14 Col. 3:12-17 John 6:41-47
January 2	*Morning:* Ps. 48;	Gen. 12:1-7	1 Kings 19:1-8
	Laudate Psalm*	Heb. 11:1-12	Eph. 4:1-16
	Evening: Ps. 9; 29	John 6:35-42, 48-51	John 6:1-14
January 3	*Morning:* Ps. 111;	Gen. 28:10-22	1 Kings 19:9-18
	Laudate Psalm*	Heb. 11:13-22	Eph. 4:17-32
	Evening: Ps. 107; 15	John 10:7-17	John 6:15-27
January 4	*Morning:* Ps. 20;	Ex. 3:1-5	Josh. 3:14–4:7
	Laudate Psalm*	Heb. 11:23-31	Eph. 5:1-20
	Evening: Ps. 93; 97	John 14:6-14	John 9:1-12, 35-38
January 5	*Morning:* Ps. 99;	Josh. 1:1-9	Jonah 2:2-9
	Laudate Psalm*	Heb. 11:32–12:2	Eph. 6:10-20
		John 15:1-16	John 11:17-27, 38-44

* *Laudate psalms: Sunday—Ps. 150; Monday—Ps. 145; Tuesday—Ps. 146; Wednesday—Ps. 147:1-11; Thursday—Ps. 147:12-20; Friday—Ps. 148; Saturday—Ps. 149*

Day	Psalm	Year 1	Year 2
Eve of Epiphany	Ps. 96; 110	Isa. 66:18-23	Isa. 66:18-23
		Rom. 15:7-13	Rom. 15:7-13

Epiphany and following

Epiphany	*Morning:* Ps. 72;	Isa. 52:7-10	Isa. 49:1-7
January 6	Laudate Psalm*	Rev. 21:22-27	Rev. 21:22-27
	Evening: Ps. 100; 67	Matt. 12:14-21	Matt. 12:14-21

The readings for the dated days after the Epiphany are used only until the following Saturday evening.

January 7	*Morning:* Ps. 46 or 97;	Isa. 52:3-6	Deut. 8:1-3
	Laudate Psalm*	Rev. 2:1-7	Col. 1:1-14
	Evening: Ps. 27; 93;	John 2:1-11	John 6:30-33, 48-51
	or 114		
January 8	*Morning:* Ps. 46 *or* 47;	Isa. 59:15b-21	Ex. 17:1-7
	Laudate Psalm*	Rev. 2:8-17	Col. 1:15-23
	Evening: Ps. 27; 93;	John 4:46-54	John 7:37-52
	or 114		
January 9	*Morning:* Ps. 46 *or* 47;	Isa. 63:1-5	Isa. 45:14-19
	Laudate Psalm*	Rev. 2:18-29	Col. 1:24–2:7
	Evening: Ps. 27; 93;	John 5:1-15	John 8:12-19
	or 114		
January 10	*Morning:* Ps. 46 *or* 47;	Isa. 65:1-9	Jer. 23:1-8
	Laudate Psalm*	Rev. 3:1-6	Col. 2:8-23
	Evening: Ps. 27; 93;	John 6:1-14	John 10:7-17
	or 114		
January 11	*Morning:* Ps. 46 *or* 47;	Isa. 65:13-16	Isa. 55:3-9
	Laudate Psalm*	Rev. 3:7-13	Col. 3:1-17
	Evening: Ps. 27; 93;	John 6:15-27	John 14:6-14
	or 114		

---

* *Laudate psalms: Sunday*—Ps. 150; *Monday*—Ps. 145; *Tuesday*—Ps. 146; *Wednesday*—Ps. 147:1-11; *Thursday*—Ps. 147:12-20; *Friday*—Ps. 148; *Saturday*—Ps. 149

DAY	PSALM	YEAR 1	YEAR 2
January 12	*Morning:* Ps. 46 *or* 97; Laudate Psalm*	Isa. 66:1-2, 22-23 Rev. 3:14-22 John 9:1-12, 35-38	Gen. 49:1-2, 8-12 Col. 3:18–4:6 John 15:1-16
Eve of Baptism of the Lord	Ps. 27; 93; *or* 114	Isa. 61:1-9 Gal. 3:23-29; 4:4-7	Isa. 61:1-9 Gal. 3:23-29; 4:4-7

Baptism of the Lord (Sunday between Jan. 7 and 13 inclusive) and following

Baptism of the Lord	*Morning:* Ps. 104; 150 *Evening:* Ps. 29	Isa. 40:1-11 Heb. 1:1-12 John 1:1-7, 19-20, 29-34	Gen. 1:1–2:3 Eph. 1:3-14 John 1:29-34
Monday	*Morning:* Ps. 5; 145 *Evening:* Ps. 82; 29	Isa. 40:12-24 Eph. 1:1-14 Mark 1:1-13	Gen. 2:4-9 (10-15) 16-25 Heb. 1:1-14 John 1:1-18
Tuesday	*Morning:* Ps. 42; 146 *Evening:* Ps. 102; 133	Isa. 40:25-31 Eph. 1:15-23 Mark 1:14-28	Gen. 3:1-24 Heb. 2:1-10 John 1:19-28
Wednesday	*Morning:* Ps. 89:1-18; 147:1-11 *Evening:* Ps. 1; 33	Isa. 41:1-16 Eph. 2:1-10 Mark 1:29-45	Gen. 4:1-16 Heb. 2:11-18 John 1:(29-34) 35-42
Thursday	*Morning:* Ps. 97; 147:12-20 *Evening:* Ps. 16; 62	Isa. 41:17-29 Eph. 2:11-22 Mark 2:1-12	Gen. 4:17-26 Heb. 3:1-11 John 1:43-51
Friday	*Morning:* Ps. 51; 148 *Evening:* Ps. 142; 65	Isa. 42:(1-9) 10-17 Eph. 3:1-13 Mark 2:13-22	Gen. 6:1-8 Heb. 3:12-19 John 2:1-12
Saturday	*Morning:* Ps. 104; 149 *Evening:* Ps. 138; 98	Isa. (42:18-25) 43:1-13 Eph. 3:14-21 Mark 2:23–3:6	Gen. 6:9-22 Heb. 4:1-13 John 2:13-22

Day	Psalm	Year 1	Year 2

Week following Sunday between Jan. 14 and 20 inclusive

Day	Psalm	Year 1	Year 2
Sunday	*Morning:* Ps. 19; 150	Isa. 43:14–44:5	Gen. 7:1-10, 17-23
	Evening: Ps. 81; 113	Heb. 6:17–7:10	Eph. 4:1-16
		John 4:27-42	Mark 3:7-19
Monday	*Morning:* Ps. 135; 145	Isa. 44:6-8, 21-23	Gen. 8:6-22
	Evening: Ps. 97; 112	Eph. 4:1-16	Heb. 4:14–5:6
		Mark 3:7-19a	John 2:23–3:15
Tuesday	*Morning:* Ps. 123; 146	Isa. 44:9-20	Gen. 9:1-17
	Evening: Ps. 30; 86	Eph. 4:17-32	Heb. 5:7-14
		Mark 3:19b-35	John 3:16-21
Wednesday	*Morning:* Ps. 15; 147:1-11	Isa. 44:24–45:7	Gen. 9:18-29
		Eph. 5:1-14	Heb. 6:1-12
	Evening: Ps. 48; 4	Mark 4:1-20	John 3:22-36
Thursday	*Morning:* Ps. 36; 147:12-20	Isa. 45:5-17	Gen. 11:1-9
		Eph. 5:15-33	Heb. 6:13-20
	Evening: Ps. 80; 27	Mark 4:21-34	John 4:1-15
Friday	*Morning:* Ps.130; 148	Isa. 45:18-25	Gen. 11:27–12:8
	Evening: Ps. 32; 139	Eph. 6:1-9	Heb. 7:1-17
		Mark 4:35-41	John 4:16-26
Saturday	*Morning:* Ps. 56; 149	Isa. 46:1-13	Gen. 12:9–13:1
	Evening: Ps. 118; 111	Eph. 6:10-24	Heb. 7:18-28
		Mark 5:1-20	John 4:27-42

Week following Sunday between Jan. 21 and 27 inclusive

Day	Psalm	Year 1	Year 2
Sunday	*Morning:* Ps. 67; 150	Isa. 47:1-15	Gen. 13:2-18
	Evening: Ps. 46; 93	Heb. 10:19-31	Gal. 2:1-10
		John 5:2-18	Mark 7:31-37
Monday	*Morning:* Ps. 57; 145	Isa. 48:1-11	Gen. 14:(1-7) 8-24
	Evening: Ps. 85; 47	Gal. 1:1-17	Heb. 8:1-13
		Mark 5:21-43	John 4:43-54

Day	Psalm	Year 1	Year 2
Tuesday	*Morning:* Ps. 54; 146	Isa. 48:12-21 (22)	Gen. 15:1-11, 17-21
	Evening: Ps. 28; 99	Gal. 1:18–2:10	Heb. 9:1-14
		Mark 6:1-13	John 5:1-18
Wednesday	*Morning:* Ps. 65; 147:1-11	Isa. 49:1-12	Gen. 16:1-14
		Gal. 2:11-21	Heb. 9:15-28
	Evening: Ps. 125; 91	Mark 6:13-29	John 5:19-29
Thursday	*Morning:* Ps.143; 147:12-20	Isa. 49:13-23 (24-26)	Gen. 16:15–17:14
		Gal. 3:1-14	Heb. 10:1-10
	Evening: Ps. 81; 116	Mark 6:30-46	John 5:30-47
Friday	*Morning:* Ps. 88; 148	Isa. 50:1-11	Gen. 17:15-27
	Evening: Ps. 6; 20	Gal. 3:15-22	Heb. 10:11-25
		Mark 6:47-56	John 6:1-15
Saturday	*Morning:* Ps. 122; 149	Isa. 51:1-8	Gen. 18:1-16
	Evening: Ps. 100; 63	Gal. 3:23-29	Heb. 10:26-39
		Mark 7:1-23	John 6:16-27

Week following Sun. between Jan. 28 and Feb. 3 inclusive, except when this Sunday is Transfiguration

Day	Psalm	Year 1	Year 2
Sunday	*Morning:* Ps. 108; 150	Isa. 51:9-16	Gen. 18:16-33
	Evening: Ps. 66; 23	Heb. 11:8-16	Gal. 5:13-25
		John 7:14-31	Mark 8:22-30
Monday	*Morning:* Ps. 62; 145	Isa. 51:17-23	Gen. 19:1-17 (18-23) 24-29
	Evening: Ps. 73; 9	Gal. 4:1-11	Heb. 11:1-12
		Mark 7:24-37	John 6:27-40
Tuesday	*Morning:* Ps. 12; 146	Isa. 52:1-12	Gen. 21:1-21
	Evening: Ps. 36; 7	Gal. 4:12-20	Heb. 11:13-22
		Mark 8:1-10	John 6:41-51
Wednesday	*Morning:* Ps. 96; 147:1-11	Isa. 52:13–53:12	Gen. 22:1-18
		Gal. 4:21-31	Heb. 11:23-31
	Evening: Ps. 132; 134	Mark 8:11-26	John 6:52-59
Thursday	*Morning:* Ps. 116; 147:12-20	Isa. 54:1-10 (11-17)	Gen. 23:1-20
		Gal. 5:1-15	Heb. 11:32–12:2
	Evening: Ps. 26; 130	Mark 8:27–9:1	John 6:60-71

Day	Psalm	Year 1	Year 2
Friday	*Morning:* Ps. 84; 148 *Evening:* Ps. 25; 40	Isa. 55:1-13 Gal. 5:16-24 Mark 9:2-13	Gen. 24:1-27 Heb. 12:3-11 John 7:1-13
Saturday	*Morning:* Ps. 63; 149 *Evening:* Ps. 125; 90	Isa. 56:1-8 Gal. 5:25–6:10 Mark 9:14-29	Gen. 24:28-38, 49-51 Heb. 12:12-29 John 7:14-36

Week following Sun. between Feb. 4 and 10 inclusive, except when this Sunday is Transfiguration

Day	Psalm	Year 1	Year 2
Sunday	*Morning:* Ps. 103; 150 *Evening:* Ps. 117; 139	Isa. 57:1-13 Heb. 12:1-6 John 7:37-46	Gen. 24:50-67 2 Tim. 2:14-21 Mark 10:13-22
Monday	*Morning:* Ps. 5; 145 *Evening:* Ps. 82; 29	Isa. 57:14-21 Gal. 6:11-18 Mark 9:30-41	Gen. 25:19-34 Heb. 13:1-16 John 7:37-52
Tuesday	*Morning:* Ps. 42; 146 *Evening:* Ps. 102; 133	Isa. 58:1-12 2 Tim. 1:1-14 Mark 9:42-50	Gen. 26:1-6, 12-33 Heb. 13:17-25 John 7:53–8:11
Wednesday	*Morning:* Ps. 89:1-18; 147:1-11 *Evening:* Ps. 1; 33	Isa. 59:1-21 2 Tim. 1:15–2:13 Mark 10:1-16	Gen. 27:1-29 Rom. 12:1-8 John 8:12-20
Thursday	*Morning:* Ps. 97; 147:12-20 *Evening:* Ps. 16; 62	Isa. 60:1-22 2 Tim. 2:14-26 Mark 10:17-31	Gen. 27:30-45 Rom. 12:9-21 John 8:21-32
Friday	*Morning:* Ps. 51; 148 *Evening:* Ps. 142; 65	Isa. 61:1-9 2 Tim. 3:1-17 Mark 10:32-45	Gen. 27:46–28:4, 10-22 Rom. 13:1-14 John 8:33-47
Saturday	*Morning:* Ps. 104; 149 *Evening:* Ps. 138; 98	Isa. 61:10–62:5 2 Tim. 4:1-8 Mark 10:46-52	Gen. 29:1-20 Rom. 14:1-23 John 8:47-59

Day	Psalm	Year 1	Year 2

Week following Sun. between Feb. 11 and 17 inclusive, except when this Sunday is Transfiguration

Day	Psalm	Year 1	Year 2
Sunday	*Morning:* Ps. 19; 150	Isa. 62:6-12	Gen. 29:20-35
	Evening: Ps. 81; 113	1 John 2:3-11	1 Tim. 3:14–4:10
		John 8:12-19	Mark 10:23-31
Monday	*Morning:* Ps. 135; 145	Isa. 63:1-6	Gen. 30:1-24
	Evening: Ps. 97; 112	1 Tim. 1:1-17	1 John 1:1-10
		Mark 11:1-11	John 9:1-17
Tuesday	*Morning:* Ps. 123; 146	Isa. 63:7-14	Gen. 31:1-24
	Evening: Ps. 30; 86	1 Tim. 1:18–2:8	1 John 2:1-11
		(9-15)	
		Mark 11:12-26	John 9:18-41
Wednesday	*Morning:* Ps. 15; 147:1-11	Isa. 63:15–64:9	Gen. 31:25-50
		1 Tim. 3:1-16	1 John 2:12-17
	Evening: Ps. 48; 4	Mark 11:27–12:12	John 10:1-18
Thursday	*Morning:* Ps. 36; 147:12-20	Isa. 65:1-12	Gen. 32:3-21
		1 Tim. 4:1-16	1 John 2:18-29
	Evening: Ps. 80; 27	Mark 12:13-27	John 10:19-30
Friday	*Morning:* Ps. 130; 148	Isa. 65:17-25	Gen. 32:22–33:17
	Evening: Ps. 32; 139	1 Tim. 5:(1-16)	1 John 3:1-10
		17-22 (23-25)	
		Mark 12:28-34	John 10:31-42
Saturday	*Morning:* Ps. 56; 149	Isa. 66:1-6	Gen. 35:1-20
	Evening: Ps. 118; 111	1 Tim. 6:(1-5) 6-21	1 John 3:11-18
		Mark 12:35-44	John 11:1-16

Week following Sun. between Feb. 18 and 24 inclusive, except when this Sunday is Transfiguration

Day	Psalm	Year 1	Year 2
Sunday	*Morning:* Ps. 67; 150	Isa. 66:7-14	Prov. 1:20-33
	Evening: Ps. 46; 93	1 John 3:4-10	2 Cor. 5:11-21
		John 10:7-16	Mark 10:35-45
Monday	*Morning:* Ps. 57; 145	Ruth 1:1-14	Prov. 3:11-20
	Evening: Ps. 85; 47	2 Cor. 1:1-11	1 John 3:18–4:6
		Matt. 5:1-12	John 11:17-29

DAY	PSALM	YEAR 1	YEAR 2
Tuesday	*Morning:* Ps. 54; 146 *Evening:* Ps. 28; 99	Ruth 1:15-22 2 Cor. 1:12-22 Matt. 5:13-20	Prov. 4:1-27 1 John 4:7-21 John 11:30-44
Wednesday	*Morning:* Ps. 65; 147:1-11 *Evening:* Ps. 125; 91	Ruth 2:1-13 2 Cor. 1:23–2:17 Matt. 5:21-26	Prov. 6:1-19 1 John 5:1-12 John 11:45-54
Thursday	*Morning:* Ps. 143; 147:12-20 *Evening:* Ps. 81; 116	Ruth 2:14-23 2 Cor. 3:1-18 Matt. 5:27-37	Prov. 7:1-27 1 John 5:13-21 John 11:55–12:8
Friday	*Morning:* Ps. 88; 148 *Evening:* Ps. 6; 20	Ruth 3:1-18 2 Cor. 4:1-12 Matt. 5:38-48	Prov. 8:1-21 Philemon 1-25 John 12:9-19
Saturday	*Morning:* Ps. 122; 149 *Evening:* Ps. 100; 63	Ruth 4:1-22 2 Cor. 4:13–5:10 Matt. 6:1-6	Prov. 8:22-36 2 Tim. 1:1-14 John 12:20-26

Week following Sun. between Feb. 25 and 29 inclusive, except when this Sunday is Transfiguration

DAY	PSALM	YEAR 1	YEAR 2
Sunday	*Morning:* Ps. 108; 150 *Evening:* Ps. 66; 23	Deut. 4:1-9 2 Tim. 4:1-8 John 12:1-8	Prov. 9:1-12 2 Cor. 9:6b-15 Mark 10:46-52
Monday	*Morning:* Ps. 62; 145 *Evening:* Ps. 73; 9	Deut. 4:9-14 2 Cor. 10:1-18 Matt. 6:7-15	Prov. 10:1-12 2 Tim. 1:15–2:13 John 12:27-36a
Tuesday	*Morning:* Ps. 12; 146 *Evening:* Ps. 36; 7	Deut. 4:15-24 2 Cor. 11:1-21a Matt. 6:16-23	Prov. 15:16-33 2 Tim. 2:14-26 John 12:36b-50
Wednesday	*Morning:* Ps. 96; 147:1-11 *Evening:* Ps. 132; 134	Deut. 4:25-31 2 Cor. 11:21b-33 Matt. 6:24-34	Prov. 17:1-20 2 Tim. 3:1-17 John 13:1-20
Thursday	*Morning:* Ps. 116; 147:12-20 *Evening:* Ps. 26; 130	Deut. 4:32-40 2 Cor. 12:1-10 Matt. 7:1-12	Prov. 21:30–22:6 2 Tim. 4:1-8 John 13:21-30

Day	Psalm	Year 1	Year 2
Friday	*Morning:* Ps. 84; 148 *Evening:* Ps. 25; 40	Deut. 5:1-22 2 Cor. 12:11-21 Matt. 7:13-21	Prov. 23:19-21, 29–24:2 2 Tim. 4:9-22 John 13:31-38
Saturday	*Morning:* Ps. 63; 149 *Evening:* Ps. 125; 90	Deut. 5:22-33 2 Cor. 13:1-14 Matt. 7:22-29	Prov. 25:15-28 Phil. 1:1-11 John 18:1-14

Transfiguration (Sunday preceding Lent) and following

Day	Psalm	Year 1	Year 2
Sunday	*Morning:* Ps. 103; 150 *Evening:* Ps. 117; 139	Dan. 7:9-10, 13-14 2 Cor. 3:1-9 John 12:27-36a	Mal. 4:1-6 2 Cor. 3:7-18 Luke 9:18-27
Monday	*Morning:* Ps. 5; 145 *Evening:* Ps. 82; 29	Deut. 6:1-15 Heb. 1:1-14 John 1:1-18	Prov. 27:1-6, 10-12 Phil. 2:1-13 John 18:15-18, 25-27
Tuesday	*Morning:* Ps. 42; 146 *Evening:* Ps. 102; 133	Deut. 6:16-25 Heb. 2:1-10 John 1:19-28	Prov. 30:1-4, 24-33 Phil. 3:1-11 John 18:28-38
Ash Wednesday	*Morning:* Ps. 5; 147:1-11 *Evening:* Ps. 27; 51	Jonah 3:1–4:11 Heb. 12:1-14 Luke 18:9-14	Amos 5:6-15 Heb. 12:1-14 Luke 18:9-14
Thursday	*Morning:* Ps. 27; 147:12-20 *Evening:* Ps. 126; 102	Deut. 7:6-11 Titus 1:1-16 John 1:29-34	Hab. 3:1-10 (11-15) 16-18 Phil. 3:12-21 John 17:1-8
Friday	*Morning:* Ps. 22; 148 *Evening:* Ps. 105; 130	Deut. 7:12-16 Titus 2:1-15 John 1:35-42	Ezek. 18:1-4, 25-32 Phil. 4:1-9 John 17:9-19
Saturday	*Morning:* Ps. 43; 149 *Evening:* Ps. 31; 143	Deut. 7:17-26 Titus 3:1-15 John 1:43-51	Ezek. 39:21-29 Phil. 4:10-20 John 17:20-26

Day	Psalm	Year 1	Year 2

1st Week in Lent

Sunday	*Morning:* Ps. 84; 150	Jer. 9:23-24	Dan. 9:3-10
	Evening: Ps. 42; 32	1 Cor. 1:18-31	Heb. 2:10-18
		Mark 2:18-22	John 12:44-50
Monday	*Morning:* Ps. 119:73-80; 145	Deut. 8:1-20	Gen. 37:1-11
		Heb. 2:11-18	1 Cor. 1:1-19
	Evening: Ps. 121; 6	John 2:1-12	Mark 1:1-13
Tuesday	*Morning:* Ps. 34; 146	Deut. 9:(1-3) 4-12	Gen. 37:12-24
	Evening: Ps. 25; 91	Heb. 3:1-11	1 Cor. 1:20-31
		John 2:13-22	Mark 1:14-28
Wednesday	*Morning:* Ps. 5; 147:1-11	Deut. 9:13-21	Gen. 37:25-36
		Heb. 3:12-19	1 Cor. 2:1-13
	Evening: Ps. 27; 51	John 2:23-3:15	Mark 1:29-45
Thursday	*Morning:* Ps. 27; 147:12-20	Deut. 9:23-10:5	Gen. 39:1-23
		Heb. 4:1-10	1 Cor. 2:14-3:15
	Evening: Ps. 126; 102	John 3:16-21	Mark 2:1-12
Friday	*Morning:* Ps. 22; 148	Deut. 10:12-22	Gen. 40:1-23
	Evening: Ps. 105; 130	Heb. 4:11-16	1 Cor. 3:16-23
		John 3:22-36	Mark 2:13-22
Saturday	*Morning:* Ps. 43; 149	Deut. 11:18-28	Gen. 41:1-13
	Evening: Ps. 31; 143	Heb. 5:1-10	1 Cor. 4:1-7
		John 4:1-26	Mark 2:23-3:6

2nd Week in Lent

Sunday	*Morning:* Ps. 84; 150	Jer. 1:1-10	Gen. 41:14-45
	Evening: Ps. 42; 32	1 Cor. 3:11-23	Rom. 6:3-14
		Mark 3:31-4:9	John 5:19-24
Monday	*Morning:* Ps. 119:73-80; 145	Jer. 1:11-19	Gen. 41:46-57
		Rom. 1:1-15	1 Cor. 4:8-20 (21)
	Evening: Ps. 121; 6	John 4:27-42	Mark 3:7-19a

Day	Psalm	Year 1	Year 2
Tuesday	*Morning:* Ps. 34; 146 *Evening:* Ps. 25; 91	Jer. 2:1-13, 29-32 Rom. 1:16-25 John 4:43-54	Gen. 42:1-17 1 Cor. 5:1-8 Mark 3:19b-35
Wednesday	*Morning:* Ps. 5; 147:1-11 *Evening:* Ps. 27; 51	Jer. 3:6-18 Rom. 1:(26-27) 28–2:11 John 5:1-18	Gen. 42:18-28 1 Cor. 5:9–6:11 Mark 4:1-20
Thursday	*Morning:* Ps. 27; 147:12-20 *Evening:* Ps. 126; 102	Jer. 4:9-10, 19-28 Rom. 2:12-24 John 5:19-29	Gen. 42:29-38 1 Cor. 6:12-20 Mark 4:21-34
Friday	*Morning:* Ps. 22; 148 *Evening:* Ps. 105; 130	Jer. 5:1-9 Rom. 2:25–3:18 John 5:30-47	Gen. 43:1-15 1 Cor. 7:1-9 Mark 4:35-41
Saturday	*Morning:* Ps. 43; 149 *Evening:* Ps. 31; 143	Jer. 5:20-31 Rom. 3:19-31 John 7:1-13	Gen. 43:16-34 1 Cor. 7:10-24 Mark 5:1-20

3rd Week in Lent

Day	Psalm	Year 1	Year 2
Sunday	*Morning:* Ps. 84; 150 *Evening:* Ps. 42; 32	Jer. 6:9-15 1 Cor. 6:12-20 Mark 5:1-20	Gen. 44:1-17 Rom. 8:1-10 John 5:25-29
Monday	*Morning:* Ps. 119:73- 80; 145 *Evening:* Ps. 121; 6	Jer. 7:1-15 Rom. 4:1-12 John 7:14-36	Gen. 44:18-34 1 Cor. 7:25-31 Mark 5:21-43
Tuesday	*Morning:* Ps. 34; 146 *Evening:* Ps. 25; 91	Jer. 7:21-34 Rom. 4:13-25 John 7:37-52	Gen. 45:1-15 1 Cor. 7:32-40 Mark 6:1-13
Wednesday	*Morning:* Ps. 5; 147:1-11 *Evening:* Ps. 27; 51	Jer. 8:4-7, 18–9:6 Rom. 5:1-11 John 8:12-20	Gen. 45:16-28 1 Cor. 8:1-13 Mark 6:13-29
Thursday	*Morning:* Ps. 27; 147:12-20 *Evening:* Ps. 126; 102	Jer. 10:11-24 Rom. 5:12-21 John 8:21-32	Gen. 46:1-7, 28-34 1 Cor. 9:1-15 Mark 6:30-46

DAY	PSALM	YEAR 1	YEAR 2
Friday	*Morning:* Ps. 22; 148	Jer. 11:1-8, 14-17	Gen. 47:1-26
	Evening: Ps. 105; 130	Rom. 6:1-11	1 Cor. 9:16-27
		John 8:33-47	Mark 6:47-56
Saturday	*Morning:* Ps. 43; 149	Jer. 13:1-11	Gen. 47:27–48:7
	Evening: Ps. 31; 143	Rom. 6:12-23	1 Cor. 10:1-13
		John 8:47-59	Mark 7:1-23

4th Week in Lent

DAY	PSALM	YEAR 1	YEAR 2
Sunday	*Morning:* Ps. 84; 150	Jer. 14:1-9 (10-16)	Gen. 48:8-22
	Evening: Ps. 42; 32	17-22	Rom. 8:11-25
		Gal. 4:21–5:1	John 6:27-40
		Mark 8:11-21	
Monday	*Morning:* Ps. 119:73-	Jer. 16:(1-9) 10-21	Gen. 49:1-28
	80; 145	Rom. 7:1-12	1 Cor. 10:14–11:1
	Evening: Ps. 121; 6	John 6:1-15	Mark 7:24-37
Tuesday	*Morning:* Ps. 34; 146	Jer. 17:19-27	Gen. 49:29–50:14
	Evening: Ps. 25; 91	Rom. 7:13-25	1 Cor. 11:2-34
		John 6:16-27	Mark 8:1-10
Wednesday	*Morning:* Ps. 5;	Jer. 18:1-11	Gen. 50:15-26
	147:1-11	Rom. 8:1-11	1 Cor. 12:1-11
	Evening: Ps. 27; 51	John 6:27-40	Mark 8:11-26
Thursday	*Morning:* Ps. 27;	Jer. 22:13-23	Ex. 1:6-22
	147:12-20	Rom. 8:12-27	1 Cor. 12:12-26
	Evening: Ps. 126; 102	John 6:41-51	Mark 8:27–9:1
Friday	*Morning:* Ps. 22; 148	Jer. 23:1-8	Ex. 2:1-22
	Evening: Ps. 105; 130	Rom. 8:28-39	1 Cor. 12:27–13:3
		John 6:52-59	Mark 9:2-13
Saturday	*Morning:* Ps. 43; 149	Jer. 23:9-15	Ex. 2:23–3:15
	Evening: Ps. 31; 143	Rom. 9:1-18	1 Cor. 13:1-13
		John 6:60-71	Mark 9:14-29

Day	Psalm	Year 1	Year 2
5th Week in Lent			
Sunday	*Morning:* Ps. 84; 150	Jer. 23:16-32	Ex. 3:16–4:12
	Evening: Ps. 42; 32	1 Cor. 9:19-27	Rom. 12:1-21
		Mark 8:31–9:1	John 8:46-59
Monday	*Morning:* Ps. 119:73-80; 145	Jer. 24:1-10	Ex. 4:10-20 (21-26) 27-31
	Evening: Ps. 121; 6	Rom. 9:19-33	1 Cor. 14:1-19
		John 9:1-17	Mark 9:30-41
Tuesday	*Morning:* Ps. 34; 146	Jer. 25:8-17	Ex. 5:1–6:1
	Evening: Ps. 25; 91	Rom. 10:1-13	1 Cor. 14:20-33a, 39-40
		John 9:18-41	Mark 9:42-50
Wednesday	*Morning:* Ps. 5; 147:1-11	Jer. 25:30-38	Ex. 7:8-24
	Evening: Ps. 27; 51	Rom. 10:14-21	2 Cor. 2:14–3:6
		John 10:1-18	Mark 10:1-16
Thursday	*Morning:* Ps. 27; 147:12-20	Jer. 26:1-16 (17-24)	Ex. 7:25–8:19
	Evening: Ps. 126; 102	Rom. 11:1-12	2 Cor. 3:7-18
		John 10:19-42	Mark 10:17-31
Friday	*Morning:* Ps. 22; 148	Jer. 29:1 (2-3) 4-14	Ex. 9:13-35
	Evening: Ps. 105; 130	Rom. 11:13-24	2 Cor. 4:1-12
		John 11:1-27 *or* John 12:1-10	Mark 10:32-45
Saturday	*Morning:* Ps. 43; 149	Jer. 31:27-34	Ex. 10:21–11:8
	Evening: Ps. 31; 143	Rom. 11:25-36	2 Cor. 4:13-18
		John 11:28-44 *or* John 12:37-50	Mark 10:46-52
Holy Week			
Passion/Palm Sunday	*Morning:* Ps. 84; 150	Zech. 9:9-12*	Zech. 9:9-12*
	Evening: Ps. 42; 32	1 Tim. 6:12-16* *or* Zech. 12:9-11; 13:1, 7-9**	1 Tim. 6:12-16* *or* Zech. 12:9-11; 13:1, 7-9**
		Matt. 21:12-17**	Luke 19:41-48**

*Intended for use in the morning   **Intended for use in the evening

Day	Psalm	Year 1	Year 2
Monday	*Morning:* Ps. 119:73-80; 145	Jer. 11:18-20; 12:1-16 (17)	Lam. 1:1-2, 6-12
	Evening: Ps. 121; 6	Phil. 3:1-14 John 12:9-19	2 Cor. 1:1-7 Mark 11:12-25
Tuesday	*Morning:* Ps. 34; 146	Jer. 15:10-21	Lam. 1:17-22
	Evening: Ps. 25; 91	Phil. 3:15-21 John 12:20-26	2 Cor. 1:8-22 Mark 11:27-33
Wednesday	*Morning:* Ps. 5; 147:1-11	Jer. 17:5-10, 14-17 (18) Phil. 4:1-13	Lam. 2:1-9 2 Cor. 1:23–2:11
	Evening: Ps. 27; 51	John 12:27-36	Mark 12:1-11
Maundy Thursday	*Morning:* Ps. 27; 147:12-20	Jer. 20:7-11 (12-13) 14-18	Lam. 2:10-18
	Evening: Ps. 126; 102	1 Cor. 10:14-17; 11:27-32 John 17:1-11 (12-26)	1 Cor. 10:14-17; 11:27-32 Mark 14:12-25
Good Friday	*Morning:* Ps. 22; 148	Wisd. of Sol. 1:16–2:1, 12-22 *or*	Lam. 3:1-9, 19-33
	Evening: Ps. 105; 130	Gen. 22:1-14 1 Peter 1:10-20 John 13:36-38* *or* John 19:38-42**	1 Peter 1:10-20 John 13:36-38* *or* John 19:38-42**
Holy Saturday	*Morning:* Ps. 43; 149	Job 19:21-27a	Lam. 3:37-58
	Evening: Ps. 31; 143	Heb. 4:1-16* Rom. 8:1-11**	Heb. 4:1-16* Rom. 8:1-11**
Easter Week			
Sunday	*Morning:* Ps. 93; 150	Ex. 12:1-14*	Ex. 12:1-14*
	Evening: Ps. 136; 117	John 1:1-18* *or* Isa. 51:9-11** Luke 24:13-35** *or* John 20:19-23**	John 1:1-18* *or* Isa. 51:9-11** Luke 24:13-35** *or* John 20:19-23**
Monday	*Morning:* Ps. 97; 145	Jonah 2:1-10	Ex. 12:14-27
	Evening: Ps. 124; 115	Acts 2:14, 22-32 John 14:1-14	1 Cor. 15:1-11 Mark 16:1-8

*Intended for use in the morning   **Intended for use in the evening

DAY	PSALM	YEAR 1	YEAR 2
Tuesday	*Morning:* Ps. 98; 146	Isa. 30:18-26	Ex. 12:28-39
	Evening: Ps. 66; 116	Acts 2:36-41 (42-47)	1 Cor. 15:12-28
		John 14:15-31	Mark 16:9-20
Wednesday	*Morning:* Ps. 99;	Micah 7:7-15	Ex. 12:40-51
	147:1-11	Acts 3:1-10	1 Cor. 15:(29) 30-41
	Evening: Ps. 9; 118	John 15:1-11	Matt. 28:1-16
Thursday	*Morning:* Ps. 47;	Ezek. 37:1-14	Ex. 13:3-10
	147:12-20	Acts 3:11-26	1 Cor. 15:41-50
	Evening: Ps. 68; 113	John 15:12-27	Matt. 28:16-20
Friday	*Morning:* Ps. 96; 148	Dan. 12:1-4, 13	Ex. 13:1-2, 11-16
	Evening: Ps. 49; 148	Acts 4:1-12	1 Cor. 15:51-58
		John 16:1-15	Luke 24:1-12
Saturday	*Morning:* Ps. 92; 149	Isa. 25:1-9	Ex. 13:17–14:4
	Evening: Ps. 23; 114	Acts 4:13-21 (22-31)	2 Cor. 4:16–5:10
		John 16:16-33	Mark 12:18-27

2nd Week of Easter

DAY	PSALM	YEAR 1	YEAR 2
Sunday	*Morning:* Ps. 93; 150	Isa. 43:8-13	Ex. 14:5-22
	Evening: Ps. 136; 117	1 Peter 2:2-10	1 John 1:1-7
		John 14:1-7	John 14:1-7
Monday	*Morning:* Ps. 97; 145	Dan. 1:1-21	Ex. 14:21-31
	Evening: Ps. 124; 115	1 John 1:1-10	1 Peter 1:1-12
		John 17:1-11	John 14:(1-7) 8-17
Tuesday	*Morning:* Ps. 98; 146	Dan. 2:1-16	Ex. 15:1-21
	Evening: Ps. 66; 116	1 John 2:1-11	1 Peter 1:13-25
		John 17:12-19	John 14:18-31
Wednesday	*Morning:* Ps. 99;	Dan. 2:17-30	Ex. 15:22–16:10
	147:1-11	1 John 2:12-17	1 Peter 2:1-10
	Evening: Ps. 9; 118	John 17:20-26	John 15:1-11
Thursday	*Morning:* Ps. 47;	Dan. 2:31-49	Ex. 16:10-22
	147:12-20	1 John 2:18-29	1 Peter 2:11–3:12
	Evening: Ps. 68; 113	Luke 3:1-14	John 15:12-27

Day	Psalm	Year 1	Year 2
Friday	*Morning:* Ps. 96; 148	Dan. 3:1-18	Ex. 16:23-36
	Evening: Ps. 49; 138	1 John 3:1-10	1 Peter 3:13–4:6
		Luke 3:15-22	John 16:1-15
Saturday	*Morning:* Ps. 92; 149	Dan. 3:19-30	Ex. 17:1-16
	Evening: Ps. 23; 114	1 John 3:11-18	1 Peter 4:7-19
		Luke 4:1-13	John 16:16-33

3rd Week of Easter

Day	Psalm	Year 1	Year 2
Sunday	*Morning:* Ps. 93; 150	Dan. 4:1-18	Ex. 18:1-12
	Evening: Ps. 136; 117	1 Peter 4:7-11	1 John 2:7-17
		John 21:15-25	Mark 16:9-20
Monday	*Morning:* Ps. 97; 145	Dan. 4:19-27	Ex. 18:13-27
	Evening: Ps. 124; 115	1 John 3:19–4:6	1 Peter 5:1-14
		Luke 4:14-30	Matt. (1:1-17) 3:1-6
Tuesday	*Morning:* Ps. 98; 146	Dan. 4:28-37	Ex. 19:1-16
	Evening: Ps. 66; 116	1 John 4:7-21	Col. 1:1-14
		Luke 4:31-37	Matt. 3:7-12
Wednesday	*Morning:* Ps. 99; 147:1-11	Dan. 5:1-12	Ex. 19:16-25
	Evening: Ps. 9; 118	1 John 5:1-12	Col. 1:15-23
		Luke 4:38-44	Matt. 3:13-17
Thursday	*Morning:* Ps. 47; 147:12-20	Dan. 5:13-30	Ex. 20:1-21
	Evening: Ps. 68; 113	1 John 5:13-20 (21)	Col. 1:24–2:7
		Luke 5:1-11	Matt. 4:1-11
Friday	*Morning:* Ps. 96; 148	Dan. 6:1-15	Ex. 24:1-18
	Evening: Ps. 49; 138	2 John 1-13	Col. 2:8-23
		Luke 5:12-26	Matt. 4:12-17
Saturday	*Morning:* Ps. 92; 149	Dan. 6:16-28	Ex. 25:1-22
	Evening: Ps. 23; 114	3 John 1-15	Col. 3:1-17
		Luke 5:27-39	Matt. 4:18-25

4th Week of Easter

Day	Psalm	Year 1	Year 2
Sunday	*Morning:* Ps. 93; 150	Wisd. of Sol. 1:1-15	Ex. 28:1-4, 30-38
	Evening: Ps. 136; 117	*or* Gen. 18:22-33	
		1 Peter 5:1-11	1 John 2:18-29
		Matt. 7:15-29	Mark 6:30-44

Day	Psalm	Year 1	Year 2
Monday	*Morning:* Ps. 97; 145 *Evening:* Ps. 124; 115	Wisd. of Sol. 1:16–2:11, 21-24 *or* Jer. 30:1-9 Col. 1:1-14 Luke 6:1-11	Ex. 32:1-20 Col. 3:18–4:6 (7-18) Matt. 5:1-10
Tuesday	*Morning:* Ps. 98; 146 *Evening:* Ps. 66; 116	Wisd. of Sol. 3:1-9 *or* Jer. 30:10-17 Col. 1:15-23 Luke 6:12-26	Ex. 32:21-34 1 Thess. 1:1-10 Matt. 5:11-16
Wednesday	*Morning:* Ps. 99; 147:1-11 *Evening:* Ps. 9; 118	Wisd. of Sol. 4:16–5:8 *or* Jer. 30:18-22 Col. 1:24–2:7 Luke 6:27-38	Ex. 33:1-23 1 Thess. 2:1-12 Matt. 5:17-20
Thursday	*Morning:* Ps. 47; 147:12-20 *Evening:* Ps. 68; 113	Wisd. of Sol. 5:9-23 *or* Jer. 31:1-14 Col. 2:8-23 Luke 6:39-49	Ex. 34:1-17 1 Thess. 2:13-20 Matt. 5:21-26
Friday	*Morning:* Ps. 96; 148 *Evening:* Ps. 49; 138	Wisd. of Sol. 6:12-23 *or* Jer. 31:15-22 Col. 3:1-11 Luke 7:1-17	Ex. 34:18-35 1 Thess. 3:1-13 Matt. 5:27-37
Saturday	*Morning:* Ps. 92; 149 *Evening:* Ps. 23; 114	Wisd. of Sol. 7:1-14 *or* Jer. 31:23-25 Col. 3:12-17 Luke 7:18-28 (29-30) 31-35	Ex. 40:18-38 1 Thess. 4:1-12 Matt. 5:38-48

5th Week of Easter

Day	Psalm	Year 1	Year 2
Sunday	*Morning:* Ps. 93; 150 *Evening:* Ps. 136; 117	Wisd. of Sol. 7:22–8:1 *or* Isa. 32:1-8 2 Thess. 2:13-17 Matt. 7:7-14	Lev. 8:1-13, 30-36 Heb. 12:1-14 Luke 4:16-30
Monday	*Morning:* Ps. 97; 145 *Evening:* Ps. 124; 115	Wisd. of Sol. 9:1, 7- 18 *or* Jer. 32:1-15 Col. 3:18–4:18 Luke 7:36-50	Lev. 16:1-19 1 Thess. 4:13-18 Matt. 6:1-6, 16-18

DAY	PSALM	YEAR 1	YEAR 2
Tuesday	*Morning*: Ps. 98; 146 *Evening*: Ps. 66; 116	Wisd. of Sol. 10:1-4 (5-12) 13-21 *or* Jer. 32:16-25 Rom. 12:1-21 Luke 8:1-15	Lev. 16:20-34 1 Thess. 5:1-11 Matt. 6:7-15
Wednesday	*Morning*: Ps. 99; 147:1-11 *Evening*: Ps. 9; 118	Wisd. of Sol. 13:1-9 *or* Jer. 32:36-44 Rom. 13:1-14 Luke 8:16-25	Lev. 19:1-18 1 Thess. 5:12-28 Matt. 6:19-24
Thursday	*Morning*: Ps. 47; 147:12-20 *Evening*: Ps. 68; 113	Wisd. of Sol. 14:27–15:3 *or* Jer. 33:1-13 Rom. 14:1-12 Luke 8:26-39	Lev. 19:26-37 2 Thess. 1:1-12 Matt. 6:25-34
Friday	*Morning*: Ps. 96; 148 *Evening*: Ps. 49; 138	Wisd. of Sol. 16:15–17:1 *or* Deut. 31:30–32:14 Rom. 14:13-23 Luke 8:40-56	Lev. 23:1-22 2 Thess. 2:1-17 Matt. 7:1-12
Saturday	*Morning*: Ps. 92; 149 *Evening*: Ps. 23; 114	Wisd. of Sol. 19:1-8, 18-22 *or* Deut. 32:34-41 (42) 43 Rom. 15:1-13 Luke 9:1-17	Lev. 23:23-44 2 Thess. 3:1-18 Matt. 7:13-21
6th Week of Easter			
Sunday	*Morning*: Ps. 93; 150 *Evening*: Ps. 136; 117	Ecclus. 43:1-12, 27- 32 *or* Deut. 15:1-11 1 Tim. 3:14–4:5 Matt. 13:24-34a	Lev. 25:1-17 James 1:2-8, 16-18 Luke 12:13-21
Monday	*Morning*: Ps. 97; 145 *Evening*: Ps. 124; 115	Deut. 8:1-10 *or* Deut. 18:9-14 James 1:1-15 Luke 9:18-27	Lev. 25:35-55 Col. 1:9-14 Matt. 13:1-16

Day	Psalm	Year 1	Year 2
Tuesday	*Morning:* Ps. 98; 146 *Evening:* Ps. 66; 116	Deut. 8:11-20 *or* Deut. 18:15-22 James 1:16-27 Luke 11:1-13	Lev. 26:1-20 1 Tim. 2:1-6 Matt. 13:18-23
Wednesday	*Morning:* Ps. 99; 147:1-11	Baruch 3:24-37 *or* Deut. 19:1-7 James 5:13-18 Luke 12:22-31	Lev. 26:27-42 Eph. 1:1-10 Matt. 22:41-46
Eve of Ascension	Ps. 9; 118	2 Kings 2:1-15 Rev. 5:1-14	2 Kings 2:1-15 Rev. 5:1-14
Ascension Day	*Morning:* Ps. 47; 147:12-20 *Evening:* Ps. 68; 113	Ezek. 1:1-14, 24-28b Heb. 2:5-18 Matt. 28:16-20	Dan. 7:9-14 Heb. 2:5-18 Matt. 28:16-20
Friday	*Morning:* Ps. 96; 148 *Evening:* Ps. 49; 138	Ezek. 1:28–3:3 Heb. 4:14–5:6 Luke 9:28-36	1 Sam. 2:1-10 Eph. 2:1-10 Matt. 7:22-27
Saturday	*Morning:* Ps. 92; 149 *Evening:* Ps. 23; 114	Ezek. 3:4-17 Heb. 5:7-14 Luke 9:37-50	Num. 11:16-17, 24-29 Eph. 2:11-22 Matt. 7:28–8:4
7th Week of Easter			
Sunday	*Morning:* Ps. 93; 150 *Evening:* Ps. 136; 117	Ezek. 3:16-27 Eph. 2:1-10 Matt. 10:24-33, 40-42	Ex. 3:1-12 Heb. 12:18-29 Luke 10:17-24
Monday	*Morning:* Ps. 97; 145 *Evening:* Ps. 124; 115	Ezek. 4:1-17 Heb. 6:1-12 Luke 9:51-62	Josh. 1:1-9 Eph. 3:1-13 Matt. 8:5-17
Tuesday	*Morning:* Ps. 98; 146 *Evening:* Ps. 66; 116	Ezek. 7:10-15, 23b-27 Heb. 6:13-20 Luke 10:1-17	1 Sam. 16:1-13a Eph. 3:14-21 Matt. 8:18-27
Wednesday	*Morning:* Ps. 99; 147:1-11 *Evening:* Ps. 9; 118	Ezek. 11:14-25 Heb. 7:1-17 Luke 10:17-24	Isa. 4:2-6 Eph. 4:1-16 Matt. 8:28-34

Day	Psalm	Year 1	Year 2
Thursday	*Morning:* Ps. 47; 147:12-20	Ezek. 18:1-4, 19-32	Zech. 4:1-14
		Heb. 7:18-28	Eph. 4:17-32
	Evening: Ps. 68; 113	Luke 10:25-37	Matt. 9:1-8
Friday	*Morning:* Ps. 96; 148	Ezek. 34:17-31	Jer. 31:27-34
	Evening: Ps. 49; 138	Heb. 8:1-13	Eph. 5:1-32
		Luke 10:38-42	Matt. 9:9-17
Saturday	*Morning:* Ps. 92; 149	Ezek. 43:1-12	Ezek. 36:22-27
		Heb. 9:1-14	Eph. 6:1-24
		Luke 11:14-23	Matt. 9:18-26
Eve of Pentecost	Ps. 23; 114	Ex. 19:3-8a, 16-20	Ex. 19:3-8a, 16-20
		1 Peter 2:4-10	1 Peter 2:4-10
Pentecost	*Morning:* Ps. 104; 150	Isa. 11:1-9	Deut. 16:9-12
	Evening: Ps. 29; 33	1 Cor. 2:1-13	Acts 4:18-21, 23-33
		John 14:21-29	John 4:19-26

On the weekdays which follow, the readings are taken from the week which corresponds to the date of Pentecost.

Day	Psalm	Year 1	Year 2
Eve of *Trinity Sunday*	Ps. 125; 90	Ecclus. 42:15-25 *or* Isa. 6:1-8 Eph. 3:14-21	Ecclus. 42:15-25 *or* Isa. 6:1-8 Eph. 3:14-21
Trinity Sunday	*Morning:* Ps. 103; 150	Ecclus. 43:1-12	Job 38:1-11; 42:1-5
	Evening: Ps. 117; 139	(27-33) *or* Deut. 6:1-9 (10-15)	
		Eph. 4:1-16	Rev. 19:4-16
		John 1:1-18	John 1:29-34

On the weekdays which follow, the readings are taken from the week which corresponds to the date of Trinity Sunday.

Week following Sunday between May 11 and 16 inclusive, if after Pentecost Sunday

Day	Psalm	Year 1	Year 2
Monday	*Morning:* Ps. 62; 145	Isa. 63:7-14	Ezek. 33:1-11
	Evening: Ps. 73; 9	2 Tim. 1:1-14	1 John 1:1-10
		Luke 11:24-36	Matt. 9:27-34
Tuesday	*Morning:* Ps. 12; 146	Isa. 63:15–64:9	Ezek. 33:21-33
	Evening: Ps. 36; 7	2 Tim. 1:15–2:13	1 John 2:1-11
		Luke 11:37-52	Matt. 9:35–10:4

DAY	PSALM	YEAR 1	YEAR 2
Wednesday	*Morning*: Ps. 96; 147:1-11	Isa. 65:1-12 2 Tim. 2:14-26	Ezek. 34:1-16 1 John 2:12-17
	Evening: Ps. 132; 134	Luke 11:53–12:12	Matt. 10:5-15
Thursday	*Morning*: Ps. 116; 147:12-20	Isa. 65:17-25 2 Tim. 3:1-17	Ezek. 37:21b-28 1 John 2:18-29
	Evening: Ps. 26; 130	Luke 12:13-31	Matt. 10:16-23
Friday	*Morning*: Ps. 84; 148	Isa. 66:1-6	Ezek. 39:21-29
	Evening: Ps. 25; 40	2 Tim. 4:1-8	1 John 3:1-10
		Luke 12:32-48	Matt. 10:24-33
Saturday	*Morning*: Ps. 63; 149	Isa. 66:7-14	Ezek. 47:1-12
	Evening: Ps. 125; 90	2 Tim. 4:9-22	1 John 3:11-18
		Luke 12:49-59	Matt. 10:34-42

Week following Sunday between May 17 and 23 inclusive, if after Pentecost Sunday

DAY	PSALM	YEAR 1	YEAR 2
Monday	*Morning*: Ps. 5; 145	Ruth 1:1-18	Prov. 3:11-20
	Evening: Ps. 82; 29	1 Tim. 1:1-17	1 John 3:18–4:6
		Luke 13:1-9	Matt. 11:1-6
Tuesday	*Morning*: Ps. 42; 146	Ruth 1:19–2:13	Prov. 4:1-27
	Evening: Ps. 102; 133	1 Tim. 1:18–2:8	1 John 4:7-21
		Luke 13:10-17	Matt. 11:7-15
Wednesday	*Morning*: Ps. 89:1-18; 147:1-11	Ruth 2:14-23 1 Tim. 3:1-16	Prov. 6:1-19 1 John 5:1-12
	Evening: Ps. 1; 33	Luke 13:18-30	Matt. 11:16-24
Thursday	*Morning*: Ps. 97; 147:12-20	Ruth 3:1-18 1 Tim. 4:1-16	Prov. 7:1-27 1 John 5:13-21
	Evening: Ps. 16; 62	Luke 13:31-35	Matt. 11:25-30
Friday	*Morning*: Ps. 51; 148	Ruth 4:1-22	Prov. 8:1-21
	Evening: Ps. 142; 65	1 Tim. 5:17-22 (23-25)	2 John 1-13
		Luke 14:1-11	Matt. 12:1-14
Saturday	*Morning*: Ps. 104; 149	Deut. 1:1-8	Prov. 8:22-36
	Evening: Ps. 138; 98	1 Tim. 6:6-21	3 John 1-15
		Luke 14:12-24	Matt. 12:15-21

Day	Psalm	Year 1	Year 2

Week following Sunday between May 24 and 28 inclusive, if after Pentecost Sunday

Day	Psalm	Year 1	Year 2
Sunday	*Morning:* Ps. 19; 150	Deut. 4:1-9	Prov. 9:1-12
	Evening: Ps. 81; 113	Rev. 7:1-4, 9-17	Acts 8:14-25
		Matt. 12:33-45	Luke 10:25-28, 38-42
Monday	*Morning:* Ps. 135; 145	Deut. 4:9-14	Prov. 10:1-12
	Evening: Ps. 97; 112	2 Cor. 1:1-11	1 Tim. 1:1-17
		Luke 14:25-35	Matt. 12:22-32
Tuesday	*Morning:* Ps. 123; 146	Deut. 4:15-24	Prov. 15:16-33
	Evening: Ps. 30; 86	2 Cor. 1:12-22	1 Tim. 1:18-2:15
		Luke 15:1-10	Matt. 12:33-42
Wednesday	*Morning:* Ps. 15; 147:1-11	Deut. 4:25-31	Prov. 17:1-20
		2 Cor. 1:23-2:17	1 Tim. 3:1-16
	Evening: Ps. 48; 4	Luke 15:1-2, 11-32	Matt. 12:43-50
Thursday	*Morning:* Ps. 36; 147:12-20	Deut. 4:32-40	Prov. 21:30-22:6
		2 Cor. 3:1-18	1 Tim. 4:1-16
	Evening: Ps. 80; 27	Luke 16:1-9	Matt. 13:24-30
Friday	*Morning:* Ps. 130; 148	Deut. 5:1-22	Prov. 23:19-21, 29–24:2
	Evening: Ps. 32; 139	2 Cor. 4:1-12	
		Luke 16:10-17 (18)	1 Tim. 5:17-22 (23-25)
			Matt. 13:31-35
Saturday	*Morning:* Ps. 56; 149	Deut. 5:22-33	Prov. 25:15-28
	Evening: Ps. 118; 111	2 Cor. 4:13-5:10	1 Tim. 6:6-21
		Luke 16:19-31	Matt. 13:36-43

Week following Sunday between May 29 and June 4 inclusive, if after Pentecost Sunday

Day	Psalm	Year 1	Year 2
Sunday	*Morning:* Ps. 67; 150	Deut. 11:1-12	Eccl. 1:1-11
	Evening: Ps. 46; 93	Rev. 10:1-11	Acts 8:26-40
		Matt. 13:44-58	Luke 11:1-13
Monday	*Morning:* Ps. 57; 145	Deut. 11:13-19	Eccl. 2:1-15
	Evening: Ps. 85; 47	2 Cor. 5:11–6:2	Gal. 1:1-17
		Luke 17:1-10	Matt. 13:44-52

Day	Psalm	Year 1	Year 2
Tuesday	*Morning:* Ps. 54; 146	Deut. 12:1-12	Eccl. 2:16-26
	Evening: Ps. 28; 99	2 Cor. 6:3-13 (14–7:1)	Gal. 1:18–2:10
		Luke 17:11-19	Matt. 13:53-58
Wednesday	*Morning:* Ps. 65; 147:1-11	Deut. 13:1-11	Eccl. 3:1-15
		2 Cor. 7:2-16	Gal. 2:11-21
	Evening: Ps. 125; 91	Luke 17:20-37	Matt. 14:1-12
Thursday	*Morning:* Ps. 143; 147:12-20	Deut. 16:18-20; 17:14-20	Eccl. 3:16–4:3
		2 Cor. 8:1-16	Gal. 3:1-14
	Evening: Ps. 81; 116	Luke 18:1-8	Matt. 14:13-21
Friday	*Morning:* Ps. 88; 148	Deut. 26:1-11	Eccl. 5:1-7
	Evening: Ps. 6; 20	2 Cor. 8:16-24	Gal. 3:15-22
		Luke 18:9-14	Matt. 14:22-36
Saturday	*Morning:* Ps. 122; 149	Deut. 29:2-15	Eccl. 5:8-20
	Evening: Ps. 100; 63	2 Cor. 9:1-15	Gal. 3:23–4:11
		Luke 18:15-30	Matt. 15:1-20

Week following Sunday between June 5 and 11 inclusive, if after Pentecost Sunday

Day	Psalm	Year 1	Year 2
Sunday	*Morning:* Ps. 108; 150	Deut. 29:16-29	Eccl. 6:1-12
	Evening: Ps. 66; 23	Rev. 12:1-12	Acts 10:9-23
		Matt. 15:29-39	Luke 12:32-40
Monday	*Morning:* Ps. 62; 145	Deut. 30:1-10	Eccl. 7:1-14
	Evening: Ps. 73; 9	2 Cor. 10:1-18	Gal. 4:12-20
		Luke 18:31-43	Matt. 15:21-28
Tuesday	*Morning:* Ps. 12; 146	Deut. 30:11-20	Eccl. 8:14–9:10
	Evening: Ps. 36; 7	2 Cor. 11:1-21a	Gal. 4:21-31
		Luke 19:1-10	Matt. 15:29-39
Wednesday	*Morning:* Ps. 96; 147:1-11	Deut. 31:30–32:14	Eccl. 9:11-18
		2 Cor. 11:21b-33	Gal. 5:1-15
	Evening: Ps. 132; 134	Luke 19:11-27	Matt. 16:1-12
Thursday	*Morning:* Ps. 116; 147:12-20	Ecclus. 44:19–45:5 *or* S. of Sol. 1:1-3, 9-11, 15-16a; 2:1-3a	Eccl. 11:1-8
	Evening: Ps. 26; 130	2 Cor. 12:1-10	Gal. 5:16-24
		Luke 19:28-40	Matt. 16:13-20

Day	Psalm	Year 1	Year 2
Friday	*Morning:* Ps. 84; 148	Ecclus. 45:6-16	Eccl. 11:9–12:14
	Evening: Ps. 25; 40	*or* S. of Sol. 2:8-13; 4:1-4a, 5-7, 9-11	
		2 Cor. 12:11-21	Gal. 5:25–6:10
		Luke 19:41-48	Matt. 16:21-28
Saturday	*Morning:* Ps. 63; 149	Ecclus. 46:1-10 *or* S. of	Num. 3:1-13
	Evening: Ps. 125; 90	Sol. 5:10-16; 7:1-2 (3-5) 6-7a (9); 8:6-7	
		2 Cor. 13:1-14	Gal. 6:11-18
		Luke 20:1-8	Matt. 17:1-13

Week following Sunday between June 12 and 18 inclusive

Day	Psalm	Year 1	Year 2
Sunday	*Morning:* Ps. 103; 150	Ecclus. 46:11-20	Num. 6:22-27
	Evening: Ps. 117; 139	*or* Ex. 6:2-13; 7:1-6	
		Rev. 15:1-8	Acts 13:1-12
		Matt. 18:1-14	Luke 12:41-48
Monday	*Morning:* Ps. 5; 145	1 Sam. 1:1-20	Num. 9:15-23; 10:29-36
	Evening: Ps. 82; 29	Acts 1:1-14	Rom. 1:1-15
		Luke 20:9-19	Matt. 17:14-21
Tuesday	*Morning:* Ps. 42; 146	1 Sam. 1:21–2:11	Num. 11:1-23
	Evening: Ps. 102; 133	Acts 1:15-26	Rom. 1:16-25
		Luke 20:19-26	Matt. 17:22-27
Wednesday	*Morning:* Ps. 89:1-18; 147:1-11	1 Sam. 2:12-26	Num. 11:24-33 (34-35)
	Evening: Ps. 1; 33	Acts 2:1-21	Rom. 1:28–2:11
		Luke 20:27-40	Matt. 18:1-9
Thursday	*Morning:* Ps. 97; 147:12-20	1 Sam. 2:27-36	Num. 12:1-16
		Acts 2:22-36	Rom. 2:12-24
	Evening: Ps. 16; 62	Luke 20:41–21:4	Matt. 18:10-20
Friday	*Morning:* Ps. 51; 148	1 Sam. 3:1-21	Num. 13:1-3, 21-30
	Evening: Ps. 142; 65	Acts 2:37-47	Rom. 2:25–3:8
		Luke 21:5-19	Matt. 18:21-35
Saturday	*Morning:* Ps. 104; 149	1 Sam. 4:1b-11	Num. 13:31–14:25
	Evening: Ps. 138; 98	Acts 4:32–5:11	Rom. 3:9-20
		Luke 21:20-28	Matt. 19:1-12

Day	Psalm	Year 1	Year 2

Week following Sunday between June 19 and 25 inclusive

Day	Psalm	Year 1	Year 2
Sunday	*Morning:* Ps. 19; 150 *Evening:* Ps. 81; 113	1 Sam. 4:12-22 James 1:1-18 Matt. 19:23-30	Num. 14:26-45 Acts 15:1-12 Luke 12:49-56
Monday	*Morning:* Ps. 135; 145 *Evening:* Ps. 97; 112	1 Sam. 5:1-12 Acts 5:12-26 Luke 21:29-36	Num. 16:1-19 Rom. 3:21-31 Matt. 19:13-22
Tuesday	*Morning:* Ps. 123; 146 *Evening:* Ps. 30; 86	1 Sam. 6:1-16 Acts 5:27-42 Luke 21:37–22:13	Num. 16:20-35 Rom. 4:1-12 Matt. 19:23-30
Wednesday	*Morning:* Ps. 15; 147:1-11 *Evening:* Ps. 48; 4	1 Sam. 7:2-17 Acts 6:1-15 Luke 22:14-23	Num. 16:36-50 Rom. 4:13-25 Matt. 20:1-16
Thursday	*Morning:* Ps. 36; 147:12-20 *Evening:* Ps. 80; 27	1 Sam. 8:1-22 Acts 6:15–7:16 Luke 22:24-30	Num. 17:1-11 Rom. 5:1-11 Matt. 20:17-28
Friday	*Morning:* Ps. 130; 148 *Evening:* Ps. 32; 139	1 Sam. 9:1-14 Acts 7:17-29 Luke 22:31-38	Num. 20:1-13 Rom. 5:12-21 Matt. 20:29-34
Saturday	*Morning:* Ps. 56; 149 *Evening:* Ps. 118; 111	1 Sam. 9:15–10:1 Acts 7:30-43 Luke 22:39-51	Num. 20:14-29 Rom. 6:1-11 Matt. 21:1-11

Week following Sunday between June 26 and July 2 inclusive

Day	Psalm	Year 1	Year 2
Sunday	*Morning:* Ps. 67; 150 *Evening:* Ps. 46; 93	1 Sam. 10:1-16 Rom. 4:13-25 Matt. 21:23-32	Num. 21:4-9, 21-35 Acts 17:(12-21) 23-24 Luke 13:10-17
Monday	*Morning:* Ps. 57; 145 *Evening:* Ps. 85; 47	1 Sam. 10:17-27 Acts 7:44–8:1a Luke 22:52-62	Num. 22:1-21 Rom. 6:12-23 Matt. 21:12-22
Tuesday	*Morning:* Ps. 54; 146 *Evening:* Ps. 28; 99	1 Sam. 11:1-15 Acts 8:1b-13 Luke 22:63-71	Num. 22:21-38 Rom. 7:1-12 Matt. 21:23-32

DAY	PSALM	YEAR 1	YEAR 2
Wednesday	*Morning:* Ps. 65; 147:1-11	1 Sam. 12:1-6 (7-15) 16-25	Num. 22:41–23:12
	Evening: Ps. 125; 91	Acts 8:14-25	Rom. 7:13-25
		Luke 23:1-12	Matt. 21:33-46
Thursday	*Morning:* Ps. 143; 147:12-20	1 Sam. 13:5-18	Num. 23:11-26
	Evening: Ps. 81; 116	Acts 8:26-40	Rom. 8:1-11
		Luke 23:13-25	Matt. 22:1-14
Friday	*Morning:* Ps. 88; 148	1 Sam. 13:19–14:15	Num. 24:1-13
	Evening: Ps. 6; 20	Acts 9:1-9	Rom. 8:12-17
		Luke 23:26-31	Matt. 22:15-22
Saturday	*Morning:* Ps. 122; 149	1 Sam. 14:16-30	Num. 24:12-25
	Evening: Ps. 100; 63	Acts 9:10-19a	Rom. 8:18-25
		Luke 23:32-43	Matt. 22:23-40

Week following Sunday between July 3 and 9 inclusive

DAY	PSALM	YEAR 1	YEAR 2
Sunday	*Morning:* Ps. 108; 150	1 Sam. 14:36-45	Num. 27:12-23
	Evening: Ps. 66; 23	Rom. 5:1-11	Acts 19:11-20
		Matt. 22:1-14	Mark 1:14-20
Monday	*Morning:* Ps. 62; 145	1 Sam. 15:1-3, 7-23	Num. 32:1-6, 16-27
	Evening: Ps. 73; 9	Acts 9:19b-31	Rom. 8:26-30
		Luke 23:44-56a	Matt. 23:1-12
Tuesday	*Morning:* Ps. 12; 146	1 Sam. 15:24-35	Num. 35:1-3, 9-15, 30-34
	Evening: Ps. 36; 7	Acts 9:32-43	Rom. 8:31-39
		Luke 23:56b–24:11 (12)	Matt. 23:13-26
Wednesday	*Morning:* Ps. 96; 147:1-11	1 Sam. 16:1-13	Deut. 1:1-18
		Acts 10:1-16	Rom. 9:1-18
	Evening: Ps. 132; 134	Luke 24:13-35	Matt. 23:27-39
Thursday	*Morning:* Ps. 116; 147:12-20	1 Sam. 16:14–17:11	Deut. 3:18-28
		Acts 10:17-33	Rom. 9:19-33
	Evening: Ps. 26; 130	Luke 24:36-53	Matt. 24:1-14
Friday	*Morning:* Ps. 84; 148	1 Sam. 17:17-30	Deut. 31:7-13, 24–32:4
	Evening: Ps. 25; 40	Acts 10:34-48	Rom. 10:1-13
		Mark 1:1-13	Matt. 24:15-31

Day	Psalm	Year 1	Year 2
Saturday	*Morning:* Ps. 63; 149	1 Sam. 17:31-49	Deut. 34:1-12
	Evening: Ps. 125; 90	Acts 11:1-18	Rom. 10:14-21
		Mark 1:14-28	Matt. 24:32-51

Week following Sunday between July 10 and 16 inclusive

Day	Psalm	Year 1	Year 2
Sunday	*Morning:* Ps. 103; 150	1 Sam. 17:50–18:4	Josh. 1:1-18
	Evening: Ps. 117; 139	Rom. 10:4-17	Acts 21:3-15
		Matt. 23:29-39	Mark 1:21-27
Monday	*Morning:* Ps. 5; 145	1 Sam. 18:5-16	Josh. 2:1-14
	Evening: Ps. 82; 29	(17-27a) 27b-30	
		Acts 11:19-30	Rom. 11:1-12
		Mark 1:29-45	Matt. 25:1-13
Tuesday	*Morning:* Ps. 42; 146	1 Sam. 19:1-18	Josh. 2:15-24
	Evening: Ps. 102; 133	(19-24)	
		Acts 12:1-17	Rom. 11:13-24
		Mark 2:1-12	Matt. 25:14-30
Wednesday	*Morning:* Ps. 89:1-18;	1 Sam. 20:1-23	Josh. 3:1-13
	147:1-11	Acts 12:18-25	Rom. 11:25-36
	Evening: Ps. 1; 33	Mark 2:13-22	Matt. 25:31-46
Thursday	*Morning:* Ps. 97;	1 Sam. 20:24-42	Josh. 3:14–4:7
	147:12-20	Acts 13:1-12	Rom. 12:1-8
	Evening: Ps. 16; 62	Mark 2:23–3:6	Matt. 26:1-16
Friday	*Morning:* Ps. 51; 148	1 Sam. 21:1-15	Josh. 4:19–5:1, 10-15
	Evening: Ps. 142; 65	Acts 13:13-25	Rom. 12:9-21
		Mark 3:7-19a	Matt. 26:17-25
Saturday	*Morning:* Ps. 104; 149	1 Sam. 21:1-23	Josh. 6:1-14
	Evening: Ps. 138; 98	Acts 13:26-43	Rom. 13:1-7
		Mark 3:19b-35	Matt. 26:26-35

Week following Sunday between July 17 and 23 inclusive

Day	Psalm	Year 1	Year 2
Sunday	*Morning:* Ps. 19; 150	1 Sam. 23:7-18	Josh. 6:15-27
	Evening: Ps. 81; 113	Rom. 11:33–12:2	Acts 22:30–23:11
		Matt. 25:14-30	Mark 2:1-12

Day	Psalm	Year 1	Year 2
Monday	*Morning:* Ps. 135; 145	1 Sam. 24:1-22	Josh. 7:1-13
	Evening: Ps. 97; 112	Acts 13:44-52	Rom. 13:8-14
		Mark 4:1-20	Matt. 26:36-46
Tuesday	*Morning:* Ps. 123; 146	1 Sam. 25:1-22	Josh. 8:1-22
	Evening: Ps. 30; 86	Acts 14:1-18	Rom. 14:1-12
		Mark 4:21-34	Matt. 26:47-56
Wednesday	*Morning:* Ps. 15; 147:1-11	1 Sam. 25:23-44	Josh. 8:30-35
		Acts 14:19-28	Rom. 14:13-23
	Evening: Ps. 48; 4	Mark 4:35-41	Matt. 26:57-68
Thursday	*Morning:* Ps. 36; 147:12-20	1 Sam. 28:3-20	Josh. 9:3-21
		Acts 15:1-11	Rom. 15:1-13
	Evening: Ps. 80; 27	Mark 5:1-20	Matt. 26:69-75
Friday	*Morning:* Ps. 130; 148	1 Sam. 31:1-13	Josh. 9:22–10:15
	Evening: Ps. 32; 139	Acts 15:12-21	Rom. 15:14-24
		Mark 5:21-43	Matt. 27:1-10
Saturday	*Morning:* Ps. 56; 149	2 Sam. 1:1-16	Josh. 23:1-16
	Evening: Ps. 118; 111	Acts 15:22-35	Rom. 15:25-33
		Mark 6:1-13	Matt. 27:11-23

Week following Sunday between July 24 and 30 inclusive

Day	Psalm	Year 1	Year 2
Sunday	*Morning:* Ps. 67; 150	2 Sam. 1:17-27	Josh. 24:1-15
	Evening: Ps. 46; 93	Rom. 12:9-21	Acts 28:23-31
		Matt. 25:31-46	Mark 2:23-28
Monday	*Morning:* Ps. 57; 145	2 Sam. 2:1-11	Josh. 24:16-33
	Evening: Ps. 85; 47	Acts 15:36–16:5	Rom. 16:1-16
		Mark 6:14-29	Matt. 27:24-31
Tuesday	*Morning:* Ps. 54; 146	2 Sam. 3:6-21	Judg. 2:1-5, 11-23
	Evening: Ps. 28; 99	Acts 16:6-15	Rom. 16:17-27
		Mark 6:30-46	Matt. 27:32-44
Wednesday	*Morning:* Ps. 65; 147:1-11	2 Sam. 3:22-39	Judg. 3:12-30
		Acts 16:16-24	Acts 1:1-14
	Evening: Ps. 125; 91	Mark 6:47-56	Matt. 27:45-54

Day	Psalm	Year 1	Year 2
Thursday	*Morning:* Ps. 143; 147:12-20	2 Sam. 4:1-12 Acts 16:25-40	Judg. 4:4-23 Acts 1:15-26
	Evening: Ps. 81; 116	Mark 7:1-23	Matt. 27:55-66
Friday	*Morning:* Ps. 88; 148 *Evening:* Ps. 6; 20	2 Sam. 5:1-12 Acts 17:1-15 Mark 7:24-37	Judg. 5:1-18 Acts 2:1-21 Matt. 28:1-10
Saturday	*Morning:* Ps. 122; 149 *Evening:* Ps. 100; 63	2 Sam. 5:22–6:11 Acts 17:16-34 Mark 8:1-10	Judg. 5:19-31 Acts 2:22-36 Matt. 28:11-20

Week following Sunday between July 31 and Aug. 6 inclusive

Day	Psalm	Year 1	Year 2
Sunday	*Morning:* Ps. 108; 150 *Evening:* Ps. 66; 23	2 Sam. 6:12-23 Rom. 14:7-12 John 1:43-51	Judg. 6:1-24 2 Cor. 9:6-15 Mark 3:20-30
Monday	*Morning:* Ps. 62; 145 *Evening:* Ps. 73; 9	2 Sam. 7:1-17 Acts 18:1-11 Mark 8:11-21	Judg. 6:25-40 Acts 2:37-47 John 1:1-18
Tuesday	*Morning:* Ps. 12; 146 *Evening:* Ps. 36; 7	2 Sam. 7:18-29 Acts 18:12-28 Mark 8:22-33	Judg. 7:1-18 Acts 3:1-11 John 1:19-28
Wednesday	*Morning:* Ps. 96; 147:1-11	2 Sam. 9:1-13 Acts 19:1-10	Judg. 7:19–8:12 Acts 3:12-26
	Evening: Ps. 132; 134	Mark 8:34–9:1	John 1:29-42
Thursday	*Morning:* Ps. 116; 147:12-20	2 Sam. 11:1-27 Acts 19:11-20	Judg. 8:22-35 Acts 4:1-12
	Evening: Ps. 26; 130	Mark 9:2-13	John 1:43-51
Friday	*Morning:* Ps. 84; 148 *Evening:* Ps. 25; 40	2 Sam. 12:1-14 Acts 19:21-41 Mark 9:14-29	Judg. 9:1-16, 19-21 Acts 4:13-31 John 2:1-12
Saturday	*Morning:* Ps. 63; 149 *Evening:* Ps. 125; 90	2 Sam. 12:15-31 Acts 20:1-16 Mark 9:30-41	Judg. 9:22-25, 50-57 Acts 4:32–5:11 John 2:13-25

Day	Psalm	Year 1	Year 2

Week following Sunday between Aug. 7 and 13 inclusive

Day	Psalm	Year 1	Year 2
Sunday	*Morning:* Ps. 103; 150 *Evening:* Ps. 117; 139	2 Sam. 13:1-22 Rom. 15:1-13 John 3:22-36	Judg. 11:1-11, 29-40 2 Cor. 11:21b-31 Mark 4:35-41
Monday	*Morning:* Ps. 5; 145 *Evening:* Ps. 82; 29	2 Sam. 13:23-39 Acts 20:17-38 Mark 9:42-50	Judg. 12:1-7 Acts 5:12-26 John 3:1-21
Tuesday	*Morning:* Ps. 42; 146 *Evening:* Ps. 102; 133	2 Sam. 14:1-20 Acts 21:1-14 Mark 10:1-16	Judg. 13:1-15 Acts 5:27-42 John 3:22-36
Wednesday	*Morning:* Ps. 89:1-18; 147:1-11 *Evening:* Ps. 1; 33	2 Sam. 14:21-33 Acts 21:15-26 Mark 10:17-31	Judg. 13:15-24 Acts 6:1-15 John 4:1-26
Thursday	*Morning:* Ps. 97; 147:12-20 *Evening:* Ps. 16; 62	2 Sam. 15:1-18 Acts 21:27-36 Mark 10:32-45	Judg. 14:1-19 Acts 6:15–7:16 John 4:27-42
Friday	*Morning:* Ps. 51; 148 *Evening:* Ps. 142; 65	2 Sam. 15:19-37 Acts 21:37–22:16 Mark 10:46-52	Judg. 14:20–15:20 Acts 7:17-29 John 4:43-54
Saturday	*Morning:* Ps. 104; 149 *Evening:* Ps. 138; 98	2 Sam. 16:1-23 Acts 22:17-29 Mark 11:1-11	Judg. 16:1-14 Acts 7:30-43 John 5:1-18

Week following Sunday between Aug. 14 and 20 inclusive

Day	Psalm	Year 1	Year 2
Sunday	*Morning:* Ps. 19; 150 *Evening:* Ps. 81; 113	2 Sam. 17:1-23 Gal. 3:6-14 John 5:30-47	Judg. 16:15-31 2 Cor. 13:1-11 Mark 5:25-34
Monday	*Morning:* Ps. 135; 145 *Evening:* Ps. 97; 112	2 Sam. 17:24–18:8 Acts 22:30–23:11 Mark 11:12-26	Judg. 17:1-13 Acts 7:44–8:1a John 5:19-29
Tuesday	*Morning:* Ps. 123; 146 *Evening:* Ps. 30; 86	2 Sam. 18:9-18 Acts 23:12-24 Mark 11:27–12:12	Judg. 18:1-15 Acts 8:1-13 John 5:30-47

DAY	PSALM	YEAR 1	YEAR 2
Wednesday	*Morning:* Ps. 15; 147:1-11	2 Sam. 18:19-33 Acts 23:23-35	Judg. 18:16-31 Acts 8:14-25
	Evening: Ps. 48; 4	Mark 12:13-27	John 6:1-15
Thursday	*Morning:* Ps. 36; 147:12-20	2 Sam. 19:1-23 Acts 24:1-23	Job 1:1-22 Acts 8:26-40
	Evening: Ps. 80; 27	Mark 12:28-34	John 6:16-27
Friday	*Morning:* Ps. 130; 148	2 Sam. 19:24-43	Job 2:1-13
	Evening: Ps. 32; 139	Acts 24:24–25:12	Acts 9:1-9
		Mark 12:35-44	John 6:27-40
Saturday	*Morning:* Ps. 56; 149	2 Sam. 23:1-7, 13-17	Job 3:1-26
	Evening: Ps. 118; 111	Acts 25:13-27	Acts 9:10-19a
		Mark 13:1-13	John 6:41-51

Week following Sunday between Aug. 21 and 27 inclusive

DAY	PSALM	YEAR 1	YEAR 2
Sunday	*Morning:* Ps. 67; 150	2 Sam. 24:1-2, 10-25	Job 4:1-6, 12-21
	Evening: Ps. 46; 93	Gal. 3:23–4:7	Rev. 4:1-11
		John 8:12-20	Mark 6:1-6a
Monday	*Morning:* Ps. 57; 145	1 Kings 1:(1-4) 5-31	Job 4:1; 5:1-11, 17-21, 26-27
	Evening: Ps. 85; 47	Acts 26:1-23	Acts 9:19b-31
		Mark 13:14-27	John 6:52-59
Tuesday	*Morning:* Ps. 54; 146	1 Kings 1:32–2:4 (5-46a) 46b	Job 6:1-4, 8-15, 21
	Evening: Ps. 28; 99	Acts 26:24–27:8	Acts 9:32-43
		Mark 13:28-37	John 6:60-71
Wednesday	*Morning:* Ps. 65; 147:1-11	1 Kings 3:1-15 Acts 27:9-26	Job 6:1; 7:1-21 Acts 10:1-16
	Evening: Ps. 125; 91	Mark 14:1-11	John 7:1-13
Thursday	*Morning:* Ps. 143; 147:12-20	1 Kings 3:16-28 Acts 27:27-44	Job 8:1-10, 20-22 Acts 10:17-33
	Evening: Ps. 81; 116	Mark 14:12-26	John 7:14-36
Friday	*Morning:* Ps. 88; 148	1 Kings 5:1–6:1, 7	Job 9:1-15, 32-35
	Evening: Ps. 6; 20	Acts 28:1-16	Acts 10:34-48
		Mark 14:27-42	John 7:37-52

DAY	PSALM	YEAR 1	YEAR 2
Saturday	*Morning:* Ps. 122; 149	1 Kings 7:51–8:21	Job 9:1; 10:1-9, 16-22
	Evening: Ps. 100; 63	Acts 28:17-31	Acts 11:1-18
		Mark 14:43-52	John 8:12-20

Week following Sunday between Aug. 28 and Sept. 3 inclusive

DAY	PSALM	YEAR 1	YEAR 2
Sunday	*Morning:* Ps. 108; 150	1 Kings 8:22-30 (31-40)	Job. 11:1-9, 13-20
	Evening: Ps. 66; 23	1 Tim. 4:7b-16	Rev. 5:1-14
		John 8:47-59	Matt. 5:1-12
Monday	*Morning:* Ps. 62; 145	2 Chron. 6:32–7:7	Job 12:1-6, 13-25
	Evening: Ps. 73; 9	James 2:1-13	Acts 11:19-30
		Mark 14:53-65	John 8:21-32
Tuesday	*Morning:* Ps. 12; 146	1 Kings 8:65–9:9	Job 12:1; 13:3-17, 21-27
	Evening: Ps. 36; 7	James 2:14-26	Acts 12:1-17
		Mark 14:66-72	John 8:33-47
Wednesday	*Morning:* Ps. 96; 147:1-11	1 Kings 9:24–10:13	Job 12:1; 14:1-22
		James 3:1-12	Acts 12:18-25
	Evening: Ps. 132; 134	Mark 15:1-11	John 8:47-59
Thursday	*Morning:* Ps. 116; 147:12-20	1 Kings 11:1-13	Job 16:16-22; 17:1, 13-16
		James 3:13–4:12	Acts 13:1-12
	Evening: Ps. 26; 130	Mark 15:12-21	John 9:1-17
Friday	*Morning:* Ps. 84; 148	1 Kings 11:26-43	Job 19:1-7, 14-27
	Evening: Ps. 25; 40	James 4:13–5:6	Acts 13:13-25
		Mark 15:22-32	John 9:18-41
Saturday	*Morning:* Ps. 63; 149	1 Kings 12:1-20	Job 22:1-4, 21–23:7
	Evening: Ps. 125; 90	James 5:7-20	Acts 13:26-43
		Mark 15:33-39	John 10:1-18

Week following Sunday between Sept. 4 and 10 inclusive

DAY	PSALM	YEAR 1	YEAR 2
Sunday	*Morning:* Ps. 103; 150	1 Kings 12:21-33	Job 25:1-6; 27:1-6
	Evening: Ps. 117; 139	Acts 4:18-31	Rev. 14:1-7, 13
		John 10:31-42	Matt. 5:13-20
Monday	*Morning:* Ps. 5; 145	1 Kings 13:1-10	Job 32:1-10,19–33:1,19-28
	Evening: Ps. 82; 29	Phil. 1:1-11	Acts 13:44-52
		Mark 15:40-47	John 10:19-30

Day	Psalm	Year 1	Year 2
Tuesday	*Morning:* Ps. 42; 146 *Evening:* Ps. 102; 133	1 Kings 16:23-34 Phil. 1:12-30 Mark 16:1-8 (9-20)	Job 29:1-20 Acts 14:1-18 John 10:31-42
Wednesday	*Morning:* Ps. 89:1-18; 147:1-11 *Evening:* Ps. 1; 33	1 Kings 17:1-24 Phil. 2:1-11 Matt. 2:1-12	Job 29:1; 30:1-2, 16-31 Acts 14:19-28 John 11:1-16
Thursday	*Morning:* Ps. 97; 147:12-20 *Evening:* Ps. 16; 62	1 Kings 18:1-19 Phil. 2:12-30 Matt. 2:13-23	Job 29:1; 31:1-23 Acts 15:1-11 John 11:17-29
Friday	*Morning:* Ps. 51; 148 *Evening:* Ps. 142; 65	1 Kings 18:20-40 Phil. 3:1-16 Matt. 3:1-12	Job 29:1; 31:24-40 Acts 15:12-21 John 11:30-44
Saturday	*Morning:* Ps. 104; 149 *Evening:* Ps. 138; 98	1 Kings 18:41–19:8 Phil. 3:17–4:7 Matt. 3:13-17	Job 38:1-17 Acts 15:22-35 John 11:45-54

Week following Sunday between Sept. 11 and 17 inclusive

Day	Psalm	Year 1	Year 2
Sunday	*Morning:* Ps. 19; 150 *Evening:* Ps. 81; 113	1 Kings 19:8-21 Acts 5:34-42 John 11:45-57	Job 38:1, 18-41 Rev. 18:1-8 Matt. 5:21-26
Monday	*Morning:* Ps. 135; 145 *Evening:* Ps. 97; 112	1 Kings 21:1-16 1 Cor. 1:1-19 Matt. 4:1-11	Job 40:1-24 Acts 15:36–16:5 John 11:55–12:8
Tuesday	*Morning:* Ps. 123; 146 *Evening:* Ps. 30; 86	1 Kings 21:17-29 1 Cor. 1:20-31 Matt. 4:12-17	Job 40:1; 41:1-11 Acts 16:6-15 John 12:9-19
Wednesday	*Morning:* Ps. 15; 147:1-11 *Evening:* Ps. 48; 4	1 Kings 22:1-28 1 Cor. 2:1-13 Matt. 4:18-25	Job 42:1-17 Acts 16:16-24 John 12:20-26
Thursday	*Morning:* Ps. 36; 147:12-20 *Evening:* Ps. 80; 27	1 Kings 22:29-45 1 Cor. 2:14–3:15 Matt. 5:1-10	Job 28:1-28 Acts 16:25-40 John 12:27-36a

Day	Psalm	Year 1	Year 2
Friday	*Morning:* Ps. 130; 148	2 Kings 1:2-17	Esth. 1:1-4, 10-19
	Evening: Ps. 32; 139	1 Cor. 3:16-23	Acts 17:1-15
		Matt. 5:11-16	John 12:36b-43
Saturday	*Morning:* Ps. 56; 149	2 Kings 2:1-18	Esth. 2:5-8, 15-23
	Evening: Ps. 118; 111	1 Cor. 4:1-7	Acts 17:16-34
		Matt. 5:17-20	John 12:44-50

Week following Sunday between Sept. 18 and 24 inclusive

Day	Psalm	Year 1	Year 2
Sunday	*Morning:* Ps. 67; 150	2 Kings 4:8-37	Esth. 3:1-4:3
	Evening: Ps. 46; 93	Acts 9:10-31	James 1:19-27
		Luke 3:7-18	Matt. 6:1-6, 16-18
Monday	*Morning:* Ps. 57; 145	2 Kings 5:1-19	Esth. 4:4-17
	Evening: Ps. 85; 47	1 Cor. 4:8-21	Acts 18:1-11
		Matt. 5:21-26	Luke (1:1-4) 3:1-14
Tuesday	*Morning:* Ps. 54; 146	2 Kings 5:19-27	Esth. 5:1-14
	Evening: Ps. 28; 99	1 Cor. 5:1-8	Acts 18:12-28
		Matt. 5:27-37	Luke 3:15-22
Wednesday	*Morning:* Ps. 65; 147:1-11	2 Kings 6:1-23	Esth. 6:1-14
		1 Cor. 5:9-6:11	Acts 19:1-10
	Evening: Ps. 125; 91	Matt. 5:38-48	Luke 4:1-13
Thursday	*Morning:* Ps. 143; 147:12-20	2 Kings 9:1-16	Esth. 7:1-10
		1 Cor. 6:12-20	Acts 19:11-20
	Evening: Ps. 81; 116	Matt. 6:1-6, 16-18	Luke 4:14-30
Friday	*Morning:* Ps. 88; 148	2 Kings 9:17-37	Esth. 8:1-8, 15-17
	Evening: Ps. 6; 20	1 Cor. 7:1-9	Acts 19:21-41
		Matt. 6:7-15	Luke 4:31-37
Saturday	*Morning:* Ps. 122; 149	2 Kings 11:1-20a	Esth. 9:1-32
	Evening: Ps. 100; 63	1 Cor. 7:10-24	Acts 20:1-16
		Matt. 6:19-24	Luke 4:38-44

Week following Sunday between Sept. 25 and Oct. 1 inclusive

Day	Psalm	Year 1	Year 2
Sunday	*Morning:* Ps. 108; 150	2 Kings 17:1-18	Hos. 1:1-2:1
	Evening: Ps. 66; 23	Acts 9:36-43	James 3:1-13
		Luke 5:1-11	Matt. 13:44-52

DAY	PSALM	YEAR 1	YEAR 2
Monday	*Morning:* Ps. 62; 145	2 Kings 17:24-41	Hos. 2:2-15
	Evening: Ps. 73; 9	1 Cor. 7:25-31	Acts 20:17-38
		Matt. 6:25-34	Luke 5:1-11
Tuesday	*Morning:* Ps. 12; 146	2 Chron. 29:1-3;	Hos. 2:16-23
	Evening: Ps. 36; 7	30:1 (2-9) 10-27	
		1 Cor. 7:32-40	Acts 21:1-14
		Matt. 7:1-12	Luke 5:12-26
Wednesday	*Morning:* Ps. 96;	2 Kings 18:9-25	Hos. 3:1-5
	147:1-11	1 Cor. 8:1-13	Acts 21:15-26
	Evening: Ps. 132; 134	Matt. 7:13-21	Luke 5:27-39
Thursday	*Morning:* Ps. 116;	2 Kings 18:28-37	Hos. 4:1-10
	147:12-20	1 Cor. 9:1-15	Acts 21:27-36
	Evening: Ps. 26; 130	Matt. 7:22-29	Luke 6:1-11
Friday	*Morning:* Ps. 84; 148	2 Kings 19:1-20	Hos. 4:11-19
	Evening: Ps. 25; 40	1 Cor. 9:16-27	Acts 21:37–22:16
		Matt. 8:1-17	Luke 6:12-26
Saturday	*Morning:* Ps. 63; 149	2 Kings 19:21-36	Hos. 5:1-7
	Evening: Ps. 125; 90	1 Cor. 10:1-13	Acts 22:17-29
		Matt. 8:18-27	Luke 6:27-38

Week following Sunday between Oct. 2 and 8 inclusive

DAY	PSALM	YEAR 1	YEAR 2
Sunday	*Morning:* Ps. 103; 150	2 Kings 20:1-21	Hos. 5:8–6:6
	Evening: Ps. 117; 139	Acts 12:1-17	1 Cor. 2:6-16
		Luke 7:11-17	Matt. 14:1-12
Monday	*Morning:* Ps. 5; 145	2 Kings 21:1-18	Hos. 6:7–7:7
	Evening: Ps. 82; 29	1 Cor. 10:14–11:1	Acts 22:30–23:11
		Matt. 8:28-34	Luke 6:39-49
Tuesday	*Morning:* Ps. 42; 146	2 Kings 22:1-13	Hos. 7:8-16
	Evening: Ps. 102; 133	1 Cor. 11:2 (3-16) 17-22	Acts 23:12-24
		Matt. 9:1-8	Luke 7:1-17
Wednesday	*Morning:* Ps. 89:1-18;	2 Kings 22:14–23:3	Hos. 8:1-14
	147:1-11	1 Cor. 11:23-34	Acts 23:23-35
	Evening: Ps. 1; 33	Matt. 9:9-17	Luke 7:18-35

DAY	PSALM	YEAR 1	YEAR 2
Thursday	*Morning:* Ps. 97; 147:12-20	2 Kings 23:4-25	Hos. 9:1-9
		1 Cor. 12:1-11	Acts 24:1-23
	Evening: Ps. 16; 62	Matt. 9:18-26	Luke 7:36-50
Friday	*Morning:* Ps. 51; 148	2 Kings 23:36–24:17	Hos. 9:10-17
	Evening: Ps. 142; 65	1 Cor. 12:12-26	Acts 24:24–25:12
		Matt. 9:27-34	Luke 8:1-15
Saturday	*Morning:* Ps. 104; 149	Jer. 35:1-19	Hos. 10:1-15
	Evening: Ps. 138; 98	1 Cor. 12:27–13:3	Acts 25:13-27
		Matt. 9:35–10:4	Luke 8:16-25

Week following Sunday between Oct. 9 and 15 inclusive

DAY	PSALM	YEAR 1	YEAR 2
Sunday	*Morning:* Ps. 19; 150	Jer. 36:1-10	Hos. 11:1-11
	Evening: Ps. 81; 113	Acts 14:8-18	1 Cor. 4:9-16
		Luke 7:36-50	Matt. 15:21-28
Monday	*Morning:* Ps. 135; 145	Jer. 36:11-26	Hos. 11:12–12:1
	Evening: Ps. 97; 112	1 Cor. 13:(1-3) 4-13	Acts 26:1-23
		Matt. 10:5-15	Luke 8:26-39
Tuesday	*Morning:* Ps. 123; 146	Jer. 36:27–37:2	Hos. 12:2-14
	Evening: Ps. 30; 86	1 Cor. 14:1-12	Acts 26:24–27:8
		Matt. 10:16-23	Luke 8:40-56
Wednesday	*Morning:* Ps. 15; 147:1-11	Jer. 37:3-21	Hos. 13:1-3
		1 Cor. 14:13-25	Acts 27:9-26
	Evening: Ps. 48; 4	Matt. 10:24-33	Luke 9:1-17
Thursday	*Morning:* Ps. 36; 147:12-20	Jer. 38:1-13	Hos. 13:4-8
		1 Cor. 14:26-33a (33b-36) 37-40	Acts 27:27-44
	Evening: Ps. 80; 27	Matt. 10:34-42	Luke 9:18-27
Friday	*Morning:* Ps. 130; 148	Jer. 38:14-28	Hos. 13:9-16
	Evening: Ps. 32; 139	1 Cor. 15:1-11	Acts 28:1-16
		Matt. 11:1-6	Luke 9:28-36
Saturday	*Morning:* Ps. 56; 149	Jer. 52:1-34	Hos. 14:1-9
	Evening: Ps. 118; 111	1 Cor. 15:12-29	Acts 28:17-31
		Matt. 11:7-15	Luke 9:37-50

Day	Psalm	Year 1	Year 2

Week following Sunday between Oct. 16 and 22 inclusive

Day	Psalm	Year 1	Year 2
Sunday	*Morning:* Ps. 67; 150 *Evening:* Ps. 46; 93	Jer. 29:1, 4-14 *or* Jer. 39:11–40:6 Acts 16:6-15 Luke 10:1-12, 17-20	Ecclus. 4:1-10 *or* Micah 1:1-9 1 Cor. 10:1-13 Matt. 16:13-20
Monday	*Morning:* Ps. 57; 145 *Evening:* Ps. 85; 47	Jer. 44:1-14 *or* Jer. 29:1, 4-14 1 Cor. 15:30-41 Matt. 11:16-24	Ecclus. 4:20–5:7 *or* Micah 2:1-13 Rev. 7:1-8 Luke 9:51-62
Tuesday	*Morning:* Ps. 54; 146 *Evening:* Ps. 28; 99	Lam. 1:1-5 (6-9)10-12 *or* Jer. 40:7–41:3 1 Cor. 15:41-50 Matt. 11:25-30	Ecclus. 6:5-17 *or* Micah 3:1-8 Rev. 7:9-17 Luke 10:1-16
Wednesday	*Morning:* Ps. 65; 147:1-11 *Evening:* Ps. 125; 91	Lam. 2:8-15 *or* Jer. 41:4-18 1 Cor. 15:51-58 Matt. 12:1-14	Ecclus. 7:4-14 *or* Micah 3:9–4:5 Rev. 8:1-13 Luke 10:17-24
Thursday	*Morning:* Ps. 143; 147:12-20 *Evening:* Ps. 81; 116	Ezra 1:1-11 *or* Jer. 42:1-22 1 Cor. 16:1-9 Matt. 12:15-21	Ecclus. 10:1-18 *or* Micah 5:1-4, 10-15 Rev. 9:1-12 Luke 10:25-37
Friday	*Morning:* Ps. 88; 148 *Evening:* Ps. 6; 20	Ezra 3:1-13 *or* Jer. 43:1-13 1 Cor. 16:10-24 Matt. 12:22-32	Ecclus. 11:2-20 *or* Micah 6:1-8 Rev. 9:13-21 Luke 10:38-42
Saturday	*Morning:* Ps. 122; 149 *Evening:* Ps. 100; 63	Ezra 4:7, 11-24 *or* Jer. 44:1-14 Philemon 1-25 Matt. 12:33-42	Ecclus. 15:9-20 *or* Micah 7:1-7 Rev. 10:1-11 Luke 11:1-13

Week following Sunday between Oct. 23 and 29 inclusive

Day	Psalm	Year 1	Year 2
Sunday	*Morning:* Ps. 108; 150 *Evening:* Ps. 66; 23	Hag. 1:1–2:9 *or* Jer. 44:15-30 Acts 18:24–19:7 Luke 10:25-37	Ecclus. 18:19-33 *or* Jonah 1:1-17a 1 Cor. 10:15-24 Matt. 18:15-20

Day	Psalm	Year 1	Year 2
Monday	*Morning:* Ps. 62; 145	Zech. 1:7-17	Ecclus. 19:4-17
	Evening: Ps. 73; 9	*or* Jer. 45:1-5	*or* Jonah 1:17–2:10
		Rev. 1:4-20	Rev. 11:1-14
		Matt. 12:43-50	Luke 11:14-26
Tuesday	*Morning:* Ps. 12; 146	Ezra 5:1-17 *or* Lam.	Ecclus. 24:1-12
	Evening: Ps. 36; 7	1:1-5 (6-9) 10-12	*or* Jonah 3:1–4:11
		Rev. 4:1-11	Rev. 11:14-19
		Matt. 13:1-9	Luke 11:27-36
Wednesday	*Morning:* Ps. 96;	Ezra 6:1-22	Ecclus. 28:14-26
	147:1-11	*or* Lam. 2:8-15	*or* Nahum 1:1-14
	Evening: Ps. 132; 134	Rev. 5:1-10	Rev. 12:1-6
		Matt. 13:10-17	Luke 11:37-52
Thursday	*Morning:* Ps. 116;	Neh. 1:1-11	Ecclus. 31:12-18,
	147:12-20	*or* Lam. 2:16-22	25–32:2
	Evening: Ps. 26; 130	Rev. 5:11–6:11	*or* Nahum 1:15–2:12
		Matt. 13:18-23	Rev. 12:7-17
			Luke 11:53–12:12
Friday	*Morning:* Ps. 84; 148	Neh. 2:1-20	Ecclus. 34:1-8, 18-22
	Evening: Ps. 25; 40	*or* Lam. 4:1-22	*or* Nahum 2:13–3:7
		Rev. 6:12–7:4	Rev. 13:1-10
		Matt. 13:24-30	Luke 12:13-31
Saturday	*Morning:* Ps. 63; 149	Neh. 4:1-23	Ecclus. 35:1-17
	Evening: Ps. 125; 90	*or* Lam. 5:1-22	*or* Nahum 3:8-19
		Rev. 7:(4-8) 9-17	Rev. 13:11-18
		Matt. 13:31-35	Luke 12:32-48

Week following Sunday between Oct. 30 and Nov. 5 inclusive

Day	Psalm	Year 1	Year 2
Sunday	*Morning:* Ps. 103; 150	Neh. 5:1-9	Ecclus. 36:1-17
	Evening: Ps. 117; 139	*or* Ezra 1:1-11	*or* Zeph. 1:1-6
		Acts 20:7-12	1 Cor. 12:27–13:13
		Luke 12:22-31	Matt. 18:21-35
Monday	*Morning:* Ps. 5; 145	Neh. 6:1-19	Ecclus. 38:24-34
	Evening: Ps. 82; 29	*or* Ezra 3:1-13	*or* Zeph. 1:7-13
		Rev. 10:1-11	Rev. 14:1-13
		Matt. 13:36-43	Luke 12:49-59

DAY	PSALM	YEAR 1	YEAR 2
Tuesday	*Morning:* Ps. 42; 146	Neh. 12:27-31a, 42b-	Ecclus. 43:1-22
	Evening: Ps. 102; 133	47 *or* Ezra 4:7, 11-24	*or* Zeph. 1:14-18
		Rev. 11:1-19	Rev. 14:14-15:8
		Matt. 13:44-52	Luke 13:1-9
Wednesday	*Morning:* Ps. 89:1-18;	Neh. 13:4-22	Ecclus. 43:23-33
	147:1-11	*or* Hag. 1:1-2:9	*or* Zeph. 2:1-15
	Evening: Ps. 1; 33	Rev. 12:1-12	Rev. 16:1-11
		Matt. 13:53-58	Luke 13:10-17
Thursday	*Morning:* Ps. 97;	Ezra 7:(1-10) 11-26	Ecclus. 44:1-15
	147:12-20	*or* Zech. 1:7-17	*or* Zeph. 3:1-7
	Evening: Ps. 16; 62	Rev. 14:1-13	Rev. 16:12-21
		Matt. 14:1-12	Luke 13:18-30
Friday	*Morning:* Ps. 51; 148	Ezra 7:27-28; 8:21-36	Ecclus. 50:1, 11-24
	Evening: Ps. 142; 65	*or* Ezra 5:1-17	*or* Zeph. 3:8-13
		Rev. 15:1-8	Rev. 17:1-18
		Matt. 14:13-21	Luke 13:31-35
Saturday	*Morning:* Ps. 104; 149	Ezra 9:1-15	Ecclus. 51:1-12
	Evening: Ps. 138; 98	*or* Ezra 6:1-22	*or* Zeph. 3:14-20
		Rev. 17:1-14	Rev. 18:1-14
		Matt. 14:22-36	Luke 14:1-11

Week following Sunday between Nov. 6 and 12 inclusive

DAY	PSALM	YEAR 1	YEAR 2
Sunday	*Morning:* Ps. 19; 150	Ezra 10:1-17	Ecclus. 51:13-22
	Evening: Ps. 81; 113	*or* Neh. 1:1-11	*or* Joel 1:1-13
		Acts 24:10-21	1 Cor. 14:1-12
		Luke 14:12-24	Matt. 20:1-16
Monday	*Morning:* Ps. 135; 145	Neh. 9:1-15 (16-25)	Joel 1:1-13
	Evening: Ps. 97; 112	*or* Neh. 2:1-20	*or* Joel 1:15-2:2
		Rev. 18:1-8	Rev. 18:15-24
		Matt. 15:1-20	Luke 14:12-24
Tuesday	*Morning:* Ps. 123; 146	Neh. 9:26-38	Joel 1:15-2:2 (3-11)
	Evening: Ps. 30; 86	*or* Neh. 4:1-23	*or* Joel 2:3-11
		Rev. 18:9-20	Rev. 19:1-10
		Matt. 15:21-28	Luke 14:25-35

Day	Psalm	Year 1	Year 2
Wednesday	*Morning:* Ps. 15; 147:1-11	Neh. 7:73b–8:3, 5-18 *or* Neh. 5:1-19	Joel 2:12-19
	Evening: Ps. 48; 4	Rev. 18:21-24	Rev. 19:11-21
		Matt. 15:29-39	Luke 15:1-10
Thursday	*Morning:* Ps. 36; 147:12-20	1 Macc. 1:1-28 *or* Neh. 6:1-19	Joel 2:21-27
	Evening: Ps. 80; 27	Rev. 19:1-10	James 1:1-15
		Matt. 16:1-12	Luke 15:1-2, 11-32
Friday	*Morning:* Ps. 130; 148	1 Macc. 1:41-63 *or* Neh. 12:27-31a, 42b-47	Joel 2:28–3:8
	Evening: Ps. 32; 139	Rev. 19:11-16	James 1:16-27
		Matt. 16:13-20	Luke 16:1-9
Saturday	*Morning:* Ps. 56; 149	1 Macc. 2:1-28 *or* Neh. 13:4-22	Joel 3:9-17
	Evening: Ps. 118; 111	Rev. 20:1-6	James 2:1-13
		Matt. 16:21-28	Luke 16:10-17 (18)

Week following Sunday between Nov. 13 and 19 inclusive

Day	Psalm	Year 1	Year 2
Sunday	*Morning:* Ps. 67; 150	1 Macc. 2:29-43 (44-48) *or* Ezra 7:(1-10) 11-26	Hab. 1:1-4 (5-11) 12–2:1
	Evening: Ps. 46; 93	Acts 28:14b-23	Phil. 3:13–4:1
		Luke 16:1-13	Matt. 23:13-24
Monday	*Morning:* Ps. 57; 145	1 Macc. 2:49-70 *or* Ezra 7:27-28; 8:21-36	Hab. 2:1-4, 9-20
	Evening: Ps. 85; 47	Rev. 20:7-15	James 2:14-26
		Matt. 17:1-13	Luke 16:19-31
Tuesday	*Morning:* Ps. 54; 146	1 Macc. 3:1-24 *or* Ezra 9:1-15	Hab. 3:1-10 (11-15) 16-18
	Evening: Ps. 28; 99	Rev. 21:1-8	James 3:1-12
		Matt. 17:14-21	Luke 17:1-10

Day	Psalm	Year 1	Year 2
Wednesday	*Morning:* Ps. 65; 147:1-11	1 Macc. 3:25-41 *or* Ezra 10:1-17	Mal. 1:1, 6-14
	Evening: Ps. 125; 91	Rev. 21:9-21 Matt. 17:22-27	James 3:13–4:12 Luke 17:11-19
Thursday	*Morning:* Ps. 143; 147:12-20	1 Macc. 3:42-60 *or* Neh. 9:1-15 (16-25)	Mal. 2:1-16
	Evening: Ps. 81; 116	Rev. 21:22–22:5 Matt. 18:1-9	James 4:13–5:6 Luke 17:20-37
Friday	*Morning:* Ps. 88; 148	1 Macc. 4:1-25 *or* Neh. 9:26-38	Mal. 3:1-12
	Evening: Ps. 6; 20	Rev. 22:6-13 Matt. 18:10-20	James 5:7-12 Luke 18:1-8
Saturday	*Morning:* Ps. 122; 149	1 Macc. 4:36-59 *or* Neh. 7:73b–8:3, 5-18	Mal. 3:13–4:6
	Evening: Ps. 100; 63	Rev. 22:14-21 Matt. 18:21-35	James 5:13-20 Luke 18:9-14

Christ the King or Reign of Christ (Sunday between Nov. 20 and 26) and following

Day	Psalm	Year 1	Year 2
Sunday	*Morning:* Ps. 108; 150	Isa. 19:19-25	Zech. 9:9-16
	Evening: Ps. 66; 23	Rom. 15:5-13 Luke 19:11-27	1 Peter 3:13-22 Matt. 21:1-13
Monday	*Morning:* Ps. 62; 145	Joel 3:1-2, 9-17	Zech. 10:1-12
	Evening: Ps. 73; 9	1 Peter 1:1-12 Matt. 19:1-12	Gal. 6:1-10 Luke 18:15-30
Tuesday	*Morning:* Ps. 12; 146	Nahum 1:1-13	Zech. 11:4-17
	Evening: Ps. 36; 7	1 Peter 1:13-25 Matt. 19:13-22	1 Cor. 3:10-23 Luke 18:31-43
Wednesday	*Morning:* Ps. 96; 147:1-11	Obad. 15-21	Zech. 12:1-10
	Evening: Ps. 132; 134	1 Peter 2:1-10 Matt. 19:23-30	Eph. 1:3-14 Luke 19:1-10
Thursday	*Morning:* Ps. 116; 147:12-20	Zeph. 3:1-13	Zech. 13:1-9
	Evening: Ps. 26; 130	1 Peter 2:11-25 Matt. 20:1-16	Eph. 1:15-23 Luke 19:11-27

Day	Psalm	Year 1	Year 2
Friday	*Morning:* Ps. 84; 148	Isa. 24:14-23	Zech. 14:1-11
	Evening: Ps. 25; 40	1 Peter 3:13–4:6	Rom. 15:7-13
		Matt. 20:17-28	Luke 19:28-40
Saturday	*Morning:* Ps. 63; 149	Micah 7:11-20	Zech. 14:12-21
	Evening: Ps. 125; 90	1 Peter 4:7-19	Phil. 2:1-11
		Matt. 20:29-34	Luke 19:41-48

Special Days

Displayed below are special days that are commonly observed in various branches of the ecumenical church. With the exception of All Saints' Day and the civil days New Year's Day and Thanksgiving, they are ordinarily not included in Reformed observance. However, there is value in including them in daily prayer. Their inclusion will recognize the work of God in these biblical events, and express our solidarity with Christians in other traditions. Psalms are those appointed for the day of the week in which a special day falls.

New Year's Eve or Day

Eccl. 3:1-13
Rev. 21:1-6a
Matt. 25:31-46

Birth of John the Baptist—June 24

Mal. 3:1-4 *or* Isa. 40:1-11
Luke 1:5-23, 57-67 (68-80) *
Matt. 11:2-19 **

Presentation of the Lord—Feb. 2

Mal. 3:1-4
Heb. 2:14-18
Luke 2:22-40

Holy Cross—Sept. 14

Num. 21:4b-9 *or* Isa. 45:21-25
1 Cor. 1:18-24
John 3:13-17 *or* John 12:20-33

Annunciation of the Lord—March 25

Isa. 7:10-14
1 Tim. 3:16
  or Heb. 2:5-10
Luke 1:26-38

All Saints' Day—Nov. 1

Isa. 26:1-4, 8-9, 12-13, 19-21
Rev. 21:9-11, 22-27 (22:1-5)
  or Heb. 11:32–12:2
Matt. 5:1-12

Visitation of Mary to Elizabeth—May 31

Isa. 11:1-5 *or* 1 Sam. 2:1-10
Rom. 12:9-16b
Luke 1:39-47

Thanksgiving Day

Deut. 8:1-10 *or* Deut. 26:1-11
Phil. 4:6-20 *or* 1 Tim. 2:1-4
Luke 17:11-19 *or* Matt. 6:25-33

---

*Intended for use in the morning   **Intended for use in the evening*

TABLE OF MAJOR CELEBRATIONS
OF THE LITURGICAL CALENDAR

TABLE OF MAJOR CELEBRATIONS OF THE LITURGICAL CALENDAR

Sunday Cycle	Daily Cycle	FIRST SUNDAY OF ADVENT	ASH WEDNESDAY	EASTER	ASCENSION	PENTECOST
A	I	November 29, 1992	February 24, 1993	April 11, 1993	May 20, 1993	May 30, 1993
B	II	November 28, 1993	February 16, 1994	April 3, 1994	May 12, 1994	May 22, 1994
C	I	November 27, 1994	March 1, 1995	April 16, 1995	May 25, 1995	June 4, 1995
A	II	December 3, 1995	February 21, 1996	April 7, 1996	May 16, 1996	May 26, 1996
B	I	December 1, 1996	February 12, 1997	March 30, 1997	May 8, 1997	May 18, 1997
C	II	November 30, 1997	February 25, 1998	April 12, 1998	May 21, 1998	May 31, 1998
A	I	November 29, 1998	February 17, 1999	April 4, 1999	May 13, 1999	May 23, 1999
B	II	November 28, 1999	March 9, 2000	April 23, 2000	June 1, 2000	June 11, 2000
C	I	December 3, 2000	February 28, 2001	April 15, 2001	May 24, 2001	June 3, 2001
A	I	December 2, 2001	February 13, 2002	March 31, 2002	May 9, 2002	May 19, 2002
B	I	December 1, 2002	March 5, 2003	April 20, 2003	May 29, 2003	June 8, 2003
C	II	November 30, 2003	February 25, 2004	April 11, 2004	May 20, 2004	May 30, 2004
A	I	November 28, 2004	February 9, 2005	March 27, 2005	May 5, 2005	May 15, 2005
B	II	November 27, 2005	March 1, 2006	April 16, 2006	May 25, 2006	June 4, 2006
C	I	December 3, 2006	February 21, 2007	April 8, 2007	May 17, 2007	May 27, 2007
A	II	December 2, 2007	February 6, 2008	March 23, 2008	May 1, 2008	May 11, 2008
B	I	November 30, 2008	February 25, 2009	April 12, 2009	May 21, 2009	May 31, 2009
C	II	November 29, 2009	February 17, 2010	April 4, 2010	May 13, 2010	May 23, 2010
A	I	November 28, 2010	March 9, 2011	April 24, 2011	June 2, 2011	June 12, 2011
B	II	November 27, 2011	February 22, 2012	April 8, 2012	May 17, 2012	May 27, 2012
C	I	December 2, 2012	February 13, 2013	March 31, 2013	May 9, 2013	May 19, 2013

A	II	December 1, 2013	March 5, 2014	April 20, 2014	May 29, 2014	June 8, 2014
B	I	November 30, 2014	February 18, 2015	April 5, 2015	May 14, 2015	June 24, 2015
C	II	November 29, 2015	February 10, 2016	March 27, 2016	May 5, 2016	May 15, 2016
A	I	November 27, 2016	March 1, 2017	April 16, 2017	May 25, 2017	June 4, 2017
B	II	December 3, 2017	February 14, 2018	April 1, 2018	May 10, 2018	May 20, 2018
C	I	December 2, 2018	March 6, 2019	April 21, 2019	May 30, 2019	June 9, 2019
A	II	December 1, 2019	February 26, 2020	April 12, 2020	May 21, 2020	May 31, 2020
B	I	November 29, 2020	February 17, 2021	April 4, 2021	May 13, 2021	May 23, 2021
C	II	November 28, 2021	March 2, 2022	April 17, 2022	May 26, 2022	June 5, 2022
A	I	November 27, 2022	February 22, 2023	April 9, 2023	May 18, 2023	May 28, 2023
B	II	December 3, 2023	February 14, 2024	March 31, 2024	May 9, 2024	May 19, 2024
C	I	December 1, 2024	March 5, 2025	April 20, 2025	May 29, 2025	June 8, 2025
A	II	November 30, 2025	February 18, 2026	April 5, 2026	May 14, 2026	May 24, 2026
B	I	November 29, 2026	February 10, 2027	March 28, 2027	May 6, 2027	May 16, 2027
C	II	November 28, 2027	March 2, 2028	April 16, 2028	May 25, 2028	June 4, 2028
A	I	December 3, 2028	February 14, 2029	April 1, 2029	May 10, 2029	May 20, 2029
B	II	December 2, 2029	March 6, 2030	April 21, 2030	May 30, 2030	June 9, 2030
C	I	December 1, 2030	February 26, 2031	April 13, 2031	May 22, 2031	June 1, 2031
A	II	November 30, 2031	February 11, 2032	March 28, 2032	May 6, 2032	May 16, 2032
B	I	November 28, 2032	March 2, 2033	April 17, 2033	May 26, 2033	June 5, 2033
C	II	November 27, 2033	February 22, 2034	April 9, 2034	May 18, 2034	May 28, 2034
A	I	December 3, 2034	February 7, 2035	March 25, 2035	May 3, 2035	May 13, 2035
B	II	December 2, 2035	February 27, 2036	April 13, 2036	May 22, 2036	June 1, 2036
C	I	November 30, 2036	February 18, 2037	April 5, 2037	May 14, 2037	May 24, 2037
A	II	November 29, 2037	March 10, 2038	April 25, 2038	June 3, 2038	June 13, 2038
B	I	November 28, 2038	February 23, 2039	April 10, 2039	May 19, 2039	May 29, 2039
C	II	November 27, 2039	February 15, 2040	April 1, 2040	May 10, 2040	May 20, 2040

ACKNOWLEDGMENTS

MATERIAL FROM THE FOLLOWING SOURCES is gratefully acknowledged and is used by permission. Adaptations are by permission of copyright holders. Every effort has been made to determine the ownership of all texts and music used in this resource and to make proper arrangements for their use. The publisher regrets any oversight that may have occurred and will gladly make proper acknowledgment in future editions if this is brought to the publisher's attention.

SCRIPTURE QUOTATIONS

Except as otherwise noted, all scripture quotations are from the New Revised Standard Version of the Bible, copyright © 1989 by the Division of Christian Education of the National Council of the Churches of Christ in the U.S.A., and are used by permission. The following quotations are altered: Ps. 25:1–2; Ps. 51:17; Ps. 96:11–13; Ps. 141:2; Zech. 14:5c, 7; Acts 1:8; Rom. 5:5; Rom. 11:33, 36; Rom. 15:13; Phil. 4:23; 2 Thess. 3:16; 1 Tim. 1:17; Heb. 2:9; Heb. 4:14, 16; Heb. 13:15; 1 Peter 2:24; 2 Peter 3:18; 1 John 4:9; Rev. 19:6–7; Rev. 22:5. *Also:* Canticle of David (1 Chron. 29:10–11); Canticle of Miriam and Moses (Ex. 15:1, 2, 11, 13, 17–18); and Christ the Servant (1 Peter 2:21–25).

The following scripture quotations are from the *Revised Standard Version of the Bible*, copyright 1946, 1952, © 1971, 1973 by the Division of Christian Education of the National

Council of the Churches of Christ in the U.S.A., and are used by permission: 2 Sam. 22:29, 33; Matt. 3:2; Luke 2:10–11; John 1:14; Phil. 4:7. *Altered:* Ps. 86:11–12; Luke 2:14; 1 Thess. 5:23; 1 Peter 1:3. *Other:* Canticle of Hannah (1 Sam. 2:1–4, 7, 8).

The following scripture quotations are from the *Good News Bible: The Bible in Today's English Version,* © American Bible Society 1966, 1971, 1976: Ps. 5:2b–3; Isa. 40:31. *Altered:* Deut. 32:11; Ps. 74:16–17; Lam. 3:22–23; 2 Cor. 4:6; 1 Tim. 6:21.

The following scripture quotations are based on more than one translation: Ps. 85:10–11 (NRSV, TEV, NEB); Ps. 86:5–6 (NRSV, TEV, NEB); Ps. 139:11–12 (TEV, JB, NRSV); Dan. 2:22–23 (TEV, NRSV); Rom. 5:8 (RSV, NRSV); 1 Peter 2:24 (RSV, PHI); Rev. 21:23–24 (TEV, NEB, JB, NRSV). *Also:* The Beatitudes (Matt. 5:3–12) (NEB, NRSV); A Canticle for Pentecost (John 14:16; 16:13a; 14:26; Acts 2:2, 4a; Rom. 8:26) (NEB, NRSV); A Canticle of Creation (Song of the Three Young Men 35–65, 34) (RSV, NEB, BCP); A Canticle of Love (1 John 4:7, 8; 1 Cor. 13:4–10; 12–13) (RSV, NEB, NRSV); A Canticle to the Lamb (Rev. 4:11; 5:9–10, 12, 13) (RSV, BCP); Christ, the Head of All Creation (Col. 1:15–20) (NEB, NRSV); God's Chosen One (Isa. 11:1–4, 6, 9) (RSV, NRSV); Jesus Christ Is Lord (Phil. 2:5c–11) (RSV, NRSV); The Mystery of Our Religion (1 Tim. 3:16; 6:15, 16) (RSV, NRSV); The Spirit of the Lord (Isa. 61:1–3, 10, 11) (NRSV, NEB); The Steadfast Love of the Lord (Lam. 3:22–26) (RSV, NEB).

The text of the Psalms section (pp. 611–783) and those psalm texts contained in the Daily Prayer section (pp. 491–572) of this book are from *An Inclusive-Language Psalter of the Christian People,* copyright © 1993 by the Order of St. Benedict, Inc., and published by license of The Liturgical Press, Collegeville, Minnesota, United States of America. All rights reserved.

LITURGICAL TEXTS

The numbers contained in the lists of prayers that follow refer to the numbers at the end of each prayer. The sources noted are the resources from which the texts in this book were taken, or sources cited in them. In many cases the particular text is not original with the source noted, since many liturgical texts that are widely shared are derived from a longer tradition and appear in a number of contemporary service books. In some instances a prayer cited from one service book may have appeared in previous editions. For example, a prayer cited from the *Book of Common Worship* (1946) may also have appeared in the 1932 and 1906 editions. Texts that have been altered are so designated or are marked (alt.).

SUPPLEMENTAL LITURGICAL RESOURCES

The following texts first appeared in one of the trial-use volumes that were published as part of the process for developing this book.

Holy Baptism and Services for the Renewal of Baptism, Supplemental Liturgical Resource 2, copyright © 1985 The Westminster Press. *Altered:* 426.

Daily Prayer, Supplemental Liturgical Resource 5, copyright © 1987 The Westminster Press: 244, 267, 301, 315, 318, 435, 436, 437, 438, 439, 440, 444, 449, 458, 459, 460, 461, 463, 465, 466, 468, 469, 474, 476, 483, 485, 486, 538, 548, 566, 592, 607, 611, 615, 618, 622, 629, 634, 642, 643, 647, 655, 659, 662. *Altered:* 131 (concluding collect), 214, 434, 441, 442, 457, 462, 464, 467, 472, 473, 475, 482, 484, 487, 490, 492, 493, 497, 541, 543, 545, 546, 551, 553, 554, 557, 562, 575, 576, 577, 578, 580, 585, 586, 589, 593, 598, 610, 613, 623, 630, 632, 637, 638, 646, 648, 651, 665.

ADDITIONAL PRESBYTERIAN CHURCH (U.S.A.) SOURCES

The Book of Common Worship, copyright, 1946, by The Board of Christian Education of the Presbyterian Church in the United States of America; renewed 1974. Used by permission of Westminster/John Knox Press: *Altered:* 2, 4, 7, 49, 67.

The Worshipbook: Services, copyright © MCMLXX The Westminster Press: 500, 505, 686, 697, 703, 705, 710, 720, 736, 739, 743, 747, 748, 760, 778, 781. *Altered:* 1, 667, 668,

671, 676, 680, 681, 690, 693, 694, 695, 696, 698, 699, 712, 713, 714, 717, 719, 721, 732, 733, 734, 744, 753, 755, 756, 759, 761, 769, 777, 785, 786, 788, 789.

INTERNATIONAL COMMISSION ON ENGLISH IN THE LITURGY

The Liturgy of the Hours: According to the Roman Rite, copyright © 1975, International Commission on English in the Liturgy, Inc. All rights reserved: 502. *Altered:* 151, 217, 314, 471, 481, 491, 514, 534, 552, 558, 564, 579, 581, 582, 583, 587, 588, 595, 596, 599, 602, 620, 624, 644, 661.

Prayers, copyright © 1983, 1986, 1987, 1988, 1990, 1992, International Commission on English in the Liturgy, Inc. All rights reserved: 450, 451. *Altered:* 448, 517.

The Roman Missal: The Sacramentary, copyright © 1973, International Committee on English in the Liturgy, Inc. All rights reserved. Used by permission of the International Commission on English in the Liturgy, Inc. Excerpts from the English translation: 268 (alt.).

OTHER SOURCES OF LITURGICAL TEXTS

The following prayers in this edition were written for the *Book of Common Worship* (1993): 480, 494, 499, 535, 537, 547, 555, 556, 570, 573, 574, 603, 612, 619, 639, 656, 664, 678, 692, 706, 708, 711, 715, 723, 725, 726, 762, 772, 773, 783.

The Art of Ministering to the Sick, by Richard C. Cabot and Russell L. Dicks, copyright © 1936 by Macmillan Publishing Company, renewed 1964 by Russell L. Dicks. Reprinted with permission of Macmillan Publishing Company: 515 (alt.).

Authorized Services, copyright © 1973 by The Church Hymnal Corporation: 509 (alt.).

Book of Alternative Services of the Anglican Church of Canada, copyright © 1985 General Synod of the Anglican Church of Canada: 519. Other prayers in this book derived from *The Book of Alternative Services* are of uncertain origin.

The Book of Common Order of the Church of Scotland, copyright © Oxford University Press, 1940: 724 (alt.).

The Book of Common Prayer, according to the use of The

514 / ACKNOWLEDGMENTS

Episcopal Church, copyright 1977 by Charles Mortimer Guilbert as custodian: 488, 506, 508, 512, 531, 688, 700, 757, 758, 768, 770, 825. *Altered:* 3, 6, 11, 95, 96, 251, 496, 501, 504, 513, 666, 669, 673, 675, 684, 687, 691, 704, 722, 728, 729, 730, 731, 735, 740, 741, 746, 749, 752, 754, 766, 774, 779, 780, 782, 790. Canticle of the Redeemed; Christ Our Passover (alt.); Daily Lectionary, pages 1050–1095 (alt.).

Daily Prayer, by Eric Milner-White and George Wallace Briggs (London: Oxford University Press, 1941): 446 (alt.).

English translations of the following texts, copyright © 1988, English Language Liturgical Consultation (ELLC): Canticle of Mary, Canticle of Simeon, Canticle of Zechariah, "Glory to God in the highest," "Jesus, Lamb of God," "Lamb of God, you take away the sin of the world," Lord's Prayer, "We praise you, O God."

Hymn to Christ the Light ("O Radiant Light"), translation © 1979 William G. Storey. All rights reserved.

Liturgy, Journal of the Liturgical Conference, vol. 10, no. 1, copyright © 1992 by The Liturgical Conference, Inc., Silver Spring, Maryland; prayer by Diane Karay Tripp: 495.

Lord Hear Our Prayer, ed. by Thomas McNally and William G. Storey. Copyright © 1978 Ave Maria Press, Notre Dame, Indiana: 784.

Lutheran Book of Worship: Minister's Desk Edition, copyright © 1978, used by permission of Augsburg Fortress: 9, 640, 652, 663, 707, 738, 742, 745. *Altered:* 245, 316, 550, 563, 590, 614, 616, 617, 621, 625, 635, 650, 660, 672, 685, 701. Texts from the Latin Roman Missal as they appear in the *Lutheran Book of Worship:* 270 (alt.). *Other texts:* Opening sentences for the Service of Light (Evening Prayer).

Markings, by Dag Hammarskjöld, translated by Leif Sjöberg and W. H. Auden, copyright © 1964 Alfred A. Knopf, Inc. (New York), and Faber and Faber Ltd. (London): 22.

Martin Luther King, Jr.: A Documentary . . . Montgomery to Memphis, ed. by Flip Schulke (New York and London: W. W. Norton & Co., 1976): 737.

Morning Praise and Evensong, by William G. Storey, D.M.S., Frank C. Quinn, O.P., and David F. Wright, O.P.

Copyright © 1973, Fides Publishers Inc., Notre Dame, Indiana: 456 (alt.).

A New Zealand Prayer Book: He Karakia Mihinare o Aotearoa, © Church of the Province of New Zealand, 1989. Reprinted with permission of the General Secretary: 447. *Altered:* 445, 470. *Also:* Canticle of Judith; Canticle of Penitence; Canticle of Thanksgiving (alt.); The Desert Shall Blossom (alt.); The New Jerusalem (alt.); Seek the Lord (alt.).

The Occasional Prayers of the 1928 Book Reconsidered, by Eric Milner-White (London: SPCK, 1930): 776.

Praise God: Common Prayer at Taizé, copyright © 1975 by Les Presses de Taizé. Published by Oxford University Press, 1977. Reprinted by permission of Oxford University Press, Inc. Texts based on the Daily Office of the Community of Taizé: 479. *Altered:* 148, 150, 170, 171, 177, 178, 213, 216, 243, 253, 269, 300, 478, 482.

Praise God in Song, ed. by John Allyn Melloh, S.M., and William G. Storey, texts by John Allyn Melloh, S.M. Copyright © 1979 G.I.A. Publications, Inc., Chicago, Illinois. Altered with permission. All rights reserved: *Altered:* 452, 453, 454, 455, 516, 518.

Praise Him! A Prayerbook for Today's Christians, © 1973 by Ave Maria Press, Notre Dame, Indiana. All rights reserved: 317.

Prayer by John Underwood Stevens, copyright © Louise Coons Stephens: 498.

Prayer by Howard Thurman, from his *Meditations of the Heart*, copyright 1953 by Harper & Row, Publishers, Inc. Paperback edition, Friends United Press, Richmond, Indiana, 1976. Copyright renewed 1981 Sue Bailey Thurman. Used with permission: 24.

Prayers for a New World, ed. by John Wallace Suter. Copyright © 1964 John W. Suter: *Altered:* 15, 702.

Prayers of the Reformers, ed. by Clyde Manschreck, copyright © 1958, Muhlenberg Press. Used by permission of Augsburg Fortress: 709 (alt.).

Prayers of the Spirit, ed. by John Wallace Suter (New York: Harper & Row, 1942): 727 (alt.).

Service Book, copyright © The United Church of Canada, 1969: *Altered:* 17.

Singing Psalms of Joy and Praise, by Fred R. Anderson (Philadelphia: Westminster Press, 1986). Copyright © 1986 Fred R. Anderson: 542 (alt.), 605 (alt.).

The Taizé Office. English translation © The Taizé Community and Anthony Brown, 1966. Published by The Faith Press, London: *Altered:* 170, 269.

Textes liturgiques, Louons Dieu et célébrons la vie. © Masamba ma Mpolo et Mengi Kilandamoko, Zaire, 1988: 677, 716.

The United Methodist Book of Worship, copyright © 1992 The United Methodist Publishing House. The following materials from this source are used by permission: Prayer attributed to Wanda Lawrence (a prayer of the Chippewa): 674.

The Uniting Church in Australia Assembly Commission on Liturgy: 682.

Uniting in Worship, © The Uniting Church in Australia Assembly Commission on Liturgy, 1988. Used by permission of The Joint Board of Christian Education, Melbourne, Australia: *Altered:* 13.

SECTION HEADING CROSSES

THE CROSS IS ONE OF THE OLDEST and most universally recognized symbols in Christianity. Those in the *Book of Common Worship, Daily Prayer* represent a variety of the many forms that have been used throughout history to represent the Christian faith.

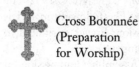 Cross Botonnée (Preparation for Worship)

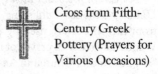 Cross from Fifth-Century Greek Pottery (Prayers for Various Occasions)

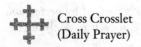 Cross Crosslet (Daily Prayer)

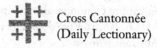 Cross Cantonnée (Daily Lectionary)

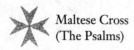 Maltese Cross (The Psalms)

Illustrations by Aavidar Design Inc.

*This book was designed
and produced by
Creative Publishing Services,
Publications Service,
Presbyterian Church (U.S.A.)
on Macintosh equipment
using Quark XPress.
All text is set in Janson.*